The Great Transformation of China

China's Economic Transformation, Innovation and Development

Series Editor

Fulin Chi, China Institute for Reform and Development, Haikou, Hainan, China

China is facing unprecedented challenges in its continued modernization process. This series brings together government insiders, academics, and policymakers in articulating specific social and political issues that China is trying to resolve, offering scholars around the world insights into what China's leadership see as the biggest challenges facing the nation and how best to resolve them. The series publishes monographs and edited volumes with contributions on a global basis dedicated to ground-breaking research on the Chinese modernization process.

More information about this series at
https://link.springer.com/bookseries/15346

Jia Kang · Liu Wei

Transformation of the Fiscal and Taxation Systems

ZHEJIANG UNIVERSITY PRESS
浙江大学出版社

palgrave
macmillan

Jia Kang
Chinese Academy of Fiscal Sciences
Beijing, China

Liu Wei
Chinese Academy of Fiscal Sciences
Beijing, China

Translated by
Du Lei
School of International Studies
Zhejiang University
Hangzhou, China

Tian Liyuan
School of International Studies
Zhejiang University
Hangzhou, China

Shang Zhilu
School of International Studies
Zhejiang University
Hangzhou, China

ISSN 2509-6001 ISSN 2509-601X (electronic)
The Great Transformation of China
ISBN 978-981-16-2592-3 ISBN 978-981-16-2590-9 (eBook)
https://doi.org/10.1007/978-981-16-2590-9

Jointly published with Zhejiang University Press
The print edition is not for sale in China (Mainland). Customers from China (Mainland) please order the print book from: Zhejiang University Press.
ISBN of the China Mainland edition: 978-7-308-15228-0

This Palgrave Macmillan imprint is published by the registered company Springer Nature Singapore Pte Ltd.
The registered company address is: 152 Beach Road, #21-01/04 Gateway East, Singapore 189721, Singapore

Series Editor's Preface: The Year 2020—A Historic Choice of Economic Transformation and Upgrading

A great nation with 13 billion people is facing a changing situation it has not ever faced for a thousand years. Change, transformation, and innovation feature the main melody of the era. In this era of high integration of growth, transformation, and reform, "great transformation" is exactly what decides the destiny of China. In other words, not only will "toxic assets" left in the traditional system have to be eliminated completely but also the new way for further growth needs to be paved quickly while letting loose the new motive force of development.

The major transformation in China's "13th Five-Year Plan" (FYP) is historically decisive. With the economic transformation as the focal point, both social transformation and government transformation are in the crucial period of transition in which innumerable thorny problems have to be tackled. Our general judgment is that the year 2020 is like a "gorge" we have to jump over. Specifically, by the end of 2020 we will have eliminated the pressure on short-term growth and changed the way for economic development while achieving a comparatively prosperous society in an all-round way and becoming one of the high-income countries in the world. If we plan well enough to make the best use of 2020, a mid-term period in the 13th FYP, we can lay a solid foundation for the medium-to-long-term peaceful and sustainable growth. If we fail to grasp the historical opportunity of 2020, we will lose the initiative of "great transformation", thus resulting in multiple systemic economic risks.

The significant breakthrough for achieving the economic transformation and upgrading in the 13th FYP period is how to cope with "four threes". Firstly, three major trends: one for industrial transformation and upgrading from "made in China" to "intellectually made in China"; one for urbanized transformation and upgrading from scale to population; and one for consumption pattern upgrading from material to service. Secondly, three major challenges: one for achieving a major breakthrough in structural reform by enhancing the structural adjustment despite the economic downturn; one for "corner overtaking" by responding to the global new round of scientific and technological revolution and increasing the ability to innovate; and one for a real and down-to-earth reform. At present, the transformation depends more on the all-round breakthrough in reform. It couldn't move forward at all without the change in systematic structure. And the growth would suffer big pressures. Thirdly, three major goals: one for industry, namely forming the service-dominated industrial structure by accelerating the process of service in manufacture; one for a major motive force, namely forming a consumption-oriented new pattern of economic growth, in which consumption guides investment and domestic consumption becomes a main force that spurs economic growth; and one for opening-up, namely forming a new open pattern dominated by service trade so as to redouble service trade in scale. Finally, three major relationships to be handled properly: one between the short term and the medium-to-long term in which the best job should be done for 2020 (the mid-term period) while resolving contradictions in the short term, basing ourselves on the mid-term and keeping our eyes on the long term; one between speed and structure which requires accelerating the structural adjustment while maintaining an increase by 7% or so; and one between policy and system in which the key is to gain a policy advantage in achieving institutional innovation under the economic pressure.

The past 40 years of reform and opening-up have left us numerable valuable assets. The most valuable one is that the more complex the situation may be and the more fundamental the change in environment, the more determined we will be in carrying out the reform and pushing through the transformation. All these require that the "great transformation" need overall arrangement and ambitious planning, need a significant breakthrough in the reform of industrial structure, urban-rural structure, regional structure, ownership pattern, open structure and administrative power structure, and need prospective planning in green sustainable development and "internet plus" development trends.

By judging the transformational reform in the 13th FYP period, China (Hainan) Institute for Reform and Development (CIRD) and Zhejiang University Press have jointly designed and published this set of series entitled *The Great Nation in Great Transformation—Economic Transformation and Innovative Development in China*. The book series has paid attention to readability based on being strategic, prospective and academic. It is our expectation that the series will offer enlightenment to readers who are closely watching the transformational reform in China while playing an active role in promoting the transformational reform in the 13th FYP period.

The authors of the series are mostly well-known scholars in their own subject areas, who wrote their respective books in their spare-time. As the director of the editorial board of the series, I wish, first and foremost, to extend my sincere thanks to the consultants, editorial board members, authors, and the leadership and editors of the press.

Last but not least, this set of series covers a wide range of subject areas, each volume representing its author's own research conclusions and academic opinions. The set does not require consistency in terms of viewpoints. Any criticism and correction from readers are truly welcome.

September 2015 Fulin Chi

Contents

About the Authors

Jia Kang, Ph.D. Advisor and Research Fellow in Chinese Academy of Fiscal Sciences. Member of the National Committee of CPPCC and Member of Subcommittee of Economy, CPPCC; Chief Economist of China Academy of New Supply-side Economics; In 2013, he edited New Supply: Chinese Innovation in Theory of Economics, initiated and established "China Academy of New Supply-side Economics" and "China New Supply-side Economist 50 Forum" (working as First President and Secretary-General). In 2015, he published a monograph named New Supply-Side Economics with Jingchun Su. In 2016, he published Supply-Side Reform—China New Supply-Side Economics, Ten Topics of Supply-Side Reform, and Crucial Challenge in front of China: How to Escape Mid-income Trap. In 2017, he headed the list in the publication of Housing System Reform and Property Tax Design in China, New Supply-Side Economics: Breakthrough in Innovative Development, Establishing the Foundation of Modern Governance: China's Fiscal and Taxation System Reform in the Past 40 Years, and so on.

Liu Wei, Ph.D. in Economics. Associate Research Fellow and Graduate Instructor in Chinese Academy of Fiscal Sciences (originally, Research Institute for Fiscal Science, the Ministry of Finance, P.R.C.); Adjunct Professor of East China University of Political Science and Law; Mainly be engaged in the research of financial theory and policies, government investment and financing, government budget performance. Liu Wei has been engaged in financial research work since 2004. Participated in or chaired more than 50 research projects of the National Social Science Fund, major national S&T special fund, the World Bank, Asian Development Bank, government departments and public institutions. Published three monographs, co-authored nine books and participated in the writing of more than ten books. Published more than 80 academic essays on journals, including Journal of the Party School of the Central Committee of The C.P.C, Economic Review, China Reform, and so on. Among them, Theoretical Interpretation and Its Practical Illustration was downloaded 45,760 times and cited 1017 times (as of the end of 30th, April, 2020) on CNKI.

List of Figures

List of Tables

1

Introduction

Fiscal and tax reform must first serve the overall interests. Its goal is not only to build a stable and strong national finance, but also to effectively support inclusive and sustainable growth and the modernization of national governance in the whole process. Over the past 30 years and more, with the establishment and improvement of the socialist market economy system, China's fiscal and taxation system reform has been promoted and deepened in an orderly manner, from "administrative decentralization" to "economic decentralization". The reform of the tax distribution system in 1994, which supported the reform of the market economy, and the public finance system, which was established and improved continuously since 1998, strongly supported the comprehensive, coordinated and sustainable development of the economy and society. The third plenary session of the 18th CPC central committee proposed that "finance is the foundation and important pillar of national governance", which established the theme and pointed out the direction for the transformation of the fiscal and taxation system: The foundation and pillar role of finance is to serve the modern market system, give full play to the positive effects of the market and make up for

J. Kang and L. Wei, *Transformation of the Fiscal and Taxation Systems*, The Great Transformation of China,
https://doi.org/10.1007/978-981-16-2590-9_1

market failure as a supplement, so as to optimize the overall allocation of resources. Fiscal and taxation system transformation is the requirement of the Times to continue to promote the economic and social transition under the concept of "modern national governance", and it is the realistic need for fiscal and taxation reform to support comprehensive reform under the new normal of economic development.

1.1 New Stage and New Challenges for China to Achieve Its Strategic Goal of Modernization and an Inevitable All-Round Reform

The Requirement of the Times to Continue to Promote Economic and Social Transition Under the Concept of "Modern National Governance"

Finance is the foundation and important pillar of national governance. First, as an important part of the national economy, finance directly serves to "stabilize growth, promote reform, adjust structure and benefit the people"; finance is also part of the administrative and political system and is supposed to promote political and administrative system reform; at the same time, finance is an important support for the "five-in-one" development of the society, culture and ecology. A slight move in one part may affect the situation as a whole. Fiscal and taxation reform must first serve the overall situation. The goal of fiscal and taxation system reform is not only to establish stable and strong national finance, but also to effectively support inclusive and sustainable growth and the modernization of national governance.

The third plenary session of the 18th CPC central committee deliberated and adopted the *Decision of the CPC Central Committee on Major Issues Concerning Comprehensively Deepening Reform* (hereinafter referred to as the decision), which has opened a new and important period of opportunities for China to comprehensively deepen reform, improve and develop the socialist system with Chinese characteristics, and greatly modernize the country's governance system and capacity. This guidance document with top-level planning significance contains a very important concept of "modern national governance", which is specifically expressed as "modernization of national governance system and governance capacity". This concept logically connects with the institutional construction requirements of "building a modern market system" that appeared several times in the document, and further connects with the fiscal and tax reform requirements of "building a modern financial system". Such a logical link is a historical "link between the past and the future" under the "five-in-one" comprehensive reform orientation established at the 18th CPC national congress. Its "inheriting from the past" can be traced back to the "revitalization of China"—a kind of modern appeal since China faced the "unchanged situation for three thousand years" and how to get rid of the backwardness and the miserable situation of being beaten. After the founding of the People's Republic of China in 1949, the concept of the "four modernizations" was clearly articulated in the 1960s and 1970s. At the beginning of the new period of reform and opening up, Deng Xiaoping clearly outlined the strategic goal of "three-step" modernization. Now, we have successfully entered the historical stage of its "third step". Under the vision of "inheriting the past", the plenum has condensed the concept of "modern national governance" that is logical and sufficient to "inspire the future", which lies in connecting the supporting reform tasks that we cannot avoid: Only through the release of institutional dividends through reform can we stimulate a series of other dividends of urbanization, scientific and technological innovation, and social management, so that we can continue to "keep pace with the Times" and connect the grand vision of the great modernization and national rejuvenation, the "Chinese dream".

In this logical chain, for the finance of "fiscal control by administration and administration through fiscal management", the decision has been expressed as "the foundation and important pillar of national governance" in the *Decision.* Theoretically speaking, finance deals with the allocation of public resources, which will inevitably pull and affect the overall allocation of resources. The modernization of China's market system is clearly stated in this document as "making the market play a decisive role in the allocation of resources" in accordance with the objective mode of market economy. Therefore, the foundation and pillar role of finance is to serve the modern market system, give full play to the positive effects of the market and supplement the market failure. The so-called "national governance" is not the same as the top-down "regulation" and "management" emphasized in the past. There are organizations and there are self-organizations; there is regulation and there is self-regulation; there is management and there is self-management. What the concept of governance emphasizes is a set of institutional arrangement and mechanism connection, intended to contain and give play to the potential of various subjects, and form the most powerful vitality and sustainability. As for finance itself, the budget revenues and expenditures in the specific management form are the scope, direction, focus and policy essentials of the activities of the state power system. We must first deal with the three basic economic and social relations between the government and the market (and enterprises as market subjects), the central and local governments, and the public power system and citizens in the arrangement of our own system. That is to say, the fiscal allocation of "fiscal control by administration and administration through financial management" should make the government neither offside nor absent. While the market plays a decisive role in allocating resources, the government should also play its role in maintaining social fairness and justice, letting market players release their vitality in fair competition, making up for market failure, assisting vulnerable groups and optimizing income distribution, so as to promote social harmony and long-term peace and stability.

Under such a set of logical links, we have made substantive progress in reforming the fiscal and taxation systems and supporting reforms to overcome difficulties. The goal is to achieve "decisive results" in supporting reform while realizing the phased goal of building a moderately prosperous society in all respects by 2020, as clearly stated in the *Decision*.

Obviously, the establishment of "modern financial system" and its associated task of deepening fiscal and taxation reform are matched with the grand blueprint of "great national rejuvenation" of China's construction of a modern country and modern society. We urgently need to put it into a set of "road map and timetable" oriented by "modernity".

On the basis of comprehensively serving the reform in the economic, political, social, cultural and ecological fields, the reform of the fiscal and taxation systems should focus on the following aspects: Reasonably defining the functions of the government, straightening out the inter-governmental financial relations, reforming the taxation system, optimizing the expenditure structure, strengthening budget management, standardizing government debts and improving the information system. At the same time, we will strengthen the coordination of fiscal and taxation reform with price, land, finance, opening up and other reforms, and implement the goal of comprehensively deepening reform.

The Realistic Need for Fiscal and Tax Reform to Support Comprehensive Reform Under the New Normal of Economic Development

After more than 30 years of rapid development, the Chinese economy has presented unprecedented new opportunities, new conditions, new imbalances and other new features. This is not only reflected in the slowdown of economic growth, but also in the transformation of growth drivers and the rebalancing of economic structure. It also means that reform and opening up have entered a new stage. In this new period of historical opportunity, it is particularly important for us to follow the law of economic development, fully understand the new situation, seek a balance of development between maintaining steady growth and adjusting the economic structure, and achieve long-term economic growth with the second-highest growth rate under the "new normal".

In November 2014, General Secretary Xi Jinping systematically elaborated the "new normal" for the first time at the Asia-Pacific Economic Cooperation (APEC) CEO Summit. Its main characteristics are from the speed, "from high-speed growth to high-speed growth"; from the perspective of structure, "the economic structure has been constantly optimized and upgraded"; from the perspective of motivation, "from factor driven, investment driven to innovation driven". It can be seen that the "new normal" means that the conditions and environment for China's economic development have undergone or are about to undergo many major changes. It will be difficult for China to repeat the high growth rate of about 10% over the past 30 years, and the traditional unbalanced, uncoordinated and unsustainable extensive growth model will certainly change. Macro-control will move toward the direction of "national governance modernization" under the "new normal". Fiscal and taxation reform will also have to consider the realistic needs of how to give play to the important role of finance in promoting the modernization of national governance. We should deal with the reality that the economy has shifted from high-speed growth to sub-high-speed growth, with more emphasis on the optimization of economic structure and the quality of economic growth and grim situation of fiscal revenue and fiscal expenditure pressure rigid.

1.2 Philosophical Thinking and Path Choice for Linking the Strategic Goals of Modernization with Inclusive Growth

Strategic Thinking and "China's Choice" from a Strategic Perspective

"Inclusive growth", first put forward by the Asian Development Bank, has been clearly affirmed by the senior leadership in China and has been discussed in academic circles for several years. It is a global strategic proposition. Finance is the distribution system of "fiscal control by administration and administration through fiscal management", which serves the whole situation. To understand and handle the financial problems well, we must first "look beyond the fiscal". In his first speech as minister of finance upon his return to the ministry of finance, Lou Jiwei convincingly demonstrated the strategic thinking of his long-renowned "academic official" with clear thinking, broad vision, bright and powerful logic and simple and simple viewpoints: Faced with the historic test of whether the "Chinese dream" can be realized, which bears on the future of the country, the destiny of the nation, the well-being of the people and the realization of the "Chinese dream", what rational choice should China make on the basic path of realizing "inclusive growth" of modernization?

Minister Lou clearly defined inclusive growth as "not diverging" as "spreading the benefits of economic development to all regions and all people". After achieving "coordinated economic and social development" in sustainable development, he went straight to the problem of how to achieve inclusive growth that is controversial and "different in everyone's mind". He first pointed out that the key to this problem is "what role should the market and the government play" in the allocation of resources, which is also closely related to the correct design of the public resource allocation mechanism reflected in the government's tax and budget arrangements. Subsequently, Minister Lou listed three representative understandings on the choice of growth path: First, with a high proportion of fiscal revenue, it supports large-scale redistribution led by the government and pursues the "fairness of results", which will lead to the compression of market role, insufficient employment and insufficient sense of struggle of the people. Happiness is not necessarily high and the economic growth rate is low. Second, the government pays more attention to the creation of development opportunities and encourages everyone to strive for development in the market. If the government properly extracts fiscal revenue and implements appropriate redistribution, the result will be full employment, people's strong sense of happiness and high economic growth rate. Third, the path of lower taxes, higher spending and higher welfare benefits for the country will expand the deficit and debt, and individuals will make less efforts to enjoy more welfare. As a result, the country will finally achieve "balance" through inflation, which actually makes it more difficult for low-income people and regions to fall into a vicious circle and middle-income trap. To the three choices represented by these three understandings, Minister Lou pointed out clearly: The second understanding is the right path to sustainable inclusive growth. Unfortunately, the first and third are "always very marketable" and are well supported. The overconfidence of government departments in their "ability to intervene" and the majority of the public agree that opportunities are fair, but when they encounter the situation of unequal opportunities in reality, the proportion of people who want to pay less and enjoy more benefits will increase, and the public opinion environment will also deteriorate. His subsequent remarks were succinct and to the point: "The first and the third are paths of no return, and it is not that we have no possibility of going astray. The second is a difficult path of reform and inclusive growth, and China is striving to move away from the possibility of being first and third and striving for the second path".

China's ongoing transition process is obviously still far from the relative stability and relative norms inherent in the concept of "mode". The real problem we are facing is actually the "China choice" issue that we cannot avoid making on the "China's path" of reform and opening up—the rational strategic orientation of "China choice" from now to the future.

The Illusion of "Government Can Do Everything" Is False, and the Process of "Welfare Catch-Up" Is Difficult to Avoid Haste

Why is taking the second path the right path to sustainability? Although this can give a lot of positive analysis and argument, but here, let us begin by examining the fundamental reasons why the first and third paths are not sustainable.

The first path of big government, high proportion of fiscal revenue and excessive emphasis on equalization of results belong to the philosophical level of falling into the "illusion of government omnipotence". It is to take government regulation and control as always rational and effective, and form a high concentration of resources and a very strong and rapid response to micro-economic activities. As Minister Lou said, the essence here is not to believe in the market's ability to repair itself, and the resulting bitterness is that the intervention measures are often counterproductive, creating volatility and reducing the role of the market in return for low vitality, so that the employment rate and growth rate are also low. For empirical evidence in this direction, we can perceive from the traditional system of "highly centralized" malpractice suffocation, magnified the painful lessons of macro decision failures, and the negative effects of the "illusion of government omnipotence" repeatedly expressed in the transition. Therefore, we must still deeply reflect on the false nature of this orientation. Even on the face of it, proponents of this approach emphasize positively the "fairness of outcomes". In fact, its misguided government is always stronger than the internal logic of the market, which will inevitably destroy the dynamic foundation of development and fail to bring about sustainable improvement of people's happiness.

However, the third path of high deficit, high debt and high welfare directly violates the "three paradoxes restriction" of financial distribution. In the past, the empirical study followed the example of several Latin American countries that fell into the middle-income trap from "welfare catch-up on a populist basis" and failed for decades. In the recent European debt crisis, some southern European countries were in danger of falling into economic and social turmoil after the failure of the euro protection umbrella. The cost and lessons are painful. But to put it bluntly, this trend is emerging in China today, often in the guise of public opinion, as the contradictions of middle-income status emerge: For example, if we regard improving people's livelihood as a guideline without talking about its basic, non-basic and rational degree, mentioning people's livelihood is like standing on the moral high ground and ignoring the matching and gradual progress of its satisfying conditions. Behind this, there is a hidden worry of "raising people's appetite but not lasting". However, when it comes to the positioning of politicians, they often naturally, intentionally, or unintentionally avoid poking through the window. The departments concerned are often reluctant to make offensive statements, or even just want to get an applause, but the difficult supporting reform and management problems related to it are delayed without discussion or resolution. Citing the principle of "holding the bottom line, highlighting the key points, improving the system and guiding public opinion" stressed by the central economic work conference, Minister Lou said in a vivid and frank way: "We should help the poor, not the lazy. We have a lot of these problems in our system". This is said to be with the authority of minister, he made public of the matters which many a man of insight would dare but discuss in private, having the public interest at heart and conversing with reason.

It should be said that from the source of motive force of "people's yearning for a better life is our goal" and the production purposes of "meet the people's growing material and cultural needs of life", with the implementation of the "three-step" modernization catch-up strategy in China, it is necessary to pursue the "welfare catch-up" of the people. But the big challenge of moving into middle-income status is this: When people's expectations for welfare improvement are further activated and accelerated, they are easily ahead of the realistic ability of the government to mobilize resources (including deepening reform and increasing institutional support) to provide effective supply. Regarding the "improve people's livelihood" orientation, the people and the government may, for a period of time, have a honeymoon-like mutual echo and inspiration, but once the momentum fails to catch up, the "welfare catch-up" will soon fall into dust from the cloud. What comes down with it is the overall momentum of economic growth and social development—and once that happens, the experience of trying to regain that momentum after a painful loss in the middle-income phase has proved much harder. Unfortunately, in this middle-income stage, policy environment, institutional construction and social justice mechanism are not yet in place, the public pressure of "eat meat, put down chopsticks and curse" is likely to force the government to implement "welfare catch-up" that goes beyond objectivity and helps the lazy. From this perspective, the major contradiction in the process of improving people's livelihood and welfare after the emerging economies enter the middle-income stage is the difficulty of "avoiding haste". Failure to avoid haste is the danger of the middle-income trap. It is urgent for us to have a clear understanding of this and rationally guide the public opinion to clarify the basic truth that "tax cuts, strict control of debt and massive increase of welfare benefits cannot be achieved at the same time".

The first and third paths are similar in form, but in terms of downplaying the role of the market and exaggerating the role of government regulation, they are all roads lead to the same destination. Neither high-tax equalitarianism nor low-tax welfarism will lead to sustainable and inclusive growth and will lead to a "no return" branch road and a dead end.

The Rational Premise of Fiscal and Taxation Services: "Let the Market Fully Play Its Role"

Since we should strive to avoid the aforementioned two roads, deviation is contempt for the market. Then back to the core issues highlighted in the report to the 18th national congress of the communist party of China and the *Plan for the Reform of Government Institutions and the Transformation of Government Functions* adopted by the NPC, we need to strike a balance between the government and the market, between the government and society, between public institutions and citizens, between the central and local governments, between local and global interests, and between the short term and the long term. On the premise of "truly making the market work", we will handle well the policy matters of deepening reform and optimizing policies to ensure that fiscal and taxation allocations serve "comprehensive, coordinated and sustainable development". We should give top priority to creating equal opportunities and upholding social justice. We should not only accelerate fiscal and taxation reform, but also actively support and cooperate with related reforms—focusing on the basic idea of establishing mechanisms to promote inclusiveness, and connecting with the top-level design and deployment of reform that the third plenary session of the 18th CPC central committee directly addressed.

On the premise of logical origin and rational understanding, how to view the market and how to make the government interact with the people rationally are nothing but the complicated reform and breakthrough innovation. With equal opportunities as the priority, we will encourage and stimulate vitality and creativity to improve people's lives and ensure people's well-being. Just as Minister Lou said, in the past 30 years and more of China's continuous market-oriented reform, the fiscal and taxation system has played a role as a breakthrough and a pioneer. Although the task of reform and policy adjustment in the future is still arduous, at the new historical starting point, with a clear direction and certain experience and theoretical preparation, we have every reason to expect a new round of fiscal and taxation reform and supporting reforms to make more substantial progress.

1.3 Support for Comprehensive Reform of Public Finance: Review and Prospect

The third plenary session of the 18th CPC central committee proposed: "Finance is the foundation and important pillar of national governance, and a scientific fiscal and taxation system is the institutional guarantee for optimizing resource allocation, maintaining market unity, promoting social equity and realizing long-term peace and stability of the country. We must improve legislation, clarify powers and responsibilities, reform the tax system, stabilize the tax burden, make budgets transparent, improve efficiency, establish a modern fiscal system and bring into full play the initiative of both the central and local governments. These requirements are rich in content, but also related to a series of difficulties in China's reform and coordination. It serves the purpose of modernizing national governance, enabling the unified market to play a decisive role in optimizing resource allocation, promoting social equity and building a system of lasting national peace and stability. It serves and supports overall reform. Prior to this, China's fiscal and tax reform accompanied by the establishment and improvement of the socialist market economy system, after more than 30 years of promotion and deepening, established a relatively complete public finance system. In particular, the reform of the tax distribution system in 1994 and the exploration of establishing the public finance system since 1998, as well as the continuous improvement of the public finance system, have strongly supported the comprehensive, coordinated and sustainable development of the economy and society.

Landmark Significance and Historic Contribution of Tax Distribution Reform in 1994

China has entered a crucial period of launching a new round of supporting reform of its economic system. Similar to previous rounds of reform, fiscal and taxation reform has once again become the starting point for discussion and promotion of supporting reform, with how to understand and deepen the tax distribution reform since 1994 as the core.

There is a general consensus in academia that: The tax system is the system arrangement that standardizes the distribution relationship between the government and enterprises, and the financial system is the system arrangement that deals with the distribution relationship between governments. If a more thorough examination is made on the level of academic theory, it can be seen that in fact this understanding is far from being in place. Finance, as a distribution system of a country's political power system "fiscal control by administration and administration through fiscal management", is studied intuitively. The first is to solve the problem of the allocation of public resources by the government to fulfill its social management power and function. What is closely related to and inseparable from it is the allocation of social resources. Therefore, for the financial system arrangement—including a series of statutory institutional, system and mechanism provisions of tax and non-tax revenue to address the government's "where does the money come from?", expenditure of "where does the money go", transfer payment and the standardized carrier of fund income and expenditure namely budget, etc.—the essential problem is to deal with the three basic relationships in economic and social life: Between the government and the enterprises of the market subject; between the central government and local governments at various levels; the distribution of financial resources and interests between the public power system and citizens.

Therefore, the financial system should first solve the problems of resource allocation based on the contract of property rights and the legal environment, the efficiency incentive under the role of the government, the response mechanism for entrepreneurship and innovation, and the fairness, predictability and sustainability of the interest distribution process, so as to serve, influence and balance the overall resource allocation. The goal model of socialist market economy established in China after Deng Xiaoping's talk in south China in 1992 actually established the irreversible orientation of legalization of various economic forms and property right norms, and the forming of fair competition market and indirect regulation system was imperative. It is thus entirely logical to lead to the coordinated reform of the "tax distribution system", which was intensified in 1993 and formally introduced on 1 January 1994. This is exactly the institutional reform that echoes the reconstruction of the overall resource allocation mechanism in China's historic economic and social transition.

As for the evaluation of the tax distribution reform in 1994, most scholars judge and affirm its great success from one of the reform goals of that year—"to increase the proportion of central fiscal revenue in fiscal revenue". Yes, this problem was one of the immediate factors that forced the "94 reforms" and provided unprecedented "political resources" for policymakers to pursue them. But taken as a whole, the landmark and historic contribution of 1994's tax distribution reform go far beyond that. The evaluation is carried out on the basic logic chain of transition and reform. Its contribution and significance lie in the fact that China's financial system has finally moved from the "administrative decentralization", which had to depart from the strict and complete meaning of unified collection and expenditure in the 1950s when the People's Republic of China was just established, to the "economic decentralization" consistent with the market economy. This breakthrough reform in the past regardless of "centralization" or "decentralization" is in accordance with the enterprise administrative subordination of the organization of financial revenue system crux. On the institutional norms of "to whom" and "to whom according to what basis", a truly fair competition environment has been formed in which all enterprises, regardless of size, regardless of economic nature, regardless of administrative level, are equal in the face of tax laws, and "state tax and local tax shall be paid accordingly". It provides a stable expectation for fostering long-term behavior on the basis of stimulating micro-enterprise vitality. Second, it makes the central and local governments say goodbye to the endless bickering under the historical stage of administrative decentralization and the continuation of the "system cycle" of bickering factors under the "contract but not do it" system, breaking the headache—inducing cycle of "once released, it will be messy, once messy, it will be tightened; once tightened, it will be dead". The opening of the new situation has formed the institutional conditions for the government to carry out macro "indirect regulation and control" on market entities, and the relatively standardized and stable sustainable institutional arrangements for the central and local governments to allocate their respective financial resources according to the tax category or the same share proportion of a certain tax category.

This "trinity" framework, which deals with the relationship between the government and enterprises, central and local governments, public rights and citizens' distribution with the orientation of unification, standardization, fairness and equity, downplays the excessive intervention and care of the governments at all levels in each specific region in the "close and distant" relationship between various enterprises and the "differential treatment" by the close and distant relationship and suppresses the bargaining mechanism between the local government and the central government and the "comparison" mechanism of the unbalance of happiness and pain between the local government and the central government. This has not only created a good market operating environment for enterprises, but also created a system atmosphere that local governments identify with standardization in their single-minded efforts to develop.

Of course, the "94 reform" with great vigor and action, under various constraints, still can only provide an initial framework for handling the three relations with the tax classification system, still with a strong color of transition. The task of deepening reform has been accomplished since then, but the task of truly implementing the tax distribution system below the provincial level is far from complete. Since 1994, China's local financial systems below the provincial administrative regions have, on the whole, failed to make the transition to a real tax distribution system, which is actually a multifarious, complicated and changeable share-cropping system and system of responsibility with strong bargaining color. The problems that people have been criticized, such as the financial difficulties at the grassroots level, the hidden liabilities at the local level and the short-term behavior of "land finance", are actually caused by the helpless operation of the share-cropping system and the system of responsibility under the provincial level, which we have known for a long time and want to change. To lay the blame for local "grassroots difficulties", "hidden liabilities" and "land finance" on the tax distribution system is to make a complete mistake, and thus negate the general direction of "94 reform". This is a big issue of right and wrong, which should not be ignored or dismissed. It must be made clear.

In a word, the "94 reform" of China's financial system has shifted from "administrative decentralization" to "economic decentralization", supporting the comprehensive significance and "milestone" nature of the reform of the market economy. In order to insist on its basic system achievement, we must face up to its "unfinished" state and work hard to deepen the reform.

The Tax Distribution System Should Be Consistent with the Market Economy

To develop a market economy, we must implement a system of tax distribution and graded finance, which is a common system and a basic mode of practice that all countries in the world share in the development of a market economy. The experience and lessons from the repeated exploration of China's financial system over the past 60 years are enough to elicit this understanding. Therefore, it is necessary to follow the basic analytical approach to examine: Why to build and perfect socialist market economy, we must insist on the direction of tax distribution reform?

The essential difference between market economy and planned economy lies in the different ways of resource allocation. The planned economy is characterized by the government's direct allocation of resources, which is reflected in the fiscal system. The government uses its power and financial power not only to provide public goods and raise fiscal revenue for providing public goods, but also to directly intervene in non-public goods and micro-economic activities in line with government regulation. Objectively speaking, with regard to the high concentration of financial power and administrative power and the resulting lack of vitality, it is not as if the top decision-makers are not paying enough attention and not thinking about change. In 1956, the decentralization thought was put forward in the exploration of "ten relations". However, the large-scale decentralization measures to local governments, which were represented by 1958 and 1970, respectively, were soon unsuccessful. In vain, they had to fall into the helpless state of "sharing the total amount and a certain amount in a year" due to the cycle process of "messy once released and dead once tightened". After 1980, in the new era of reform and opening up, the decentralization of power with the figurative name of "the system of dividing revenue and expenditure between the central and local governments", the "delegation of power and transfer of benefits" to enterprises with multiple "local responsibility" combined with the overall progressive reform and the pattern of regulation and control was changed from "rule by rule" to "block by block". After loosening the old system and opening up certain space for reform, the crux of the old system of organizing fiscal revenue and controlling enterprises by administrative subordination has not been touched. Soon, "tax reduction and concession of part of the profits" were exhausted, but enterprises could not survive, and local governments evolved into "vassal economy". The failure of the central government's regulation and control functions and the difficulty in performing their duties have become politically and economically unacceptable, which finally forced the 1994 tax distribution reform toward economic decentralization.

It must be emphasized that the tax distribution reform in 1994 is based on the establishment of socialist market economy target model after Deng Xiaoping's southern talk. The market economy, which is based on the mechanism of market allocation of resources, requires the government to focus on maintaining social fairness and justice and making up for market failures and deficiencies. Therefore, the government's administrative power and financial power are mainly positioned in the public sphere. "Production and construction finance" should be transformed into "public finance", with the provision of public goods and services as the main goal and focus of work. Therefore, it is necessary to change the tax classification system based on the rule of fiscal revenue of administrative subordination organizations and move toward the legal background of the tax distribution and classification system so that the enterprise can cross the subordination relations, cross the administrative region merger and reorganization upgrading optimization without barriers and release the potential, vitality, full and fair competition. At the same time, the relationship between governments also follows the principle of norms and efficiency. The government at all levels performs the function of public finance in a standardized way and divides the administrative power and financial power reasonably among governments at all levels. In addition, the financial balance mechanism is the transfer payment mainly based on the "top-down flow" of funds. This framework is the fiscal decentralization framework under the concept of "economic decentralization", which is similar to the international experience of "fiscal federalism" in the form of tax distribution and classification financial system arrangement.

Tax distribution system is the abbreviation of tax distribution and fiscal classification system. Its system includes, first of all, the rational division of administrative power (expenditure responsibility) and financial power (broad tax base allocation) among governments at all levels. To establish fiscal budgets for raising funds and managing expenditures at different levels according to tax revenues, then, it logically leads to the hierarchical property rights management and debt management, as well as the transfer payment system. The tax distribution system not only meets the internal requirements of the government to maintain market order and provide public products under the market economy, but also meets the public needs of standardized and predictable division of labor and cooperation among governments at all levels to improve the efficiency of public resource allocation.

Therefore, in a word, the fiscal system of tax distribution is consistent with the market economy. On the journey of deepening the reform of the socialist market economic system, promoting comprehensive and coordinated reform and realizing the Chinese dream of modernization in a "five-in-one" way, it is unshakable for us to stick to the direction of the reform of the tax-sharing fiscal system. Based on the basic facts since 1994, problems such as county and township financial difficulties, hidden liabilities, land finance and "money from the ministry" in the operation of local finance in recent years are not caused by the tax distribution system. It is precisely because the reform of tax distribution system has not been implemented yet, especially at the provincial level. Faced with the problems and disadvantages in real life related to difficulties at the grassroots level, local hidden liabilities and short-term behaviors of "land finance", in addition to the misconception that the 1994 tax reform (in essence, it will negate the general direction of financial reform and transformation matching with the market economy) was to blame for these negative factors without knowing actual situation below provincial levels, there is another kind of proposition that, although it does not completely negate the direction of tax distribution in terms of expression, it puts forward "tax distribution between the central government and provinces, no tax distribution below provinces", "tax distribution in non-agricultural regions, and no tax distribution in agricultural regions" from the perspective of emphasizing "adapting measures to local conditions". The author once summarized it as the design idea of "two vertical sections and two horizontal sections (two categories)" and wrote different opinions. This design idea seems to be oriented toward "seeking truth from facts", the key is that it fails to understand the inherent requirement of resource allocation of market economy, and breaks away from the base line of Chinese economy society shunt and the maneuverability in real life. It is a kind of thinking direction that makes the pattern of financial system return to "division by sections" and "various forms of responsibility systems", and fails to grasp the "real problem" of deepening reform completely: How can the system arrangement of non-barrier flow of various elements required by a unified market be so "adapted to local conditions" while both horizontal and vertical are cut?

If there is no tax distribution below the provincial level, in fact, this is exactly the reality that has been formed and criticized since the "94 reform" due to impeded deepening of reform. The real problem is how to get out of this "No way out" bad dilemma. If we say "agricultural regions do not engage in tax distribution system", then apart from how to reasonably divide China into various large and small "agricultural regions" that are only a line from non-agricultural regions in the actual operation plan, just think about it: How will the enterprises in each region form the chain of deduction for the first kind of value-added tax in China and how will the local governments deal with the right of claim for enterprise income tax in their respective jurisdictions in the state of system division and segmentation? The real problem behind the completely unacceptable disorder state is the resource allocation optimization mechanism of the unified market, which inevitably requires the tax distribution system to implement the full coverage of its institutional arrangements "horizontally to the border and vertically to the end"—the inherent requirement of the system innovation of the tax distribution reform is the same. The management system innovation and information system innovation related to and corresponding to the reform should be covered from the horizontal to the border and from the vertical to the end.

A Complete and Accurate Understanding of Several Important Points That Should Be Clarified in the Tax Distribution System

The fiscal system of tax distribution system is a system framework with clear logical hierarchy and systematic connection with market economy and modern social form. It is necessary to start with the "core issue" of the relationship between the government and the market, and understand it completely and accurately under the orientation of "letting the market play a full role", so as to eliminate many differences and seek basic consensus.

First, the logical starting point of the tax distribution system is the government's function positioning and the right of revenue and expenditure under the orientation of the market economy target model. In the market economy, the government should give up the role of direct allocation of resources under the planned economy to play a role mainly in the field of market failure, providing public goods and services, and maintaining social equity and justice. The common scope of the government's power depends largely on the boundary of public goods. In order to perform the public duties of the government, the society must authorize and endow the government with the power to allocate (obtain and control) resources, which includes the power to obtain funds and the power to control funds in the allocation of economic resources. Modern society usually presents as the authorization of the legislature. Among them, income right includes two kinds: One kind is to collect taxes (fee) right, and one kind is to hold creditor's rights. The former is the property right in the common sense, while the latter is actually the contingency factor of the "paid" way supplemented by the property right in the form of "free" to obtain income. Accordingly, the types of government revenue are divided into tax, fee and debt, among which tax is the main one (debt can be borrowed if cross-time and cross-generation public goods are provided for financing). As regards taxation, it is necessary to take into account both the objective of adequate income and the maximum possible non-distortion of the market, as well as the appropriate "take from those who have much and give to those who have little" of the interests of members of the community. This objectively requires tax system design to be unified, standardized, fair and efficient, and to form necessary differences ("treat differently while concerning oneself with facts and not with individuals"). In the arrangement of the tax system, it is required to keep the tax "neutral" as far as possible, so as to avoid distorting the allocation of resources. However, to give full play to the guiding role of the market and the macro-control role of the government, it is inevitable to add appropriate differentiated design of tax system. Therefore, in the agricultural era with underdeveloped commodity economy, agricultural tax based on cultivated land usually becomes the first choice. With the rise of commodity economy, the turnover tax based on the turnover of commodities is favored by many countries. When the economy further developed in modern times, the income and property tax base was paid more attention by all countries. For the overall design of the tax distribution system, it is necessary to take what should the government do and what should it not do in modern society, and how should the government regulate the market players and taxpayers as the origin. That is to respect the market and service and guide the market economy of the government function positioning and appropriate way to perform their duties as a logical starting point, and coordinate the rationalization of fiscal authority (expenditure responsibility) and the rationalization of tax base allocation of compound tax system in the arrangement system of classification collection authority system.

Second, the scope of government power plays a major role in the premise of government revenue scale (generalized macro tax burden).

The income right of the government provides the possibility for the government to actually raise income. However, the actual amount of income to be raised first depends on the scope of government power, or on the boundary of public functions under the influence of specific national conditions, stages, strategic design and other factors. This reflects a kind of regular understanding brought by the government's financial management thought of "income is determined by expenditure". At the same time, it can also comment on and respond to the argument about the high or low macro tax burden in China in recent years from this perspective. Excluding fiscal expenditure efficiency and objective differences in the supply cost of public goods among countries, the so-called macro tax burden is high or not high, which first and foremost depends on the positioning of government functions and the scope of power. From the practical situation of various countries after the industrial revolution, the long-term performance of the proportion of government expenditure presents an upward trend, which is concluded by the famous "Wagner's law". The fundamental reason is that with the social development, economic and social public affairs tend to be complex and services upgrade, and the scope of government's public functions is gradually expanded.

The boundaries of the scope of power and function of the government in China are generally beyond those of mature market economy countries under the traditional system (there is no discussion on the situation of public services in some villages under the pattern of "urban–rural separation"). Notwithstanding some convergence since the reform and opening up, significant differences are still registered. In addition to the factors such as offside, absence and low capital efficiency caused by incomplete transformation of government functions, it also includes: The specific reform cost in the process of transition; specific economic development responsibilities undertaken to implement the catching-up strategy and realize the great rejuvenation of the nation; China strives to speed up the industrialization and urbanization process in mature market countries over the past hundred years, resulting in provision of public goods (basic system conducive to market development, infrastructure for economic development and livelihood guarantee for social stability and harmony); and other factors in other countries. They interweaved and overlapped intensively during China's reform and opening up over the past 30 years.

The above analysis does not deny that the market reform is not in place, the government is offside, and the expenditure efficiency is low, which leads to the improper allocation of public resources and waste of "useless" government expenditure or higher administrative costs. The main point is to show that the scope of government's power is the framework of the macro tax burden. Different countries have different development stages and national conditions, so the static macro tax burden among countries is not very comparable. China's specific national conditions and the current special stage lead to a wide scope of government power. In addition to some improper factors, there are also certain objective inevitability and rationality in the proportion of established macro tax burden and government expenditure.

The above analysis shows that market failure requires the government to perform its public duty (power), and it should be given corresponding power to acquire and control (allocate) economic resources (right of income and right of expenditure). However, the scale of income (government available financial resources /GDP ratio) obtained by the government through the right to income depends on the scope of power. Of course, the scale of actual income also depends on economic development, tax collection and management ability, tax system design and policy, government credibility and other factors. Accordingly, the power of administration and the financial power that conforms to it are the "quality" framework defining factors. It more reflects the arrangement of the financial system, and the scale of financial resources and the macro tax burden are the result of the "quantity" generated by the combined action of various factors under the premise of the power administration and the financial power.

Third, the division of power is the initial and basic link of system design and whole process optimization in deepening the reform of tax distribution system.

The financial system of tax distribution system includes three parts: Division of power of, division of income and expenditure and transfer payment. Among them, the division of powers reflecting the rational positioning of government functions is the initial and basic link, and is the major premise of the allocation of financial powers and resources and the transfer payment system. Therefore, we should avoid discussing the superficial view of how income is divided when we talk about tax distribution reform but should discuss how to deepen the reform of tax distribution system in a complete and logical order.

Similar to the need to define a reasonable scope of powers before discussing the overall revenue scale of the government, the powers between governments at all levels must be reasonably divided before discussing the rationalization of financial scale and expenditure responsibility of governments at all levels. This is consistent with the first level to support the principle of "income is determined by expenditure". Only when the division of powers among governments at all levels is rationalized can the responsibility for expenditure be rationalized, and then how to ensure that the financial resources at all levels are neither too much nor too little can be discussed. That is, the feasible scheme that "financial power and administrative power are compatible (consistent with each other), and financial power and administrative power are matched". Assigning administrative power to a certain level of government not only means that the level of government is responsible for expenditure, but also for the quality, quantity and cost of public goods. Therefore, the two concepts of "administrative power" and "expenditure responsibility" are not exactly the same. Expenditure responsibility is more similar to the concept expression of "accountability system" and "performance appraisal" under the framework of administrative power. The essential requirement of public finance is to carry out reasonable and effective institutional regulation of public service responsibility behind the appearance of "distribute" and "spend" in order to seek the maximization of public interests.

Generally speaking, the division of power among different levels of government should take into account such factors as the nature of public goods and the coverage of their "spillover", the complexity of relevant information, the incentive-compatibility mechanism consistent with the maximization of overall interests, and the supply efficiency of public goods. National public goods should be provided by the central government. Regional public goods should be provided by local governments. The specific expenditure responsibilities should be reasonably corresponded to and respectively assigned to the central and local governments. At the same time, local governments have more information advantages than the central government and better understand the needs of local residents. Therefore, when both the central government and the local government can provide some public services, based on efficiency, they should be more inclined to be provided by the local government.

Fourth, the division of broad tax base income mainly depends on the attributes and characteristics of tax categories and requires the general standardization of the framework of tax base allocation among regions. However, the actual tax abundance in different regions is inevitably different, and there exists the "horizontal imbalance" of fiscal revenue in China.

After the rational division of administrative powers, the logical links are the allocation of financial rights (generalized tax base division arrangement), budget and expenditure management, as well as the allocation of property rights and debt rights corresponding to the subject at the corresponding level. So let's look at the tax base.

The division of income according to tax types (i.e., the allocation of tax base) belongs to the due subject and key characteristics of the subject under the framework of fiscal system of tax distribution system. Taxes that are closely related to national sovereignty and overall macro-control functions, or that are based on a single market with high liquidity, should be assigned to the central government; However, taxes closely related to regional characteristics, with no or weak liquidity in tax base, and with a more regional tax base, which will not cause excessive inter-regional tax competition, and which need to be "adapted to local conditions", shall be assigned to local tax. No matter how the tax categories (tax bases) are allocated among governments and whether the income is not shared or shared, the principles and methods of distribution and the proportion of sharing should be consistent and standardized within a country. Even those that cannot be exclusively shared by the central or local governments, but have to be shared for transitional or even long-term reasons (such as China's current value-added tax, enterprise income tax and individual income tax), also need to implement a unified sharing method and sharing proportion nationwide. If we fail to adhere to the most basic "national uniformity", the foundation of our tax distribution system, which was formed in 1994, will be shaken. Imagine, for example, raising the 25% share of value-added tax (or the 40% share of income tax) in less developed areas to "adjust measures to local conditions" to alleviate local difficulties, which sounds "reasonable" as proposed by some comrades. Suppose, then, that if one province were to be set at 50%, the other would immediately make a long list of demands for 60%, and the least developed outlying provinces might ask for more than 70%. The middle and developed regions will soon be equally indignant with a long list of reasons and "difficulties" for changing the ratio. In this way, the actual rules of the system will be transformed into a "one place, one rate" and bargaining system, and the basic framework of the tax distribution system will collapse. Problems such as "crying kids get milk", "endless bickering", "money from the ministry" and "public relations" under the table, which used to be rife with malpractice and uneven happiness, will come back again. The basic logic of dividing central and local income by tax would be lost. In this way, the fiscal system in reality is not a "tax distribution system" that is consistent with the unified market, fair competition environment and stable and normative system. Therefore, even if sharing tax, its sharing method must be the same throughout the country. "Adapt to local conditions" depends on the transfer payment to deal with. This has actually become the bottom line to safeguard the achievements of China's "94 reform" basic system.

It needs to be emphasized that the uniform allocation of tax base, the same sharing method and the same sharing proportion in different regions do not mean that the actual tax abundance (the amount of income per capita that can be realized in a certain tax) in different regions is leveled, but there will be different situations due to the differences in regional economic development level and other related factors. This situation is particularly significant in China where the regional disparity is great, objectively forming a stronger demand for balanced transfer payment system than the general economy.

Fifth, because income and expenditure are divided among governments according to different principles, tax abundance and supply cost are necessarily different in different regions. It is impossible for the central and local governments to make both ends meet, so it is objectively necessary to adjust the "horizontal imbalance between regions" with the top-down transfer payment system based on the "vertical imbalance between central and local governments".

The standard institutional arrangement inherently requires the uniformity of tax types and sharing proportion in different regions, but the actual tax abundance varies greatly due to the difference of regional economic development level and other related factors, which is destined to produce the significant "horizontal imbalance" of fiscal revenue abundance between regions. At the same time, the supply cost of public goods required by local governments to provide "equalization of basic public services" will produce another "horizontal imbalance" in expenditure burden due to huge regional differences, making less developed provinces (districts) face greater difficulties. It is precisely in places with low tax abundance that the per capita cost of public goods is very high because most of them are sparsely populated, plateau and mountainous areas with harsh natural conditions. On the other hand, places with high tax abundance are generally places with dense population, high level of urbanization, good natural conditions and living environment, and low per capita cost of providing public goods. The fiscal revenue abundance is low and the expenditure cost is high. This is a difficult situation generally faced by underdeveloped areas. Therefore, the solution to this problem under the framework of tax distribution system mainly relies on the "top-down" transfer payment system arrangement of the central finance and provincial finance for the less developed regions to form a sustainable overall plan to adjust regional differences.

The Proposal of Public Finance and the Construction of Public Finance System

1. The proposal of public finance and its essentials

In China, the concept of "public finance" is put forward in the process of economic and social transition. In the process of the transformation from the traditional system to the socialist market economy system, it is objectively necessary to form a basic orientation of fiscal function and fiscal form adjustment. After more than 10 years of exploration, this guidance is summarized as the guidance of public finance, which was clearly put forward by leading comrades of the financial department and the State Council in 1998. Subsequently, the requirements for the establishment of a framework for public finance were written into the documents of the plenum of the CPC central committee and the documents of the national development plan. The public finance proposed step by step from the original supply-oriented finance, production-construction-oriented finance and the "revitalization of finance" explored in the process of transition is a fiscal form that adapts to the requirements of the Times and can match the requirements of the new socialist market economy system and overall economic and social development in the new era.

As the name suggests, the key internal orientation of public finance is to emphasize the publicity of finance. Therefore, the basic characteristics of public finance should be reflected in at least the following four aspects.

First, to meet social and public needs as the main goal of financial allocation and focus of work. The core problem in this aspect is how to correctly handle the relationship between publicity and class. In short, the basis of the historic transformation that took place in China after the reform and opening up in the 1980s was an honest recognition that we must focus on economic development rather than class struggle. Now, it is necessary to further promote the scientific outlook on development, that is, the correct understanding that economic development is the central task and development is the absolute principle, and further promote the scientific development that is comprehensive and coordinated among the economy, society and nature. This general idea and direction, as the "absolute principle", is the strategic core of the basic line, which Deng Xiaoping stressed to hold fast and unswervingly for a hundred years. Lenin once pointed out that after the establishment of the socialist regime, the state becomes a quasi-state and a semi-state in a certain sense—that is, it enters the process of the so-called demise of the state. Now, it seems that although this will be a long historical process, but the class content is gradually thinning, we must grasp the dominant public needs and emphasize the meeting of social public needs as the main goal and focus of the financial system.

The second basic feature is that finance should take the provision of public goods and services that cannot be effectively provided by the market as the basic way to meet social public needs. The essential problem contained in this basic feature is to reasonably grasp the division of labor and cooperation between the government and the market.

The market should be the basic mechanism of resource allocation, but it also has some failure areas, which need the government to intervene and adjust accordingly. Among them, it is very important to provide public goods and services that the market cannot effectively provide. Only in this way, the government and the market form a reasonable complementary division of labor complementary relationship, which can be conducive to the full liberation of productivity, the overall optimization of resource allocation and the maximization of the overall social benefits and welfare.

The third basic feature is the standard public choice based on the premise of equal civil rights and political power balance, as the decision-making and supervision mechanism of financial allocation (i.e., the allocation of public resources). The essential content of this basic feature is to ensure the democratization, legalization and constitutionalism of financial management, the scientization of decision-making and the maximization of public needs. Normative public choice is also a basic path of political civilization construction. Compared to the state of finance that we didn't get into before, and the decision-making mechanisms for the state of finance in the old state and the new state, the essential improvement of public finance can be attributed to the establishment of a set of institutional framework for regulating public choice of power balance in the process of democratization of public affairs and promotion of political civilization interaction. In China's rapid economic and social transition, the "golden period of development" and the "period of prominent contradictions", all kinds of contradictions are intertwined in a complex way. This requires us to actively consider from the perspective of the system how to use the institutional space in the direction of political civilization development, alleviate contradictions, handle public affairs well, fully reflect the public will as far as possible and accomplish the modernization process with relative smoothness and without great social cost.

The fourth basic feature is that in the management and operation of public finance, the basic management system should be the budget with openness, transparency, integrity, pre-determination and strict implementation in the modern sense. The "openness" here still has a direct echo with the expression of public finance. The budget, with its logical beginning, integrity and normative modern significance, will become the realization carrier of all concepts, principles, objectives and institutional elements of public finance. The essence of this feature is to prevent the distortion of public power, regulate government behavior, implement the public will and pursue the maximization of public interests by means of an elaborate and perfect financial management system.

2. Review of management system support and management reform of public finance system construction

In 1998, the framework of building public finance in China was put forward. It was in line with the Deng Xiaoping's goal model of socialist market economy established after the southern talk in 1992 and a major reform of the tax distribution system introduced in 1994. The macro "indirect regulation" framework required by the objective market economy logically leads to the milestone reform of China's fiscal system from the administrative decentralization of "the system of dividing revenue and expenditure between the central and local governments (local responsibility)" to the "economic decentralization" in the form of tax distribution and classification. Under the framework of tax distribution established in 1994, the relationship between government and enterprise finally broke out of the control paradigm of administrative subordination, and the government no longer organizes fiscal revenue according to the administrative subordination of enterprises. Instead, all enterprises, regardless of size, administrative level or economic nature (state-owned or non-state-owned), shall pay national and local taxes to governments at different levels according to law. To compete on a level playing field with each other, at the same time, the so-called "system cycle" no longer exists between the central and local governments. An unprecedented and stable and standardized fiscal system based on "tax distribution" has been formed. This reform achievement becomes the system support which further launches the public finance reform.

Since the establishment of public finance framework in 1998, China has actively promoted a series of reform measures within the financial system, in order to implement the system innovation, management innovation and technology innovation required by public finance. Its main contents are:

(1) Implement departmental budget (comprehensive budget) reform. The core requirement of departmental budgets is that, in preparing and reporting their budgets, all government financial resources, including both budgetary and extra-budgetary funds, should be fully accounted for, so as to ensure the integrity of their budgets. The reform began in 1999. Within a few years, the department budget framework compatible with the socialist market economy system has been basically formed. The reform also extends to the depth and advances the project budget rolling management and so on. The reform of departmental budgets has gradually made government budgeting more complete, transparent, standardized, fair and efficient. It has significantly changed the outdated, less transparent and less binding budgeting methods in China, and provided the most important and fundamental institutional guarantee for the construction of public finance.

(2) The reform of centralized receipt and payment of the state Treasury in a single account was carried out, and a centralized receipt and payment system of the state Treasury conducive to the whole process supervision of financial funds and the pursuit of efficient operation was established. The reform began in August 2001 in the central government and was fully implemented in 2008, which was implemented in all central government departments and their more than 10,000 grassroots budget units; general budgetary funds at the central level, government-managed funds and budgetary funds for the operation of state capital will all be paid from the state treasury, and the reform will be gradually expanded to include some special transfer payments from central government subsidies to local governments. The vast majority of central budget departments have carried out the pilot reform of official business cards at their respective levels to further standardize and reduce cash expenditures. The reform at the local level has also made significant progress.

(3) Carry out the reform of "income and expenditure line". In recent years, the basic content of the reform of "two lines of revenue and expenditure" is that the various charges and incomes from fines and confiscations of the units exercising the public power are no longer linked with the unit's expenditure and welfare treatment, but enter the special financial account and are classified as the overall planning of the budget. The expenditures of the imposing unit shall be arranged in accordance with the budget. In this reform, progress has been made in standardizing the management of fee-charging funds, cleaning up government-managed fund projects when they are due, and in curbing arbitrary fees for education and reducing the burden on farmers. In general, non-tax government revenue, such as administrative fees, government-managed funds, revenue from the paid use of state-owned resources (assets), revenue from state-owned capital operations, lottery funds, and revenue from fines and confiscations, should be included in the "two lines of revenue and expenditure" management.

(4) Reform the government procurement system represented by centralized procurement through tendering and bidding. Since 1999, China has increased the content of centralized government procurement in the department budget of central government units. The reform of the government procurement system has been comprehensively carried out in state organs, institutions and organizations at all levels. The scope of application of some government centralized procurement projects was clarified in the *Catalogue and Standards of Central Budget Units for Centralized Government Procurement in 2005*, expanding the scope of departmental centralized procurement projects and enhancing their operability. The current open bidding for bulk government procurement makes the government procurement behavior compatible with the market mechanism constrained and optimized, improves the efficiency of the use of funds, significantly inhibits corruption and improves the level of regulation. The size of government procurement increased from 32.8 billion Yuan in 2000 to 599.09 billion Yuan in 2008 and more than 1 trillion Yuan in 2012, with a saving rate of about 11%.

(5) Actively promote the reform of the financial transfer payment system. China's financial transfer payment system has made great progress after the reform of tax distribution system in 1994 and has been further improved and perfected in the process of building the public finance framework thereafter. In recent years, China's financial transfer payment system has been constantly improved, especially the establishment and improvement of financial transfer payment, which has changed the financial management system mode of "one-to-one" negotiation and "bargaining" between central finance and local finance before the reform of fiscal management system of tax distribution system, enhanced the systematic-ness and rationality of financial management system and reduced the arbitrariness in determining the amount of local subsidies. The growing scale of transfer payments has supported the administrative operations and social programs in the economically underdeveloped central and western regions, and promoted equal access to basic public services among regions. At the same time, special transfer payments are mainly used to support weak links in economic and social development. The newly increased special transfer payments are mainly used to support agriculture, education, science, culture, health, social security and other fields related to people's livelihood, which reflects the requirements of public finance.
(6) Reform the classification of government revenues and expenditures in line with international standards. The government revenue and expenditure classification reform implemented in China on January 1, 2007, brings the classification and subject system of budget revenue and expenditure in line with international standards, and it is also an infrastructure construction of the framework of public finance system. Its contents include the unified classification of government revenue, the establishment of a new functional classification system of government expenditure and a new classification system of expenditure economy. The ministry of finance will compile the budget according to the new government revenue and expenditure accounts. In November 2007, the ministry of finance and the people's bank of China adjusted the classification of government revenue and expenditure in 2008 in combination with the budget reform of state-owned capital operation. Since then, according to the needs of the

reform, the government revenue and expenditure classification subject is constantly revised. In the next step, we will continue to deepen the reform of classifying government revenue and expenditures, and establish a unified and standardized system of government revenue and expenditures accounts that are jointly implemented by finance departments at all levels.

(7) Discuss and explore the methods of financial performance evaluation system and the gradual construction of performance budget. Paying attention to performance is an inevitable requirement of the deepening of budget reform, which is intended to effectively improve the efficiency of government management and the effectiveness of financial funds. In recent years, the financial department actively studies and formulates standardized performance evaluation management methods, strives to clarify the scope, object and content of performance evaluation, strives to establish a preliminary performance evaluation system and gradually introduces the concept and method of performance budget into the fiscal expenditure management of China. At present, a number of projects have been selected by the central government and many local governments for pilot budget performance evaluation. On the basis of summarizing the work experience of budget performance evaluation of all departments, the pilot scope will be appropriately expanded, and the results of performance evaluation will be combined with the department budget preparation in an attempt to change the phenomenon of "heavy distribution, light management" in the previous budget fund arrangement.

(8) Actively implement the "golden financial project". China's ministry of finance is organizing and implementing the construction of the "gold financial project", namely the "government financial management information system (GFMIS)", aiming to establish an information platform for financial management and financial supervision that comprehensively reflects the government's financial resources and supports scientific decision-making of public finance in order to realize revision and improvement of department budgeting system, technical support and application service from the central to the local departments. The planning and implementation of the "gold financial project" is a major project in the reform of the financial management

system. Its comprehensive promotion can enable financial management departments at all levels to improve the level of budget revenue and expenditure management, eliminate the system distortion and public fund benefit loss caused by subjective, profit-driven or human error with objective and institutional norms, and significantly improve the performance of public finance operation.

3. The change of fiscal expenditure structure in strengthening the "public" orientation

Since China took the construction of public finance as the goal of fiscal transformation to adapt to the socialist market economic system in 1998, the concepts of "publicity" and "equalization of public services", which correspond to the construction of socialist market economic system, the realization of comprehensive, coordinated and sustainable development of social economy and the construction of a harmonious society, have become increasingly clear. While the public revenue system has been developed and improved through the reform of taxes and fees, the structure of fiscal expenditure has also changed significantly.

(1) Basic livelihood security became the focus of fiscal expenditure. Since 1998, under the guidance of public finance, the focus of fiscal expenditure has been on making up for the market failure areas, namely non-profit and non-competitive areas, gradually correcting the "offside" and "absence" of the government, and continuously strengthening and improving people's livelihood. Especially after the 16th national congress of the communist party of China, with the establishment of "people-oriented", "five overall planning", "building a harmonious society" and other governance and administration concepts, it has become the focus of the government to solve some of the most concerned, the most direct, the most realistic interests of the people. In the financial sector, a series of fiscal and taxation policies and measures have been introduced and actively explored to meet the needs of the people and improve their overall welfare. People's livelihood has become the focus of expenditure restructuring. For example, we will

increase fiscal support for farmers, increase public spending on education and health care, give more priority to public education and health resources in rural areas, the central and western regions, poor areas, border areas and ethnic minority areas, and ensure equal access to basic public services. We have vigorously supported the development of the social security system, ensured that the subsistence allowance system is in line with the employment and reemployment policies, formulated and implement fiscal and taxation preferential policies for employment and reemployment, adjusted and raise pensions for enterprise retirees, and extended the subsistence allowance system to rural areas, expanded the coverage of the new type of rural cooperative medical care and raised the level of government input and launched reform of the universal healthcare system in 2009, and so on. For example, in terms of supporting the development of education, the national financial expenditure on education increased from 335.2 billion Yuan in 2003 to 901 billion Yuan in 2008, an increase of about 1.7 times in six years, and rose to 1043.8 billion Yuan in 2010, an increase of 15.8% over 2008. Of this, the central government spent 198.14 billion Yuan on education, an increase of 23.6%. For another example, in terms of supporting the development of medical and health undertakings, the national financial expenditure on medical and health care increased from 83.1 billion Yuan in 2003 to 275.7 billion Yuan in 2008, more than tripled, and jumped to 399.4 billion Yuan again in 2010, with an annual growth rate of 44.9%. At the same time, from the perspective of the direction of capital construction expenditure of the central government, the trend of concentrated investment in the fields of people's livelihood is also very obvious, such as projects to improve rural production and living conditions, rural water conservancy and other major infrastructure projects and construction projects that involve the vital interests of the masses and need to be promptly addressed. *The Proposal of the Central Committee of the Communist Party of China on Formulating the 12th Five-Year Plan for National Economic and Social Development*, which was adopted at the fifth plenary session of the 17th central committee of the communist party of China, clearly sets forth the requirements for the formation of a system of basic public services during the 12th five-year plan period.

(2) Promote coordinated and sustainable socio-economic development. With the development of reform and opening up, in view of some deep-seated contradictions in China's economic and social development, such as the imbalance between regions, the obvious gap between urban and rural areas, the backward and extensive mode of economic development and so on, the government has made great efforts to increase investment in fiscal distribution, and implemented measures to alleviate contradictions and promote coordination. In terms of regional coordination, the central budget for local transfer payments reached 2,560.66 billion Yuan in 2010, of which general transfer payments increased from 2.1 billion Yuan in 1995 to 1,229.57 billion Yuan in 2010, an increase of 585 times. The overall level of central transfer payments to local standard income and expenditure gap has rapidly increased from 9.6% in 2000 to 81% in 2007. In terms of spending on agriculture, for the first time since 2003, the central government spent more than 200 billion Yuan on agriculture, rural areas and farmers, reaching 214.4 billion Yuan. From 2003 to 2007, the central government spent 2,153.67 billion Yuan on agriculture, rural areas and farmers. From 2008 to 2010, with the relaunch of the proactive fiscal policy, the central government's input in agriculture, rural areas and farmers hit a new high. In 2009, the expenditure increased by more than 20% to 716 billion Yuan. Spending on agriculture, forestry and water resources hit a new high in 2010, up 19.8%. From 2003 to 2008, the central government spent 457 billion Yuan on science and technology to support independent innovation, energy conservation and emissions reduction. In addition, we vigorously support ecological construction and environmental protection. On the basis of certain achievements in key ecological projects, such as the protection of natural forests, the return of farmland to forests and grassland, and the prevention and control of desertification, we will continue to increase financial input, actively promote follow-up policy adjustments for returning farmland to forests, establish a system of compensation funds for forest ecological benefits and support the

pilot reform of the management system of state-owned forest farms and the system of state-owned forest rights.

(3) Support the cultivation of market economic entities. Fiscal allocation actively serves the overall interests of building a socialist market economic system, increases input in cultivating market players and takes support measures for enterprises of different ownerships. In terms of supporting state-owned enterprises, we have invested a lot in stripping off the social functions of central enterprises, separating the main and auxiliary functions of state-owned enterprises and reforming them into subsidiary businesses, and reforming the system of monopolized industries. From 2004 to 2007, with the exception of agricultural reclamation and forestry enterprises, the social functions of the separate offices of central government enterprises were fully completed. For this purpose, the central government has approved a total of 9.68 billion Yuan in subsidies for 2,640 institutions and 4.77 billion Yuan in assets. In 2004, the state council decided to gradually solve the problem of large collectives run by factories in northeast China in accordance with the principle of "pilot projects first, and then promote". The central government set up special subsidy funds to actively support the pilot reform. From 2003 to 2007, a total of 76 central enterprises received approval and financial support for the overall plan and implementation of the reform and diversion of the main and auxiliary sectors, involving 675,000 workers who had their labor contracts terminated and 29.54 billion Yuan in economic compensation paid.

(4) In terms of supporting the non-state-owned economy, the focus of fiscal expenditure is mainly on small and medium-sized enterprises. In line with the characteristics of the development of small and medium-sized enterprises, and in accordance with the national macroeconomic goals and industrial development plans, we will gradually establish fiscal and capital policies for all types of small and medium-sized non-public enterprises. During the tenth five-year plan period, the central government allocated a total of 8.5 billion Yuan of special funds to support small and medium-sized enterprises to promote the rapid development of non-public small and medium-sized enterprises. According to statistics, by 2007, more than 30

provincial financial departments had set up about 160 special funds to support the development of small and medium-sized enterprises. In addition, by increasing the investment in environmental construction of small and medium-sized enterprises, we have encouraged service agencies, guaranteed agencies and venture capital enterprises for small and medium-sized enterprises, actively provided non-public SMEs with services such as technology sharing, information sharing and financing guarantee, and guided private capital to invest in small and medium-sized enterprises in their initial stage of development, so as to create favorable conditions for their development.

(5) The basic ideas and essentials of deepening the reform of the financial system in the course of comprehensive reform.

China's economy has entered the new normal. In 2015, the comprehensive deepening of reform began to enter the implementation stage after the formulation of top-level design. It is the "difficult period of difficult period"; power and resistance coexist. As the conclusion of the 12th five-year plan is approaching and the 13th five-year plan is in preparation, the breakthrough way to comprehensively deepen reform is to grasp the strategy and make timely adjustments. Reform of the fiscal system will be a key step in comprehensively deepening reform. In the deepening of reform, improve the fiscal system of China's tax system. In line with the flattening of the government level and the integration and streamlining under the orientation of "big ministry system", we should follow the three-level framework of the central government, provinces and cities and counties and the principles of "first-level political power, first-level administrative power, first-level financial power, first-level tax base, first-level budget, first-level property right and first-level debt raising". With the transfer payment system from top to bottom at the central and provincial levels and from horizontal to horizontal at the regional level, a fiscal system should be established that is compatible with the market economic system in terms of administrative power and financial power, as well as financial resources and expenditure responsibilities.

According to the outstanding contradictions and real problems in the deepening reform of tax distribution system since the "94 reform", the future reform should focus on at least:

1. Actively and gradually promote the implementation of the sub-provincial tax distribution system in the "minimum package" supporting reform; through the reform of direct provincial management of county, township financial management and comprehensive supporting system, the original five levels of government in China are flattened into three levels of central government, provincial government and city and county government (different regions may have the first and then), which serves as a framework basis for the transformation from "mountains and rivers" to "a bright future".
2. Adjust and straighten out the division of powers at the central and local levels under the top-level planning. Then, according to the attributes and logic principles of government affairs, reasonably and clearly divide the responsibility of inter-governmental expenditure, and start the work of forming a detailed list of administrative power and expenditure responsibility from rough to detailed as soon as possible, and then dynamically optimize and strengthen the performance evaluation constraints. Local governments should withdraw from the investment field of general competitive projects, the judicial power of economic cases should be concentrated at the central level, etc.
3. With the tax reform as the coordination, actively improve the income distribution system at all levels, which is mainly based on tax allocation; vigorously promote reform of resource taxes and legislation on real estate taxes; expand the scope of collection of consumption tax and adjust the collection of consumption tax on some items and transfer part of the income from consumption tax items to local governments; classify the vehicle purchase tax as local income; in actively promoting the reform of replacing business tax with value-added tax, the central government takes the increase of VAT revenue as the source of general transfer payments from the central government to local governments.
4. Optimize the equalization formula of transfer payment according to factors such as population, geography, service cost and functional area positioning, and strengthen financial support for underdeveloped local governments; appropriately reduce the proportion of

special transfer payments in total transfer payments, merge and integrate similar items in special projects or merge projects; try to make the specific information arrive at the local level as early as possible, and in principle cancel its "local supporting funds" requirements, in order to facilitate the overall preparation and serious implementation of the local budget; in addition, actively explore ways to optimize the cross-regional transfer payment systems such as "give assistance to an oriented area" and "ecological compensation".

5. Deepen the reform of budget management at all levels in combination with the supporting reform, and actively try to compile the rolling budget in the middle of 3–5 years from the central level under the premise of full-caliber budget; the single account Treasury centralized collection and payment system was developed into "horizontal to the border, vertical to the end"; in addition, it supports and optimizes the scientific decision-making of the allocation of public resources in the whole society represented by the budget system with the construction of a complete set of modern information systems in the form of "golden finance project" and "golden tax project". It is necessary to accelerate the construction of public debt and municipal debt system for local sunshine financing, and gradually replace hidden liabilities such as local financing platforms with insufficient transparency, lack of standardization and high risk prevention cost and difficulty; the construction of local state-owned assets management system should also be actively promoted in combination with the construction of state-owned capital operation budget system.

6. Under the path dependence of "gradual reform" and the multiple constraints and logic orientation of "building a country under the rule of law" and "strengthening public knowledge and participation", gradually and actively and rationally promote the construction of fiscal and taxation laws, master the balance between "innovation and development in the standard" and "innovation and development in the standard" under the premise of serving the overall situation, strengthen and optimize top-level planning and continue to encourage pilot projects, and in the historical period of economic and social transition, the stable rules that can be looked into constantly and timely have been legislated.

(6) Public finance lays a good foundation for the establishment of a modern financial system

Financial system arrangement reflects the relationship between the government and the market, between the government and society, and between the central government and the local government, involving economy, politics, culture, society, ecological civilization and other aspects. In 1994, the tax distribution reform adjusted the financial relationship between the central and local governments on the basis of raising the "two proportions", emphasizing the initiative of the central and local governments and forming the basic framework of China's existing financial system. It has become an important breakthrough in the reform of China's market economic system in the twentieth century and laid the foundation for the rapid development of China's social economy in the past 20 years. The synchronized tax system reform further standardized the relationship between the government and the market, released the vitality of micro-market subjects, effectively promoted the operation of the market economy system and improved the government's ability to regulate and control the economy. As mentioned above, the exploration of establishing public financial system since 1998 focused on the improvement of expenditure system and adjustment of expenditure structure, and the focus of fiscal expenditure shifted from the field of economic construction to the field of people's livelihood. In 1999, the reform of the budget system was initiated, and the framework of the modern budget system was initially established through the introduction of departmental budgets, centralized treasury receipts and payments, and government procurement. The construction and improvement of the public finance system have standardized the relations between the central and local governments, the state and enterprises, the government and the market, and laid a good foundation for the construction of the modern financial system.

Different from the public finance emphasized since 1998, the connotation of modern financial system is richer. Modern financial system is the inheritance and development of traditional financial system. The rise of market economy has inherent conflict with the traditional financial system. Because the contradiction between the market, capital and the government is more and more conflicted, it is urgent to construct a new fiscal system that can restrain the revenue and expenditure of the government. The modern government budget system is established under this background. Modern financial system itself is also in constant evolution and increasingly highlights the concept of national governance. The third plenary session of the 18th PC central committee adopted the *Decision of the CPC Central Committee on A Number of Major Issues Related to Comprehensively Deepening Reform.* For the first time, it is clear from the perspective of national governance that finance is the foundation and important pillar of national governance, and the establishment of a modern financial system is an important strategic orientation. It also puts forward the key points of constructing modern financial system from three aspects: Establishing a complete, standard, transparent and efficient modern government budget management system; to build a unified tax system conducive to scientific development, social equity and market; to establish a system in which administrative power and expenditure responsibility are compatible. Thus, it can be seen that the characteristics of the modern financial system are as follows: The modern financial system is a system that adapts to the national modernization and is a democratic and legalized financial system that adapts to the needs of dynamic financial governance.

1.4 The International Practice of Tax Distribution System and Reference to China

As the distribution system of a country's "fiscal control by administration and administration through fiscal management", the first problem is to solve the problem that the government allocates public resources to fulfill its social management power and function. What is closely related to and inseparable from it is the allocation of social resources. Therefore, the essence of financial system arrangement is to deal with the three basic relationships in economic and social life: The distribution of financial resources, resources and interests between the government and market subjects, between the central government and local governments at all levels, and between the public power system and citizens. The relationship of rights, responsibilities and interests between the government and tens of millions of enterprises, between the central government and local governments at all levels, and between the public power system and citizens or taxpayers is inevitably reflected and converged in the financial system. In terms of financial allocation of "fiscal control by administration and administration through fiscal management", the institutional arrangement should first solve the problems of resource allocation based on property right contract and legal environment, efficiency incentive under the role of the government, entrepreneurship and innovation response mechanism, as well as the fairness, predictability and sustainability of the interest distribution process, so as to serve, influence and balance the overall resource allocation.

Tax distribution system is the abbreviation of tax distribution and classification system. From an international perspective, the following basic observations can be made: In the stage of development of human society to the modern civilization, the fiscal system of tax distribution and classification is a common system and basic practice mode in the development of market economy. Its system includes, first of all, the rational division of administrative power (expenditure responsibility) and financial power (broad tax base allocation) among governments at all levels; to establish fiscal budgets for raising funds and managing expenditures at different levels according to tax revenues; then the hierarchical property rights management and debt management, as well as the transfer payment system. The tax distribution system not only meets the internal requirements for the government to maintain the market order under the market economy, to form a long-term mechanism of fair competition among market subjects in the legalized environment and to provide the function positioning of public products, but also meets the public needs for the standardization and predictable division of labor and cooperation among governments at all levels to improve the efficiency of public resource allocation.

The market economy, which is based on the mechanism of market allocation of resources, requires the government to focus on maintaining social equity and justice and making up for market failures and deficiencies. Therefore, the government's administrative power and financial power are mainly positioned in the public sphere, with the provision of public goods and services as the main goal and focus of work. In the inter-governmental financial relations, the principle of externality, complexity of information processing and compatibility of incentives should be followed. The government at all levels shall perform the function of public finance in a standardized way and divide the administrative power and financial power reasonably among the governments at all levels. It is accompanied by the financial balance mechanism, namely the transfer payment dominated by the "top-down flow" of funds. This framework is the fiscal decentralization framework under the concept of "economic decentralization", which is also the fiscal system arrangement in the international experience of "fiscal federalism".

The Basic Situation of the US Tax Distribution System

The United States is a typical federal market economy country, with government agencies divided into three levels: Federal, state and local (county, city, town, school district, special district, etc.). In the history of the United States, it experienced the development process from the confederation to the federation. After continuous practice and improvement, it basically formed a relatively standardized inter-governmental financial relationship. That is to say, governments at all levels have clear administrative power and financial power, and implement the tax distribution system characterized by separate legislation, revenue sharing and top-down transfer payment system between governments.

1. Division of powers of governments at all levels

American governments at all levels follow the following principles in the division of powers: First, the principle of scope of benefits. In other words, different project beneficiaries and the scope of benefits are taken as the basis to distinguish the functions of governments at all levels. The federal government shall be responsible for any public project that has a macroscopic and overall situation and benefits the whole country and the whole people. State or local governments are responsible for projects that benefit only one region and are part of a whole. Second, the principle of improving efficiency. In other words, the government with the lowest investment cost and the highest work efficiency is responsible for a certain business or project. Third, the principle of unification of administrative power and financial power. That is to say, the administrative power of the first-level government should be compatible with the financial power of the first-level government, and the financial capacity should be reasonably distributed among the governments at all levels. According to the above principles, the state government mainly provides public goods and services that benefit from the state. Mainly include: State administration, social welfare, education, debt, infrastructure, management of state businesses and transportation, etc. In line with its scope of administrative power, the state government's expenditure responsibilities include: Expenditure on public works, basic education, medical and health care, income insurance, public welfare programs, fire protection, police, gas and water supply, servicing of state debts, etc. Local governments in the United States (here refers to the government below the state level, different from the meaning of local government in China) are mainly responsible for local administration, public security, fire protection, traffic management, public utilities, local education, local infrastructure investment and construction, family and community service management.

The authority and responsibility of governments at all levels are determined in legal form, thus laying a foundation for dividing the expenditure scope of finance at all levels. Generally speaking, the fiscal expenditure of the state government is mainly used for the development of education, public welfare, highway construction and medical and health undertakings, while the fiscal expenditure of the local government is mainly used for public security, fire control, sanitation and other aspects.

2. Tax division of governments at all levels

The federal, state and local governments all compile and implement their own independent budgets, have the right to set and change their own tax categories and tax rates according to law, and have their own relatively stable sources of income.

The federal constitution clearly stipulates the responsibility of financial power at all levels. The authority of federal finance mainly includes: Taxation power and expenditure function. The federal constitution provides that congress has the power to levy taxes for the repayment of the debt, the defense of the nation and the general interest of the United States. This overall interest is interpreted to include not only general objectives such as defense, justice, etc., but also highly selective programs that target specific regions or demographic groups, such as aid grants and transfer payments. The principle of uniform taxation, the federal constitution stipulates that "duties, duties on domestic goods and other duties shall be uniform throughout the country". Tax uniformity requires states to pay the same tax at the same rate, not at the same rate. Equal treatment is required for the same taxpayer, regardless of the size of the region and tax source, which are taxed in proportion.

The federal, state and local governments have their own relatively independent tax systems and enjoy the right to set, design and manage their own tax rates. Parliaments at all levels may determine their own tax laws and systems within the scope of the constitution, and governments at all levels may decide on the types of taxes and the standards for their collection. The three levels of government respectively exercise the tax legislative power, judicial power and executive power, which makes the United States form a unified federal tax system and different state and local tax systems coexist. Governments at all levels have some taxes of their own, and governments at all levels have their own main taxes. Take the income tax as an example. Each level of government has its own income tax law and independently collects its own income tax. State and local governments can decide for themselves what kind of deductions to make to taxpayers. Like the federal income taxes that are paid by the taxpayers, 25 states and the federal governments have adopted a "'Unified tax base, fraction collection' and no deduction has been made for what the taxpayer has paid. 16 states allow the deduction of prepaid federal income taxes. In the United States, the method of taxation and tax rate are also decided by governments at all levels".

Federal taxes include personal income taxes, corporate income taxes, social security payroll taxes, excise taxes, sales taxes, inheritance and gift taxes, and tariffs. Among them individual income tax is main tax category. State taxes include sales taxes, personal income taxes, corporate income taxes, excise taxes and royalties. Sales tax is the main tax category. This kind of tax is a price excluded in tax, which is closely related to economic development and commodity circulation. It is suitable as the main tax of the independent state government. Local government taxes include property taxes, sales taxes, income taxes and some user fees, mainly property taxes. Property taxes are levied on all types of property, including real and personal property. The real tax is mainly real estate property tax. The tax base is the property value at specific time points. The tax rate is determined according to a certain proportion of the monetary value of the property. At the same time, governments at all levels divide tax revenue by sharing tax sources and tax rates. That is through the individual income tax with the federal level as the focus of the multi-level same-origin sharing levy; the separate collection of many other taxes well handled the financial relationship between the governments of the United States, a big federal country, and provided a fund guarantee system for the governments at all levels to fulfill their functions and realize their goals of social development and economic regulation and provide a funding guarantee system. The division of fiscal revenue with the same tax and tax revenue sharing in United States is unique in the financial systems of all countries in the world.

In terms of the distribution of tax revenue, the United States implements the distinctive share-sharing system, that is, except that each fiscal level has a main tax type as the main source of revenue, most of the remaining tax sources are jointly collected by fiscal authorities at all levels at different rates. As mentioned above, the federal government is mainly based on individual income tax (45% of the federal government's income), supplemented by consumption tax, estate tax and tariff. The state government takes consumption tax as the main body (accounting for more than 30% of the state government income), supplemented by income tax and goods tax; local governments are dominated by property taxes and supplemented by other taxes. In terms of the division of main taxes, the United States combines the nature of taxes with the characteristics of different levels of government. Moreover, the higher the government level is, the more taxes it has. This not only enables governments at all levels to have stable and reliable sources of income, but also facilitates the implementation of macro-control policies by the federal government.

3. Transfer payments from governments at all levels

Transfer payments between governments at all levels are carried out from top to bottom.

The federal government controls the major taxes and income sources, concentrates a large amount of financial resources, arranges a considerable part of funds in its annual budget, grants various forms of subsidies to the state and local governments and forms a relatively complete intergovernmental transfer payment system. The purpose of implementing this system is to adjust and alleviate the difference of public service level between regions. On the other hand, the purpose is to promote state and local government allocation behavior in line with the federal government's macro policy objectives.

Transfer payment in the United States can be divided into several types according to different conditions of use: First, earmarks. The state or local government that receives the grant must use it for the specified purpose and manner. The largest earmarks are for social security, medicare, education and training, and transportation. Such grants directly reflect the regulatory intent of the federal government. Second, supporting appropriations. In earmarks, the federal government requires the recipient state or local government to allocate a set proportion of its own funds to projects to guide the delivery of public services in line with federal goals. Third, non-earmarked funds. The purpose of the grant is to narrow the differences in the level of public services between different regions due to their different tax capacities and to enhance their capacity for self-development. Fourth, tax expenditures. In other words, the federal government gives a deduction for some items of state and local income tax, which is actually a subsidy for related items. For example, interest on state and local government bonds is exempt from federal income tax. The transfer payment method in the United States is relatively standardized. On the one hand, most of the appropriations are calculated according to the established formula, which fully takes into account the per capita income, urban population and tax collection situation, avoids human intervention and influence, and has strong transparency and impartiality. On the other hand, the federal government is gradually adopting the representative tax system, that is, the allocation of funds based on tax capacity, tax effort and other efficiency factors instead of per capita factors. In addition to the federal government, states also transfer payments to local governments.

Basic Situation of German Tax Distribution System

Germany is a federal country with a parliamentary system and a three-level system of federal, state and local taxation for fiscal relations between governments. Germany's fiscal decentralization is coordinated and operated in a standardized way and is guaranteed by the *Basic Law* as the national constitution. First of all, according to the principle of moderate concentration and relative decentralization, the expenditure scope of governments at all levels is determined, and the governments at all levels are endowed with certain tax authority. Sharing tax and exclusive tax coexist, and sharing tax is the main mode to divide tax revenue. In addition, the system of vertical and horizontal transfer payments was also implemented to adjust the surplus and deficit of financial funds between the federal government and various states. The standardization and legalization of German fiscal decentralization, as well as the measures to ensure the leading role of the federal government in macro-control, are worthy of our reference.

1. Division of powers of governments at all levels

Germany implements the three-level management system of federal, state and local governments, and adopts the mode of decentralization, autonomy and moderately centralized division of fiscal and tax authority. Germany is a country with a fiscal federalism. In fiscal theory, the scope of government expenditure at all levels is determined according to the benefit range of public goods, and it is believed that the responsibility of income distribution and the responsibility of economic stability have national significance, and the central government should implement this policy nationwide. Local governments can play a greater role in regional resource allocation.

The *Basic Law* of Germany first stipulated the administrative power of the federal government in the division of expenditure. The administrative powers of the federal government mainly include: Federal administration, financial administration and national customs affairs; state security and armed forces; foreign affairs and international relations; nationwide communications, post and telecommunications; major scientific research and development programs, such as space technology, nuclear energy and marine development; part of the cost of social security, including health care, unemployment, pensions and welfare payments. In addition, by law, the federal bank of Germany is responsible for the issuance and management of money. The main responsibilities of the state government include: Administrative affairs and financial management at the state level; to maintain social order and judicial administration; educational and social and cultural undertakings; medical and health care; environmental protection. In addition, under the principle of high efficiency and low cost, the responsibilities of federal highway construction, shipping, energy development and utilization can be transferred to the state government after the approval of the legislative body. The primary responsibility of sub-state governments is to provide public goods and services with a strong regional character. The specific scope includes: Administrative affairs management, infrastructure construction, social relief, cultural and educational undertakings, local public security protection, public transportation and urban development planning at the local level. At the same time, the *Basic Law* also takes into account the intersecting issues of business and expenditure. It also provides that the responsibility shared by the federal government and the state government shall be determined by the two parties through an agreement on the proportion of their respective expenses. All expenses for matters entrusted to the federal government by the states shall be borne by the federal government, but the states shall ensure that they shall be used exclusively.

2. Tax revenue division of governments at all levels

The tax authority mainly includes tax legislative power, tax levying power, adjustment power and reduction power. Germany's tax authority is divided according to the mode of centralization of legislative power and decentralization of executive power. At the federal level, Germany naturally has separate legislative power on federal taxes such as tariffs and enjoys priority legislative power on shared taxes. State and local governments have greater power over local taxes, such as property taxes, and can set their own tax rates, deductions and surcharges. Germany's federal tax administration collects tariffs and federal excise taxes, while other federal and local taxes are collected by state and local tax authorities. When there is a conflict between the federal and state tax laws, the federal government makes the final decision. In addition, German law stipulates that taxes already levied by the central government cannot be levied by local governments. This is different from countries such as the United States and Canada, which are also federalist.

Germany divides all taxes into shared and exclusive. The shared tax is shared by the federal, state and local governments, or the federal and state governments. It is distributed among the governments at all levels in accordance with a certain proportion. The exclusive tax is the fixed income of the governments at all levels. Shared taxes include: Personal income tax (distributed among federal, state and local governments in the proportions of 43%, 43% and 14%), corporate income tax and value-added tax (50% federal and 50% state), and business tax (20%, 20% and 60% between federal, state and local governments). The exclusive taxes of the federal government mainly include tariff, salt tax, monopoly tax, insurance tax, capital flow tax, federal consumption tax and tax imposed by the European Economic Community. The state government's exclusive taxes mainly include: Property tax, estate tax, beer tax, fire tax, motor vehicle tax, horse race tax and lottery tax. The exclusive taxes of local government mainly include: Land tax, capital and gains tax, entertainment tax, beverage tax, etc. The main feature of German tax-sharing system is sharing tax, which accounts for more than 2/3 of the total tax revenue. With the exception of the European Economic Community (EEC), which takes 3% of the fixed income of governments at all levels plus their share of the shared tax, the share of all tax revenues is 48.7% at the federal level, 34.7% at the state level and 16.6% at the local level. Of course, according to the actual changes, once every two to four years, the above sharing proportion shall be adjusted as necessary through legal procedures.

3. Transfer payments between governments at all levels

German governments at all levels implement vertical and horizontal financial transfer payment system.

Germany's vertical fiscal balance, including federal transfer payments to the state and state transfer payments to the local. Among them, the federal transfer payment to the state government takes the form of direct allocation of a part of shared income to the state. The second is to support one or more causes in the state to achieve the stated policy objectives. State transfer payments to local governments usually take the form of general subsidies and special subsidies. General subsidies usually do not specify the specific use and general investment of funds, nor do they require local governments to provide corresponding supporting funds. Instead, they grant local governments greater freedom in the use of funds, so that local governments can flexibly arrange capital investment according to local actual conditions. Germany's general subsidies, which are designed and implemented in accordance with the requirements of the factor law, account for more than 50% of the total vertical allocations from the central government to local governments. When calculating the amount of subsidy, the financial demand is calculated first, which is equal to the per capita fiscal income of each place in the state multiplied by the weighted per capita population of that place. Second, figure out the financial capacity of the place. Then, according to the actual situation in the state, an adjustment coefficient is calculated, which is about 0.5~0.9. According to the result of the given formula "(financial demand number − financial capacity number) × adjustment coefficient", if the local financial capacity is greater than its financial demand, the state usually does not consider to implement general subsidies for it; if the number of local financial needs is greater than the number of financial capacity, a certain degree of transfer subsidies will be given according to the specific requirements. Special subsidies, as a kind of allocation for designated purposes, shall not be used for other purposes. From the perspective of local finance, special subsidies do increase fiscal revenue, but at the same time of increasing financial resources, they do not get corresponding financial powers. Special subsidies from German states to local governments are mainly used for infrastructure, schools, public transportation and social security.

The federal parliament made it a rule that all the economically developed states in the east should pay money to the federal government as a balance fund to be transferred to the economically backward states in the south. After mutual support, if there is still insufficient financial resources, the federal government will take a certain proportion from the share of value-added tax as compensation.

On the premise of achieving vertical financial balance, Germany also adjusts the wealth gap between states and between regions through balanced funds. This is mainly manifested in the fact that the states with better financial conditions directly allocate financial resources to the regions with poor financial conditions according to the institutional approach. The basic approach is to work out the financial capacity and financial balance index of each state according to the requirements of the factor law, so as to realize the scientific transfer of interstate financial resources. This horizontal fiscal balance process is mainly composed of four related links: First, calculate the fiscal (revenue) capability index of each state based on tax elements. Second, on the premise of comprehensive consideration of factors such as population size, population density and age structure, the fiscal balance index of each state is obtained. Then, compare the fiscal capacity with the fiscal balance index and determine three levels of the situation. First, the states with good financial conditions should pay the horizontal transfer payment funds; second, states that can balance their finances; third, the states that need to accept horizontal financial transfer payments. On this basis, the federal government and the states that should pay the balance fund will allocate funds to the recipient states at the end of each quarter according to the system, and summarize and liquidate at the end of each year.

Basic Information of Japan's Tax Distribution System

Japan is a typical unitary country, where the powers of the central and local governments are uniformly stipulated by the constitution. In terms of the division of powers between the central and local governments, local governments at all levels are relatively independent. The central government is the first level, 47 prefectures are the second level, and 3,253 municipalities and towns are the third level.

1. Division of powers of governments at all levels

Japan's administrative agencies are divided into the central government, prefectures and municipalities (legally known as "local autonomous groups" in Japan). The principle of the distribution of powers among Japanese governments at all levels is as follows: First, clearly define the principle of administrative responsibility. In other words, the power of the three-level government should be completely divided, and the affairs closely related to the local people should be transferred to the local governments at all levels. The affairs related to the overall situation of the country or the interests of other places should be assigned to the central government, while the affairs that local governments cannot afford should be coordinated by the state. Second, the principle of giving priority to cities and towns. In order to protect the interests of the people, all kinds of affairs should be handled by the municipal and village governments that can best reflect the public opinion and have the least administrative power. Third, the principle of efficiency. For trans-regional affairs requiring coordination, high efficiency and low cost shall be taken as the standard for the division of power. According to these principles, the scope of the central government's powers mainly includes: National administrative affairs, financial management and national customs affairs; national defense; foreign affairs and international relations; nationwide communications, post and telecommunications; major scientific research and development programs, such as space technology and Marine development; price index control. In addition, according to the law, the central bank is responsible for the issuance and management of money. As a local government, prefectures and municipalities have the following responsibilities: Local administrative affairs; to maintain social order and judicial administration; infrastructure; educational and social and cultural undertakings; medical, health and social welfare; environmental protection. In addition, in accordance with the principle of high efficiency and low cost, some functions of the central government can be delegated to local governments after the approval of the legislature. Fiscal decentralization in Japan highlights the importance of local finance, known as "big local government", where about 70% of government spending is arranged through local budgets.

On the basis of reasonably and clearly defining the scope of power, the scope of expenditure should be scientifically divided. Japan's *Local Finance Law* stipulates that, in principle, local autonomous groups shall bear all the operational expenses required by them and their institutions. In the division of administrative powers, the central government shall bear all or part of certain operating expenses, public operating expenses, disaster relief and other expenses of which the state and local governments have an interest. Local public investment accounts for a large proportion in Japan's national fiscal expenditure, and a considerable part of local fiscal expenditure is invested in infrastructure, so local public investment accounts for a large proportion in Japan's overall investment. It can be said that this is a feature of fiscal decentralization under the Japanese fiscal management system.

2. Tax revenue division of governments at all levels

Japan's tax revenue division mainly follows three principles: One is based on the division of power; second, the bulk of the tax source to the central government; third, taxes related to macro policies are transferred to the central government, while those with obvious benefits are transferred to the local government. National taxes are collected by the national taxation bureau of ministry of finance. Local taxes are divided into prefectural taxes and municipal taxes, which will be collected by the tax authorities under the finance bureau at the corresponding level. It is worth adding that when local finance fails to make ends meet, non-statutory taxes can be established. Of course, such taxes need to go through strict and complicated examination and approval procedures before collection.

Japan has many taxes and a complicated tax system. Listed as national taxes are: Personal income tax, corporate tax, inheritance tax, gift tax, consumption tax, tobacco tax and land value tax. The taxes belonging to prefecture mainly include: Prefecture resident tax, enterprise tax, real estate acquisition tax, prefecture tobacco tax, golf course tax, special local consumption tax, car tax, coal well tax and hunting registration tax. On top of that, the prefectural government has also introduced a vehicle-income tax and a vehicle-distribution tax for road spending, as well as a hunting tax for the protection of birds and livestock, as well as for the management of hunting expenses. Among the above taxes, enterprise tax and resident tax in prefecture account for the highest proportion, accounting for 47 and 32.8% of the total tax revenue of prefecture, respectively, and motor vehicle tax and gasoline distribution tax account for about 8.3 and 5.4%, respectively. The rest taxes are lower. The major taxes of the municipality are: Resident tax, fixed asset tax, light motor vehicle tax, tobacco tax, mineral product tax and special land ownership tax.

In addition to these general taxes, highly urbanized areas, such as Tokyo and Osaka, as well as cities with a population of more than 300, 000, have introduced special business and office taxes designed to improve the urban environment. In municipalities with mineral springs, mineral springs taxes have been levied to protect mineral springs and improve health facilities, fire prevention facilities and tourism conditions. If necessary, the municipal government may also levy a town planning tax or other taxes. Among the taxes collected at the municipal level, the municipal residents pay the highest tax rate, accounting for 53.4% of the total tax revenue, followed by fixed assets tax, accounting for 34.8%. It can be seen that Japanese local taxes take income tax and property tax as the main taxes.

Japan's central government, prefectures and municipalities have their own taxes. The main taxes of the central finance are individual income tax and corporate income tax. The main taxes of prefecture are enterprise tax and resident tax. The main taxes of the municipalities are resident tax and fixed assets tax.

3. Transfer payments from governments at all levels

Japan's fiscal transfer payment is not only large in scale, but also relatively perfect in system. Its transfer payment basically consists of three parts: Local (national) transfer tax, local (national) transfer tax and national Treasury expenditure. This is the outstanding feature of Japan's fiscal operation mechanism of "central finance raising funds and local finance spending money", and it is also determined by the local autonomy system under the unitary system.

Local transfer tax is convenient for some taxes to be uniformly collected by the state, but part of the tax should be directly used for local expenditures. So after collected by the national tax bureau, and decomposed in accordance with the provisions of the proportion, part is transferred to local governments, which can be regarded as sharing taxes. At present, road tax, car tonnage tax, liquefied petroleum gas tax, aviation fuel tax and special tonnage tax belong to this situation. Among them, the first three are transferred to places as the funds for construction and maintenance of roads, and the amount of transferred funds depends on the length of roads and the size of occupied area, which is not necessarily related to the collection sites of the three taxes. An aviation fuel tax is a tax levied by the central government on the fuel that aircraft owners load into their aircraft, and is earmarked for local governments to repair airport facilities and prevent noise pollution. Special tonnage tax is an addition to tonnage tax (a tax levied on net tonnage of a Marine ship entering a Japanese commercial port), which is levied in full by the local government but does not specify the specific purpose of the earmarks.

Different from the local (national) transfer tax, which focuses on the use of funds or the return of funds to the expropriated land, the local delivery (national) tax is aimed at balancing the local financial resources and allocates part of the national tax, such as income tax, corporate tax and liquor tax, to the local government. It neither provides for the specific use of funds nor attaches other conditions, and can play a role in bridging regional differences. Local tax refers to the tax collected by the central government and then distributed among different parts of the country according to certain standards. The total tax is determined by a certain proportion of the total national tax of income tax, corporate tax and liquor tax, which is now 32%. There are ordinary and special local taxes. 94% of the local tax is ordinary tax, which is distributed according to the insufficient fiscal revenue calculated by objective standards. The rest is special tax, which is used for emergencies such as disasters. In this way, the general tariff constitutes the central element of the local tax delivery system, which is distributed according to the difference between the base fiscal needs and the base fiscal incomes of local governments.

The baseline financial requirement is the sum of the costs necessary for each administrative item, such as fire, police, education, etc. The necessary cost of each administrative project is calculated by the following method: First, determine the measuring unit that can reflect the financial needs of each administrative project. For example, fire cost is measured in terms of population, road cost in terms of road area and length, and education cost in terms of number of schools and staff. The second is to determine the unit cost of each measurement unit. It is decided mainly according to the standard planning of prefecture and municipality, with reference to the local budget and final accounts. Third, the amount of measurement units and unit costs of the calculation of financial base needs. Fourth, coefficient adjustment. In view of the different circumstances of different projects and the different characteristics of different regions, the calculated base financial requirements could also be adjusted by multiplying the correction factor. This kind of coefficient adjustment is divided into adjustment of type of unit of account, adjustment of climate, adjustment of class, adjustment of density and adjustment of social and economic development.

The base fiscal revenue is calculated according to the predicted revenue or tax capacity of local governments, but the predicted value of local tax revenue does not equal to the base fiscal revenue, but only takes part of it as the base fiscal revenue. This part is 80% in prefecture and 75% in municipality. The above provisions mainly take into account the possible existence of other financial needs not included in the baseline financial needs. If the former is less than the latter after calculating the base fiscal needs and the base fiscal income of each local government, the general delivery tax will not be paid to the local government. On the contrary, for those regions where the base fiscal need is larger than the base fiscal income, the central government has to pay the general delivery tax to make up the fiscal gap. Since the purpose of local tax payment is to balance local financial revenues and expenditures, it is similar to general or unconditional subsidies in other countries, and its effect of balancing local financial resources is also obvious.

The expenditure of the state treasury is the subsidy provided by the central government to local governments according to specific purposes and conditions. Treasury expenditure can be divided into three types according to the nature of expenditure: Treasury burden, treasury trust and treasury subsidy. Treasury burden money refers to the funds allocated by the central government to local governments in proportion to their share of the financial burden in the affairs jointly undertaken by the central government and local governments. Treasury trust money refers to the funds paid by the state when it is needed to entrust the local government to handle the affairs, which should be borne by the state. A treasury grant is a grant to be paid by the state for local affairs which the state deems necessary for encouragement and assistance. Grants or bursaries are divided into: A portion of the cost of a service or project that is fully subsidized or shared by the Treasury; a portion of the cost of a business or project that is subsidized and shared by a percentage paid by the treasury. The fund transfer payment system implemented by the central government to local governments in Japan has played an important role in achieving the vertical and horizontal fiscal balance between the central government and local governments at all levels.

Inspiration from Tax Distribution System of Market Economy Countries

1. The division of powers between the central and local governments is clear and guaranteed by law

The division of powers of the central and local governments of each country is specific and clear, and the division of powers and expenditure responsibilities, tax authority and tax categories, and transfer payment system of each country have all established a strict and sound legal system through legislation. For example, the US constitution and other laws clearly stipulate the administrative and financial powers of the central and local governments. The *Basic Law* of Germany clearly stipulates the powers of the federal government and divides government expenditure at all levels accordingly. The division of administrative powers in Japan has been stipulated and confirmed in the law, so that the effective operation of the financial system has the necessary guarantee. In terms of tax division, both federalist countries and unitary countries have stipulated the tax authority and the dominating relationship of each tax category from the central government to the local authorities through legislation. For example, *Russia's Budget Code* and *Tax Code* play an important role in adjusting tax division. In terms of transfer payment, a relatively scientific transfer payment system that can take various factors into consideration has been designed to reduce or even eliminate the blindness and arbitrariness in transfer payment. In the process of transfer payment policy implementation, there is also a sound legal system to protect, so as to reduce the interference and influence of human factors.

2. Divide the financial power according to the administrative power

The division of financial power is based on the division of administrative power, which is a common practice abroad and one of its most successful experiences. In the form of laws, each state delimit the scope of the powers of the central and local governments. The central authorities shall have jurisdiction over all matters related to the overall interests of the state, such as national defense, foreign affairs and currency issuance; matters that are only directly related to the interests of local residents, such as basic education, social welfare services and public security, are under the jurisdiction of local governments and are entirely decided and managed by local governments. If it is related to the overall interests of the state, but must be implemented by local authorities, the central authorities shall still have the power to exercise their powers. The central government can exercise its power through three ways: The central government can execute through its local agencies, supervise and guide local implementation in accordance with uniform standards, and the central government entrusts local execution to exercise its power. On the basis of the division of powers, each country shall divide its financial powers accordingly and put the important national revenues and expenditures under the central government and the local revenues and expenditures closely related to the residents' lives under the local government. This division of financial power by administrative power is conducive to the full implementation of the legal functions of the central and local government departments at all levels on the basis of living within their means, and to the balance between the central and local financial revenues and expenditures.

3. Establish a stable source of local government revenue in the form of tax distribution system

In handling the financial distribution between the central and local governments, all the above-mentioned countries have implemented the tax distribution system. The characteristic of tax distribution system is to divide the revenue system of central government and local government according to tax categories and establish stable revenue sources for governments at all levels. Although each country's local tax elasticity is small, the tax amount is small, but each country all guarantees by the legal form each level local government to have the independent management authority to the local tax, which has provided a stable source for each level local government's financial revenue. The separation of tax revenue between the central and local governments at all levels is conducive to distinguishing the financial resources between the governments at all levels, easing the tension between the central and local financial relations, and meeting the requirements of decentralization and autonomy of local governments at all levels to a certain extent.

4. Local governments all have independent and clear main taxes

No matter what kind of tax distribution mode is adopted, all countries are able to reasonably divide central and local taxes according to their national conditions, especially to ensure that local governments have clear main taxes. When dividing taxes of governments at all levels according to law, the establishment of local taxes should be paid more attention. On the one hand, property tax plays an important role in the local tax system of various countries. Although the names of property taxes vary from country to country, there are local property taxes and so on in the United States; immovable property acquisition tax and fixed assets tax in Japan; in Germany, state and local governments have property tax and land tax, etc., but they all have the common characteristics of property tax and strong locality, and are suitable local taxes. On the other hand, each country has its own characteristic circulation tax and income tax. As the transfer tax is closely related to the specific economic structure and industrial structure of each country, relatively speaking, there are such taxes in the main local taxes, but the specific taxes are different. For example, Germany is a big beer country, and the tax source of beer tax is relatively stable. Therefore, among the local taxes in Germany, there are beer taxes that are not available in other countries. It is also worth noting that most Western countries have three-level governments and corresponding three-level finance, which is one of the reasons for the rational division of tax categories. However, China's five-level finance will inevitably affect the effective division of limited tax categories in local four-level governments.

5. Establish a scientific, standardized and effective inter-governmental transfer payment system

Countries with a well-functioning tax distribution system have a complete set of transfer payment system corresponding to it. The division of tax types and tax revenues is only the initial basic distribution. As the transfer payment system of fiscal redistribution, it can adjust and balance the financial relations between the upper and lower levels of government and between regions, and achieve the vertical balance between the central and local finance and the horizontal balance between local finance. All countries that establish a tax distribution system should pay attention to the redistributive role of finance. On the premise of ensuring the central government to concentrate its major financial resources, local governments should balance their fiscal revenues and expenditures. On the other hand, a standard central allocation system should be established to supplement each other by means of tax distribution and subsidy system. Dividing the fiscal revenue between the central and local governments into fixed income of governments at all levels, tax-sharing income of governments at all levels and different forms of subsidies from higher governments to lower governments makes all the income of the lower-level governments and the subsidies from the central government to the local governments become the basic means for the central government to exercise fiscal and economic control over the local governments.

6. Highly centralized and moderately decentralized financial power

Although the practical trend of the reform of local financial system varies from country to country, the goal is the same, which is to achieve moderate concentration and reasonable decentralization of financial power. In the decentralization system, local governments have relatively large financial power, which needs to be moderately concentrated. In a centralized country, the fiscal power of local governments is relatively small, which requires reasonable decentralization. As far as the financial power of local government is concerned, the differences between the two systems are gradually narrowing down, which indicates that the development of modern social economy requires the moderate concentration and reasonable decentralization of financial power. A high degree of centralization and rational decentralization of financial power will help bring the initiative of the central and local governments into full play.

[Column 0.1]

Financial and tax management systems in South Korea and Hong Kong, China and their experiences: Asian Development Bank Technical Assistance Grant Program ADB TA—8379 PRC, *Research Report on Fiscal and Tax Management Systems in South Korea and Hong Kong*, research group of institute of fiscal science, ministry of finance, September 2014.

Overview of Fiscal and Tax Management Systems of the Republic of Korea and Hong Kong, China

1. Fiscal and tax management system of South Korea

South Korea is a market economy country with private ownership as the main body. Politically, it implements local decentralization and autonomy, and economically, it is highly centralized. This determines that there is no administrative subordination or restriction between the central government and the local government, and local autonomy is highly independent. The administrative and financial powers between the central government and the local government are all regulated by the state and local laws.

(1) The division of financial powers between the central and local governments

For a long time, the biggest characteristic of the division of financial power in South Korea is that the fiscal revenue is highly concentrated in the central government, while the expenditure is just the opposite, mainly responsible by the local government. At present, the ratio of national tax to local tax is 8:2, and the ratio of actual fiscal expenditure between central government and local government is 4:6.

(2) Tax system

South Korea implements a thorough tax distribution system between the central government and local governments. The tax legislative power, collection power and management power are concentrated in the central government. Local governments have no tax legislative power, but only partial management power. South Korea is a country based on direct tax, tax is divided into central tax and local tax, no sharing tax. Central tax (national tax) includes: Individual income tax, corporate income tax, social security tax, value-added tax, special consumption tax, inheritance and gift tax, wine tax, stamp duty, securities transaction tax, transportation tax, education tax, special tax on rural development, comprehensive real estate tax, etc. Local taxes include property acquisition tax, registration and license tax, leisure tax, local consumption tax, resident tax, property tax, motor vehicle tax, local income tax, tobacco consumption tax, public facilities tax and local education tax. In 2014, South Korea's budget revenue was 352 billion US dollars, and tax revenue (VAT, income tax, etc.) was 206 billion US dollars, accounting for 59%. Fund income (pensions, employment insurance, etc.): $120 billion, accounting for 34%; other revenue (asset sales dividends, fines, etc.): $26 billion, or 7%.

(3) Inter-governmental financial transfer payment

According to the law of South Korea, the expenses for local governments to perform their duties should, in principle, be solved by themselves. However, due to the different economic development status and financial resources distribution among regions, the local tax and non-tax revenue cannot meet the necessary expenses of local governments in general, so it needs to be subsidized by the central government. Specific practice includes: It is system of local pay tax. In order to ensure the minimum necessary expenditure of local governments, the central government will subsidize a certain proportion (40%) of national tax revenue to local governments. Local tax can be divided into general tax, special tax, decentralization tax and real estate tax. The second is to set up the transfer fee system. In order to meet the needs of specific undertakings (water source protection, road repair, etc.), the central government shall transfer all or part of the income from the specific taxes of national taxes to the local government, and the local government shall set up projects and implement them independently.

(4) Budget procedures

South Korea's budget process consists of three stages: Budget preparation (planning), implementation and review. The first year is budget preparation and approval, the second year is budget implementation, and the third year is budget implementation result review. The budget preparation stage mainly includes: First, the financial planning department issues guidelines for budgeting based on the principles and indicators of the five-year rolling plan to determine the budget principles for the new fiscal year and to limit the ceiling of the competent departments. Second, the competent departments shall, in accordance with the principles of budgeting issued by the financial planning department, put forward their own budget expenditure plans including detailed existing project planning and new project planning, and then submit to the financial planning department for review and adjustment. Third, through repeated communication, coordination and adjustment, the draft budget submitted to the congress must be submitted to the congress 90 days before the beginning of the fiscal year (the first few days of October each year). Fourth, after the preliminary examination by the standing committee and the comprehensive examination by the conference committee, the National People's Congress shall vote by the plenary session, and the budget shall be determined 30 days before the beginning of the new fiscal year. In the budget implementation stage, the financial planning department allocates the budget and arranges the funds according to the budget approved by the congress, and then the competent departments spend the money according to the relevant legal system. In the budget review stage, the first is the self-inspection by the competent departments (at the end of February), then the comprehensive review by the ministry of planning and finance (on April 10), and finally, the final report (on April 10 to May 20) is submitted to the congress for review and approval (at the end of May).

2. Financial and tax management system of Hong Kong, China

During the research in Hong Kong, the research group had a key understanding of the basic framework of finance and tax in Hong Kong, budget "envelope", annual budget process and tax system.

(1) Basic framework

In accordance with the *Basic Law of the Hong Kong Special Administrative Region of the People's Republic of China*, the Hong Kong special administrative region shall maintain its financial independence. The budget is budgeted by living within its means, with a view to balancing the budget, avoiding deficit, keeping pace with the growth rate of GDP and implementing an independent tax system.

According to the organization chart of the HKSAR government, the Financial Secretary, which is directly under the chief executive of the HKSAR, is responsible for the allocation and management of financial resources in the region. The Financial Secretary comprises four policy bureaus, namely the Commerce and Economic Development Bureau, the Development Bureau, the Financial Services and the Treasury Bureau, the Hong Kong Monetary Authority, and the Economic Analysis and Business Facilitation Branch. The Financial Services and the Treasury Bureau comprises the Inland Revenue Department, the Treasury Department and other specific administrative agencies. In addition, departments directly under the chief executive, such as the Independent Commission against Corruption (ICAC) and the National Audit Office, are responsible for financial supervision.

(2) Budget "envelope" and annual budget process

Before preparing the next financial year's budget, the Financial Secretary issues the departmental budget totals for the next financial year to the heads of departments on the basis of the resources required for the provision of existing services. This amount is usually written in an envelope, hence the name "envelope". The essence of the envelope is a performance-based budget system based on results. After accepting the envelope, the money spent by each bureau will generally not be regulated, but the service results performed by the envelope will be held accountable.

Hong Kong's annual budget process consists of the following stages, which are repeated: First, the allocation of resources (May to October of the previous year). The Treasury Bureau reviewed the expenditure guidelines for the next five years and issued a provisional expenditure envelope. The Bureau submitted funding applications for the new initiatives, senior resource meetings allocated new resources and the Financial Secretary issued a final expenditure envelope. The second is the annual budget preparation stage (from October of the first year to February of the current year). The department prepares budget and the Financial

Secretary decides on the necessary revenue and expenditure measures and the Treasury examines the budget. Third, the review and formal approval of the budget stage (February to April that year). The estimates and *Appropriations Bill* will be tabled at the legislative council. The Finance Committee will consider the draft estimates of expenditure at a special meeting. The council will approve the estimates of expenditure and passed the *Appropriations Bill*. The annual budget process for Hong Kong is shown in Fig. 1.1.

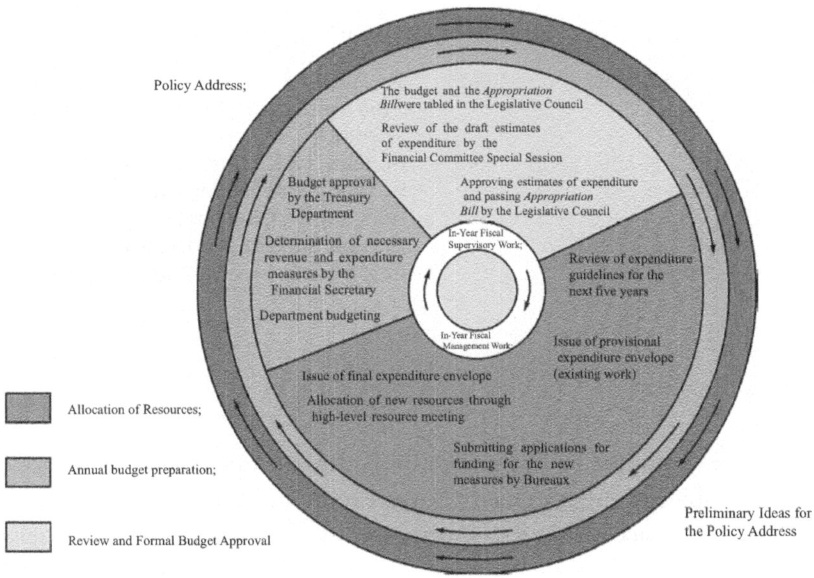

Fig. 1.1 Hong Kong annual budgeting process (香港周年预算流程)

施政报告	Policy Address
施政报告的初步构思	Preliminary Ideas for the Policy Address
库务科审定预算	Budget approval by the Treasury Department
财务司司长决定所需的收入及开支措施	Determination of necessary revenue and expenditure measures by the Financial Secretary
部门编制预算	Department budgeting

发出最终开支封套	Issue of final expenditure envelope
高层资源会议分配新资源	Allocation of new resources through high-level resource meeting
各局就新措施提交拨款申请	Submitting applications for funding for the new measures by Bureaux
发出暂定开支封套 (现有工作)	Issue of provisional expenditure envelope (existing work)
复核未来五年的开支指引	Review of expenditure guidelines for the next five years
立法会核准开支预算及通过《拨款条例草案》	Approving estimates of expenditure and passing *Appropriation Bill* by the Legislative Council
财务委员会特别会议审议开支预算草案	Review of the draft estimates of expenditure by the Financial Committee Special Session
预算及《拨款条例草案》提交立法会省览	The budget and the *Appropriation Bill* were tabled in the Legislative Council
年度内的财政监察工作	In-Year Fiscal Supervisory Work
年度内的财政管理工作	In-Year Fiscal Management Work
资源分配	Allocation of Resources
周年预算编制	Annual budget preparation
审核及正式核准预算	Review and Formal Budget Approval

(3) Tax system

Hong Kong adopts a low-tax policy, and its tax system is relatively simple. It does not distinguish between residents and non-residents, and taxes are levied according to the principle of geographical origin. There is no capital appreciation and capital transfer taxes. It is taxed at one level, without VAT, sales tax and tariff.

The relevant current taxes include direct (profits tax, salaries tax, property tax) and indirect (stamp duty, lottery duty, rates, government rent, dutiable commodities tax, motor vehicle first registration tax, etc.). Profits tax, salaries tax and stamp duty account for a large proportion of Hong Kong's tax revenue. Of the 243.549 billion Hong Kong dollars in tax revenue in 2013–2014, profits tax accounted for 49.6%, salaries tax 22.8% and stamp duty 17.0%.

In addition to taxation, land price income and other operating income also constitute an important source of fiscal revenue in Hong Kong. In the 2014–2015 Hong Kong budget revenue, land price revenue accounted for 16.3%, and other operating revenue accounted for 26.2%, as shown in Fig. 1.2.

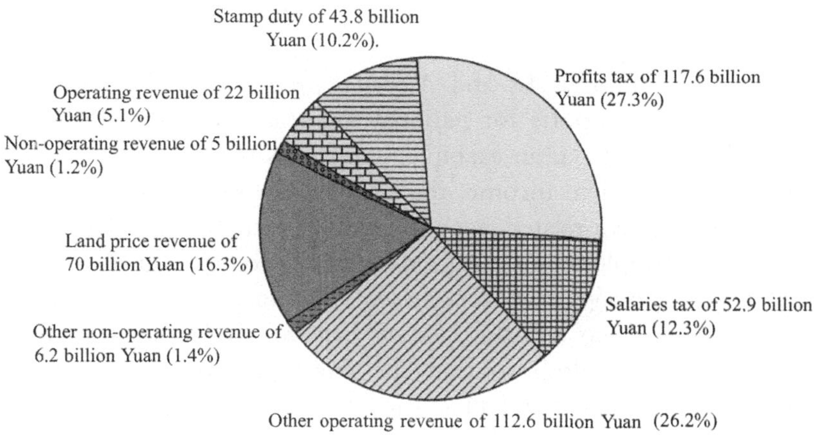

Fig. 1.2 Hong Kong's 2014–2015 annual budget revenue (香港2014-2015年度预算收入)

印花税438亿元 (10.2%)	Stamp duty of 43.8 billion Yuan (10.2%)
利得税1176亿元 (27.3%)	Profits tax of 117.6 billion Yuan (27.3%)
薪俸税529亿元 (12.3%)	Salaries tax of 52.9 billion Yuan (12.3%)
其他经营收入1126亿元 (26.2%)	Other operating revenue of 112.6 billion Yuan (26.2%)
其他非经营收入62亿元 (1.4%)	Other non-operating revenue of 6.2 billion Yuan (1.4%)
地价收入700亿元 (16.3%)	Land price revenue of 70 billion Yuan (16.3%)
投资收入	Investment revenue
经营收入220亿元 (5.1%)	Operating revenue of 22 billion Yuan (5.1%)
非经营收入50亿元 (1.2%)	Non-operating revenue of 5 billion Yuan (1.2%)

(2) Characteristics of the fiscal and tax management systems of the republic of Korea and Hong Kong, China

1.Characteristics of South Korea's fiscal and tax management system

(1) Sound legal system and act in strict accordance with legal norms

The *National Assembly Act* and *National Finance Act* of South Korea are strong legal supports for national financial execution. Taking the *National Finance Act* as an example, it includes three parts, namely the legal system related to income, the legal system related to expenditure and the legal system related to national debt, each of which has its own system. For example, in the legal system related to expenditure, there are the *Law on the Budget and Management of Transfer Fees*, the *Budget Law for Government Units* and the *Law on Government Procurement*. In the daily fiscal and tax administration, the above laws and regulations shall be strictly implemented and all acts in accordance with the law.

(2) The financial power is highly concentrated in the central government, and the central government implements a high transfer payment system for local governments

South Korea's fiscal revenue is highly concentrated in the central government (80% of the national tax revenue), while the expenditure is on the contrary, mainly in the charge of the local government (60% of the expenditure), and the central government implements transfer payment to the local government (40% of the national tax revenue). South Korean law requires local governments to pay for their own operations as they perform their duties. However, due to the different distribution of economic development and financial resources among regions, the local tax and non-tax income in some places cannot meet the necessary expenditure of local governments. Therefore, the reality of South Korea is to transfer part of the central government's income to the local government through transfer payment forms such as local tax payment and transfer payment.

(3) Divide the basic income sources of the central and local governments according to tax types, and there is no sharing tax

There are more than 20 kinds of taxes in South Korea, which are divided into central tax and local tax. There is no sharing tax. National taxes (individual income tax, corporate income tax, social security tax, value-added tax, special consumption tax, inheritance and gift tax, etc.) are at the disposal of the central government, while local taxes (property acquisition tax, registration and license tax, leisure tax, local consumption tax, resident tax, property tax, tobacco consumption tax, etc.) are at the disposal of the local government. According to the above division, the national tax revenue in 2013 was 271.1 trillion won, among which the national tax was 216.4 trillion won, accounting for 80%. Local taxes were 54.7 trillion won, or 20%.

(4) Low tax burden and low government debt

Compared with the low tax burden and high government debt of the United States and Japan and the high tax burden and low government debt pattern of European countries, South Korea maintains the pattern of low tax burden and low government debt. In 2010, South Korea's tax revenue as a percentage of GDP was 19.3%, slightly higher than the United States (18.5%) and Japan (16.3%), lower than the UK (28.2%), Germany (22.0%) and Sweden (34.1%); government revenue as a share of GDP is 25.1%, slightly higher than that of the US (24.8%) and significantly lower than that of the UK (34.9%), Germany (36.1%) and Sweden (45.5%). Government debt is 34.3% of GDP, which is not only lower than the UK (85.6%), Germany (86.3%) and Sweden (49.3%), but also more lower than the United States (97.8%) and Japan (192.7%).

(5) Carried out extensive and in-depth reform of the fiscal and taxation management system

In 1998, the financial crisis fundamentally changed the fiscal situation of South Korea. The ratio of government debt to GDP increased from less than 12% in 1997 to 25% in 2004. South Korea's economic restructuring has led to rising unemployment and a widening income gap, requiring the government to play a more active role in fiscal policy. In the twenty-first century, South Korea's population is aging rapidly, which requires corresponding changes in the nature and scale of government expenditure to meet the rapidly increasing welfare expenditure. To this end, in 2004, the Korean government initiated a major fiscal reform aimed at improving the fiscal system and improving the efficiency of fiscal expenditure. The scope of these reforms is comprehensive, and medium-term fiscal expenditure framework, top-down budget allocation, performance management system, digital budget and accounting system are the four major parts of this comprehensive fiscal reform.

A national fiscal strategy meeting chaired by the President and attended by all cabinet members shall be held in April or May each year to establish a five-year national fiscal management plan (i.e., medium-term fiscal expenditure framework), which shall be revised annually and connected with the annual budget. At the same time, the top-down budget allocation method is introduced in the budget preparation, and the budget quota is implemented for the departments in charge of each industry to expand the autonomy of each department. In addition, performance management system should be implemented to implement performance management for budget projects. Performance evaluation should be conducted for 1/3 of the budget projects every year, and all budget projects should be evaluated within 3 years, and the performance should be linked to the annual budget. In addition, in order to effectively integrate financial information and apply it to all aspects of financial management, South Korea has established a comprehensive financial information management system—"Digital Budget and Accounting System (DBAS)". The system uses constantly updated government financial data to improve the transparency and efficiency of national financial management.

2. Characteristics of financial and tax management system in Hong Kong, China

(1) Prudent financial management philosophy

The government's financial philosophy is prudent, living within its means, committed to avoiding deficits, not allowing government spending to grow faster than the economy, and maintaining a simple and clear low tax regime. Hong Kong pursues the above financial management philosophy mainly for the following purposes: Maintaining adequate financial reserves; ensuring that the public sector does not over-commit social resources; ensuring the government's ability to invest in infrastructure and improve public services in line with economic growth trends; ensuring the confidence of investors at home and abroad to make long-term investments in Hong Kong.

Hong Kong's macro tax burden is relatively low. Although there is no clear provision in the budget law, there is a basic consensus that the macro tax burden shall not exceed 20%. Despite the low level of macro tax burden, Hong Kong's fiscal position is sound. Since the handover, except for the deficit in some years hit by the Asian financial crisis, most fiscal years in Hong Kong have been in comprehensive surplus. This is thanks to Hong Kong's precise budget, public expenditure savings, open and transparent procedures and a sound supervision system. The financial situation of Hong Kong since its handover is shown in Fig. 1.3.

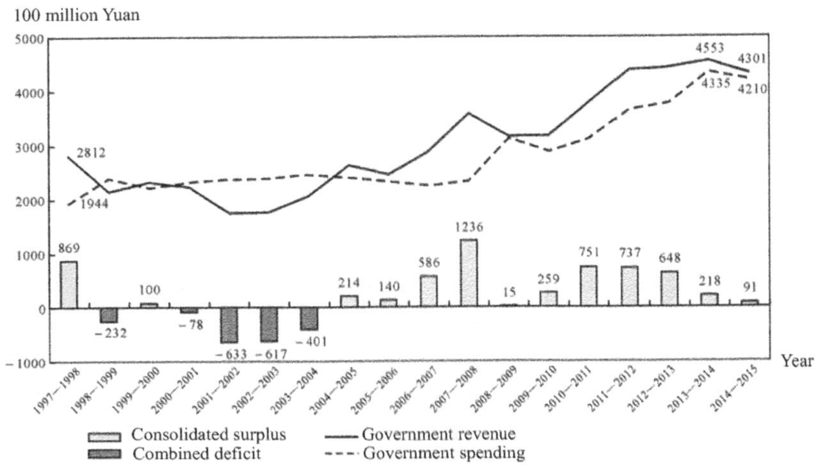

Fig. 1.3 Hong Kong's fiscal position since the handover (回归以来香港的财政状况)

亿元	年100 million Yuan
年份	Year
综合盈余	Consolidated surplus
政府收入	Government revenue
综合赤字	Combined deficit
政府开支	Government spending

(2) Standardized and orderly budget management

All government revenues and expenditures in Hong Kong are subject to budgetary management and are divided into general revenue accounts and fund accounts. To compile the medium-term forecast of fiscal revenues and expenditures for the next five years, predict the trend of economic growth and fiscal revenues and expenditures, and assess the impact of future expenditure and tax measures on fiscal affairs. Annual budget preparation spans the entire budget year, that is, starting from the new fiscal year in April to prepare the budget for the next year.

Hong Kong's expenditure budget is relatively rigid. The scope of each head and subhead of expenditure should be clearly defined. All expenditure should be consistent with it. All changes in the expenditure budget (including supplementary appropriations) must be approved by the legislative council. Hong Kong's remaining balance of expenditure can be carried forward. Pro-active inclusion of unspent funds into the next fiscal year's expenditure envelope will encourage departments to strictly control their expenditure. The system of centralized collection and payment is implemented. The account is composed of general income accounts and 8 funds. The income is directly paid into the corresponding account, and the financial allocation is directly paid to the final use link by Treasury. Hong Kong's cash and accrual accounts provide a more accurate picture of the government's balance sheet. The Hong Kong fiscal reserve budget for 2014–2015 is shown in Table 1.1.

In the course of the implementation of the budget, any amendment to the budget in respect of any major or well-received issue shall be subject to the approval of the finance committee of the legislative council. However, to a certain extent, with the devolution of powers by the legislative council, government departments can make changes to their budgets to avoid unnecessary procedures and respond to public demands in a timely manner to provide better services.

(3) Long-term planning for a rainy day

Table 1.1 Hong Kong fiscal reserve budget for 2014–2015 (unit: 100 million Yuan)

Government general income book	4028
Earmarked funds	1332
Capital works reserve fund	798
Capital investment fund	20
Civil service pension reserve fund	270
Disaster relief fund	less than 100 million Yuan
Innovation and technology fund	18
Loan fund	14
Lotteries fund	212
Land fund	2197
Total	7557

With an aging population and a shrinking workforce, Hong Kong's economy and government revenues will grow more slowly, while spending is likely to rise sharply. In 2013, the Financial Secretary of Hong Kong established the "long-term financial planning working group", which invited economists, accounting, tax and actuarial experts to study how to plan for public finance to cope with an aging population and long-term financial commitments. Looking at the current state of public finances, the panel made projections for the fiscal position up to 2041–2042, taking into account demographic trends, economic growth and current policies, as shown in Fig. 1.4.

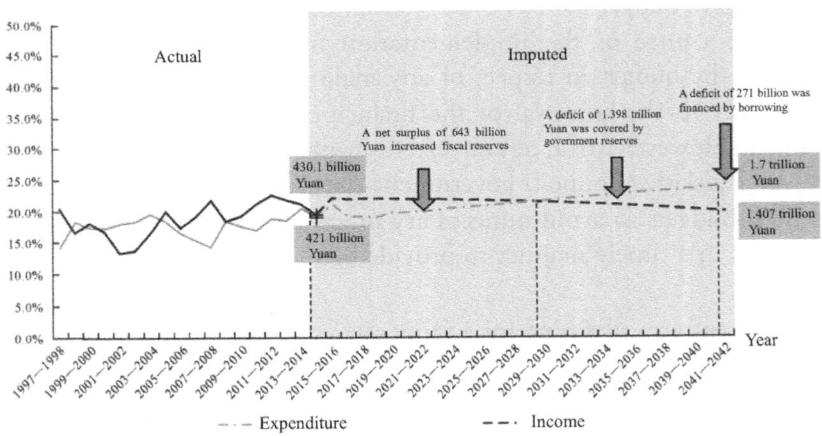

Fig. 1.4 Hong Kong's fiscal outlook at current economic growth and current service levels (按目前经济增速和现有服务水平的香港财政展望)

实际	Actual
推算	Imputed
6430 亿元的净盈余令财政储备增加	A net surplus of 643 billion Yuan increased fiscal reserves
13980 亿元的赤字由财政储备应付	A deficit of 1.398 trillion Yuan was covered by government reserves
2710 亿元的赤字由借贷应付	A deficit of 271 billion was financed by borrowing
17000 亿元	1.7 trillion Yuan
14070 亿元	1.407 trillion Yuan
4301 亿元	430.1 billion Yuan

4210 亿元	421 billion Yuan
年份	Year
开支	Expenditure
收入	Income

The group's calculations and analysis provide a clear warning to the financial and Hong Kong community. The panel makes clear that spending growth continues to outpace growth in the economy and incomes, and that structural fiscal deficits are inevitable. The panel's key recommendations are that the government should control expenditure growth, safeguard income and prepare for future hunger by stockpiling resources for the next generation to meet future financial challenges in a multi-pronged manner.

3. Inspiration from fiscal and tax management systems in South Korea and Hong Kong, China

(1) Attach importance to the balance between the central and local financial relations, and reasonably divide the powers of the central and local governments

However, South Korea implements the local autonomy system, but in the financial aspect highly centralizes. The ratio of central and local income is 8 to 2, while the ratio of central and local expenditure is 4 to 6. In terms of income division, South Korea's central and local taxes are clearly divided, without sharing taxes. Nearly half of centralized income is spent by local governments through taxes and transfers. In terms of the division of powers, South Korea has clearly enumerated various powers of local governments in the local autonomy law. If the powers are not clear or new powers cannot be determined to be assumed by the central or local governments, the corresponding courts will decide the ownership of powers.

In dealing with the relationship between the central government and local finance in China, we should define the responsibility of inter-governmental expenditure on the basis of the clear division of inter-governmental powers. We should learn from the practical experience of South Korea, consider increasing the scale and proportion of general transfer payments, especially balanced transfer payments, and reduce or standardize special transfer payments. On the basis of reasonably defining the administrative power, we should further straighten out the financial distribution relationship between governments at all levels. First, the central and local governments should properly delineate their powers and spending responsibilities. On the basis of transforming government functions and reasonably defining the boundary between government and market, we will take full account of the scope of public benefits, the complexity and asymmetry of information, as well as the autonomy and initiative of local governments, and clarify the powers and expenditure responsibilities of governments at all levels, appropriately increase and strengthen the central government's powers and spending responsibilities, increase the proportion of its powers directly exercised by the central government, manage the central government's responsibilities and reduce the number of entrusted tasks. At the same time, the central and local personnel institutions, fiscal expenditure responsibility and guarantee mechanism should be adjusted accordingly, so as to achieve the unification of financial responsibility and personnel organization allocation, thus greatly reducing special transfer payment and local intervention, and promoting market unification, judicial justice and equal access to basic public services. Second, we will further improve the division of income between the central and local governments. According to the characteristics of tax categories, the tax categories should be reasonably divided according to the principles of fairness, convenience and efficiency. We will maintain overall stability in the pattern of financial resources between the central and local governments, and provide institutional support for fully mobilizing the initiative of both governments. Third, we will improve the transfer payment system. We will improve the mechanism for the steady growth of general transfer payments, clean up, integrate and standardize special transfer payments, substantially reduce the number of transfer payments, merge overlapping projects, gradually eliminate special projects in competitive fields and supporting local funds, and strictly control special projects for guidance, relief and emergency response. We will identify the reserved special projects and include items which belong to local affairs and whose amount is relatively fixed, in general transfer payments, and timely sort out special transfer payment projects according to economic and social development.

(2) Improve legislation and establish the concept of financial rule of law.

South Korea and Hong Kong have a very strong concept of financial rule of law. The government has the corresponding legal basis for taxation and government expenditure and strictly follows the law. For example, in South Korea, there are 12 corresponding laws in the 15 categories of national taxes. Although local taxes are not divided according to tax categories, there are also three laws for uniform norms, including the *Basic Law on Local Taxes*, the *Local Tax Law* and the *Law on Special Local Taxes*. Profits tax, salaries tax and property tax are clearly regulated in the *Inland Revenue Ordinance*. The scope of each head and subhead of expenditure is clearly defined in the Hong Kong expenditure budget. All expenditure should be consistent with it. All changes in the expenditure budget (including supplementary appropriations) must be approved by the legislative council.

We should learn from the "high, comprehensive, detailed and strict" legal system construction in South Korea and Hong Kong of China, establish the concept of rule of law, establish and improve the fiscal and taxation laws and regulations that public departments and market players must abide by, so as to standardize various financial distribution relations and behaviors, and promote the orderly and coordinated operation of the government and market. We will comprehensively carry out financial planning and tax administration in accordance with the law, and bring public finance into the legal system. At the same time, in accordance with the requirements of building a sunshine government and a responsible government, we should speed up the disclosure of final accounts and budgets and gradually implement a comprehensive and standardized budget disclosure system. We will ensure that citizens have the right to know, to participate in and to supervise their financial activities. We will modernize our capacity for democratic financial management and national governance. Considering the current critical period of comprehensively promoting the construction of China under the rule of law, we should speed up the promulgation of the *Fiscal Law*, raise the legislative level of relevant laws and regulations, improve the system of fiscal budget laws and regulations, and act in strict accordance with the law on this basis. In particular, we will conscientiously implement the relevant provisions of the newly revised *Budget Law* so that China's fiscal, taxation and budgetary management will move forward on the right track under the rule of law.

(3) Attach importance to long-term fiscal planning and promote sustainable fiscal development

Both South Korea and Hong Kong attach great importance to the issue of fiscal sustainability. South Korea began to work out a five-year medium-term fiscal development plan in 2004 and rolled it out annually. The preparation of the annual budget shall be based on the medium-term budget. In Hong Kong, fiscal guidelines for the next five years are also prepared over a period of five years as the basic basis for the annual budget. Not only that, but Hong Kong is also aware of the impact of an aging population and slowing economic growth on its finances. The working group on long-term fiscal planning has been set up to work out fiscal projections for as far as 2041–2042.

An aging population, slowing economic growth and increasing fiscal pressure are also important issues facing the Chinese government. Drawing on the experience of South Korea and Hong Kong, we must strengthen our research and take proactive measures in advance. In order to improve the annual budget control method, the focus of budget examination and verification should be extended from the balance state of fiscal revenue and expenditure and the size of deficit to expenditure budget and policy, and the constraint of expenditure budget should be hardened. At the same time, we will establish a cross-year compensation mechanism to make fiscal policy more forward-looking and sustainable.

(4) Clean up preferential tax policies and impose strict financial and economic discipline

Historically, in order to promote the development of enterprises and create jobs, South Korea has also formulated some preferential policies for enterprises, which have played an important role. But at present, some preferential policies become the solidified interests of enterprises. To change that, the government is launching a comprehensive review of tax incentives and plans to eliminate a number of inappropriate ones. Hong Kong also has clear legal provisions on preferential tax policies, which are strictly implemented in accordance with the law and will not be opened casually. Drawing on the experience of the republic of Korea and Hong Kong, we will comprehensively evaluate the preferential tax policies in the future. Violations of laws and regulations are strictly prohibited, and preferential policies that do not comply with laws and regulations shall be stopped. In accordance with the requirements of the third plenary session of the 18th CPC central committee and in accordance with the principles of uniform tax system, fair tax burden and promotion of fair competition, we should strengthen the standardized management of preferential tax policies, especially regional preferential tax policies.

(5) Establish a modern integrated financial management information system

The modernization of integrated financial management information system is an important means to improve the level of financial management and the efficiency and transparency of financial management. South Korea has established an integrated information management system, digital budget and accounting system (DBAS), which has improved the transparency and efficiency of national financial management. In view of this, China must establish an integrated financial management information management system among the financial department, the tax department, the Treasury Department of the People's Bank of China, the Treasury Agency and the budget and expenditure department. It should include: Budget preparation system and budget implementation management system to ensure the allocation of budget funds in line with the budget arrangement and expenditure schedule requirements; revenue management system to monitor tax warehousing;

the treasury cash management system to timely reflect the treasury daily income and expenditure and balance situation; the general ledger system of treasury receipts and expenditures, so that all the receipts and expenditures accounts are reflected in a system; debt management system, which fully reflects the situation of national debt issuance, repayment and balance; electronic bank clearing system to shorten the time for financial fund allocation.

(6) Improve the mode of fiscal investment in science and technology and promote innovation-driven development

It can be seen from the investigation of South Korea and Hong Kong that both of them attach great importance to the role of innovation in economic development. The South Korean government recently released the *Third Basic Plan for Science and Technology* (2013–2017), which increased the contribution of research and development to economic growth from 35.4% in 1981–2010 to 40% in 2013–2017. South Korea's new basic science and technology program has a research and development budget of 92.4 trillion won (about 83 billion US dollars), and proposes to promote the development of 120 national strategic technologies (including 30 key technologies) in five fields. Education, science and technology also account for a large proportion of fiscal expenditure in Hong Kong. If promoting innovation is like growing mushrooms, the "release guideline-organization declaration-expert review-appropriation of funds-project acceptance" behavior pattern is just like the government is busy planting mushrooms, while the "risk environment" behavior pattern of optimizing innovation environment is to provide the environment (such as temperature, humidity and nutrient quality) needed for mushroom growth. We know from the investigation in South Korea that the government of South Korea also supports enterprise innovation, but the way of support is not to directly give financial funds to enterprises, but to create and provide more learning opportunities for enterprises, so as to improve the innovation ability of enterprises. It is under this mode of government-supported enterprise innovation that South Korea has cultivated enterprises with strong innovation ability and great influence in the world, such as Samsung and Hyundai. Drawing lessons from the experience of South Korea, it is suggested that our country should construct the innovation incentive system of science and technology finance on the basis of innovation financial support mode. We should give full play to the guiding and supporting role of financial funds in technological innovation and expand it from direct subsidies for R&D activities to post-subsidy, "angel investment" guidance, purchase of services, learning opportunities and other flexible and diverse support methods. And we shall strengthen the direct investment and tax, finance, government procurement and other policies, to achieve the combination of promoting technology supply and driving market demand. For things that are in line with the direction of reform and development, we need to focus on spending money on mechanisms to improve the financial performance of science and technology.

International practice and enlightenment on medium-term budget framework: *International Practice of Medium-Term Budget Framework and Its Implications for China, Research Report of Institute of Fiscal Science, Ministry of Finance*, 3rd issue, 2015 (total No. 1834).

At present, the preparation of medium-term budget has become a common practice in many foreign countries, especially OECD countries. In many years of practice, they have accumulated a lot of valuable experience, which is worth our reference. Since the 1960s, as the society increasingly emphasizes the importance of understanding and mastering the long-term trend of the change of fiscal revenue and expenditure, some developed countries in Europe and America began to break through the annual limitation of the traditional fiscal budget, and then compile the medium-term budget in addition to the annual budget, or directly transform the original annual budget into the medium-term budget. Since then, the reform of annual budget management system implemented by many countries in order to achieve sustainable fiscal development has constituted an important part of the new financial management mode in Western countries.

(1) Motivation for preparing the medium-term budget framework abroad

Generally, European and American developed countries have to prepare the multi-year budget, mainly in order to further improve the mechanism of action of fiscal plan, make up for the annual budget in reflecting the changes in balance of payments, control spending growth, adjust the expenditure structure, coordinate the relationship between revenues and expenditures, and carry out the policy of finance and economic aspects of functional defects, so as to promote financial revenue and expenditure of scientific decision and strengthening the government's macroeconomic control. The British government has implemented a five-year plan for defense and infrastructure spending since the 1950s, but most government spending is still budgeted on an annual basis. By comparing the annual budget with the five-year plan for some of the expenditure items already implemented, the British government believes that the multi-year budgeting method is both useful and feasible. Thus, it was decided to prepare a five-year public expenditure plan, the public expenditure survey (PES), consisting of several expenditures, beginning in 1961 and becoming a recurrent system by 1969.

Germany and France draw up multi-year budgets first and foremost in response to the economic crisis. In the mid-1960s, the federal economy experienced its first post-war recession after more than ten years of rapid growth. In 1966, GDP growth fell by 4.4% from the average in the 1950s, and unemployment rose by 2.1%. As a kind of counter-cyclical system construction, the German federal parliament passed the *Law on Promoting Economic Stability and Growth* in June 1967, which stipulates that the federal government and the states should formulate a five-year fiscal medium-term plan, so as to predict and analyze the economic development trend and fiscal revenue and expenditure dynamics, and propose alternative policy measures. In France, the original annual budget used to include a multi-year budget element, but it was limited to the total amount of investment in larger construction projects that would take years to complete. At the end of 1980s, the French economy fell into crisis again, and negative growth appeared in 1993. The recession worsened the fiscal position and the fiscal deficit rose rapidly as a share of GDP. To this end, the French government has taken a series of measures centering on tax increase to gradually improve the financial situation. But at the same time, the economic recovery has been slow because of the increased tax burden. After reflection, the French government believes that if the revenue and expenditure are reasonably arranged as early as possible in the form of multi-year fiscal budget to avoid excessive tax increase, the economy may get out of the predicament sooner. With this in mind, France began formally drawing up its medium-term fiscal plan over a three-year period in 1998. In addition, due to the aging age structure of French civil servants and the implementation of the policy of "one step forward and one step back", the current and future period of civil servants' salary and social insurance expenditure accounted for a larger proportion of fiscal expenditure, and the growth was relatively fast. It is also one of the important starting points of France's medium-term fiscal plan to make early prediction and adjust the expenditure structure, so as to ensure that the salary and pension can be fully paid in due time without fiscal passivity.

In the United States and Canada, the impetus for medium-term budgets has been to rein in government spending and deficits. After World War II, the United States continued to stimulate the economy by means of expanding government spending. In addition, the expansion of social welfare programs and the competing tax cuts of various governments for the consideration of political elections led to the continuous expansion of budget expenditure and the difficulty of fiscal revenue to grow in line with expenditure. As a result, fiscal deficit became a normal state. Especially since the second half of the 1960s, spending and deficits have become irreversible, increasing even as the economy booms. This situation not only led to the re-selection of macro policies, but also put forward the requirement for the reform of the budgeting method. One of the important measures to achieve this requirement is to adopt the medium-term budget. In 1970, the *Legislative Reform Act* passed by the congress of the United States stipulated that the budget authorizations and expenditures proposed by the executive departments of major programs to be implemented or expanded should be predicted for five years. In 1974, the *Congressional Budget and Seizure Control Act* further required the President, the congressional budget committee and the congressional budget office to make multi-year financial projections during the budget process. Since then, successive federal governments have prepared medium-term budgets of varying duration. In addition to the federal government, about 40% of state governments have adopted medium-term budgeting methods to better control their spending. In Canada, after the mid-1970s, changes in the international situation further expanded the scope of government functions. In addition, the rise of international oil price had a huge impact on economic development. As a result, the proportion of government revenue decreased, the deficit and debt expanded, financial difficulties intensified, and the role of planned project budgets in the management of expenditure projects decreased day by day. In this context, the federal government introduced a new spending management system in 1979, introducing a five-year fiscal plan.

The EU also attaches great importance to the role of the medium-term budget for the purposes of coordinating the budget policies of member states, strengthening the supervision of member states' financial conditions and seeking regional economic stability. The *Stability and Growth Pact* of the European Union clearly stipulates that each member state shall prepare and submit its medium-term fiscal plan to the European commission every year, so as to ensure that the fiscal deficit of each member state does not exceed the convergence standard of 3% of GDP, so that the economy of each member state can be within the range of safe fluctuations.

(2) The implications of the medium-term budget framework

1. Medium-term fiscal framework, medium-term budget framework and medium-term expenditure framework

The so-called medium-term budget framework (MTBF) is a rolling, binding aggregate budget framework that usually lasts three to five years (some countries are longer), with spending limits at its core. In the *Revised Handbook on Fiscal Transparency* (2001), the international monetary fund (IMF) defines the "medium-term budget framework" as a framework that links the fiscal aggregate forecasting system with a disciplined process of ministries and commissions reflecting detailed medium-term budget estimates of current government policies, thereby unifying medium-term fiscal policy with medium-term budget preparation. Among them, the forward estimate of expenditures becomes the basis for budget negotiations in the post-budget year and is coordinated with the final result of budget implementation. According to the development stage of the medium-term budget framework, we can divide the medium-term budget framework into the following three progressive levels:

(1) Medium-term fiscal framework, MTFF. Medium-term fiscal framework is the starting point and the first step of medium-term budget framework generally includes a fiscal policy statement, a series of medium-term macroeconomic and financial targets and projections, focusing on medium-term macroeconomic operation state and financial revenue and expenditure target analysis and prediction, as the medium-term budget framework and medium-term spending framework provide the basis for the compilation of and support. Consistent with the medium-term budget objectives, MTFF actually reflects the total fiscal control of the medium-term budget, which is conducive to the strengthening of fiscal discipline. Regardless of the perfection of the medium-term budget framework, the medium-term fiscal framework is an indispensable and important component.
(2) Medium-term budget framework (MTBF). On the basis of the medium-term fiscal framework, the budget estimation of each expenditure institution forms the medium-term budget framework at the micro-level. The objective of the medium-term budget framework is to allocate budgetary resources based on national strategic priorities to ensure that budget allocations are consistent with overall fiscal objectives. It requires a degree of predictability for spending agencies while ensuring overall fiscal discipline. In fact, the medium-term budget framework based on the medium-term fiscal framework is the most basic form of the medium-term expenditure framework.
(3) Medium-term expenditure framework (MTEF). The medium-term expenditure framework is formed by adding financial fund "activities" and "output" on the basis of the medium-term budget framework. Like the medium-term budget framework (MTBF), the

medium-term expenditure framework (MTEF) is also at the micro-level. In addition to strengthening fiscal discipline and improving resource allocation, MTEF focuses on the improvement of expenditure performance, which is consistent with the operational performance objectives of modern budget management and conducive to improving the efficiency of fiscal expenditure and realizing fiscal strategy. According to the *World Bank Handbook of Public Expenditure Management* (1998), the medium-term expenditure framework consists of a top-down resource scope, a bottom-up estimation of the current and medium-term costs of existing policies and the matching of costs and available resources. The top-down resource horizon is essentially a macroeconomic model that represents fiscal targets, revenue forecasts and spending forecasts, as well as government debt and costly administrative reforms. In fact, we can regard the medium-term expenditure framework as the medium-term budget framework with performance budget added. It is the typical existence form that medium-term budget frame is more perfect.

2. Realization of medium-term budget framework and budget management objectives

In a general sense, any budget system or procedure is committed to achieving the objectives of three levels of budget management: Total financial constraints at the macro-level, resource allocation based on policy priorities at the intermediate level and operational performance at the micro-level. The most important significance of introducing the medium-term budget framework on the basis of annual budget is to establish a direct connection mechanism between policy, planning and budget, so as to lay a foundation for achieving the three objectives of budget management.

(1) The medium-term budget framework is conducive to the control of fiscal aggregate. The budget process starts from the determination of fiscal aggregate, and fiscal constraint provides an external constraint framework for the determination of fiscal aggregate, enabling the

budget to complete the operation of fiscal aggregate. The medium-term budget framework establishes clear fiscal constraints for the coming year (usually three to five years after the budget year). It sets limits on government spending to politicians, interest groups and other applicants for public funds in order to limit the need for spending. The medium-term budget framework does not usually elaborate on the government's policy intentions, but it clearly indicates the government's fiscal trends or the direction in which the government intends to go in the coming years and helps the public and other stakeholders to judge the credibility of the government's fiscal commitments. In the process of forming and determining budget policies, the medium-term budget framework can act as a constraint on public expenditure requirements at the beginning of the annual budget process.

(2) The medium-term budget framework can provide the basis for the optimization and adjustment of expenditure structure. The optimization and adjustment of the structure of public expenditure (i.e., the adjustment of the priority of public expenditure policies) are almost impossible to complete within the annual framework, because the annual budget has a short time span and the financial resources available in a year are limited. However, it is completely different under the medium-term framework. The budget under the medium-term framework can provide an operational time base and resource base for the optimization and adjustment of expenditure structure. In the absence of a medium-term budget framework, spending adjustments that need to be made quickly in response to environmental change tend to reduce inputs and activities, such as the maintenance and upkeep of public infrastructure, that are easy to cut (and thus less resistant) in the short term. It is clear that such spending adjustments are not based on government policy and therefore often deviate from policy objectives and priorities. By clarifying the expenditure to be arranged in the medium term for the implementation of current policies, the medium-term budget framework enables the government to evaluate the cost effectiveness of various policies and determine whether the corresponding expenditure plan is chosen because of "policy priority" or because of "easy to cut".

(3) The medium-term budget framework is conducive to the performance evaluation and improvement of government budget. Under the annual framework, due to the time-delay effect of fiscal policy, some expenditure items cannot reflect the degree of its impact in the short term, so that their performance cannot be truly evaluated. However, if such evaluation is placed in the medium-term framework, the current and future projects can be better evaluated through the information of financial revenue and expenditure in the medium and long term. The medium-term budget could also encourage a wider allocation of public resources. In the annual budget, most items are fixed and have little room for adjustment. The government can only spend according to the budget arrangement and the legal contract with suppliers. However, under the medium-term budget framework, the government can carry out inter-temporal and timely budget control according to the economic and financial situation. At the same time, the department can also independently and rationally arrange expenditure within the medium-term range, which is conducive to optimizing resource allocation and comprehensive evaluation of expenditure performance. In Australia, for example, departments are required to submit annual budget report documents together with a "contract" report detailing the services they need to provide. The financial department inspects and evaluates the quality, quantity, time schedule and cost of the tasks completed by various government departments according to the arrangement of various indicators in the budget of each department and the financial plan "contract", which serves as the main basis for examining the performance of government departments.

(3) Typical country cases of the medium-term budget framework

1. The British Public Expenditure Survey (PES)

As early as 1961, Britain pioneered medium-term budget reform with the introduction of the multi-year "public expenditure survey" (PES). The core of the medium-term budget is to pursue budget discipline, policy rationality and expenditure efficiency by putting expenditure decisions in the medium-term framework. The emphasis on fiscal discipline and spending efficiency in the medium-term budget is not unique to the UK, but also exists in the budgets of Australia, Canada, New Zealand and other countries due to their historical links and interactions with each other.

In Britain, the formation of the annual budget and the medium-term budget strategy begins in the late spring and early summer, when the chancellor of the exchequer, together with his senior advisers and the heads of the internal revenue service and the customs and excise service, presents a fiscal strategy for the next three years. The government's medium-term fiscal strategy will guide the development of the medium-term budget, which will be formally unveiled when the annual budget is presented to parliament in November. Once a fiscal strategy is in place at the start of the summer, the cabinet's public spending committee will set medium-term limits on total spending and departmental spending to keep it in check. The government then reviews its existing spending commitments for the next two fiscal years and forms a new projection for the third year, in a process known as the public expenditure survey (PES).

In Britain, ministries are responsible for setting priorities within limits set by the Treasury, as is common in other commonwealth countries. Departments are given a wide range of power to transfer budget resources in the budget formation process, such as providing funds for projects with higher priority and reducing or canceling low-priority projects completely. This approach forces departments to adhere to total spending controls, while identifying not only their spending limits but also their operating costs, such as payroll. In recent years, the ministry of finance has restricted administrative and wage spending in government departments and introduced "cost saving" activities in government units. The general principle is that expenditure and price growth should be offset by efficiency improvement to improve the efficiency of the public sector.

The UK's medium-term budget is not presented as a separate document. Rather, it is fully integrated into the annual budget and presented to parliament as part of a "fiscal statement and budget report" (FSBR). In addition to the annual budget, the FSBR includes the government's medium-term fiscal strategy, short-term economic forecasts, analysis of tax measures in the budget and analysis of public finances including public sector borrowing needs.

The UK first introduced the Comprehensive Spending Review in 1998. CSR is at the core of the UK's public spending plan and control framework and is a direct manifestation of the medium-term budget framework. Comprehensive expenditure review mainly includes two aspects: One is to review the long-term government expenditure and second, review the allocation of departmental budget resources in the next three years. The review includes: (1) To evaluate the expenditure growth and public service reform since the implementation of the first CSR, which will provide an information basis for setting new targets for the next 10 years; (2) examine key trends and challenges in the coming decade, including population, socio-economic change, globalization, climate and environmental change and technological change, and assess how public services will respond to them; (3) to arrange budgetary resources to respond to the above changes and to continue to seek maximum efficiency in public expenditure during the comprehensive expenditure review period (three years) and to assess the effectiveness of the long-term policy objectives of the present government through a zero-base review of the sectorial expenditure baseline; (4) on the basis of identifying areas of expenditure reduction, continue to develop efficiency planning and integrate the savings resulting from such efficiency planning into departmental expenditure plans.

2. Germany's medium-term macroeconomic plan and fiscal strategy

German law requires that, along with the submission of the draft budget, a five-year fiscal plan (i.e., a quantitative description of the fiscal policy strategy) be submitted to the legislature for use in the budget debate in parliament (Sect. 50 of the *Budget Principles Act*). The fiscal plan is drawn up by the government itself (Sect. 9 of the *Stabilization and Growth Act*) and sent to parliament only to inform it. The first year of the fiscal plan is for the current fiscal year, the second year is for the budget year, and the next three years are included. By law, the federal secretary of the Treasury is responsible for drawing up financial plans that are updated annually according to the state of economic development (Sect. 9 of the *Economic Stability and Growth Promotion Act*). Federal ministers are responsible for the preparation of investment plans in their areas of responsibility that reflect the direct annual expenditure of projects and federal financial subsidies for third-party investments (Sect. 10 of the *Economic Stability and Growth Promotion Act*).

For the federal government, in addition to the draft federal budget, the federal Treasury has to submit a report on the current state of the public finances and their potential impact on the economy as a whole in the future (article 31 of the *Federal Budget Code*). The financial report is a core budget document that describes the assessment of budget proposals. The law does not specify its specific content, usually including: Budget summary and description; federal medium-term fiscal plan; statement of macroeconomic conditions and tax policies; description of the financial relations of the federal, state and municipal governments; financial relations with the EU; liabilities, commitments and obligations of the federal government; federal special purpose fund; information on government assets and participation in private economic activities; etc.

With regard to the medium-term fiscal plan, it is customary, not legal, for the federal Treasury to forecast changes in macroeconomic indicators over the next three years based on possible developments over the previous two. To distinguish between two types of expenditure, one kind of expenditure must have certain legal provisions to provide for, and the other kind of expenditure is only general provisions (such as wage expenditure); the forecast of fiscal revenue and expenditure should consider the direction of future policy changes. The fiscal plan contains about 40 categories of functional expenditures, but federal, state and municipal administrations will compile further details of 7,000 to 8,000 expenditures and 1,100 revenues.

3. New Zealand's medium-term budget

In New Zealand, the budget process is characterized by a high degree of "downshifting", with a large part of responsibility and financial management at the departmental level. Following this logic, the medium-term estimates for New Zealand are also carried out by the linear sector.

Since 1991, New Zealand has adopted an incremental budget, requiring expenditure agencies to update their expenditure baseline projections for the previous year, with additional requests for funds thus considered a change to the baseline level. Baseline estimates of departmental expenditures submitted to the Treasury cover the budget year and the following two years.

Medium-term expenditures are expected to be guided by Treasury guidelines to enhance fiscal discipline and efficiency. Departments are usually required to raise funds for new projects from their departmental budgets and are not normally compensated for increased input costs, with additional funds available only for legal requirements or for major new government projects.

To improve transparency, the following three important documents need to be provided throughout the year of the budget cycle. First, when the budget is reviewed by parliament for the second time, the government must submit a "statement of budget policy", which gives a brief introduction of the government's short-term fiscal plan and medium-term fiscal strategic policy objectives. Second, when the budget is presented to parliament for the last time, the "fiscal strategy report" must be published, which includes the latest financial estimates and explains the differences between the budget and the strategic objectives in the "budget policy statement". Third, multi-year fiscal and economic forecasts (economic and financial updates to the budget) are published twice a year and compared with independent estimates from outside the government.

(4) Effectiveness of the medium-term budget framework in international practice

After years of practical exploration, the medium-term budget framework has been adopted by many countries and achieved good results in practice.

1. It is conducive to maintaining the consistency of policies and promoting sustainable development

The medium-term budget could shift the focus of government decision-making away from the short-term and toward thinking about future sustainability. Modern financial management is endowed with the function of fiscal policy protection and regulation, and the positioning of fiscal policy in national policies determines that its policy effect must be sustainable. Therefore, the medium-term budget is the basis of stable and consistent fiscal policy and sustainable development. Since the traditional annual budget only arranges the fiscal revenue and expenditure of the country according to a budget year, it is often easy to make the cross-year fiscal decisions fail to meet the future expenditure needs after meeting the financial security of a budget year. Therefore, the budget guarantee and control of the implementation of fiscal policies should be extended to a longer period, and overall coordination, foresight and unified arrangement should be carried out in the medium-term vision.

Around the world, a common cause of implementing medium-term budgets in some countries since the mid-1980s has been the economic crisis. Under the framework of the medium-term fiscal plan, in case of a crisis, the "drawer project" (some alternative investments to cope with the fluctuations of the economic cycle) in the medium-term fiscal plan can be used to deal with economic fluctuations and alleviate the economic crisis.

2. Make the government budget more forward-looking and prevent and defuse public risks

As it is usually necessary to consider the spending arrangements and policy planning for the next 3–5 years after the budget year, the medium-term budget is more forward-looking than the annual budget, and forward-looking is one of the most important characteristics of a good budget system. Unlike the annual budget, the medium-term budget is not a statutory multi-year budget allocation scheme, but it can provide clear spending guidance or targets for the government and government departments in the coming years. This advantage is important for managing financial risk.

One of the main flaws of the annual budget is that it ignores potential fiscal risks. Many current policies or government commitments imply fiscal risks that lead to a sharp increase in future expenditures or losses. However, under the annual budget framework, as these expenditures cannot be reflected in the budget, they are often ignored in the budget process and the possibility of high costs is high. By the time policymakers start noticing these risks, it may well be too late. As a result, annual budgets do not motivate policymakers to identify risks at an early stage and take appropriate action to prevent them. By contrast, a prominent advantage of the medium-term budget is that it focuses on the long-term sustainability of current policies, enabling adverse spending trends to be identified and discovered at an early stage so that they can be anticipated, stopped and slowed in time, and funded as early as possible.

3. Create a monitoring mechanism to enhance budget transparency

Government budget is a tool to realize the fiduciary responsibility of government through political process. In the annual budget system, there will inevitably be "short-term behavior" and "adverse selection" and other moral hazards, such as "small Treasury", "ask the ministry for the money", "year-end surprise spending" and other phenomena. The medium-term budget is conducive to regulating budgetary behavior and improving the transparency of fiscal policies and budget arrangements. An important goal of the implementation of the medium-term budget is to make the government and the functional departments of the allocation of financial funds in a certain period of time to consider, so that there will be a stable fiscal revenue and expenditure expectations, so as to improve the predictability of the budget and the use of financial funds efficiency. At the same time, it can make the society have a clear expectation for the future trend of national fiscal policy and promote stable economic growth and sustainable fiscal development.

At the same time, the medium-term budget decision-making process is more accountable and reliable, and the political responsibility of all parties can be strengthened on the management level by increasing transparency. First, politicians need to understand their priorities and the social will to finance them. At the same time, managers of functional departments should assume more responsibilities, because the priorities and resource allocation of each functional department are set in the medium-term expenditure framework; that is, all budget arrangements are put on the table, which is conducive to public supervision and inspection. Of course, accountability can only be achieved if the medium-term budget is released to the public, not just an internal technical document. Many countries now publish medium-term budget frameworks that allow people to play a greater role in reform.

(5) International experience in the medium-term budget framework and its implications for China

Through a comprehensive review of the practical experience of the medium-term budget framework of countries around the world, the following six points of consensus have been reached for China's reference.

1. Attach great importance to the role of the medium-term budget and improve its binding force on the annual budget

From the perspective of international practice, countries all over the world attach great importance to the role of the medium-term budget, which has a strong binding force on the annual budget. Relevant laws of all countries stipulate the legal status and role of the medium-term budget. The *EU Treaty* also explicitly requires all member states to prepare the medium-term budget and submit it to the European commission for supervision. This not only improves the guiding role of the medium-term fiscal plan on economic operation, ensures the implementation of the medium-term fiscal plan, but also strengthens the binding force of the medium-term fiscal plan on the annual budget. At present, although China also formulates medium- and long-term financial plans, they are mainly internal reference documents and have no clear legal status, so it is difficult to give full play to their role. It is one of the important tasks of the new round of fiscal and taxation reform in our country to adapt to the requirements of the development of the socialist market economy, formulate the medium-term budget framework and establish the inter-annual budget balance mechanism.

2. The medium-term budget framework should adapt to national conditions

At present, the medium-term budget frameworks of countries around the world are more or less different, and these differences are specifically designed to adapt to the specific policy needs and policy contexts of individual countries. For example, in preparing detailed medium-term tax and spending plans, the German federal fiscal plan is a good way to achieve a multi-year budget, which in many ways improves the budget process. It is true that the overall application of German medium-term fiscal planning also has many defects and cannot be widely used outside Germany. New Zealand's medium-term budget framework is representative and worthy of other countries' reference. But in New Zealand, where many budgetary responsibilities, including the provision of medium-term budget forecasts, are delegated through a formal system of contracts to spending agencies, contracts within government departments are trusted because the country has a strong private sector, it has put in place a contractual mechanism, a highly transparent mechanism for allocating public resources and an efficient mechanism for controlling public expenditure. In developing countries and countries in transition, these mechanisms are far from perfect, and the medium-term budget model based on them cannot be copied.

From the existing form, the world's medium-term budget is divided into two kinds: One is the medium-term fiscal plan or planning, and one is a direct medium-term budget. The former includes Britain's public spending plan, Germany's five-year medium-term fiscal plan and France's three-year medium-term fiscal plan. The medium-term budget in this form is a reportorial document examining financial developments. Its main purpose is to try to forecast the government's fiscal expenditure and revenue in the next few years and incorporate it into the budget process as an important reference and basis for the preparation of annual budget. Unlike the former, the latter is a direct extension of the traditional annual budget. The main country taking this form is the United States. In the United States, federal budgets since the late 1970s span at least three years: The previous budget year, the current budget year and the next budget year. In recent years, the US federal budget has typically been more than three years long. Taking the federal budget for the 1985 budget year as an example, in addition to the actual figures for the 1983 budget year, the approvals for the 1984 budget year and the budgets for the 1985 budget year, the projections for the next four budget years are shown.

From China's point of view, in order to make use of the existing basis and easy to operate, on the whole, the medium-term budget framework of our country should be compiled and standardized according to the first medium-term budget form adopted by most European and American countries. Considering that China is currently in a critical period of centralized adjustment of economic structure, rescheduling of economic growth rate and comprehensively deepening reform, there are many uncertain factors, and the choice of the medium-term budget framework should not be prolonged for the time being. In the near future, it may be considered to limit the three-year period of the two years after the addition of the newly compiled budget year, and gradually increase the time span with the accumulation of experience in the future. However, the forecast and analysis time of major planned projects and statutory expenditure projects can be appropriately extended.

3. Accurate and scientific forecasting is the basis for the preparation of the medium-term budget framework

As a fiscal policy and a management tool, the success or failure of the medium-term budget framework depends on the government's forecasting ability to a large extent. The central link of the preparation and implementation of the medium-term budget is all about the prediction. The updated macroeconomic situation is the premise of formulating corresponding policies and making scientific forecast of fiscal revenue and expenditure. The Swedish ministry of finance forecasts and revises all macroeconomic indicators 4–5 times a year. In addition, the ministry of finance also tracks and evaluates income and expenditure items, and forecasts fiscal expenditure 5–6 times a year from a medium-term perspective. The forecast of fiscal expenditure needs the support of computer technology. For this reason, the Swedish government introduced the integrated budget management system, which can complete the prediction and evaluation of each expenditure, and this budget management system is open to the ministry of finance and all government agencies.

At present, due to many uncertain factors in China's economic development, the macroeconomic situation should be predicted objectively and cautiously in order to prevent inaccurate forecasts and increase the difficulty of future budget target adjustment and failed payment of committed funds.

4. Content and procedural specifications for the medium-term budget framework

From the perspective of content, according to the studies of the World Bank (WB) and the international monetary fund (IMF), the key contents and compilation points of the medium-term budget framework include: (1) The medium-term budget framework should be based on the medium-term macroeconomic framework, a report on fiscal (and economic) policy objectives and formal fiscal constraints (e.g., the ratio of deficits to GDP); (2) a report on fiscal and economic policies; (3) a medium-term macroeconomic and fiscal forecast; (4) expenditure estimates for departments/agencies for the next two to four years after the next budget year, broken down by function (e.g., education and health) and by economic nature (e.g., capital expenditures and recurrent expenditures); (5) the preparation process of the medium-term budget framework should correspond to the annual budget preparation process (six stages), especially in accordance with the annual expenditure limit; (6) the medium-term budget framework is prepared by the government as a whole, but all government departments should follow the spending limits set for each department in the medium-term budget.

From the programming point of view, countries in the world usually start with a three-year rolling forecast of total sectorial expenditure, then introduce bottom-up planning for some projects based on in-depth analysis, and then gradually expand to other projects and complete the medium-term budget framework from the bottom up. Specifically, the standardized medium-term budgeting process includes the following steps: First, the formation of a macroeconomic framework. Forecasts of medium-term income, expenditure and macroeconomic conditions. Second, the formation of sector planning. Agreement on sectorial objectives, outputs and behavior; the formulation and review of master plans and sub-plans; forecast of planning costs. Third, the formation of a strategic expenditure framework. Internal and inter-departmental trade-offs are agreed upon in the strategic allocation of resources. Fourth, make clear the allocation of departmental resources and set an upper limit on departmental budgets in the medium term. Fifth, the preparation of departmental budgets. Departmental medium-term planning based on budget caps. Sixth, audit. Submit interim budget reports to the legislature.

From China's point of view, drawing on international experience, the medium-term budget framework can be prepared in accordance with the budget for several years, rolling forward for another year, and consistent with the annual budget in terms of the content and structure of revenue and expenditure. At least it should be specific to the section level subjects of the annual budget and combine the preparation of the medium-term budget framework with the elaboration of the annual budget. The specific preparation procedure is as follows:

The first step is to make macroeconomic forecasts (economic forecasts that serve the purpose of fiscal policy) and formulate medium- and long-term fiscal management plans. The forecast must be cautious, which may draw lessons from Canada's practice, with an increase of 0.5 to 1 percentage point above the forecast rate.

The second step is to formulate fiscal policies, targets and budget aggregates and their limits. Budget aggregates are based on macroeconomic and fiscal goals as well as social and political needs, as well as new sectorial needs and updated cost projections.

Third, set departmental limits, including targets and departmental spending ceilings. Departmental quotas should be based on national policy priorities and kept within the overall budget of the previous level.

Fourth, major government leaders convene meetings to agree on macroeconomic forecasts, long-term plans, fiscal targets, total spending and department limits.

Fifth, the linear department makes a budget request, that is, prepares the budget proposal under the above guidelines.

Sixth, review and document the budget, that is, whether the budget requests of the linear departments are within the departmental limits and conform to the policy priorities.

5. Clear division of labor and cooperation among related organizations

In the preparation of the medium-term budget framework, the division of responsibilities among relevant departments is relatively clear. In France, the medium-term budget framework is completed jointly by the forecasting division of the ministry of finance and the budget division, which is responsible for forecasting the trends of fiscal and economic development and proposing the basic principles of planning arrangements and major fiscal reform measures. The budget division is responsible for testing the specific situation of fiscal revenues and expenditures, preparing annual budgets and fiscal revenue and expenditures plans, and proposing specific fiscal policies and measures. In Germany, the fiscal medium-term plan is the responsibility of the fiscal planning committee, and the specific work is completed by the ministry of finance in conjunction with relevant comprehensive economic departments. The fiscal management functions of the Australian federal government are shared between the State Treasury and the ministry of finance, the former of which is mainly responsible for macroeconomic policy and tax management. The ministry of finance is mainly responsible for fiscal expenditure management and budget preparation. In the preparation of the medium-term budget framework, the State Treasury and the ministry of finance are both independent and accountable to each other, but also work closely together by forming a joint working group. This kind of division of labor and cooperation is conducive to brainstorming and leveraging the strengths of each department.

In order to do a good job in the preparation of China's medium-term budget framework, we must first further standardize the preparation process of the medium-term budget framework. In addition, on the basis of defining the financial department as the functional department for compiling the medium-term budget, the functions of the ministry of finance, relevant departments and departments and bureaus within the financial department should be specified, so that all departments can form synergy and improve the scientificity of the medium-term budget.

6. Pay attention to the status and role of the legislature

From the experience of various countries, the legislature plays an important role in the formation and entry into force of the medium-term budget framework. In Sweden, each September, before passing a detailed annual budget, congress sets a multi-year spending limit, usually setting a level for the next three years. In other words, on top of the three-year rolling spending limit, congress will add up the numbers for the new year. Spain's *General Budget Act 47/2003* also calls for a legally binding limit on total spending. In most countries, the law does not require the legislature to formally approve the medium-term budget framework. Except in individual cases, the legislature is only aware of this information and does not formally approve the total amount. For example, the German *Law Promoting Economic Stability and Growth Act of 1967*, an earlier law requiring medium-term budget framework planning, requires the government to make a five-year plan but only submit it to both houses of parliament.

(6) Two issues that need to be paid special attention to

1. Integrate plans, policies and budgets, and improve the budget decision-making mechanism

The prerequisite for improving the efficiency of public resource allocation is that the government can strategically allocate resources, allocate scarce resources to the most critical areas in each period and solve the most urgent social and economic problems in this period. To do this, medium-term plans, policies and budgets must be integrated, which is precisely the strength of the medium-term budget framework. However, in view of the current situation in China, there is a clear disconnect between plans, policies and budgets. Adjustments are urgently needed to meet the needs of medium-term budget preparation. At present, the national economic and social development plan compiled every five years in China is in theory a guiding plan that can influence the formulation of policies and budgets. In reality, it is indeed a basis for departments to apply for funds, but it is only one of the bases. During the planning period, on the one hand, the party committee and the government will still introduce major policies beyond the plan and have an impact on the budget; on the other hand, the projects arranged in the plan may not receive sufficient financial support, and the connection between the plan and the budget is not high. There are two issues that need to be addressed if the plan and budget are to be well aligned: First, the relationship between the financial department and the planning department can be considered to establish a more effective coordination mechanism on the premise of maintaining the status quo of the powers and responsibilities of the two institutions, or to establish a decision-making mechanism with higher authority on top of the two. Second, the political tenure and planning cycle should be consistent. In other words, there should be no five-year development plan for the next leader before the previous one leaves office.

At the same time, we should further improve the status of the financial sector and make it a true core budget agency. Since the budget reform, with the promotion of comprehensive budget and budget refinement and other reforms, budgetary authority and expenditure management began to be centralized to the financial department, the situation of budget "fragmentation" before the reform began to be improved, and the financial department also began to move toward the "core budget institution" as modern public budget calls it. However, "fragmentation" has not fundamentally changed. Within the government, the position of the financial sector is still not very high. Outside the financial sector, other departments still control the distribution of certain funds, which are essentially "quasi-budgetary agencies". In order to build the financial department into a real "core budget institution", it can be considered to completely concentrate the right of capital distribution in the financial department, so that the financial department can completely go beyond the current accounting-oriented function positioning, reshape itself into a policy analysis institution and establish its authoritative position in budget allocation.

2. Gradually introduce baseline prediction method instead of cardinal number method

The application of baseline forecasting in micro-budget management has a long history. The funding department used the baseline as a basis for securing additional resources, while the finance department used it as a starting point for a balanced budget. In the 1970s, baseline forecasting was revived with changes in the macroeconomic situation, but this time it was applied more in the field of macroeconomic budget management, focusing on both aggregate and structure. In 1974, the *Congressional Budget and Seizure Control Act* explicitly required the President to specify the current service budget.

The primary purpose of baseline forecasting is to provide a basis for budgeting and management by predicting the future costs of government services. The main contents of the baseline forecast include: First, eliminate one-off factors, make clear the government service that will continue in the future and calculate its cost; second, predict future economic conditions, social conditions, price level, government performance and other factors, estimate the future cost of current services, and form a baseline for budget preparation and management; third, demonstrate the impact of policy adjustment on baseline volume and structure. Baseline projections can dispense with the notion and practice of viewing current income and expenditure levels as baselines (vested interests). The total size of government expenditures and the budgetary arrangements of expenditure departments are not dependent on baselines, but on environmental parameters, budget schedules and policy changes. If there is no change in policy, but only changes in environmental parameters and budget schedule, then reasonable revenue (projections) and expenditure requirements (estimates) form the baseline of the budget. Of course, the current policies cannot remain unchanged. Some of them need to be stopped and some new policy measures need to be implemented. This change in revenues and expenditures purely due to policy changes forms the budget increment from the baseline forecast perspective.

2

Problem Orientation: Prominent Problems Facing China's Fiscal and Taxation System

Under the "trinity" framework of unified, standardized, fair and equitable handling of the relationship between the government and enterprises, the central and local governments, and the distribution of public rights and citizens, the system dividend of the tax distribution reform in 1994 was released, and the overall sustainability of the operation of the socialist market economy was improved. However, restricted by various objective conditions, the fiscal and taxation system reform in 1994 still had a strong transitional color, leaving some institutional problems unresolved. In the following 20 years, the financial system has been constantly improved, but there are still some reforms are not in place, supporting measures are not timely followed up, especially since the concept of "modern national governance" was put forward, the systematic construction of the modern financial system is extremely urgent. This paper focuses on the analysis of the current practical problems in the system of tax sharing and related issues of fiscal sustainability, and discusses the resistance and obstacles to the reform, in order to pave the way for the proposal of the reform plan.

J. Kang and L. Wei, *Transformation of the Fiscal and Taxation Systems*, The Great Transformation of China,
https://doi.org/10.1007/978-981-16-2590-9_2

The tax distribution reform in 1994 was the fundamental reform of macro indirect regulation and control in the development of China's socialist market economy, and finally realized the decisive change from the administrative decentralization that was repeatedly explored but always failed to go through to the "economic decentralization" that could make the path go wider and wider. In the following 20 years, while constantly improving the tax system, we also adjusted and improved the fiscal system for many times on the basis of maintaining the basic framework of tax distribution. However, the current financial system still has many problems and reform obstacles, and we need to further study and analyze, in order to "suitably" make improvements.

2.1 Problems to Be Straightened Out of China's Current Fiscal System of Tax Distribution

The tax sharing reform in 1994 not only "increased the proportion of the central government's revenue in the total revenue", but also made a significant milestone and historic contribution to the development of China's socialist market economy, which makes China's financial system finally move from the "administrative decentralization" in the 1950s, when it had to say goodbye to the "administrative decentralization" which means strict and complete unification of revenue and expenditure but can never be achieved despite repeated explorations, to the "economic decentralization" consistent with the market economy. First of all, it has made a breakthrough in transforming the previous institutional crux of financial revenue of enterprises in accordance with their administrative subordination, regardless of whether "centralization" or "decentralization" is based on. Unprecedented institutional arrangement has been formed that all enterprises, regardless of their size, regardless of their economic nature, regardless of their administrative levels, are equal and non-discriminatory in the face of tax laws. This truly level playing field provides stable expectations for fostering long-term behavior on the basis of stimulating the vitality of micro enterprises. At the same time, the central and local governments have bid farewell to the "institutional cycle" of endless bickering under the historical stage division system of administrative decentralization, and the continuation of the factors of bickering under the "contract without doing" system under the "contract without doing" system, no longer entering the head-aching vicious cycle of "once released, it will be messy, once messy, it will be tightened; once tightened, it will be dead" (i.e., "release, messy, tightened and dead"). It has formed the institutional conditions for the government to carry out macro "indirect regulation and control" on market entities, and a relatively standardized and stable sustainable institutional arrangement for the central and local governments to allocate their financial resources according to the tax or the same proportion of a certain tax.

It is under this "trinity" framework where unified, standardized, fair and equitable approach is adopted to deal with the government and enterprises, central and local, public rights and the distribution of citizens (in the context of finance and taxation, citizens are natural persons who have the obligation to pay taxes); in 1994, the system dividend of the tax distribution reform was released, and the overall sustainability of the socialist market economy was improved.

However, restricted by some objective conditions, the fiscal and taxation system reform in 1994 still had a strong transitional color, leaving some institutional problems unresolved. Over the next 20 years, the fiscal system improved, but some reforms were still not in place. Especially since the concept of "modern national governance" was put forward, the systematic construction of modern financial system is extremely urgent.

Issues Concerning Administrative Power and Expenditure Responsibility

The important principle of the tax distribution reform in 1994 was "the combination of administrative power and financial power", but the actual reform focused on the "income" end, establishing a relatively stable relationship between central and local income distribution. This means that taxes necessary for safeguarding state sovereignty, allocating national resources and exercising macro-control will be transferred to the central government, and the central government will receive the lion's share of the country's fiscal revenue, which also follows the general practice of market economy countries. In terms of expenditure, however, the existing division of inter-governmental responsibility for expenditure prior to the reform in 1994 is not clearly defined. In particular, the responsibility for expenditure related to the overall allocation of resources is largely divided among provincial and sub-provincial governments. The division of governmental power and expenditure responsibility is unreasonable, unclear and non-standard, which has become the main problem in the current financial system.

First, some things that should be centrally managed are left to local authorities, including social security, national social infrastructure, national protection of natural resources and prevention and control of pollution (such as protection of international boundary rivers, management of large rivers across river basins, prevention and control of trans-regional pollution, handling of trans-regional economic disputes and management of the use of sea areas and oceans). In mature market economy countries, this kind of public affairs, like national defense and foreign affairs, is usually under the overall responsibility of the central government, from personnel to specific decision-making, financing, budget, implementation, management and supervision. However, in China, except for some institutions (such as the central bank, the state administration of taxation, etc.), the central government does not have its own civil service at the local level. The above public affairs are basically decided and standardized by the central government, and local governments are responsible for expenditure, management, performance and implementation under the central command.

Second, the central government has taken on a greater share of the responsibility for expenditure in matters under local administration. The direct embodiment is that the special transfer payment has a wide variety of types and a growing scale, involving general public services, public security, education, science, culture and health, energy conservation and environmental protection, agriculture, forestry and water conservancy, transportation, commercial services, finance, land and resources, housing, social security, employment and other fields. For some local projects, ranging from major regional infrastructure projects to small projects to renovating toilets in rural areas, relevant departments of the central government often provide financial subsidies. These matters that should be managed by local governments, with too much involvement of the central government, may not be well managed due to the influence of information complexity and other factors. On the contrary, local governments will generate a sense of dependence and be restricted from playing a better role in local affairs.

Third, the responsibilities of the central and local governments overlap and there are many matters under joint management. The central and local governments share responsibility for social security, public health, compulsory education and other matters and expenditure. This also induces the central and local governments to play games through various forms, which may easily lead to unclear responsibilities and crowding each other out. “Sharing responsibility” has become neither the responsibility nor accountability of either party.

Inter-governmental Income and Taxation Issues

1. There are defects in the division of intergovernmental income

The tax distribution reform carried out in 1994 is based on the principles of fair competition for all types of enterprises to pay taxes in accordance with the law, the central and local governments to obtain fiscal revenue according to the allocation of tax bases, and the coordination of administrative and financial powers. The central and local tax revenues are divided according to the tax categories, and the tax categories necessary for safeguarding the rights and interests of the state and implementing macro-control are classified as the central tax; the main taxes directly related to economic development are divided into central and local shared taxes; taxes suitable for local collection and administration are classified as local taxes, and enriched to increase local revenue. This reform breaks away from the previous administrative decentralization limitations of “sharing in revenue by category”, “sharing in revenue in total amount” and “fiscal responsibility system” by “economic decentralization", and determines the overall framework of China's inter-governmental tax division system. Since then, with the change of the economic environment and the implementation of a number of tax reform, China has adjusted and improved the tax division system for many times on the basis of stabilizing the basic framework of the fiscal system of tax distribution, thus forming the current inter-governmental tax division system framework (see Table 2.1).

However, the main focus of the tax distribution reform is to improve the centralization of the central finance on the basis of straightening out the distribution relationship between the central and local governments. Therefore, major taxes with large tax bases and abundant tax sources will be assigned to or shared by the central government. At the same time, the jurisdiction of tax legislation and management is highly centralized in the central government, while the consideration of local tax system is relatively insufficient. After a long period of operation, China has accumulated many contradictions and problems in the construction of central and local financial relations and local tax system, which cannot fully adapt to the new situation of economic and social development and needs to be further improved.

(1) The construction of local tax system lags behind seriously and local financial resources are insufficient

Up to now, China does not have a clear local tax system, and local governments lack the main tax types with stable income sources, so the local fiscal revenue is far from meeting the fiscal expenditure needs, and they have to rely heavily on the transfer payment from the central government. Before the tax distribution reform in 1994, the proportion of local fiscal revenue was much higher than that of the central government, and the proportion of local fiscal revenue remained between 60 and 80% for a long time, so did the proportion of fiscal expenditure. Therefore, the central and local governments have basically balanced their fiscal revenues and expenditures. The tax distribution reform has increased the proportion of the central fiscal revenue in the national fiscal revenue, but it has not changed the allocation relationship of fiscal expenditure responsibility, resulting in the local fiscal revenue which is

Table 2.1 Framework of China's current inter-governmental tax division system

No	Subject
The central government fixed income	Tariff, consumption tax and value-added tax levied by the customs on behalf of the government, consumption tax, business tax and urban maintenance and construction tax paid centrally by the head offices of Banks and insurance companies, vehicle purchase tax and central enterprise income tax not included in the shared scope
Central and local shared revenue	The central government shares 75% of the domestic value-added tax, while local governments share 25%. The central government will share 60% of the corporate income tax and individual income tax, and the local government will share 40%. The resource tax is divided according to different resource types. The offshore oil resource tax is the central income, and the rest is the local income. The central government shares 97% of the stamp duty on securities transactions, while Shanghai and Shenzhen share 3%
Local government fixed income	Business tax (excluding the business tax paid by the head offices of Banks and insurance companies), urban land use tax, urban maintenance and construction tax (excluding the part paid by the head offices of Banks and insurance companies), property tax, vehicle and ship tax, stamp tax (excluding securities transaction stamp tax), farmland occupation tax, deed tax, tobacco tax, land value-added tax

Note central enterprises not included in the sharing scope include State Post, Industrial and Commercial Bank of China, Agricultural Bank of China, Bank of China, China Construction Bank, China Development Bank, Agricultural Development Bank of China, Export-Import Bank of China and offshore oil and gas enterprises.

far from meeting its fiscal expenditure needs. In 2012, local government revenue was 6,896.9 billion Yuan, while local government expenditure reached 1,1927.2 billion Yuan. The local self-sufficiency coefficient was only 0.58 (see Fig. 2.1). This means that nearly half of local fiscal expenditure depends on transfer payments from the central government to local governments. Such a huge fiscal transfer payment is not only easy to trigger rent-seeking behavior, but also the local governments are often not as responsible in the use of central fiscal allocation as they are in the treatment of local income, resulting in inefficient fiscal expenditure.

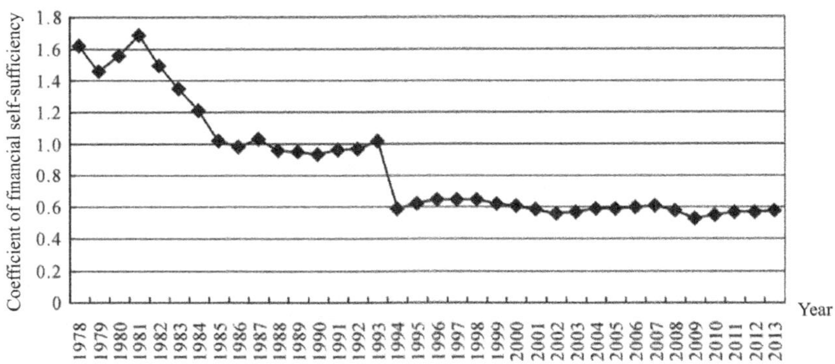

Fig. 2.1 Local Fiscal Self-Sufficiency from 1978 to 2013. 注: 财政自给系数 = 本级一般预算收入/本级一般预算支出 *Note* coefficient of financial self-sufficiency = General budget at the corresponding level/general budget expenditure at the corresponding level (资料来源: 根据《中国统计年鉴2013》和《2013 年财政收支情况》(财政部网站) 中的相关数据计算而得 *Source* calculated according to relevant data in *China Statistical Yearbook 2013* and *Fiscal Revenue and Expenditure in 2013* (website of the Ministry of Finance)

财政自给系数	Coefficient of financial self-sufficiency
年份	Year
图 1–1 1978–2013	年地方财政自给能力情况

(2) The income structure of local governments is unreasonable, lacking of main taxes and highly dependent on Shared taxes

Currently, local taxes include business tax, urban land use tax, urban maintenance and construction tax, property tax, vehicle and ship tax, stamp tax, farmland occupation tax, deed tax, tobacco tax, land value-added tax, etc. Although there are many kinds of taxes, they lack the main taxes that can provide long-term and stable income, and local governments highly rely on shared tax for income. At present, the most important tax in the local tax system is the business tax, but the business tax paid by the head offices of Banks and insurance companies belongs to the central government. Apart from the business tax, the other two main sources of local government tax revenue are the shared share of VAT and enterprise income tax. In 2012, the business tax, value-added tax and enterprise income tax revenues of local governments were 1554.3 billion Yuan, 673.8 billion Yuan and 757.2 billion Yuan, respectively, accounting for 63.1% of the local tax revenue (4731.7 billion Yuan) and 48.9% of the local fiscal revenue (6107.7 billion Yuan). This shows that local fiscal revenue is highly dependent on shared taxes.

This problem is more obvious in the inter-provincial tax division. There are too few main taxes to provide sufficient income, making it even more difficult to divide them among provincial, municipal, county and township governments. As a result, most regions follow the practice between the central and provincial governments and "share" several taxes with higher income among governments at all levels. In fact, there are various and often adjusted as sharing and responsibility system. For the main provider of public services, the county (city) level of government, there are only a few small taxes. The current tax division below the provincial level is shown in Table 2.2.

(3) Tax administration is highly centralized in the central government, and local governments lack necessary tax power

At present, China's tax legislation power is exclusive to the central government. In terms of tax administration, the central government has delegated to the local authorities the power to levy and suspend the abattoirs and banquet taxes (both taxes have been suspended), and delegated to the local authorities the power to formulate detailed rules for the

Table 2.2 Current tax division under provincial level

No	Subject
The stable income and large-scale taxes are generally shared by provinces and cities	Such as Beijing, Tianjin, Hebei, Shanxi, Inner Mongolia, Liaoning, Jilin, Shanghai, Henan, Hainan, Chongqing, Sichuan, Shaanxi, Tibet and Qinghai. The taxes shared by provinces and cities and counties are mainly value-added tax (25%), enterprise income tax, business tax and individual income tax (40%), urban land use tax and resource tax. The proportion of shared income between provinces and cities and counties mainly includes "five to five", "four to six", "three to seven", etc.; most provincial share proportion is slightly lower than that of cities and counties
Generally, small taxes are exclusively enjoyed by cities and counties	Mainly including urban construction tax, property tax, farmland occupation tax, vehicle and vessel use and license tax, stamp duty, land value-added tax, deed tax, etc.
According to the combination of taxation and industry	Zhejiang, Heilongjiang, Jiangsu, Anhui, Fujian, Shandong, Jiangxi, Hubei, Hunan, Guangdong, Guangxi, Guizhou, Gansu, Ningxia and Xinjiang Uygur Autonomous Region provinces according to the combination of tax types and industries. At the same time, it is stipulated that the tax revenue of major industries, pillar industries or key enterprises shall be exclusively enjoyed by the provincial level: As specified in Shandong, key enterprise VAT is designated as the provincial-level tax; Ningxia designated taxes from 31 key electric power and chemical enterprises as provincial-level value-added tax; in addition, there are 9 provinces and cities designating financial insurance business tax as a provincial fixed income

Source Li Ping, Ed. *Illustration of Inter-governmental Financial Relations in China*, China Financial and Economic Press, 2006

implementation of property tax, vehicle and vessel tax, urban maintenance and construction tax, and urban land use tax. However, in general, the legislative power, the power of interpretation, the power of tax items and rates adjustment and the power of tax reduction and exemption are highly concentrated in the hands of the central government. Local governments have only very limited administrative authority. Under this highly unified tax management system, on the one hand, local governments are unable to adjust the tax system according to local conditions, which weakens the initiative of local governments to organize income and regulate economy. On the other hand, local governments often use non-standard preferential means such as financial returns, which easily leads to the abuse of government funds and unfair distribution.

Under the current fiscal system framework of tax distribution system, tax reform will inevitably have a profound impact on the relationship between local fiscal revenue and government finance. Taking the reform of replacing business tax with value-added tax as an example, "replacing business tax with value-added tax" will replace business tax originally belonging to local government revenue with value-added tax, which will inevitably cause the redistribution of interests between central and local governments. Although the pilot regulations stipulate that after the change of the original business tax to value-added tax, the VAT revenue still belongs to local governments, which will not affect the tax division between the central government and local governments in the short term, this transitional policy arrangement is difficult to solve some contradictions inherent in the financial system. After the abolition of business tax, which is the largest local tax, local governments are weak in financial self-sufficiency, and the contradiction between relying more on transfer payment and sharing tax will be magnified, which is not conducive to the establishment of a standardized relationship between the central government and local governments. Therefore, the comprehensive promotion of "replacing business tax with VAT" further highlights the importance of accelerating the improvement of local tax system, which will inevitably force the comprehensive deepening of fiscal and tax reform.

2. Problems in tax system

(1) The tax system is weak in progressivity and lacks effective means of adjusting income distribution

Since the reform and opening up, with the rapid development of China's economy, the income gap is also expanding. From the perspective of Gini coefficient, China's Gini coefficient was 0.317 in 1978, which exceeded the warning level of 0.4 in the world from 2000, and then continued to rise, reaching the highest value of 0.491 in 2008. Since 2009, the Gini coefficient has dropped. In 2013, the Gini coefficient was 0.473, the lowest in 10 years, but still far above the warning level of 0.4 (see Fig. 2.2).

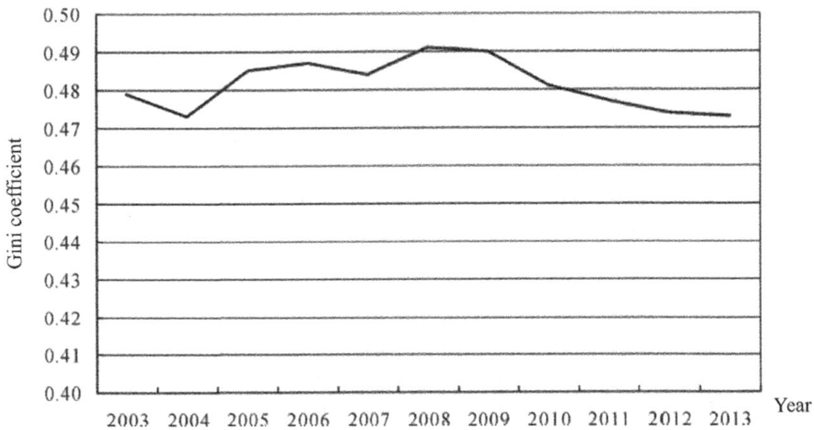

Fig. 2.2 Gini Coefficient of China from 2003 to 2013 (资料来源: 国家统计局 *Source* National Bureau of Statistics)

基尼系数	Gini coefficient
年份	Year
图 1-2 2003–2013	年地方财政自给能力情况

There are many reasons for the widening income gap, among which the absence of tax policy is an important factor. Tax policy is an important tool for adjusting income distribution, but it has not played its due role in regulating income distribution for a long time. This is mainly reflected in the following aspects.

First, the proportion of indirect taxes is obviously high, which is not conducive to play the function of tax system to adjust income distribution. From the perspective of income distribution, direct tax is better than indirect tax. However, the current structure of China's tax system is that the proportion of indirect tax is obviously high and the proportion of direct tax is too low, resulting in the weak ability of adjusting income distribution. As shown in Table 2.3 and Table 2.4, China's indirect taxes accounted for over 65% of all taxes from 2008 to 2012, far higher than

Table 2.3 Proportion of indirect tax and direct tax in China from 2008 to 2012

Year	2008	2009	2010	2011	2012
Proportion of indirect taxes	68.8	68.9	69.6	68.3	67.5
Proportion of direct tax	31.2	31.1	30.4	31.7	32.5

Note: Indirect taxes include value-added tax, consumption tax, business tax, resource tax, stamp duty, vehicle purchase tax, tariff, tobacco tax, urban maintenance and construction tax and education surcharge. Direct taxes include enterprise income tax, individual income tax, property tax, urban land use tax, land value-added tax, vehicle and ship use tax, ship tonnage tax, farmland occupation tax and deed tax
Source calculated according to relevant data in *China Statistical Yearbook 2013*

the average level of OECD countries. Indirect tax is a neutral tax with regressive nature. From the perspective of individual tax burden, the tax burden on lower-income earners is higher as a share of their income than it is on higher-income earners, thus substantially widening the income gap.

Secondly, the unreasonable setting of related taxes in direct taxes weakens the government's ability to adjust income distribution. In the direct tax, the highest income is the enterprise income tax, but the enterprise income tax is levied on the enterprise, the primary function is to raise fiscal revenue, and it does not have the individual income distribution function itself. Individual income tax is the most important type of tax to regulate individual income distribution. However, the coverage of current individual income tax in China is relatively narrow, and the proportion of income in total tax revenue is relatively low, which limits the space for its role. From the perspective of the element setting of individual income tax system, the over-progressive taxation mechanism with the strongest function of income adjustment only applies to the income from wages and salaries, and the range of collection only includes 7% of wage earners (2% of all residents), which has seriously lost the income distribution adjustment function which the individual income tax should have.

Finally, some taxes are missing. The lack of property tax, estate tax, gift tax, social security tax and other taxes that regulate personal income and wealth from different aspects in the link of personal property ownership makes the ability of tax system to adjust income gap extremely limited.

Table 2.4 Proportion of indirect and direct taxes in OECD countries (unit: %)

Year	1965	1970	1975	1980	1985	1990	1995	2000	2004	2005	2008
Proportion of indirect taxes	38.4	36.1	32.8	32.5	33.7	31.9	32.4	31.7	32.2	31.9	31.5
Proportion of direct tax	61.6	63.9	67.2	67.5	66.3	68.1	67.6	68.3	67.8	68.1	68.5

Source calculated from relevant data of OECD, Revenue Statistics 1965–2008

(2) The unreasonable tax system of goods and services is not conducive to the transformation of economic development mode

With the development and improvement of China's market economy and the continuous refinement of social division of labor, the current tax system for goods and services, which separately collects value-added tax and business tax, has gradually shown its inherent irrationality and defects. The increasingly prominent constraint on the development of the tertiary industry is not conducive to the major adjustment of economic structure and the fundamental transformation of economic development mode. This constraint is reflected in the following three aspects.

First, the combination of VAT and business tax violates the "neutral" and "fair" principles of the commodity tax system.

Modern tax theory holds that VAT is the most "neutral" tax and has the least distortion of resource allocation. Value-added tax (VAT) is a new tax on defects in the original turnover tax, such as product tax and sales tax. Turnover tax is levied in full on the circulation of commodities in all links such as production and circulation, which has serious disadvantages of double taxation. Although VAT is also levied in every link of production and consumption, through the deduction mechanism, only the value-added part of the circulation amount is taxed at each link in the middle, thus effectively avoiding the problem of double taxation, which realizes tax neutrality, ensures fair tax burden of goods and services in all links of circulation, and avoids unfair tax burden due to the different division of labor of production and operation.

The current parallel practice of value-added tax and business tax breaks the uniformity of the mode of taxation of goods and services circulation and destroys the neutrality and fairness of value-added tax. First, in the current tax system, the construction industry of the secondary industry and most of the tertiary industry are subject to business tax rather than value-added tax. As a result, the scope of value-added tax is relatively narrow, leading to the interruption of the VAT deduction chain in the economic operation, which cannot completely eliminate the factor of repeated taxation, and the neutral effect of value-added tax is greatly reduced. Second, excluding some industries from the scope of VAT does not accord with the principle of tax fairness. Although these industries do not collect value-added tax, they inevitably need a large number of purchased goods and services in the process of production and operation. Due to the fact that their input tax cannot be deducted, this part of tax burden is actually borne by enterprises, aggravating their tax burden and forming a situation of unfair taxation of value-added tax and business tax industries.

Second, the combined collection of value-added tax and business tax has had a very negative impact on the development of the service industry.

From the perspective of industrial development and economic structure adjustment, most third industries are excluded from the scope of value-added tax, which greatly hinders the development of the service industry. Industries are excluded from the scope of VAT, which greatly hinders the development of the service industry. This is mainly manifested in three aspects. First, the business tax contained in outsourcing services of manufacturing enterprises cannot enter the VAT deduction chain, resulting in an increase in the tax burden of enterprises. Enterprises tend to produce their own services rather than outsourcing services, which is not conducive to the expansion of the demand for the service industry. Second, the business tax taxes the turnover in full and cannot be deducted, which will inevitably lead to double taxation and inhibit the professional division of labor in the service industry and the development of service subcontracting. Third, the value-added tax and business tax contained in the purchasing cost of the service industry cannot be refunded when the service industry exports, which lead to the export of services with tax, reduce the competitiveness of China's service export and are not conducive to the expansion of China's service trade export.

Finally, the development of industrial specialization makes the enterprise's production of goods and service closely integrated, difficult to distinguish and define, increasing the difficulty of tax collection and management.

From the perspective of tax collection and management, the two sets of tax systems in parallel have caused some difficulties in the practice of tax collection and management, especially with the emergence of diversified business and new economic forms; tax collection and management is also facing new problems. For example, in the modern market economy, the bundling of goods and services is becoming more and more numerous and complicated, and it is increasingly difficult to accurately divide the proportion of goods and services, which challenges the standard of dividing the two taxes. For another example, with the development of information technology, some traditional commodities have been service-oriented, and the distinction between commodities and services has become more and more blurred. It is difficult to clearly define the two, and the problem of whether to apply value-added tax or business tax arises, thus increasing the cost of tax collection and management, resulting in resource waste.

(3) The tax system has a weak regulating effect on resources and environment

After more than 30 years of reform and development, China has not only made great achievements in the economic field, but also faced great challenges in the field of resources and environment. At present, the pressure of resource constraint is increasing, environmental pollution is becoming more and more serious, and the ecological system is continuously degraded. The ecological environment is facing a very serious situation, which has become a major problem restricting the sustainable and healthy economic development. The *Decision of the Central Committee of the Communist Party of China* on several major issues concerning comprehensively deepening reform adopted at the third plenary session of the 18th CPC central committee clearly states that we need to accelerate the establishment of an ecological civilization system and improve the system and mechanism for developing land space, conserving and utilizing resources, and protecting the ecological environment.

With the continuous deterioration of the situation of China's resources and environment, China's consideration of green environmental factors in the reform and adjustment of the tax system is also increasing, and has established a series of resources and environment tax system, which plays a certain positive role in promoting environmental protection and resource conservation. However, generally speaking, the current tax system has obvious problems and deficiencies in regulating resources and environment, and the system construction is not yet perfect, which cannot meet the urgent requirements of accelerating the transformation of economic development mode, promoting resource conservation and environmental protection. First, a complete environmental tax system has yet to be built.

Although China has initially formed an environmental tax system in terms of the tax categories and fees levied on resources, pollutant discharge, refined oil products and motor vehicles, China's environmental tax system is far from perfect compared with the relatively perfect environmental tax system abroad.

One is the absence of separate taxes on pollutants and carbon dioxide emissions. From the point of view of ecological environment protection, the special taxes on pollutant discharge, ecological environment destruction or products have the main position in the environmental tax system. However, China lacks specific targeted taxes, such as sulfur tax, nitrogen tax, sewage tax and carbon dioxide tax, which are directly related to pollutant emissions. As a result, on the one hand, it is difficult to form a tax revenue source dedicated to environmental protection; on the other hand, it is limited in policy options, and some tax policies with stronger effectiveness cannot be considered, designed and regulated. Second, there is a lack of coordination between the existing taxes related to the environment. Due to the lack of overall design of the environmental tax system, the current tax categories related to the environment are only limited to the repair and adjustment of the original tax system, and they have a weak connection with each other and lack of coordination. The environmental tax system lacks systematic-ness, which makes it difficult to form synergy and has insufficient regulatory effect on environmental protection.

Secondly, there are defects in the tax system setting of taxes related to resources and environment.

In the current tax system, the main taxes related to resource and environmental protection are resource tax, consumption tax, vehicle and vessel tax and vehicle purchase tax. However, from the perspective of the tax system setting of these taxes, some of them are not perfect in the tax system setting, resulting in insufficient regulation and control of resources and environment, which need to be further strengthened.

From the perspective of resource tax, the main purpose of the current resource tax is to regulate the differential income of resources and promote the rational development and utilization of resources. From the perspective of promoting resource conservation, the main problems of resource tax are: First, the low tax burden fails to fully reflect the intrinsic value of resources, leading to the excessive exploitation and use of resources. On the basis of the reform of AD valorem resource tax on coal, it is urgent to accelerate the reform of AD valorem resource tax on other items to fully reflect the intrinsic value of resource goods and environmental costs. Second, the scope of tax collection is narrow. Currently, the resource tax is mainly levied on mineral resources, without including renewable resources such as water resources, forest resources and grassland resources in the collection scope. Therefore, the role of resource tax in protecting natural resources and ecological environment cannot be fully played.

From the point of view of consumption tax, after many reforms and adjustments, the current consumption tax has a higher environmental protection factor, and the adjustment of environmental protection is increasingly strengthened. However, compared with the consumption tax system of developed countries, there is still a big gap, mainly manifested in: First, the scope of taxation is too narrow. Some high-energy consumption, high pollution, high emissions of products, such as coal, thermal power, Freon, large motor vehicles and so on are included into the tax scope. Second, the tax rate is not reasonable, and the overall level of tax burden is low, which cannot reflect the external economic cost of taxable product consumption behavior. Taking the consumption tax on refined oil as an example, the unit tax on unleaded gasoline in China is 1 Yuan/liter, and the unit tax on leaded gasoline is 1.4 Yuan/liter. In 2012, the average unit tax on unleaded gasoline in the EU 27 countries is 0.52 euro/liter, and the average unit tax on leaded gasoline is 0.58 euro/liter, which is more than three times higher than that in China. From the perspective of vehicle purchase tax, the current vehicle purchase tax adopts a single tax rate of 10%, which does not take into account the energy efficiency, pollution emissions and other situations of vehicles to formulate different tax rates, and cannot play a regulating role in high-energy consumption and high-emission vehicles.

(4) Tax administration efficiency needs to be improved

Tax collection and management system reform and tax reform complement each other. Since the 1980s, the reform of tax collection and management system and the reform of tax system complement each other. Since the 1980s, our country has made arduous exploration on establishing scientific and strict tax collection and management system. Since the twentieth century, our country has carried on the arduous exploration to the establishment of scientific strict tax collection management system. Especially after the tax reform in 1994, in order to meet the requirements of the new tax collection and management system, the state administration of taxation put forward the new tax collection and management mode of "centralized collection and key inspection based on tax declaration, tax payment and optimized service, relying on computer network", which started a new journey of deepening the tax collection and management reform. With the gradual improvement of the market economy system, tax collection and management reform have never been interrupted. It has gradually established the taxpayer's own tax return system and service system, management and monitoring system, inspection system and organization system. We will implement scientific and fine tax administration and strengthen the reform of weak links in tax collection and administration. We will vigorously carry out specialized and information-based tax administration, carry out trials of specialized tax source administration and constantly explore new methods and measures for tax administration. Significant progress has been made in the reform of tax collection and management. A system for taxpayers to report and pay taxes on their own has been basically established. Major changes have been made in the concept of tax service. Breakthroughs have been made in the informatization of tax administration, the deterrent of tax inspection has been enhanced, and the quality and efficiency of tax collection and administration have been significantly improved, which has effectively promoted steady and rapid growth of tax revenue, ensured the effective use of tax revenue to regulate the economy and regulate distribution, and played an important role in supporting economic and social development.

However, due to the late start of China's tax collection and management system construction, in the process of rapid development and improvement of the market economy, the current tax collection and management has exposed many problems and does not adapt to the situation of economic development.

First of all, the legal system of tax collection and management is not perfect, and the legal effect needs to be improved. There are still many problems in the content and operation of the current *Law on the Administration of Tax Collection*, which need further revision. Relevant provisions on tax administration, tax inspection and tax agency are all in the form of departmental rules and regulations, with low legal effect and irregular content.

Secondly, the informatization level of tax collection and management is relatively low, and the sharing mechanism has not been formed. Due to the weak basic work of tax informatization, the new tax collection and management mode requires to rely on computer network and take informatization and specialization construction as the goal; due to the wide coverage of basic tax work, data collection is not comprehensive and accurate enough to meet the needs of tax collection and management and tax source monitoring. Finally, the consciousness of tax service is weak and the relationship between tax collection and payment is not harmonious. First, the service concept of "taxpayers-oriented" has not been established. Since the starting point of the work is not to satisfy taxpayers, the publicity of tax laws and regulations is not in place, and the new tax policy has not been timely delivered to taxpayers, it is difficult to respond quickly to the changes and needs of taxpayers in the tax collection and payment process. Second, while requiring taxpayers to pay taxes in good faith, the credit system and evaluation mechanism of tax authorities to collect taxes in good faith are not perfect, making it difficult to build a harmonious tax collection and payment relationship.

Problems in the Transfer Payment System

First, the scale of transfer payments continues to expand. Due to the current fiscal system, especially the imperfect division of powers and excessive decentralization of expenditure responsibilities, it is difficult for local governments to meet the basic needs of their financial power, which is mainly solved by transfer payments between the upper and lower levels of governments. As a result, the scale of transfer payments continues to expand, and the proportion of transfer payments in central fiscal revenue and expenditure increases year by year. Transfer payments from the central government to local governments (excluding tax rebates) increased from 1.4017 trillion Yuan in 2007 to 3.9912 trillion Yuan in 2012, representing an annual growth rate of 26.9%. In 2012, 71.1% of central government revenue was used for transfer payments to local governments (excluding tax rebates), higher than 56% in 2010 and 67.87% in 2011.

Secondly, due to the lack of clear division of governmental powers and expenditure responsibilities, the design of China's transfer payment system is messy, and the characteristics of general transfer payment being "special" and special transfer payment being "general" are increasingly obvious. According to the *2012 Classification of Government Revenue and Expenditure*, "general transfer payment income" includes 27 major items. It not only includes transfer payments for equalization, transfer payments in ethnic minority areas, transfer payments for adjustment of wages, transfer payments for rural tax reform and other non-prescribed purposes, but also includes "quasi-special" transfer payments, such as subsidies to defuse debts, transfer payments to education, transfer payments to social security and employment, transfer payments to medical and health care, transfer payments to agriculture, forestry and water conservancy, and other forms of payment with clear scope and purpose. Correspondingly, special transfer payments tend to be generalized. Also, in the 2012 government revenue and expenditure classification, "special transfer payment revenue" includes 24 major items, such as general public services, diplomacy, national defense, public security, education, science and technology, culture, sports and media, social security and employment, medical and health care, energy conservation and environmental protection, urban and rural community affairs, agriculture, forestry and water affairs, transportation, which almost cover all major public services.

Third, the structure of transfer payments is not reasonable, the proportion of general transfer payments is relatively small, and the number of special transfer payments continues to increase. The project is multifarious and funds are dispersed. In 2010, of the total 2.73 trillion Yuan in transfer payments from the central government, 1.41 trillion Yuan were special transfer payments, and 262.22 billion Yuan in general transfer payments for specific purposes, totaling 61.7% of total transfer payments were for specific purposes. That's down from 62.54% in 2009, but up 8.3% from 2008. From November 2011 to March 2012, the national audit office organized an audit investigation on the financial funds of 54 counties (cities, districts and flags, hereinafter referred to as counties with the financial strength of each accounting for about one-third) in 18 provinces (autonomous regions and municipalities directly under the central government). It is found that county-level finance is highly dependent on transfer payments from higher authorities. 49.39% of public finance expenditure comes from transfer payments from higher authorities, among which 61.66% comes from 45 counties in central and western China. It is found that county-level finance is highly dependent on transfer payments from higher authorities. 49.39% of public finance expenditure comes from transfer payments from higher authorities, among which 61.66% comes from 45 counties in central and western China. In 2011, 54 counties received 73.818 billion Yuan in transfer payments from their superiors, of which 50.8% were special transfer payments. In addition to the funds earmarked in general transfer payments, 68.40% of the total transfer payments are earmarked.

In addition, special transfer payment projects are complex and messy, with backward system construction and management and poor performance. Special transfer payments generally have the problem of "focus more on distribution but less on management", and even the phenomenon of "split". The allocation of funds for some special transfer payments lacks institutional norms, and the implementation of projects lacks reports. In the process of use, the constraints are not strong, and there is a lack of performance evaluation method, which is not only easy to form the "leakage and venting" of transfer payment funds, but also difficult to ensure the realization of the policy objectives set for the transfer payment project at the beginning. In terms of budget management, there are also problems. Transfer payments from superiors have not been fully incorporated into local budgets. Meanwhile, the distribution of special funds and special transfer payments is not standardized and transparent, and the supervision mechanism is weak. Corruption cases abound. Looking through the *Warning Record of CaiYuan- Selected Cases of the National Financial System*, the illegal and disciplinary cases in the field of special funds and special transfer payment allocation occupy a large space.

Financial System Problems Below the Provincial Level

The financial system below the provincial level, which belongs to the concept of "local" in China, is an important part of the national financial system. It is the implementation and extension of the central government's local financial system, which affects the behavior space of local governments and the supply level of basic public services. In 1994, the fiscal system of tax sharing established the fiscal distribution relationship between the central government and local governments under the framework of large tax sharing system. In accordance with the central government's system of tax distribution to local governments, local governments have adjusted their financial systems at all levels below the provincial level and established a transfer payment system. Since the reform of tax sharing system is based on overcoming or eliminating the defects of the original system, standardizing the financial distribution relationship between the central government and the provinces, and rapidly enhancing the central government's financial resources, it makes China's current tax sharing system only solves the contradiction between the central government and the local government in the division of financial rights, and the financial relationship below the provincial level has not yet been straightened out. Generally speaking, the real tax sharing system has not been realized. The division of income between governments below the provincial level is varied, complex and variable. Total amount sharing and revenue and expenditure responsibility systems and so on which divide income by tax category with great bargaining color all exist to varying degrees. The more underdeveloped the grassroots, the more inclined to adopt responsibility system. Even in regions that divide income by tax categories, some provinces and cities and counties have too many tax categories to share, and some still divide income by enterprise affiliation or industry, which violates the principle of tax sharing. Governments at all levels below the provincial level are divided into different levels of tax sharing, the lower the level, the less financial resources. The lower the administrative power, the heavier the administrative power. In addition, the reform of transfer payments has not been fully implemented, which has led to difficulties in county and township finance and unbalanced basic public services.

1. Tax revenue division below the provincial level

The tax categories below the province are divided roughly into the following situations.

(1) Tax categories below the provincial level

One is that taxes with stable incomes and large scale are shared between provinces and cities and counties. Most provinces have adopted this model. At present, the main types of revenue sharing taxes between provinces and cities and counties are value-added tax (25%), business tax, enterprise income tax and individual income tax (40% shared by local governments), and urban land use tax.

Second, cities (counties) should be the only ones to enjoy taxes with lower incomes. At present, the fixed income tax mainly includes resource tax, urban construction tax, property tax, vehicle and boat use and license tax, farmland occupation tax, stamp duty, deed tax, land value-added tax, etc.. As a city or county (city), although there are many fixed income taxes, the income scale is generally small, without many main taxes. This is especially true after the state abolished agricultural taxes and taxes on special agricultural products except tobacco.

Third, while some provinces and cities divide their incomes according to the above two ways, it also stipulates that the tax revenue of major industries or pillar industries shall be exclusively enjoyed by the provincial level. More provinces and cities adopt this way of division. As specified in Tianjin, the value-added tax, business tax, enterprise income tax, individual income tax, urban construction tax, education fee additional, as well as the airport, port, cigarette, automobile, sky steel, sky iron, steel pipe and venture environmental protection company's value-added tax, business tax, enterprise income tax, individual income tax and so on from the traffic and transportation, postal communications, petroleum and petrochemical, financial insurance and other industries are included into the revenue of the city. Hebei Province will include value-added tax, business tax paid by petroleum, petrochemical, nonferrous metals, electric power enterprises and power enterprises with provincial investment as the provincial income. Shaanxi Province made it clear when the system was adjusted in 2004 that value-added tax on electric power enterprises in the whole province (excluding small hydropower), power VAT refunded at the provincial level, urban construction tax and education surcharge levied with the wheeling charges VAT of Northwest Power Grid Co., Ltd., business tax on financial insurance (including non-bank financial institutions) and the accompanying urban construction tax and educational surcharge, provincial highway tolls business tax and the accompanying urban construction tax and educational surcharge are taken as the provincial fixed income. In addition, 20 other provinces use the financial insurance business tax as the provincial fixed income.

(2) Sharing types of tax sharing

Tax sharing can be divided into the following three types:

One is proportional sharing. Currently, a total of 15 provinces, including Beijing, Tianjin, Hebei, Shanxi, Liaoning, Jilin, Heilongjiang, Henan, Shandong, Hubei, Guangxi, Chongqing, Hainan, Shaanxi and Gansu, have adopted this method to divide income sharing between provinces and cities and counties. The proportion of sharing income between provinces and cities and counties is mainly divided into "five to five", "four to six" and "three to seven". The sharing proportion of most provincial governments is slightly lower than that of cities and counties, which reflects the principle of downward inclination of financial resources and plays a positive role in alleviating financial difficulties at the grassroots level.

Second, it is divided according to the subordination relationship. At present, Shanghai, Zhejiang, Anhui, Jiangxi and other four provinces still use this way of division. For example, Zhejiang Province divides the income of value-added tax, business tax and enterprise income tax into provincial income and city and county income according to the subordination of enterprises. It needs to be noted that all provinces are divided into provincial-level fixed income and municipal and county fixed income according to the subordination relationship for state-owned assets operating income, planned loss subsidy, administrative fee income, confiscation income and special income.

Third, cross-division by proportion and affiliation. Currently, 12 provinces and regions, including Inner Mongolia, Jiangsu, Fujian, Hunan, Guangdong, Yunnan, Sichuan, Guizhou, Tibet, Qinghai, Ningxia and Xinjiang, divide their shared income in this way. As in Guangdong, the value-added tax revenue is divided according to the subordination relationship of enterprises. The income tax revenue from state-owned enterprises is divided according to the subordination relationship of enterprises. The income tax revenue from non-state-owned enterprises is shared between provinces and cities on the basis of "four to six" ratio, and business tax and individual income tax on the basis of "four to six" ratio. The financial system of some provinces (excluding Guizhou) below the provincial level is shown in Table 2.5.

2. Transfer payments below the provincial level

In recent years, with the gradual improvement of the transfer payment system provided by the central government to local governments and the continuous expansion of the scale, local governments have also established the transfer payment system of provincial-level transfer payment in line with the central government's measures and their own conditions. The provincial transfer payment consists of financial transfer payment and special transfer payment. Among them, financial transfer payments

Table 2.5 Financial system conditions below the provincial level in 2013

Region	Province	Year of promulgation of the current system	Whether to tax according to the type of tax	The provincial tax sharing of major taxes	Proportion of provincial major tax shares				
					VAT sharing ratio at the provincial level	Business tax sharing ratio at the provincial level	Enterprise income tax sharing ratio at the provincial level	Individual income tax sharing ratio at the provincial level	Other taxes or fees
Eastern region	Jiangsu	2008	Yes	Value-added tax, enterprise income tax, cultivated land occupation tax, local and urban land use tax, land value-added tax, property tax and deed tax	12.5% Increment concentration	—	Increment concentration 20%	—	The tax on cultivated land occupation is 50%, and the tax on land use in local cities and towns is 30%, tax on land value-added tax is 30%, tax on property tax is 30% and deed tax is 30%
	Zhejiang	2008	No	Total amount sharing					20% Provincial total amount sharing of the increment part is 20%
	Shandong	2005	Yes	Business tax, enterprise income tax and individual income tax	—	20%	8%	15%	5% Increased revenue from compensated land transfer

Region	Province	Year of promulgation of the current system	Whether to tax according to the type of tax	The provincial tax sharing of major taxes	Proportion of provincial major tax shares				
					VAT sharing ratio at the provincial level	Business tax sharing ratio at the provincial level	Enterprise income tax sharing ratio at the provincial level	Individual income tax sharing ratio at the provincial level	Other taxes or fees
	Guangdong	2011	Yes	Business tax, enterprise income tax, individual income tax, land value-added tax	—	50%	20%	20%	50% Land value-added tax
	Fujian	2002	No	Total amount sharing					
	Liaoning	2010	No	Based on the final accounts of sharing tax revenue of provinces and cities in 2008, the sharing tax base of provinces and cities in the base year (namely year 2009) is calculated according to the annual growth rate of the three years from 2006 to 2008. The proportion of provincial sharing tax base drawn on each city to the provinces and cities sharing tax bases of each city is the proportion of total amount sharing of each city turned over to provincial finance with one rate for one city					
Central region	Shanxi	2002	Yes	Value-added tax, business tax, enterprise income tax, individual income tax, resource tax, urban land use tax	8.75%	35%	14%	14%	Resource tax 35%, urban land use tax 35%
	Jilin	2004	Yes	Value-added tax, business tax, enterprise income tax, individual income tax	12.50%	50%	16%	16%	—

(continued)

Table 2.5 (continued)

Region	Province	Year of promulgation of the current system	Whether to tax according to the type of tax	The provincial tax sharing of major taxes	Proportion of provincial major tax shares				
					VAT sharing ratio at the provincial level	Business tax sharing ratio at the provincial level	Enterprise income tax sharing ratio at the provincial level	Individual income tax sharing ratio at the provincial level	Other taxes or fees
	Heilongjiang	2006	Yes	Business tax	—	50%	—	—	—
	Anhui	2004	Yes	Enterprise income tax, individual income tax	—	—	15%	15%	—
	Jiangxi	2003	Yes	Resource tax, urban land use tax, stamp tax, land value-added tax, individual income tax, property tax	—	—	—	16%	Resource tax, urban land use tax, stamp tax, land value-added tax, property tax in 2002, 40% of the stock
	Henan	2004	Yes	Increment sharing at the provincial level of business tax, enterprise income tax, individual income tax	—	20% Incremental sharing	20% Incremental sharing	20% Incremental sharing	—

Region	Province	Year of promulgation of the current system	Whether to tax according to the type of tax	The provincial tax sharing of major taxes	Proportion of provincial major tax shares				
					VAT sharing ratio at the provincial level	Business tax sharing ratio at the provincial level	Enterprise income tax sharing ratio at the provincial level	Individual income tax sharing ratio at the provincial level	Other taxes or fees
	Hubei	2011	No	The tax revenue shared by the province under the fiscal management system in 2002 shall be based on the provincial tax revenue approved by all cities and counties in 2010. It increases and decreases at the same rate as the local tax revenues of cities and counties. No more sharing of VAT, business tax and income tax					Urban construction tax, cultivated land occupation tax, urban land use tax, stamp duty, resource tax, urban education fee surcharge will continue to be paid per quota
	Hunan	2010	Yes	Enterprise income tax, individual income tax, resource tax, urban land use tax, land value-added tax	4.25%	25%	12%	12%	Resource tax 25%
	Hainan	2007	Yes	Value-added tax, business tax, enterprise income tax, individual income tax, land value-added tax and deed tax	13.75% Haikou city 8.75% Sanya 6.25% Others	55% Haikou city 35% Sanya 25% Others	22% Haikou city 14% Sanya 10% Others	22% Haikou city 14% Sanya 10% Others	Haikou city: land value-added tax and deed tax 35% Sanya land value-added tax and deed tax 25% Other areas: land value-added tax and deed tax

(continued)

Table 2.5 (continued)

Region	Province	Year of promulgation of the current system	Whether to tax according to the type of tax	The provincial tax sharing of major taxes	Proportion of provincial major tax shares				
					VAT sharing ratio at the provincial level	Business tax sharing ratio at the provincial level	Enterprise income tax sharing ratio at the provincial level	Individual income tax sharing ratio at the provincial level	Other taxes or fees
	Heibei	2005	Yes	Value-added tax, business tax, enterprise income tax, individual income tax, sewage charge	10%	10%	20%	10%	Sewage charge 10%
Western region	Sichuan	2000	Yes	tax, business tax, individual income tax, resource tax, property tax, stamp duty, urban land use tax, deed tax	8.75%	35%	—	14%	35% Resource tax, property tax, stamp duty, urban land use tax, deed tax
	Guizhou	2013	Yes	Value-added tax, resource tax, urban land use tax	5%	20%	8%	8%	20% Resource tax, urban land use tax

Region	Province	Year of promulgation of the current system	Whether to tax according to the type of tax	The provincial tax sharing of major taxes	Proportion of provincial major tax shares				
					VAT sharing ratio at the provincial level	Business tax sharing ratio at the provincial level	Enterprise income tax sharing ratio at the provincial level	Individual income tax sharing ratio at the provincial level	Other taxes or fees
	Yunnan	2005	Yes	tax, individual income tax, cultivated land occupation tax, additional income from education fees of cigarette enterprises at the county level	—	—	24%	24%	Cultivated land usage tax 30%, cigarette enterprise educational surcharges 60%
	Shanxi	2004	Yes	Value-added tax, business tax, urban land use tax, property tax, resource tax	7.50%	30%	20%	20%	30% Urban land use tax, property tax, resource tax
	Gansu	2003	Yes	Value-added tax, business tax, enterprise income tax, individual income tax	Cities and provinces with good economic conditions 17.5% and other cities and provinces 5%	30%	20%	20%	—

(continued)

Table 2.5 (continued)

Region	Province	Year of promulgation of the current system	Whether to tax according to the type of tax	The provincial tax sharing of major taxes	Proportion of provincial major tax shares				
					VAT sharing ratio at the provincial level	Business tax sharing ratio at the provincial level	Enterprise income tax sharing ratio at the provincial level	Individual income tax sharing ratio at the provincial level	Other taxes or fees
	Qinghai	2004	Yes	Value-added tax	12.50%	—	—	—	Resource tax, cultivated land occupation tax, land use tax, fixed asset investment orientation adjustment tax, foreign enterprise income tax quota payment (1997 base)
	Ningxia	1995	Yes	Enterprise income tax, individual income tax, property tax, land use tax, resource tax	—	—	20%	20%	50% Property tax 30% and resource tax
	Xinjiang	2004	Yes	Resource tax	—	—	—	—	Resource tax 75%
	Guangxi	2005	Yes	Value-added tax, business tax, enterprise income tax, individual income tax	8%	40%	10%	15%	—

Region	Province	Year of promulgation of the current system	Whether to tax according to the type of tax	The provincial tax sharing of major taxes	Proportion of provincial major tax shares				
					VAT sharing ratio at the provincial level	Business tax sharing ratio at the provincial level	Enterprise income tax sharing ratio at the provincial level	Individual income tax sharing ratio at the provincial level	Other taxes or fees
	Inner Mongolia	2012	Yes	Value-added tax, business tax, enterprise income tax, individual income tax, resource tax	7.5%	10%	10%	10%	Resource tax 65%

Note (1) As of June 2013. (2) Filing according to the sample provincial (district) financial system. (3) Zhejiang and Fujian provinces adopt the system of total amount sharing, and the proportion of total amount sharing is 20%. Liaoning and Xinjiang join the total amount sharing type and share as per market per rate. (4) Compared with the situation in 2006, 9 out of 26 provinces and regions have made institutional adjustments, among which four of the six eastern provinces adjusted their systems, accounting for 66.7% of the total; three of the 10 provinces in the central region have adjusted their systems, accounting for 30% of the total. Two of the 10 provinces and regions in the western region have adjusted their systems, accounting for 20% of the total. The eastern region is significantly higher than the central and western regions. In addition, there have been no changes in the share ratio and method of downward payment in Zhejiang Province, but in 2008 the provincial government issued a document to adjust the system and redesign the transfer payment from the province to the downward payment. In 2006, three eastern provinces (Jiangsu, Zhejiang and Fujian) adopted the method of sharing 20% of the total amount. By 2013, four provinces (Zhejiang, Fujian, Liaoning and Hubei) have adopted the total amount sharing method, while Jiangsu has withdrawn the total amount sharing method and adopted the tax sharing method. However, Liaoning exited from the tax sharing, adopted the total amount sharing per market per rate. Hubei also exited from tax sharing and adopted total amount sharing. From the perspective of financial allocation, the main bodies of provinces and regions that have implemented the adjustment have concentrated their financial resources at the provincial level, such as Guangdong, Inner Mongolia, Guizhou, Hainan and Hunan mainly include general transfer payments, adjusted transfer payments for wages, transfer payments for rural tax reform, transfer payments for ethnic minority areas, awards and subsidies to ease the financial difficulties of counties and townships ("three awards and one subsidy"), and incentive transfer payments issued by local governments. The incentive transfer payment issued by local governments refers to the incentive subsidy implemented to fully mobilize the enthusiasm of county and township to develop economy and strengthen financial management by establishing scientific index system and reward and penalize the poor. Special transfer payment from province to lower level refers to special subsidy funds set up by provincial governments to achieve specific policy objectives and compensate some affairs entrusted to lower-level governments. The recipient of the fund shall use the fund for specified purposes and use the fund exclusively.

After the central government introduced the transitional transfer payment method in 1995, all localities implemented the general transfer payment from the provincial level to the lower level in accordance with the central government's method and local conditions and in accordance with the principles of objectivity, fairness and standardization. According to the nature of general transfer payments, local governments generally aim to narrow the financial gap within their jurisdictions and promote the equalization of basic public services between regions. However, restricted by objective conditions, 19 provinces in the central and western regions, including Hebei and Ningxia, have clearly stipulated that the main goal of general transfer payments in the near future is to ease the prominent contradiction in the financial operation of counties and townships, mainly including ensuring the payment of salaries of government organs and public institutions and the normal operation of grassroots political power. Ningxia Hui autonomous region stipulates: "by standardizing the form of fund allocation, the financial difficulties of cities and counties will be gradually alleviated, the financial differences between regions will be adjusted, and the basic public service capacity of local governments will be equalized. At present, the financial foundation of governments at all levels is still relatively weak, the transfer payment funds are mainly used to ensure basic expenditures for the payment of salaries and the normal operation of government organs and public institutions, and to promote the development of agriculture, science and technology, education and other necessary undertakings, so as to achieve balanced development between regions and between urban and rural areas".

In addition, Anhui, Hubei, Qinghai and other provinces have also given full play to the policy guiding function of general transfer payments, guiding and encouraging municipal and county governments to increase revenue, reduce expenditure and develop local economies. According to the regulations of Anhui Province, in accordance with the requirements of "accelerating development, enriching the people and strengthening the province, building a well-off society in an all-round way", meeting the needs of the reform of county financial system directly under the province's control, on the basis of increasing the general transfer payment for financial difficulties and improving their basic financial guarantee capacity, we should give full play to the guiding role of the general transfer payment policy, establish an incentive and restraint mechanism, encourage counties to rely on themselves, accelerate their development, strengthen their financial and economic strength and form a group of financially and economically strong counties as soon as possible. According to the regulations of Qinghai Province, "through the implementation of general transfer payments, the initiative of cities and counties to increase income and reduce expenditure and achieve fiscal balance can be mobilized". In practice, Hubei Province has divided general transfer payment into equalization transfer payment, incentive transfer payment and policy transfer payment according to its different policy functions, calculation factors and distribution methods.

On the whole, the vast majority of regions follow the central government's general transfer payments to local governments. The amount of transfer payment shall be determined according to the standard balance of revenue and expenditure and transfer payment coefficient of cities and counties within the jurisdiction, namely "transfer payment amount of a certain region = (standard fiscal expenditure of the region - standard fiscal revenue of the region) × transfer payment coefficient". However, there are some exceptions. Shanxi, Guizhou and Tibet provinces and autonomous regions provide full subsidies to the standard fiscal revenue and expenditure gap of local governments. The calculation formula is:

"transfer payment amount of a certain region = standard fiscal expenditure of that region - standard fiscal revenue of that region". On the basis of county-level and city-level per capita disposable financial subsidy of 10,800 Yuan and 15,000 Yuan, respectively, based on the compiled figures, Guangdong Province made up for the cities and counties below the subsidy standard. Jiangsu Province listed the counties (cities) with the standard per capita financial resources of less than 11,000 Yuan in 1999 as the transfer payment scope, and subsidized 50% of the difference between the standard per capita financial resources of various regions and 11,000 Yuan.

Although the general transfer payments of all provinces are calculated at the county and city level, Shandong, Gansu, Jiangxi, Qinghai, Tibet and other provinces implement secondary distribution through the prefectural and municipal level. Hebei stipulates that 22 pilot counties are directly assigned by the provincial government, while other counties are redistributed by municipal finance. In order to ensure the effective use of transfer payment funds, these provinces implementing secondary distribution have made clear provisions. The prefectural (municipal) level shall not further adjust or reduce the amount of transfer payment subsidies to the counties (cities or districts) it belongs to, and shall require the prefectural (municipal) level, on the basis of verifying the transfer payments of each county (city or district), to increase the support to the counties it belongs to, especially those with financial difficulties, by raising necessary funds according to local conditions.

In terms of the use of funds, it is generally stipulated that transfer payments should be mainly used to ensure the payment of salaries to employees of administrative institutions, the normal operation of institutions, social security and other basic public expenditures, and to repay debts when due. At the same time, the subsidy funds shall not be used for "image projects" or "vanity projects"; otherwise, the general transfer payment funds of the next year will be deducted as appropriate. In terms of funds supervision, governments at all levels are required to strengthen supervision over transfer payments and improve the efficiency of the use of funds. Governments at the prefectural and municipal levels should actively raise funds, increase the scale of general transfer payments, increase support to counties and townships with financial difficulties, and help alleviate the financial difficulties of counties and townships by optimizing the structure of fiscal expenditure, reducing their own expenditures and special appropriations.

2.2 Insufficient Support of Management System Needed for Policy Optimization and Performance Improvement

Full-bore Budget Problem

Modern government budget requires all government funds to be included in the budget, subject to budget process constraints. This is known as the principle of budget comprehensiveness. Since the budget reform in 1998, with the progress of the departmental budget reform, the centralized payment of the national Treasury and the classification of government revenues and expenditures, various kinds of extra-budgetary revenues and expenditures have been gradually brought under budgetary control, and the comprehensiveness of the budget has been constantly improved. In 2007, the state capital operation budget was prepared on a trial basis, and the profits handed over by central enterprises were included in the budget. The land transfer fee is fully incorporated into the budget management of local funds, and a thorough "revenue and expenditure line" is implemented. In 2011, all extra-budgetary funds were abolished, and all extra-budgetary revenue was put under general budget management or into the management of government-managed funds.

However, the comprehensive budget reform has not been completed, and a considerable part of public funds has not been included in the budget management. This includes funds, such as social security funds, that are not required under current reforms to be included in budgetary management. It also includes the funds required by the state but not fully included in the budget management in the implementation process, such as government funds and the contribution of state-owned capital operation income. At the local level, the state capital management budget has not been fully promoted. The current budget for state capital operation is still only a budget for "small state assets", and the income generated by other types of state assets (such as financial assets and mineral assets) is still beyond the budget management. At the same time, although governments at all levels have been strengthening the control of extra-budgetary funds, especially those beyond the system, the phenomenon of private "small Treasury" has not been put an end to.

Performance Management and Accountability Mechanism

Performance budget is the inevitable development direction of modern budget reform and government efficiency improvement. Since 2003, the central and local governments at all levels have carried out a number of decentralized performance evaluation pilot projects. In 2005, the ministry of finance issued the *Measures for the Performance Evaluation and Management of Central Department Budget Expenditure*, which actively promoted the reform of budget performance management, and local financial performance evaluation was also actively carried out, making great progress. However, there is still a considerable distance between the full implementation of the performance budget reform, which is mainly reflected in the following aspects:

Although the concept of performance has been initially established, the long-term formation of the "focus more on distribution and less on performance" has not changed fundamentally.

Plans, policies and budgets are still not well aligned. The plan for national economic and social development, which is drawn up every five years, can hardly be integrated with the annual budget. After the introduction of the plan, governments at all levels will still introduce a large number of policies and have an impact on the budget. The government's budget formulation lacks a medium- and long-term vision, and it is difficult to consider the effective connection between the government's policy objectives and the annual budget from a medium- and long-term perspective.

Accountability systems for departments and personnel have not yet been established. Results-oriented performance budget reform requires that the dereliction of duty of relevant departments and personnel can be effectively investigated and institutionalized, namely the implementation of accountability system. The budget reform of more than ten years emphasizes administrative control and hard budget constraint, and establishes the “external control” system to supervise the income and expenditure behavior of various departments, which is also the foundation of modern public budget system. However, from the direction of performance budget reform, departments should be given some autonomy in budget implementation in the future, so they should not rely excessively on external control for a long time. While continuing to improve the external control, establish a standardized internal control system in each department to urge each department to control itself. If there is a problem, it can be traced to the relevant departments and personnel.

The Reform of Government Accounting System

Over the years, there has been no substantive reform in government accounting. The target positioning of the government accounting system is unclear, the accounting system is segmented, the accounting information is scattered, the accounting function is incomplete (e.g., the accounting scope is relatively narrow), the accounting basis is single, and the whole process and comprehensive accounting supervision of the government revenue and expenditure cannot be conducted, which cannot meet the needs of financial management and performance evaluation. At the same time, the current budget accounting system is not conducive to the management of assets and liabilities by government departments and administrative institutions, nor is it conducive to preventing and reducing financial risks and improving the government’s ability to provide public services. Especially in the accounting basis, the simple cash system cannot accurately and comprehensively reflect the rights and responsibilities of the government. The accrual accounting system can be gradually introduced to improve the transparency of government finance and control financial risks.

Imperfect Audit and Supervision System

Independent auditing is an integral part of modern public budgets. At present, the national audit office belongs to the state council department and is an internal government institution. The *Audit Law* stipulates that audit institutions must report audit results to people's congresses at the same level. This makes auditing a part and a link of budgetary supervision. However, fundamentally speaking, China's audit system belongs to administrative audit. In order to improve China's audit system, special audit committees can be set up within the NPC. This will not only improve the auditing system, but also strengthen budgetary supervision by the NPC.

In addition, problems such as too short time and lack of professionalism still exist in the budget review process. The NPC, in particular, has to review the national budget within a few days of its meeting. More professionals should be hired to assist the NPC and its standing committee in reviewing and supervising the budget.

2.3 Issues Related to Fiscal Sustainability

After more than 30 years of rapid growth, the Chinese economy is undergoing a phase transition. The growth rate is slowing down and more emphasis is being placed on "sustained and healthy economic development". The report to the 18th national congress of the communist party of China said, "China's development is still in an important period of strategic opportunities during which much can be done". We should accurately judge the changes in the connotation and conditions of the important period of strategic opportunities. The transformation of the stage of economic development also poses new challenges to the sustainability of finance. After the transition of economic development stage, it will inevitably affect the fiscal revenue and expenditure, and then put forward new challenges to the fiscal system and policy. Investigation of international and domestic practices, the following characteristics are embodied.

The Economic Slowdown Has Brought Down the Growth Rate of Fiscal Revenue

China's economy has entered a new normal, which is mainly manifested in the slowdown of economic growth, transformation of growth drivers and rebalancing of economic structure. These new characteristics determine that China's economic operation has entered a new relatively stable second high growth rate normal stage. After the economic growth rate changes from high speed to medium speed or even low speed, the increase of fiscal revenue will be under pressure, especially in the economies with income tax as the main source of tax revenue, which is also the embodiment of the role of fiscal "automatic stabilizer". The period of significant revenue growth is also over.

The "Lewis Turning Point" Appears and the Demographic Dividend Disappears

The transition from a developing economy to a developed one usually takes place at the lewis turning point, the point at which excess Labor turns into shortages in industrialization. This theory was put forward by William Arthur lewis, winner of Nobel Prize in economics, which was widely recognized by academia and supported by many countries. Japan's "lewis turning point" occurred around 1960, and South Korea's around 1975. The arrival of "lewis turning point" indicates that the unlimited supply of surplus labor is coming to an end, and the "demographic dividend" brought by cheap labor to economic development will gradually disappear. For example, after Japan passed the "lewis turning point", the shortage of labor factors caused a rapid rise in wages. From 1966 to 1975, the average annual increase of manufacturing wages was 16.4%. With the acceleration of population aging, China's labor cost has been increasing year by year in recent years, and some labor-intensive industries have begun to shift to Southeast Asia.

Infrastructure Investment Space Is Still Considerable, Social Spending Pressure Increased

Large-scale infrastructure construction is often concentrated in the period of rapid economic growth. After the transformation of economic development stage, the investment scale, investment focus and field will also change.

With the improvement of the level of economic development, along with the aging of the population and the irreversibility of the welfare level, the pressure on social expenditure such as social security and medical care will continue to increase; especially, the expenditure on medical and health care will continue to accelerate.

Compared with developed countries, the transformation of China's economic development stage brings more severe challenges, mainly manifested in: The historical process of urbanization is still accelerating, and there is still considerable room for future rounds and multi-focus infrastructure investment (such as the construction of public transportation system in a large number of central cities, rural water conservancy facilities and special regional construction represented by "Sansha infrastructure"). Meanwhile, China's population is aging rapidly, and we are facing a big dilemma of pension gap before getting rich. The rapid increase of wages and the shortage of low-end labor force make the contradiction of labor supply and demand more prominent. Regional development is still very uneven. This requires us to actively and reasonably deal with the problem of sustainable fiscal development in China.

Accumulation of Financial Risks

At the end of 2012, the balance of central government Treasury bonds stood at 7756.57 billion Yuan, accounting for only about 15% of the GDP of the year, while the national deficit in 2012 was 800 billion Yuan, accounting for 1.5% of the GDP of the year. The national budget deficit for 2013 was 1.2 trillion Yuan, or 2.1% of GDP. If we refer to the warning lines of EU deficit ratio and debt ratio (3 and 60% of GDP, respectively), China's fiscal health is good.

In the near future, China's financial risks are concentrated in the local government debt risk. According to the national audit office's audit notice on local government debt released in 2011, by the end of 2010, the total outstanding local government debt at the provincial, municipal and county levels was 10.72 trillion Yuan, with the exception of 54 county-level governments that had no government debt. 79% came from bank loans, or 8.46 trillion Yuan, 70% of the debt matures around 2015. Of the 10.72 trillion Yuan of debt, 62.6% is owed by the government, 21.8 percent is contingent, and 15.6% is under salvation of the government.

Local government debt can be traced back to 1979, when eight counties and districts borrowed money from the government to repay debts, according to authorities. From the late 1980s to the early 1990s, many local governments issued local bonds in order to raise funds to build roads and bridges and build infrastructure. Some are even interest-free, to support in the name of national construction apportion to the units. But in 1993, it was stopped by the state council because of doubts about the ability of local governments to deliver on their promises. Article 28 of the *Budget Law of the People's Republic of China* promulgated later clearly stipulates that "unless otherwise stipulated by law and the state council, local governments shall not issue local government bonds". While the law does not allow local governments to borrow and run deficits, it does not prohibit companies set up by local governments from borrowing. In the 1990s, most local governments sidestepped the law by setting up financing vehicle companies, which borrowed from the financial sector or issued bonds to the public. These local financing vehicles actually constitute the liabilities of local governments, which are not reflected in their budgets and are not known to higher authorities. As a result, local governments are using companies to circumvent the law. After implementing stimulus packages in response to the global financial crisis in 2008, local governments also relied more on financing platforms to raise funds. According to data released by the national audit office in 2012, there were 6,576 financing platform companies involved in local government debt.

Previous announcements by the national audit office showed that since 1979, land transfer revenue has been the main source of local government debt repayment. In 2011, the audit of national local government debt found that 12 provinces, 307 cities and 1,131 counties pledged to use land transfer revenue as the source of debt repayment, accounting for 37.96% of the debt. Other sources of debt repayment funds include the income of the debt-paying institutions, such as the tuition income of colleges and universities; operating income, such as vehicle tolls. However, these expected revenues, whether from land sales or fees, are extremely unstable, so some local governments have been caught in a cycle of "robbing Peter to pay Paul" and "raising new debts to repay old debts". According to research and calculation, if no effective solution is adopted for the 8.46 trillion Yuan of local outstanding bank loans, there may be 2.54 trillion Yuan of potential non-performing assets if the 30% non-performing ratio is calculated.

In the medium and long term, China's financial risks include railway debt, environmental governance costs, pension gap and rising medical and health costs, in addition to local government debt generated by local financing platforms.

2.4 Analysis of Resistance and Obstacle Factors of the Reform

The *Decision of the CPC Central Committee on Several Major Issues of Comprehensively Deepening Reform* adopted at the third plenary session of the 18th CPC central committee clearly defines that finance is the foundation and important pillar of national governance from the perspective of national governance, and takes the establishment of modern financial system as an important strategic orientation. Fiscal reform involves political, economic, social, cultural and ecological progress. There are major obstacles and barriers to establishing a modern financial system and deepening the reform of the financial system.

Solidification of the Concept/Understanding

The fixed concept is actually a thinking pattern. In this way of thinking, people always subconsciously judge and treat new things based on past thinking and knowledge when looking at some things and phenomena, and always consciously or unconsciously ignore or resist extremely. Due to the influence of the planned economy system in the past and the fact that China's market mechanism is not yet perfect, China is still in the process of economic transition. At present, there are still ideological problems in comprehensively deepening reform and modernization of national governance, which seriously hinder and affect China's economic and social transformation and the realization of the "Chinese dream" of modernization. Thought is the forerunner of action. The great practice of reform and opening up over the past 30 years shows that the emancipation of the mind is the most fundamental emancipation, the general switch of all theories, routes, principles and policies, and the driving force for the innovation and development of all work. The new round of reform of the fiscal and tax systems is a profound reform that will affect the modernization of China's governance system and capacity. Therefore, we must strengthen the overall situation awareness and sense of responsibility, dare to break through the barriers of thought and shoulder the important task of reform.

Legal Restriction and Absence

From the division of central and local powers, countries are usually based on constitutional provisions. The constitution of our country basically covers the same range of government functions at all levels with only different jurisdictions. The constitution only makes vague statement on the division of powers of governments at all levels, but does not make systematic and clear provisions. Administrative organs at all levels are responsible in both directions, with the state council as their top leader and also responsible and report on their work to people's congresses at the same level and administrative organs at the next higher level. The constitution also gives the state council the power to adjust the functions of provincial administrative organs and to change inappropriate decisions of administrative organs at all levels. The division of functions and powers between the central and local state organs follows the principle of giving full play to the initiative and enthusiasm of local governments under the unified leadership of the central government, but it is not clear in which areas local governments should take the initiative and enthusiasm. The specific functions and responsibilities of state administrative organs are mainly reflected in relevant state council documents or departmental regulations. Due to the lack of top-level design of the system, the intergovernmental authority and expenditure responsibilities are divided into overlapping, blurred boundaries and unclear responsibilities.

China's fiscal system is relatively weak in terms of legal system construction. Known as the "economic constitution", the *Budget Law* was formally implemented in 1995. For more than 40 years before that, China had no special budget laws, but administrative regulations of the state council. It took 10 years to revise the *Budget Law*, spanning three sessions of the National People's Congress (NPC), four trials and four rounds of repeated trials, until August 31, 2014, the tenth session of the standing committee of the twelfth National People's Congress finally adopted it, and it came into effect on January 1, 2015. In terms of tax legislation, only three of China's 18 tax categories have been legislated by the National People's Congress, and the rest are implemented in the form of regulations of the state council. The background is that since 1985, the National People's Congress authorized the state council to push forward the reform of the tax system in the form of tax regulations during the reform of the system. The advantage of this approach was that it was conducive to the rapid establishment of China's tax system, but the disadvantage was the randomness of some taxes. Especially with the economic system reform into the "deep water area", the weakness of the legal basis of taxation is further highlighted.

Constraints/Generated by Path Dependence

Since the reform and opening up, China's reform generally relies on the following two paths: First, crisis drives the reform. Over the past three decades, reform has often been crisis-oriented. Food is not enough to eat, so there is a contract responsibility system; the central government has no money to spend, so there is a tax distribution system; rural unjustified financial levies and random fund-raising leads to social instability, so there are rural tax reform; state-owned enterprises suffered heavy losses, hence the "invigorate large enterprises while relaxing control over small ones"; growing regional disparities and local protectionism have led to income-sharing reforms.

Second, gradual reform. The so-called incremental reform refers to the incremental reform carried out by utilizing existing organizational resources without touching vested interests. In order to ensure local vested interests, the system of refunding VAT and consumption tax has been implemented. During income tax sharing reform, income tax base return is introduced; during the reform of taxes and fees on refined oil products, the central government provided a fixed amount of rebates to local governments for the revenue they received from abolishing the "six fees". These are typical products of incremental reform. This path dependence based on crisis promotion and gradual reform promoted and ensured the smooth implementation of the reform at that time, but it also inevitably brought problems such as reduced efficiency of reform and inability to make a single step. Some reforms that had been mentioned on the agenda were not implemented.

The next step is to deepen the reform of the fiscal and tax systems. We need to crack the hard nut. Inertia, constraints and even shackles caused by path dependence will become obstacles to the reform.

Resistance from People with Vested Interests

Premier Li Keqiang once mentioned that he would carry out the reform with To the determination of a strong man to cut his wrist, the spirit of the last stand, which is a profound illustration of the great resistance we face in deepening reform. Among them, vested interests have become the biggest risk and resistance to reform, and the vested interests in fiscal and tax reform are likely to include the government and government departments themselves. Resistance from vested interests is the inertia of those who benefit from the existing structure to block reform. Establish a complete, standardized, transparent and efficient modern government budget management system, involving the disclosure of government departments' budget, power and administration, as well as the establishment of accountability system. In the reform of inter-governmental fiscal system, it involves the re-division of central and local governments' financial resources, powers and expenditure responsibilities. In the tax reform, the reform of value-added tax, resource tax, consumption tax and property tax will involve the vital interests of different social groups and industries. The reform will surely touch the cake of some people, and resistance from vested interests should not be underestimated.

3

Goal Lead: The General Idea, Basic Goal and Path of Fiscal and Taxation System Reform

At the third plenary session of the 18th CPC central committee, innovative positioning and incisive exposition of the core concept of governance have been carried out, namely modernization of national governance and the relationship between finance and national governance has been defined in an innovative manner, that is finance is the foundation and important pillar of national governance. This requires us to set up a modern financial system as the goal, speed up the reform of the fiscal and tax systems, to meet the objective requirements of the new stage of development. Under the framework of the "five-sphere integrated plan": a plan to promote coordinated economic, political, cultural, social and ecological advancement and the "the Four-Pronged Comprehensive Strategy" top-level design, we will make system and institutional innovations that are "problem-oriented" in connection with fiscal reform and development. This paper mainly puts forward the general idea, basic goal and path of China's "13th five-year plan" fiscal system reform.

As mentioned above, there are still many problems in the current fiscal system, and the deep-seated contradictions and problems in the deep-water areas of reform cannot be solved by mere tinkering and adjustment.

J. Kang and L. Wei, *Transformation of the Fiscal and Taxation Systems*, The Great Transformation of China,
https://doi.org/10.1007/978-981-16-2590-9_3

This requires us to press ahead with fiscal and tax reform in a resolute, prudent, firm and sustained manner in the new situation at home and abroad. The third plenary session of the 18th CPC central committee proposed that "the overall goal of comprehensively deepening reform is to improve and develop the socialist system with Chinese characteristics, promote the modernization of national governance system and governance capacity", and "finance is the foundation and important pillar of national governance". In the guidance document at the highest level, innovation orientation and incisive exposition of the core concept of governance-national governance modernization, and innovation orientation of the relationship between finance and national governance requires us to establish a modern financial system as the goal, promote the realization of the goal of comprehensive deepening of reform, to meet the objective requirements of the new stage of development.

3.1 General Idea

Under the framework of the "five-sphere integrated plan": a plan to promote coordinated economic, political, cultural, social and ecological advancement and the "the Four-Pronged Comprehensive Strategy" top-level design, we shall link the financial reform and development of the "problem-oriented" system mechanism innovation construction and improve China's tax sharing financial system. The general idea of the reform of the tax sharing financial system during the 13th five-year plan period in China is as follows: On the premise of clarifying the transformation and reasonable positioning of government reform functions, and in line with the flattening of government levels and the integration and simplification of the "big ministry system" orientation, a "flattening" financial hierarchical framework is established to reasonably divide the powers and expenditure responsibilities of the central government, provinces, cities and counties, and improve the transfer payment system. According to the principle of "first-level political power, first-level administrative power, first-level financial power, first-level tax base, first-level budget, first-level property right and first-level creditor's right", it is equipped with transfer payments from the top down at the central and provincial levels and necessary and reasonable horizontal transfer payments. It is necessary to establish a fiscal and tax system that conforms to the financial rights and administrative rights of the market economy system and matches the financial resources and expenditure responsibilities. Deepen the reform of the budget management system; implementing tax reform to promote the transformation of growth pattern; meanwhile, performance orientation should be strengthened.

3.2 Basic Goal

The fiscal revenue and expenditure mechanism and arrangement should fully reflect the intention of national governance under the framework of the "five-sphere integrated plan": a plan to promote coordinated economic, political, cultural, social and ecological advancement "and the "the Four-Pronged Comprehensive Strategy". In reforming the fiscal and tax systems, equal opportunities and social justice must be given top priority. At the same time, it will actively support and coordinate fiscal and taxation reform, focus on establishing mechanisms and promoting inclusiveness, and ensure that governments at all levels follow through on their fiscal and administrative powers and match their financial and spending responsibilities. This will serve the top-level design and deployment of the reform at the third plenary session of the 18th CPC central committee.

Clearly Define Government Functions and Responsibilities and Financial Functions

Proper handling of the relationship between government, market and society determines the rationalization of government functions, and government functions, responsibilities and responsibility authority determine the responsibility of government expenditure. Therefore, the core of fiscal and tax system reform is to correctly handle the relationship between the government, the market and the society, to draw a clear boundary between the government, the market and the society, and to respect the law of the market. Let the market play its full role, maximize the public interest and safeguard social justice as the basis, give full play to the decisive role of the market in the allocation of resources, and give play to the role of the government in an appropriate and suitable way. The principle of "market and society first" should be followed, and what the market and society can do well should be left to the market and society. Where the market and society can do but fail to do so, the government shall play an auxiliary role. Where the market and society fail to do so, the government shall take the lead in undertaking or organizing the allocation of relevant resources. We will make innovations in the way the government performs its functions, fully introduce market mechanisms, and give full play to the role of fiscal policy. The positioning of government function and financial function is: Respect the market, serve and guide the market economy, and serve the construction of modern national governance system on the basis of the rationalization of the classification of financial authority (expenditure responsibility) and the rationalization of the classification allocation tax base of the composite tax system.

Improve the Division of Governmental Powers and Expenditure Responsibilities

Division of authority, division of income, expenditure and transfer payment is the core content of fiscal and tax system reform. The rational division of governmental power and expenditure responsibility is the fundamental premise of the system of financial power and financial resources allocation and transfer payment. It is necessary to divide the powers among governments at all levels in the process of actively improving legislation. The basic principles of inter-governmental division of powers are: First, divide powers and expenditure responsibility according to the level of public goods and the scope of benefits. National public goods and services should be provided by the central government to cover the whole country; the benefit scope of local public goods and services is limited to local areas and should be provided by local governments. Local public goods and services with spillover may be jointly provided by the central government and local governments, or provided with subsidies by the central government or directly provided by the central government. It is worth noting that the externality of local affairs can be solved by expanding the scope of central authority or by means of local consultation mechanism. Given the complexity of information processing, local governments know more about local conditions than the central government does, so it is not necessarily reasonable for the central government to assume too much responsibility for affairs and expenditure. Second, according to the efficiency of public service delivery, authority and expenditure responsibility are divided. Taking into account historical and cultural traditions, it is more efficient for the central government to provide responsibility for income distribution and economic stability. However, in the implementation of income distribution responsibilities, different countries rely on the power of local governments. Therefore, the division of governmental authority and expenditure responsibility in our country should fully consider the historical and cultural tradition factors, and then determine the expenditure responsibility sharing mechanism easily accepted by governments at all levels. Third, divide power and expenditure responsibility according to the principle of economies of scale. As for the division of governmental powers and expenditure responsibilities, we should also pay attention to the problem of scale economy. Certain responsibilities that may not achieve economies of scale if undertaken by local governments; if it is borne by the central government, it can play a cost-saving role. Fourth, we should minimize sharing of powers among governments. We should try our best to ensure that most of the powers of governments at all levels are independently assumed, and reduce the powers shared by all, supplemented by a small number of powers entrusted by superiors and leading authority.

Reasonably Divide the Tax Base/Tax Rate in Combination with Tax Reform

All regulations and behaviors of the government should be based on the criteria of not affecting or minimizing the free flow of production factors and the independent decision-making of market subjects. The corresponding income (tax base) division needs to consider the impact of tax categories on the flow of production factors, as well as the realization of macro and meso regulatory functions at the central and local levels. The division of tax categories between the central and local governments, namely the allocation of tax bases, is generally considered to follow the following basic principles: Taxes that are closely related to national sovereignty and overall macro-control functions, or whose tax base covers the unified market and has great liquidity, should be classified into the central government. Tax categories that are closely related to regional characteristics, that have no mobility or weak mobility of tax base, and that are relatively regional, do not cause excessive tax competition among regions and need to be "adapted to local conditions" should be assigned to local areas. According to this principle, customs duties, personal income tax, value-added tax, social security tax and other taxes should be assigned to the central, such as real estate tax, resource tax, specific regional taxes should be assigned to the local.

In terms of the specific practice of each country, different countries have some flexibility in respect of individual taxes based on their own conditions while basically following the above principles. For example, the individual income tax in the United States is shared by the federal government, state and local governments in accordance with the tax base sharing and tax sharing method (mainly at the federal level, implementing excess progressive tax rate; supplemented by state and local, with low or even low rates of proportional taxation). In the UK, residential property tax (known as council tax) is a local tax, while non-residential property tax (known as business tax) is a source of central tax and central transfer payments to local governments, which are returned to each region according to the number of residents. After the "94 reform", China considered to mobilize the enthusiasm of local governments in terms of income division, and took the large tax base or several large taxes (value-added tax, enterprise income tax, individual income tax) as the shared tax. However, these main tax categories, which are directly related to economic development and have obvious characteristics of tax base mobility, are designated as sharing taxes between the central and local governments. To some extent, it violates the due principle of income division, and the result is to stimulate local governments to undertake more economic development responsibilities, and to implement excessive tax competition between each other (in the form of competition for investment and tax sources, etc.). Therefore, "splitting financial power (tax base)" and "splitting financial power (income)" both have scientific rules to follow and an objective internal negotiation mechanism to be based on, rather than simply acting in accordance with people's subjective will and preference. In this respect, artificial control is very limited.

Adjust the Fiscal Relationship Between the Central and Local Governments and Improve the Transfer Payment System

Whether considering the socialist nature of "achieving common prosperity" or the requirement of "equalization of basic public services" proposed by citizens based on "equal human rights" in a society ruled by law, it is objectively necessary to use transfer payment system to regulate the surplus and shortage of financial funds among governments from top to bottom. The basic premise of the effective operation of this transfer payment is that the central government obtains financial resources commensurate with its macro-control function in "vertical imbalance", so as to adjust the "horizontal imbalance" among regions. After two or three decades of development that "let some people and some regions get rich first", China has faced huge differences in economic development levels among regions due to its different natural geographical environment. It is still a long way to go to "achieve common prosperity". In the new era, the central government has an important responsibility that cannot be avoided, that is, to "enrich and replenish the leanness" in a reasonable way and to curb the widening gap between regions. This kind of material premise for the central government to fulfill the responsibility of regulating regional differences against "horizontal imbalance" is to form a reasonably designed and sustainable financial distribution framework of "vertical imbalance" between the central and local governments.

The construction goals of China's transfer payment system include balancing local basic public service capacity (general transfer payment) and realizing specific macro-control goals (special transfer payment).

Improve the Budget Management System and Improve the Government Budget System

The budget system is the core of the modern financial system. The reform of budget management should promote the construction of the modern national governance system and improve the way the country raises, distributes and uses funds. A good modern budget system should follow 10 internationally recognized basic principles: comprehensiveness, principle, legality, flexibility, predictability, deliberability, authenticity, transparency, information and integrity. This is also the direction and goal of the improvement of China's budget management system, including the realization of budget comprehensiveness, that is, all public funds are required to be included in the budget, the establishment of a full-caliber public budget system. We will improve the transparency of the budget, namely, the openness of the budget, and expand the scope and detail of the openness of the budgets of governments at all levels, especially the specific contents such as the three public expenses, as well as the calculation and determination methods of intergovernmental transfer payments. We will implement medium-term fiscal planning and management, overcome shortsightedness in the annual budget, provide favorable conditions for improving macro-control under the new normal, and provide an operational time and resource basis for optimizing and adjusting the expenditure structure.

3.3 Path

According to the outstanding contradictions and real problems in deepening the reform of tax distribution system since the "94 reform", under the background of improving national governance capacity and governance modernization, the path to establish a modern fiscal and tax system should include:

Take the Government Flattening Reform as the Framework

In recent years, great progress has been made in financial "flattening" reform, starting with the pilot reform of "County Administrated by Province" and "County Control over Rural Finance" in some areas. In June 2009, the ministry of finance gave a timetable for the reform of "direct provincial administration of counties". The overall goal is to promote the reform of County Administrated by Province by the end of 2012, except in ethnic autonomous areas. By the end of 2013, a total of 27 provinces (autonomous regions) and 1,080 counties (cities) had implemented the financial management system under direct provincial administration. The current financial reform of "County Administrated by Province" has also laid a foundation and created conditions for the reform of "County Administrated by Province" system and "reduction of administrative hierarchy". With the development of economy and society, "County Administrated by Province" will inevitably deepen the reform of administrative system that reduces the administrative hierarchy in the direction of local conditions. At the same time, the simplification of administrative levels will be conducive to the transformation of government functions and further clarify the functional scope and expenditure responsibilities of governments at all levels, so as to realize the service-oriented government transformation in line with the market economy system. The overall significance and extensibility of this reform are quite obvious. We should continue to promote the flat reform of "County Control over Rural Finance" and "County Administrated by Province", reduce the financial entity level to three levels and promote the reform of tax sharing system below the provincial level. Its significance is to promote the implementation of the sub-provincial tax sharing system that has not been implemented since 1994. Originally, it turns out that the tax distribution below the province did not actually "transition" in place. It has become multifarious, complex and variable sharing system and responsibility system with bargaining feature and obvious malady. If the tax sharing system can be implemented below the provincial level, other supporting reforms can be substantially promoted. In the past, there was a problem of how to divide about 20 kinds of taxes in China. After years of exploration, no matter how well they were divided, many short-term behaviors of local governments criticized by people now, which are contrary to their reasonable functions, should be reformed along with the change of institutional conditions.

On the whole, the reform of "direct provincial administration of counties" in China can be divided into three steps: The first step is to do what the current provincial pilot is doing, The provincial government is mainly in charge of the finance of the county directly, and the economic management power is delegated to the lower level but still maintain the administrative leadership of the city to county; The second step is the division of cities and counties, unified by direct provincial administration, repositioning the functions of cities and counties, some cities adjacent to the county can be changed to municipal districts; the third step is the municipal reform. While reasonably expanding the scope of municipal districts, the organization and personnel should be reasonably adjusted. The general direction should be to abolish the prefecture-level cities in the traditional sense (the level can be retained, but the personnel can be gradually adjusted), and fully implement the split distribution of cities and counties and the direct supervision of counties by provinces. In the above process, we can also vigorously promote the reform of the financial system of towns and townships. For the towns and townships with underdeveloped economy and small fiscal revenue, we can try out the method of unified management of fiscal revenue and expenditure by county finance, and implement the mode of "County Control over Rural Finance" for general towns and townships. Under the premise of maintaining the ownership and use right of funds and the financial approval right of the towns and villages, the management mode of "budget compilation, account establishment, centralized collection and payment, procurement and management, and bill management" is adopted.

The Matching Logic Is Based on Reasonable Adjustment of Power

Under the top-level planning, the division of administrative power between the central government and the local government should be adjusted and straightened out, including the power of the central government, the power of the local government, the power of the central government to share administrative power with the local government, the power of the central government to entrust affairs, and the power of the central government to guide and encourage affairs. Then, according to the attributes and logic principles of government affairs, it makes reasonable and clear division of inter-governmental expenditure responsibilities, and starts to form a detailed list of central, provincial, city and county administrative powers and expenditure responsibilities as soon as possible, and then dynamically optimizes and strengthens performance appraisal constraints. As soon as possible, the basic pension system, the judicial system, food and drug safety, border defense, maritime areas and trans-regional watershed management will be assigned to the central government. Local governments should withdraw from the general investment field of competitive projects and regulate the division of administrative power of the governments below the provincial level.

Drive Tax Reform and Inter-governmental Income Distribution Reform with the Construction of Local Tax System

We will build and improve the local tax system, and, in line with the reform of the tax system, actively improve the income distribution system at all levels based on the allocation of tax categories. We will implement the *Interim Regulations on the Registration of Immovable Property*, actively promote the unified registration of immovable property and establish a unified urban and rural immovable property registration system. We will actively push forward the legislation of real estate tax, strive to enter the legislative process of real estate tax from 2015 to 2016, and accelerate the legislation and implementation process. The goal is to make it the main tax of local government. We will vigorously advance the reform of resource taxes, with the focus on extending the price-based collection mechanism to coal, and further expand the scope of resource taxes. A separate environmental tax would be introduced, with revenues divided locally. We will expand the scope of excise tax collection, adjust the collection of some items of excise tax and allocate revenue from some items of excise tax to local governments. The vehicle purchase tax shall be assigned to the local income. In the process of replacing the business tax with a value-added tax, the central government will use the increase in value-added tax revenue as a source of general transfer payments to local governments.

Embody the Principle of Priority of Power in a Standard Transfer Payment System

We will optimize the equalization formula for transfer payments in accordance with population, geography, service costs, location of functional zones and other factors, and strengthen financial support for underdeveloped local governments. Appropriately reduce the proportion of special transfer payments in the total transfer payments, and merge and integrate similar or mergeable items in special projects. The specific information should reach the local level as far as possible in advance, and the requirement of "local supporting funds" should be cancelled in principle to facilitate the overall preparation and serious implementation of the local budget. In addition, efforts should be made to optimize the system of cross-regional transfer payments such as "counterpart support" and "ecological compensation".

Establish a Modern Public Budget Management System as the Basic Support

In combination with the requirements of establishing a modern financial system, under the premise of a full-caliber budget, the central government began to actively compile a rolling budget in the middle of three to five years. Develop the single account Treasury centralized collection and payment system into "horizontal to the side, vertical to the end". It supports and optimizes the scientific decision-making of the allocation of public resources of the whole society represented by the budget system through the construction of a complete set of modern information system in the form of "golden financial project" and "golden tax project". We will implement the provisions of the new budget law on local government debt, accelerate the development of the system of local government bonds and municipal bonds financed by local governments, and gradually replace or substitute hidden liabilities such as local financing platforms that are not transparent or standardized, but have high risk prevention costs and great difficulty. The construction of local state-owned assets management system should also be actively promoted in combination with the construction of state capital operation budget system. Under the multiple constraints and logical orientations of "gradual reform" path dependence, "building a country under the rule of law" and "strengthening public knowledge and participation", gradually and actively and rationally promote the construction of fiscal and taxation legal system, grasp the balance between "regulate through innovation and development" and "innovate and development in standard" under the premise of overall situation, strengthen and optimize top-level planning and continue to encourage pioneering efforts. In the historical period of economic and social transition, the stable rules that can be observed should be legislated in a timely manner.

Taking the Administration of Creditor's Rights and Property Rights as Important Elements

The sharing and classification fiscal system required by market economy contains the necessity and rationality of local government borrowing moderately. Borrowing powers is the proper financial power of governments at all levels under the tax sharing and classification system. In most market economy countries, the local government bond market has been relatively mature and perfect, becoming an important way of local financing and an organic part of the capital market, and playing a very important role in the national economic development, especially the development of local economy. The new *Budget Law* gives local governments the right to moderately borrow and allows them to borrow on an appropriate scale and raise necessary construction funds through standardized legal procedures and under conditions of transparency and supervision. This helps local governments cope with high expenditures on municipal construction and other aspects in the short term in the operation of classified budgets. The expenditure peak should be spread over a longer period of time, and the function of providing quasi-public goods should be utilized by social funds and market mechanisms, so as to make up for the insufficient revenue of local governments effectively and broaden the path for further deepening the reform of fiscal system.

Property rights management is one of the important divisions between central and local governments. As the cornerstone of the property rights system of the modern market system of "modern national governance", mixed ownership has opened the space for the reform of state-owned economic sectors and the reconstruction of state-owned assets management system. Based on the logic chain of "modern state governance-modern market system-modern enterprise system-mixed ownership", the breakthrough statement of the third plenary session of the 18th CPC central committee on the understanding of "mixed ownership" actually emphasizes that in the context of modern state governance and the rule of law, property rights of any market entity can be handled in accordance with mixed ownership under the joint-stock system framework, so as to achieve the maximum inclusiveness, win–win and all-win and substantially advance reform.

4

Practical Operation: Build a Modern Fiscal and Taxation System Suitable for the Modernization of National Governance

The construction of a modern fiscal and tax system that adapts to the modernization of national governance should be further promoted from the following aspects: First, the formation of scientific and standardized inter-governmental financial distribution relations; Second, improve the budget management system, improve the government budget management system; Third, deepen tax reform and accelerate the establishment of a sound local tax system. Fourth, further deepen the reform of fiscal expenditure management; Fifth, improve the government debt management system. At the same time, this paper also presents in the form of a column the practical cases of local fiscal reform, the basic understanding and international experience of medium-term fiscal planning, the observation and understanding of macro tax burden, and the international practice of local debt management.

Finance is an important part of the economy, which directly serves to transform the growth model and adjust the structure. Finance is also an administrative and political component that will constrain or promote administrative and political restructuring; At the same time, finance is also an important support in social, cultural and ecological fields. A

J. Kang and L. Wei, *Transformation of the Fiscal and Taxation Systems*, The Great Transformation of China,
https://doi.org/10.1007/978-981-16-2590-9_4

slight move in one part may affect the situation as a whole. Therefore, in the process of modernization of the national governance system, the establishment of a modern financial system and the deepening of the reform of the fiscal and tax systems should proceed from serving the overall situation. On the basis of comprehensively serving the reform in economic, political, social, cultural and ecological fields, we will make further progress in properly defining government functions, rationalizing inter-governmental financial relations, reforming the tax system, optimizing the structure of expenditure, strengthening budget management, standardizing government debt, and improving the information system. At the same time, we will improve the financial and economic legal system, and strengthen fiscal and tax reforms in line with reforms in pricing, land, finance and opening-up.

4.1 Form a Scientific and Standardized Inter-governmental Financial Distribution Relationship

For improving the financial system, on the whole, inter-governmental powers and expenditure responsibilities should be scientifically divided on the basis of reasonably defining the boundary between the government and the market. We will strengthen the central government's functions related to overall development, including the unified market, social security and environmental protection. We will weaken intervention in local governments, appropriately adjust the division of revenue among governments, improve the unified, standardized and transparent system of transfer payments, further improve the financial system below the provincial level, and strengthen the ability of county-level governments to provide financial support for basic public services.

Clearly Define the Functions and Responsibilities of the Government, and Scientifically Divide the Inter-governmental Powers and Expenditure Responsibilities

The goal of straightening out the inter-governmental financial relations is to establish the division system of responsibilities and financial rights among the central government, provinces, cities and counties under the "flattening" framework.

According to the standards of responsibility subjects, government responsibilities can be divided into four categories: independent responsibility, shared responsibility, entrusted responsibility of superior government and leading responsibility of superior government. From the reference of international intergovernmental financial relations, the crystallization of human wisdom and typical experience is: Among governments at all levels, "to run one's own affairs with one's own finance is the most efficient; Take other people's money for your own business is the second efficient. Take other people's money for other people's business is the least efficient." Therefore, the general principle of intergovernmental fiscal relations is to reduce the sharing of responsibilities and reduce the sharing of taxes as much as possible. Governments at all levels shall be endowed with corresponding financial powers to meet their needs of assuming responsibilities.

1. Basic thinking on the division of intergovernmental responsibilities and expenditure responsibilities

First, the types of responsibilities should be refined to ensure that governments at all levels clearly own most of the responsibilities independently, reduce the number of shared responsibilities, supplemented by a small number of delegated responsibilities and leading responsibilities of superiors.

Second, some of the responsibilities undertaken by existing local governments will be retaken by the central government, including the expenses for the work facilities of central law enforcement agencies such as the judiciary, border protection, border protection, customs and national taxes.

Third, the central government should strive to fulfill the responsibilities independently undertaken by itself, and set up its own vertical agencies at the regional, provincial and municipal levels to supervise direct and entrusted expenditures in a less shared manner.

Fourth, responsibilities are divided according to the internationally accepted administrative structure of three levels of government. The central government is responsible for providing the bottom line, and transfer payment support is provided from the central government to the provincial level to make the government system (including local governments in remote and underdeveloped areas) assume the responsibility of providing basic public services. For example, basic education (primary and secondary schools), basic medical care, basic old-age care, basic housing, basic unemployment, basic public health, basic employment, and basic living allowances for urban and rural residents. At the same time, we should implement the municipal and county governments, clarify their functions, and aim to provide improved public services, municipal infrastructure, and local public security.

2. Scheme for the division of intergovernmental responsibilities and expenditure responsibilities

Drawing on international experience and following the basic principles of the scope of benefits, capacity, efficiency, economies of scale, externalities, information adequacy and incentive compatibility, governments at all levels should assume their responsibilities as much as possible, minimize the sharing of responsibilities, and gradually change the situation of central government directives and local implementation. The central government's own agencies shall perform the duties assumed by the central government alone; If the central government's own institutional capacity is insufficient, we should first strengthen the central government's own capacity building. The division of responsibilities is as detailed and executable as possible. The central government focuses on major issues and issues that affect the overall situation, and local governments should delegate as much responsibility as possible to local governments. We will accelerate reform of the administrative system at the central level, at the provincial level and below, adjust administrative divisions, and reform of the financial system, and provide legislative guarantees accordingly to improve the stability of the division of responsibilities and powers among governments (see Table 4.1).

First, the responsibilities of the central government. First, state sovereignty and regime operation. It includes: membership in international organizations, multilateral and global negotiations, international cooperation; foreign affairs, national defense (army), national security, border defense, customs and counter-terrorism; The National People's Congress, the national political consultative conference, the ruling party, the central government, the courts and the procuratorates; Public security, fire and armed police. Second, people's livelihood and public services. Ensuring the safety of drinking water, air and food and other basic living conditions of the people; Provide basic minimum standards for education, public health, medical care, culture, science and technology, and social security; National key higher education; National disease prevention and control, national first-class hospitals, and major public health emergencies; National and basic scientific research projects in high-energy physics, aerospace, mathematics and mechanics; National nature reserves; sources protection of the three rivers, shelterbelts building in the three north areas, and bringing desertification under control. Third, public facilities and municipal works. National trans-regional and trans-basin water conservancy facilities, national power grids, trunk postal and telecommunications networks, high-speed railways and trunk railways, national ports, national and regional aviation hubs; Interregional resource protection and development; National strategic reserves of crude oil, rare earth, grain and other materials. Fourth, market supervision and economic regulation. Regulate micro-behavior, maintain market order, and ensure the market environment for micro-subjects to operate; Adjust the economic cycle, maintain economic growth, adjust the industrial structure, achieve full employment, stabilize prices and balance of international payments; National economic and social development plan, national economic restructuring, fiscal and monetary policies, financial supervision, and

Table 4.1 Definitions of intergovernmental responsibilities and expenditure responsibilities

The central government assumes its responsibilities independently	State sovereignty and regime operation	[1] International cooperation, international organizations, international affairs and international relations: membership in international organizations, multilateral and global negotiations, international cooperation in health, education, science, technology and culture [2] Responsibilities for serving national sovereignty: diplomacy, national defense (army), national security, border defense, customs, and counter-terrorism [3] National legislation, judiciary and administration: National People's Congress, national political consultative conference, ruling party, central government, court and procuratorate [4] Responsibilities for maintaining social order: public security, fire control, armed police
	People's livelihood and public utilities	[5] People's basic living conditions: the safety of drinking water, air and food [6] Basic livelihood security: Basic minimum standards of basic public utilities, including basic education, (such as preschool education, primary and secondary schools, special education), basic public health (such as infectious diseases, mental illness prevention and treatment) and basic medical and health, (such as comprehensive and specialized subject hospital, community hospitals, township health center), basic culture, mass culture, intangible cultural heritage), basic social security (basic endowment insurance, basic medical insurance, housing) [7] General public services: state-level key higher education; national-level disease prevention and control, national-level hospitals (third-class A-level hospitals), major public health emergencies; national-level and basic scientific research projects (such as high-energy physics, aerospace, Mathematics, mechanics, etc.); national nature reserves; cross-regional environmental protection (such as the protection of the Three Rivers source, the construction of the Three North Shelterbelt, desertification control, etc.)

	Public facilities and municipal works	[8] Basic industries and infrastructure: national and trans-regional infrastructure construction (national trans-regional and trans-river water conservancy facilities, national power grid, trunk post and telecommunication network, high-speed railway and main trunk ordinary railway, national port, national and regional aviation hub); Interregional resource protection and development; national strategic material reserves (such as crude oil, rare earth, grain, etc.)
	Market supervision and economic regulation	[9] Market rules: regulate micro-behaviors, maintain market order, and ensure the market environment for micro-entities to operate [10] Macroeconomic regulation: Adjust the economic cycle, maintain economic growth, adjust the industrial structure, achieve full employment, stabilize prices and balance of international payments; National economic and social development plan, national economic restructuring, fiscal and monetary policies, financial supervision, and economic operation order and stability; National agricultural development (such as agricultural economic restructuring, land consolidation, grain acquisition, national poverty alleviation); Basic statistics nationwide; cross-regional cooperation on comprehensive economic development; Other matters of trans-regional cooperation [11] Adjust income distribution: Adjust the distribution structure of the state, enterprises and individuals, as well as the distribution relations among the three departments, and adjust the distribution relations among governments, industries, individuals, urban and rural areas, and regions; National policies for regulating employment and income distribution
	State-owned assets and public resources	[12] Operational state-owned assets: central financial and non-financial enterprises [13] State-owned assets of administrative institutions: central level [14] Natural resources: National and trans-regional natural resources, including state-owned land, minerals, water resources, forests, grasslands, tidal flats, air and air space, etc

(continued)

Table 4.1 (continued)

	Responsibilities entrusted to provincial/municipal/county governments	[15] The central government provides financial support, and the provincial/city/county governments are responsible for coordinating the promotion and implementation. It includes: subsistence allowance for urban and rural residents; Primary and secondary education and school bus services; Community hospitals and township health centers; Rescue and reconstruction after major disasters; Social relief and special care; Economic construction projects; Census
Provincial governments undertake and execute independently	State sovereignty and regime operation	[16] International cooperation, international organizations, international affairs and international relations: provincial international cooperation [17] National legislation, judiciary and administration: provincial people's congress, provincial political consultative conference, provincial party committee, provincial government, provincial court and provincial procuratorate [18] Responsibilities for maintaining social order: provincial public security (including police)
	General public services	[19] General public services: The basic public service standards shall be appropriately increased above the lower limit of the national basic public service standards and in light of the financial situation of this province; Provincial higher and specialized secondary education; Provincial disease prevention and control and environmental health, health and medical system construction, provincial hospitals, provincial public health emergencies; Scientific research and technology research and application, provincial scientific research projects; Provincial nature reserves; Environmental protection within provinces and across cities and counties (including prevention and control of lakes, rivers and air pollution); basic housing

	Public facilities and municipal works	[20] Basic industries and infrastructure: Provincial and cross-city and county infrastructure construction and maintenance (including water conservancy facilities, feeder power facilities, feeder post and telecommunication network, national and provincial highways, feeder railway, port, provincial aviation hub); Protection and utilization of provincial resources; Provincial reserves of important materials (grain, cotton, edible oil, etc.)
	Market supervision and economic regulation	[21] Market rules: stable market order at the provincial level, and financial supervision at the provincial level (supervision of non-public and non-deposit financial institutions and guidance of private finance at the provincial level)
		[22] Macroeconomic regulation: Provincial development planning and adjustment of provincial economic structure; Provincial agricultural development (including provincial mountain and river basin development, provincial poverty alleviation); Province-wide data statistics; Cross-city and county cooperation projects
		[23] Adjustment of income distribution: adjustment of income distribution at the provincial level and promotion of employment
	State-owned assets and public resource	[24] Operational state-owned assets: provincial finance and non-financial enterprises
		[25] State-owned assets of administrative institutions: provincial level
		[26] Natural resources: natural resources across cities and counties
	Responsibilities entrusted to the municipal and county governments	[27] Provincial governments contribute funds, and the municipal and county governments are responsible for coordinating the promotion and implementation. It includes basic housing security; Economic construction projects
The municipal and county governments undertake and execute independently	State sovereignty and regime operation	[28] National legislation, justice and administration: municipal and county people's congresses, municipal and county political consultative conferences, municipal and county party committees, municipal and county governments, municipal and county courts, and municipal and county procuratorates
		[29] Responsibilities for maintaining social order: public security and social stability within the jurisdiction

(continued)

Table 4.1 (continued)

	people's livelihood security and public utilities	[30] General public services: basic public service standards that are above the lower limit of the national basic public service standards and may be appropriately increased according to the financial situation of the city or county; Secondary hospitals; Cultural and sports facilities at the municipal and county levels; Kindergarten education, primary and secondary education, adult education; Population and household registration administration; Community service
	Public facilities and municipal works	[31] Municipal public facilities: municipal and county-level infrastructure construction (provincial and county-level highway construction); Urban roads; Construction and operation of public transportation network within the jurisdiction; Urban and county planning; Municipal public utilities (including water supply, drainage, power supply, gas supply, heating, public transportation, energy utilization, landscaping), garbage and sewage treatment, environmental sanitation, environmental protection and pollution treatment
	Market regulation and economic regulation	[32] Market rules: the market order in municipal and county districts is stable
		[33] Macroeconomic adjustment: development planning of cities and counties, adjustment of economic structure of cities and counties; City and county data statistics
		[34] Regulate income distribution: employment promotion in cities and counties
	State-owned assets and public resources	[35] Operational state-owned assets: municipal and county-level financial and non-financial enterprises
		[36] State-owned assets of administrative institutions: city and county level
		[37] Natural resources: natural resources within the jurisdiction of cities and counties

Note: in addition, there are some guiding duties. It means that the central government encourages provincial/municipal or provincial governments to assume certain responsibilities. In this case, the higher government provides some funds and the lower government provides some funds, but the guiding responsibility itself is the responsibility of the lower government. It includes: strategic emerging industry development, with local characteristics of industrial development economic operation order and stability; National agricultural development; Cross-regional cooperation on comprehensive economic development; To regulate the distribution structure of the state, enterprises and individuals, as well as the distribution relations within the three departments. To regulate the distribution relations among government levels, industries, individuals, urban and rural areas, and regions. Fifth, state-owned assets and public resources. State-owned assets of central financial and non-financial enterprises; State-owned assets of central administrative institutions; National and trans-regional natural resources, including state-owned land, minerals, water resources, forests, grasslands, tidal flats, air and air space, etc..

Second, the responsibilities of provincial governments. First, state sovereignty and regime operation. It includes: International cooperation at the provincial level; Provincial people's congresses, provincial political consultative conferences, provincial party committees, provincial governments, provincial courts and provincial procuratorates; Provincial public security (including police). Second, people's livelihood and public services. The basic public service standards shall be appropriately increased above the lower limit of the national basic public service standards and in light of the financial situation of this province; Provincial higher and specialized secondary education; Provincial disease prevention and control and environmental health, health and medical system construction, provincial hospitals, provincial public health emergencies; Scientific research and technology research and application, provincial scientific research projects; provincial nature reserves; Environmental protection within provinces and across cities and counties; basic housing. Third, public facilities and municipal works. Provincial and cross-city and county infrastructure construction and maintenance (including water conservancy facilities, feeder power facilities, feeder post and telecommunication network, national and provincial highways, feeder railway, port, provincial aviation hub); Protection and utilization of provincial resources; Provincial reserves of important materials (grain, cotton, edible oil, etc.). Fourth, market supervision and economic regulation. Stable market order at the provincial level, provincial financial supervision (supervision of non-public, non-deposit financial institutions and private financial guidance at the provincial level); Provincial development planning and adjustment of provincial economic structure; Provincial agricultural development (including provincial mountain and river basin development, provincial poverty alleviation); Province-wide data statistics; Income distribution and employment promotion at the provincial level. Fifth, state-owned assets and public resources. State-owned assets of provincial-level financial and non-financial enterprises; State-owned assets of provincial administrative institutions; Natural resources across cities and counties.

Third, the responsibilities of municipal and county governments. First, state sovereignty and regime operation. It includes: Municipal and county people's congresses, municipal and county political consultative conferences, municipal and county party committees, municipal and county governments, municipal and county courts, and municipal and county procuratorates; Public security and social stability within the jurisdiction. Second, people's livelihood and public services. The basic public service standards shall be appropriately increased above the lower limit of the state's basic public service standards according to the financial situation of the cities and counties; Secondary hospitals; Cultural and sports facilities at the municipal and county levels; Kindergarten education, primary and secondary education, adult education; Population and household registration administration; Community service. Third, public facilities and municipal works. Municipal and county-level infrastructure construction (provincial and county-level highway construction); Urban roads; Construction and operation of public transportation network within the jurisdiction; Urban and county planning; Municipal public utilities (including water supply, drainage, power supply, gas supply, heating, public transportation, energy utilization, landscaping), garbage and sewage treatment, environmental sanitation, environmental protection and pollution treatment. Fourth, market supervision and economic regulation. Stable market order in municipal and county districts; City and county development plans and economic restructuring; Statistics of data within the limits of cities and counties; Employment promotion in cities and counties. Fifth, state-owned assets and public resources. State-owned assets of municipal and county level financial and non-financial enterprises; State-owned assets of municipal and county-level administrative institutions; Natural resources within the jurisdiction of cities and counties.

Fourth, delegated and guiding duties. This part of the responsibility is less, only play a supporting role. The first is delegated responsibility. Central government funds, provincial/city/county governments are responsible for the coordination and implementation. It includes: Minimum living allowances for urban and rural residents; Primary and secondary education and school bus services; Community hospitals and township health centers; Rescue and reconstruction after major disasters; Social relief and special care; Economic construction projects; Census. Provincial governments contribute funds, and municipal and county governments are responsible for coordinating the promotion and implementation. It includes: basic housing security; Economic construction projects. The second is leading duties. To encourage and guide the lower level governments to undertake certain duties, the higher level governments should provide some funds and the lower level governments should provide some funds. It includes: strategic emerging industry development, with local characteristics of industrial development (Table 4.1).

Improve the Division of Government Revenue to Meet the Needs of Changing the Growth Model

Compared with the international level, China's central government financial concentration is not high at this stage. On the premise of dividing administrative power and expenditure responsibility into basic directions of reform, it is necessary to improve the market economic system and transform the development mode to promote tax reform and make necessary and reasonable adjustments to income distribution.

The Decision of the Central Committee of the Communist Party of China on Several Major Issues Concerning Comprehensively Deepening Reform puts forward that "the current financial structure of the central and local governments shall be kept stable on the whole, and the division of revenue between the central and local governments shall be further straightened out in light of the tax reform and the nature of tax categories". This requirement comprehensively takes into account the actual situation of local governments in China assuming administrative power and expenditure responsibility. It is conducive to ensuring that the central government performs its functions and implements major policy decisions. It is also conducive to protecting local vested interests, cultivating local tax categories, and mobilizing local initiatives, so as to form consensus on reform and ensure the smooth progress of reform. To implement the requirements of the *Decision of the CPC Central Committee on Several Major Issues Concerning Comprehensively Deepening Reform*, tax categories should be reasonably divided according to their nature and characteristics and in accordance with the principles of fairness, convenience and efficiency. Taxes with large periodic fluctuations in income, strong redistribution effect, uneven distribution of tax bases, large mobility of tax bases and easy to be transferred should be classified as central taxes, or with a larger proportion Shared by the central government. In order to fully mobilize the two initiatives and provide institutional guarantee for the realization of the "five-in-one" comprehensive well-off society, the tax categories with obvious benefits and regional characteristics that have no direct or significant impact on the operation of the macro economy are classified as local taxes or divided into a larger proportion by local governments. Specifically, it includes the following aspects.

1. Further improve the basic idea of revenue division between central and local governments

The allocation of financial power in the financial system is an important institutional arrangement to ensure governments at all levels to perform their duties effectively. On the whole, the division of financial rights should take into account the nature of taxes, give consideration to the distribution of interests among different regions, straighten out the division of income between the central and local governments, and promote the transformation of economic development mode and the formation of a unified market. On the whole, efforts should be made to make the division of the tax base scientific and rational, reduce shared taxes as appropriate. We will determine the tax categories with strong tax base liquidity, easy to cause the transfer of tax sources, inequality of distribution across regions, conducive to adjusting income distribution, promoting the transformation of economic development pattern, promoting the sustainable use of resources and the formation of a single market as the central fixed income. To be specific, for performing the function of macro-control, the central government should master: Taxes that are conducive to maintaining the unified market, have strong liquidity, are not suitable for segmentation, have the function of income redistribution and macroeconomic "stabilizer", such as individual income tax; Taxes that facilitate the implementation of industrial policies, such as excise taxes; Taxes related to national sovereignty, such as tariffs. In order to fulfill their functions of providing regional public goods and optimizing the investment environment of their jurisdictions, local governments should have weak liquidity, information advantages and tax collection and management advantages, and form incentive compatible and virtuous circle taxes, such as real estate taxes, to fulfill their functions.

According to the inherent nature of tax revenue, mature market economy countries generally divide the tax base with strong liquidity, uneven distribution among regions, large annual fluctuations, easy tax burden transfer and income distribution, such as value-added tax and income tax, into the central government revenue. The tax base shall be more localized, and the tax revenue, which can be well controlled by the local government, shall be assigned to the local revenue. On the premise of further standardizing the tax system, the current inter-governmental income division can be adjusted as follows: the inter-governmental income division should consider the tax category attribute, the division status of administrative power and expenditure responsibility, the degree of inter-regional financial difference and other factors. The centralized revenue of the central government should not only ensure the central government to fulfill its functions and expenditure responsibilities, but also facilitate the effective implementation of macro-control and promote equal access to basic public services. The following reform ideas can be considered: Value-added tax, will change from the central and local sharing revenue, into the central revenue, and the central government will pay the export tax rebate in full. In order to reduce the impact on local revenue, we can consider redistributing the VAT revenue Shared by local governments according to population and other objective factors without changing the distribution pattern of central and local VAT revenue, so as to change the current situation of sharing VAT revenue by source areas. Or reduce the VAT rate and change it to a central tax, while allowing local governments to collect retail sales tax within the original share of VAT. This tax is levied in the retail sector, not in production and distribution, and does not include the local pursuit of quantitative expansion mechanism, which is conducive to the realization of urbanization. Local governments can set their own tax items and tax rates according to local characteristics. For example, they do not levy taxes on basic foodstuffs, generally implement low tax rates on general goods and services retail sales, and implement high tax rates on cigarettes and alcohol. As a project to promote income distribution, the progressive income tax is closely related to the economic cycle and has strong fluctuation between the years. It should not be used as the income of local governments. We may consider changing the proportional sharing system between the central government and the local government to the sharing system based on the approved tax base, with the local government collecting taxes on a fixed proportion and the central government collecting progressive taxes. In principle, resource tax is suitable for central government revenue. However, in China, resources are mainly distributed in poor areas in central and western China. In order to support the development of these regions, resource tax can be left to local governments, but it is better to stay at the provincial level, so as to avoid the occurrence of unbalanced financial distribution caused by uneven distribution of resources and resources, leading to new conflicts. In addition, the source of equalization transfer payment should be clearly defined. One tax category or all or a certain proportion of some taxes can be designated as the source of equalization transfer payment.

2. Specific programs for the division of intergovernmental income

Based on the international experience and the idea of "more exclusive tax and less sharing tax", the following principles should be adhered to in the division of government revenue at the central, provincial and municipal levels: First, it is based on the principles of efficiency, fairness, convenient collection and management and adequate income. Second, we need to minimize the sharing of taxes and increase the scale of exclusive income at all levels. Third, we will expand direct and local taxes. In practice, it should be coordinated with the reform of the tax system and the construction of the local tax system. For example, we should consider increasing the resource tax, environmental tax, real estate tax and other types of property tax, increase the proportion of direct tax, and support the construction of the local tax system. See Table 4.2 for the specific plan of intergovernmental revenue division.

First, improve central taxation. It is mainly value-added tax, export tax refund, excise tax levied by the customs on import and value-added tax, customs duty, resource consumption tax (tobacco, alcohol), fuel consumption tax (such as in the production link), tonnage tax, offshore oil and gas resource tax, inland oil and gas and extra-large mineral resource tax (the central government may share appropriately), Individual income tax (appropriate sharing by the central government, the proportion should be more than 50%), enterprise income tax (appropriate sharing by the central government, such as 50%), inheritance tax (not yet levied, appropriate sharing by the central government), securities trading stamp duty (maintain the current distribution ratio); Payment of basic endowment insurance and basic medical insurance; Basic endowment insurance payment, the basic medical insurance premium; Government-managed funds at the central level, in which revenue from land transfer funds (appropriately centralized, such as 30%); The portion turned over from the state-owned capital operation at the central level; Central level non-tax income.

Second, we will adjust and gradually reduce the sharing of taxes between the central and local governments. We will cancel the "two-tax" rebate method and eliminate VAT sharing. After the transition period of replacing business tax with value-added tax (VAT), we will stop transferring VAT revenue from pilot industries to local governments. Its corresponding interests are guaranteed in the reform of expanding local taxes, retaining the financial industry after replacing the business tax with a value-added tax, business tax on the living service industry, which has no connection with the value-added tax chain or has little connection with it, standardizing the tax sharing system between the central and

Table 4.2 Intergovernmental income sharing program

Type of government	Type of fiscal revenue
Central government	customs duties, customs on behalf of the import of consumption tax and value-added tax, value-added tax (excluding the pure retail link), export tax rebate (excluding final consumer goods), resource consumption tax (tobacco, alcohol), fuel consumption tax (if collected in production), tonnage tax, offshore oil and gas resource tax, inland oil and gas and extra-large mineral resource tax (appropriately Shared by the central government), individual income tax (above 50% of the central government), enterprise income tax (50% of the central government), inheritance tax (not yet levied), securities trading stamp duty (maintain the current distribution ratio). Basic endowment insurance payment, basic medical insurance premium. Central government-managed funds, of which land transfer revenue (central 30%). The state capital operating income at the central level shall be turned over. Central level non-tax income
Provincial government	fuel consumption tax (such as in the retail link), non-resource consumption tax (large displacement cars, golf courses, etc.), Inland oil, gas and large mineral resources tax (provincial 30%), small and medium-sized mineral resources tax (provincial 50%), individual income tax (provincial 60%), enterprise income tax (provincial 60–70%), inheritance tax (ot yet levied 60%), stamp duty on securities trading (maintain the current distribution ratio), environmental tax (water resources, forests and beaches, not yet levied), value-added tax (pure retail link), export tax rebate (final consumer goods), business tax (life service industry after the "business tax replaced with VAT"), tobacco tax (provincial 40%), tax on large and medium-sized cars and ships. Industrial injury insurance premium, maternity insurance premium, unemployment insurance premium. Provincial government-managed funds, including land transfer funds (provincial 30%). Part of the income from state capital operation at the provincial level. Provincial non-tax revenue, including vehicle license and parking royalties (50%)

(continued)

local governments, and improving the transfer payment system. In the share ratio of enterprise income tax and individual income tax between

Table 4.2 (continued)

Type of government	Type of fiscal revenue
Municipal and county governments	tobacco tax (city and county 60%), small car and boat tax, real estate tax, land value-added tax, deed tax, farmland occupation tax, urban land use tax, urban maintenance and construction tax. Part of the income turned over from state capital operation at the city and county level. Non-tax income at the city and county level. Land transfer fee (city and county 40%)

the central government and local government, the share of local government can be appropriately increased, for example, the enterprise income tax is adjusted to 50–50 share.

Third, stabilize provincial income. It includes: value-added tax for small-scale taxpayers, business tax on financial industry and living services, consumption tax on refined oil (such as in the retail link), and non-resource consumption tax, non-resource consumption tax (large displacement car, golf course, luxury goods, fireworks, car tires, motorcycle, wooden disposable chopsticks, solid wood floor), Trans-provincial inland oil and gas and large mineral resources tax (less than 30%), small and medium-sized mineral resources tax (provincial below 50%), individual income tax (50%), enterprise income tax (50%); Provincial government-managed funds, of which land transfer revenue (30%); The portion turned over from state-owned capital operations at the provincial level; Non-tax revenue at the central level, including vehicle license plates and parking fees (50%).

Fourth, to enrich the city and county taxes. Including: tobacco tax (cities and counties 60%), small car and boat tax, real estate tax, land value-added tax, deed tax, farmland occupation tax, urban land use tax, urban maintenance and construction tax; The portion turned over from the state-owned capital operation at the city or county level; Non-tax income at the city and county level; Land transfer fee (40%).

Fifth, the establishment of central and local sharing fees. State land transfer fees shall be unified into land use fees after deducting compensatory costs, which shall be shared by the central government, provinces, cities and counties. Specific sharing ratio is to be studied and calculated, taking into account of the distribution of adjustment of each item.

Sixth, endow the localities with certain powers of taxation. It mainly includes the right to choose some local taxes, the right to adjust tax rate and the right to set up tax legislation according to local conditions.

Further Deepen Reform of the Fiscal System at and Below the Provincial Level

China is a big country with five levels of government. The regulation of intergovernmental financial relations should not only stay at the level of central and provincial governments, but also go deep into the level of provincial governments. The fiscal system at or below the provincial level shall be unified and stipulated by the central government in principle, and the proportion of revenue sharing, the requirements for vertical and horizontal balance at or below the provincial level, and the encouragement measures of the central government shall be specified. We will further adjust and improve the financial management system at and below the provincial level, balance regional and vertical financial resources, strengthen the capacity of grassroots support, optimize the distribution of regional financial resources, and promote equal access to public services. It is necessary to focus on the following aspects: first, to strengthen the responsibility of provincial governments, provincial governments should reasonably grasp the proportion of provincial government revenue in the province's income, increase regional financial regulation, and gradually narrow the gap between local governments below the province's financial resources. Second, we need to clarify the powers and expenditure responsibilities of governments at and below the provincial level. We need to divide expenditure responsibilities at and below the provincial level in accordance with the principles of externality, complexity of information and compatibility of incentives. We need to set up relevant provincial institutions and establish a transfer payment system at and below the provincial level based on the division of revenues at and below the provincial level. Third, we should unify the division of income below the provincial level, clarify the main tax categories of the governments below the provincial level, and reduce the negative impact of inter-regional income division on fair competition of enterprises. We will resolutely prohibit tax breaks or exemptions for enterprises, promote the rational flow of factors of production and promote healthy competition among enterprises. Fourth, we will further improve the mechanism for ensuring basic funding for county-level governments, adjust the level of funding in light of policy changes, constantly improve the system of awards and subsidies, and increase guidance and assistance to all regions. Fifth, we will continue to push forward the reform of direct provincial management of county finance, constantly enrich and improve the content and mode of reform, strengthen the township finance management, give full play to the function of township finance. In addition, in the supporting reform, we should actively and gradually promote the implementation of the tax sharing system below the provincial level. We should also flatten China's original five government levels into three levels: central government, provincial government, city and county government (different regions may be successively) through the direct provincial management of counties, rural financial management of counties and comprehensive supporting reform of townships.

Improve the System of Transfer Payments and the Mechanism for Ensuring Grassroots Financial Support

On the whole, to improve transfer payments, we need to reduce the size of transfer payments and streamline their programs on the basis of institutional reform in line with relevant powers and expenditure responsibilities. Focus on improving the effectiveness of transfer payment policies; We will reshape the rules of distribution and make them more normative, law-based and transparent.

1. Design the transfer payment system based on the clear division of inter-governmental powers and expenditure responsibilities

As mentioned above, the direction of fiscal reform is to strengthen the central government's administrative power and expenditure responsibility, clarify the scope of government's administrative power and expenditure responsibility at all levels, and reduce interference in local administrative power and expenditure projects. Accordingly, the current transfer payment structure should be adjusted. First, we will strengthen general transfer payments, promote equal access to basic public services, and incorporate the existing adjustments to special transfer payments within the scope of local spending responsibilities into general transfer payments. Second, special transfer payments should mainly address externalities, joint expenditure responsibilities, and achieve the specific policy objectives of the central government. Matters within the scope of the central government's powers and expenditure responsibilities shall be disbursed by the central government instead of through special transfer payments. In principle, local governments will have greater autonomy in matters within the scope of their powers and spending responsibilities through general transfer payments arrangements, and the central government will no longer interfere by arranging special transfer payments.

2. We will improve the system of general transfer payments

We will set up general transfer payments and special transfer payments in a scientific way, give full play to their respective functions, gradually increase the size and proportion of general transfer payments, and give better play to the advantages of local governments that are close to the community and manage them nearby. We will balance financial resources among different regions, focusing on increasing transfer payments to old revolutionary base areas, ethnic minority areas, border areas, and poor areas. In principle, general transfer payments will be used to bridge the gap in local financial resources caused by the central government's policy of reducing revenue and increasing spending. We should set targets for equalization of basic public services in the long, medium and short term, and define the areas and issues of public services. According to the target of different period, choose feasible policy path. We will further improve the framework of the general transfer payment system, identify the sources of funds for transfer payments, and reduce the arbitrariness of determining the total size of transfer payments. We will improve the way funds are allocated for general transfer payments, continue to give full play to the advantages of selecting objective factors and allocating funds according to formulas over the years, and reduce the randomness of fund allocation. We will optimize the equalization formula for transfer payments based on factors such as population, geography, cost of services, and location of functional zones, and strengthen financial support for underdeveloped local governments. We will give priority to making up the gap in revenue and expenditure in areas where development is prohibited or restricted, and promote equal access to basic public services.

3. Improve the system of special transfer payments

Special transfer payments should be classified, standardized and consolidated according to the responsibilities of inter-governmental expenditures. We will significantly reduce the number of transfer payment items, reduce the proportion of special transfer payments in all transfer payments, and merge and integrate duplicate and overlapping items in special items as well as similar or merge-able items. We will gradually eliminate special programs and local funds in competitive areas, strictly control programs for guidance, relief, and emergency response, and identify those programs that belong to local affairs and have a relatively fixed amount to be included in general transfer payments, and promptly clean up special transfer payments in light of economic and social development. We will set thresholds and access mechanisms for special transfer payments. We will eliminate projects that do not live up to their name or are outdated, merge projects that overlap with each other, and strictly control the scale of special transfer payments. In principle, the allocation of transfer payments by governments at all levels should be directly addressed to the public and the ultimate beneficiaries, and the procedures should be open and transparent. At the same time, the specific information should reach the local level as early as possible, and in principle, the "local supporting funds" requirement should be cancelled, so as to facilitate the overall preparation and serious implementation of the local budget.

4. Improve the management system and supervision mechanism of financial transfer payments

We will improve the system for managing transfer payments and eliminate the need for multiple departments to manage and distribute transfer payments. We will improve the unity and integrity of transfer payments between governments, make it clear that the financial sector is the only entity implementing and managing transfer payments, and eliminate the practice of transfer payments within the system. The special funds exchanged between the higher and lower levels of government departments shall all be included in the financial transfer payment, arranged by the financial department to the specific expenditure departments, included in the departmental budget management, and subject to the supervision of the financial department and the audit at the same level. At the same time, we should improve the supervision mechanism of transfer payments. As for general transfer payments, since the central government does not specify their specific uses, they are controlled by local governments themselves. The supervision and management of the use of these funds should be mainly realized through the review of local governments' budgets and final accounts and the supervision of budget implementation.

5. We will advance legislation on transfer payments and improve laws and regulations on transfer payments

At present, the management system of transfer payment belongs to departmental rules and regulations, which are relatively decentralized, with low legislative level and weak constraint. It is urgent to strengthen the legislation of financial transfer payments to standardize the behaviors of all parties in the budgeting, project management, especially the project establishment, distribution, management and supervision of special transfer payments, rationalize working mechanisms and decision-making procedures, promote openness and transparency, and give better play to the role of transfer payments. At present, we should study and formulate the *Financial Transfer Payment Law*. As a practical choice under transitional measures and realistic conditions, transfer payment can be regulated in the form of special regulations of the state council. Through laws, regulations and systems, it shall clarify the rules of the game, determine the financial transfer payment policy objectives, sources of funds, distribution standards, distribution procedures, to ensure the legality and seriousness of the rules, to ensure the financial transfer payment policy effect.

6. We will continue to improve community-level financial support mechanisms

The development of a mechanism to ensure basic funding for county-level governments began in 2010. The main goal is to ensure the basic expenditure of workers' salaries, maintain normal operation and implement the national unified policy on people's livelihood and guide all localities to provide support for county-level governments. The *Opinions on Establishing and Improving the Basic Financial Support Mechanism for County-Level Governments* (C.Y. [2010] No. 443) of the Ministry of Finance explicitly put forward the main goal of ensuring the wages, operation and livelihood of county and township governments, and comprehensively promoting the construction of the basic financial support mechanism for county-level governments. The main content of the basic financial support mechanism for county-level governments is as follows: each year, the central government formulates the scope and standards of basic financial support for county-level governments in accordance with relevant national policies. The scope of protection includes the wage policy and livelihood policy formulated by the state, as well as public funds and local subsidies of government organs and public institutions. Among them, the guarantee standards of the first two items shall be implemented in accordance with the unified provisions of the state, while the guarantee standards of the second two items shall be approved by provinces according to the financial status of each region. On this basis, calculate and determine the basic financial security needs of counties throughout the country, and compare with the same caliber of fiscal expenditure of counties, check and ratify the expenditure gap. Incentive awards shall be given to areas that are well protected; For regions with financial gaps, guaranteed rewards shall be given according to the digestion of the gaps. For those regions that still have a shortage of basic financial resources at the county level by the end of 2012, the equalization transfer payment or tax refund for the region in 2013 will be deducted and direct subsidies will be provided to the counties with insufficient financial resources. The central government will adopt incentives and constraints to guide provincial finance to fulfill its responsibility by improving the financial system below the provincial level and increasing transfer payments to county-level governments.

By the end of 2012, we had basically achieved the policy goals of "ensuring wages, ensuring operations, and ensuring people's well-being." county-level governments had significantly increased their financial resources, and had significantly improved ability to provide basic public services, and achieved initial progress. However, the current financial capacity of county-level governments is still far from strengthening the governance capacity of grass-roots governments, promoting equal access to basic public services, and promoting the building of a moderately prosperous society in all respects.

We will further improve the mechanism for ensuring basic funding for county-level governments, and establish a long-term mechanism that ensures accountability at different levels, provides dynamic support, pays attention to performance, and is open and transparent. We will continue to raise the level of financial support for county-level governments so that their financial resources are matched dynamically with their basic spending responsibilities. We need to adopt a series of policies and measures, including raising security standards, improving the financial system and transfer payment system below the provincial level, advancing the reform of direct provincial management of county finance, and establishing a mechanism for county-level basic financial resources to ensure steady growth of funds. We will ensure the sound operation of county finance and optimize the distribution of financial resources. We need to strengthen the connection between pilot reforms of the system under direct provincial control of counties. On the basis of steadily advancing the reform of direct provincial management of county finance, we will

improve relevant policies and measures, guide and encourage provincial and municipal governments to grant county-level governments more economic and social management power, and enhance county-level governments' ability to coordinate, independently make decisions and provide public services for regional economic and social development.
[Column 3.1].
Local practices:
Zhejiang province issues *Trial Measures on Transfer Payment for Ecological and Environmental Protection.*

(1) The object and nature of financial transfer payments

The object of financial transfer payment is the city, county (city) that has a large area and the source of the first-grade tributaries of the eight river trunk streams and basins with an area of more than 100 square kilometers in Zhejiang Province. And it takes the financial settlement unit of the provincial financial system to the city and county as the object of calculation, assessment and distribution of transfer payment funds. The transfer payment of provincial ecological and environmental protection funds shall be coordinated and arranged by the municipal and county (city) governments, including expenditures for local environmental protection.

(2) Method of distribution of transfer payments

1. Indicator setting
Relevant indicators are set according to two major factors, such as ecological function protection and environmental (water and gas) quality improvement. (1) two indicators of ecological function protection: ecological forest area above the provincial level; Large and medium-sized reservoirs. (2) two indicators of environmental quality improvement: water quality of major river basins; Air quality.
2. Weight distribution
(1) 50% of the ecological function protection category, including 30% of the public welfare forests above the provincial level and 20% of the large and medium-sized reservoirs. (2) 50% environmental

quality improvement, including 30% water quality in major river basins and 20% air quality.
3. Assessment coefficient and calculation method
(1) ecological function protection. (1) ecological forest area above the provincial level: calculate according to the ratio of public welfare forest area to the whole province area of each city and county above the provincial level during annual assessment confirmed by the provincial forestry department. (2) large and medium-sized reservoirs: calculate according to the ratio of converted area of large and medium-sized reservoirs to the whole province area. But the available amount of each city or county (city) is no more than 20% of the total amount distributed.
(2) environmental quality improvement. Warning indicators are set for the outgoing water quality and atmospheric environment of major river basins, that is, the warning indicator of water environment is the water environment functional zone standard, and the warning indicator of atmospheric environment is the number of days with API value less than 100, which accounts for no less than 85% of the number of days in the whole year. If the quality is higher than the warning index, a certain subsidy and reward shall be given for each level raised; if the quality is lower than the warning index, a certain deduction and compensation shall be given for each level lowered.
(1) water environment quality in major river basins: Calculate and evaluate in different cases according to the exit water quality at the junction section of main river basins in cities and counties confirmed through the provincial environmental protection bureau monitoring and the annual average surface water runoff confirmed by provincial water resources department. (1) for all the exit water quality at the junction sections of the main river basins in cities and counties that has reached the warning level or above, 1 million Yuan of incentive fund subsidies will be granted. At the same time, if the exit water quality reaches the third class water standard, the coefficient is 0.6. The coefficient is 0.8 when reaching the second class water standard; for the first class water standard, the coefficient is 1. Where there are multiple rivers and interfacial

sections, the coefficients shall be weighted and averaged according to the corresponding standards. The subsidy funds are distributed according to the proportion of each city, county (city) coefficient multiplied by its average surface water runoff for many years in the province. (2) according to the annual assessment of exit water quality at the junction of cities and counties (cities) compared with the previous year's changes, implement the reward and punishment mechanism for improving or lowering water quality. That is, the coefficients of four types of water, five types of water and inferior five types of water are set as 0.4, 0.2 and 0.1 respectively. The total coefficients of each city, county (city)in the assessment year and the previous year are calculated and compared according to the abovementioned method. For every 1 percentage point increased over the previous year, a reward subsidy of 100,000 Yuan will be given; On the contrary, for every one percentage point reduction, a subsidy of 100,000 Yuan will be deducted, and so on.

(2) atmospheric environment quality: Calculate and evaluate the air pollution index (API value) of each city, county (city) confirmed by the provincial environmental protection bureau. (1) for cities and counties with an API value less than with the percentage(set to X) reached alarming index standard (85%) of 100 days to the days in the year and above, a certain amount of incentive funds will be allocated. When the X value is equal to 100%, set the coefficient as 1, and calculate the subverted coefficient by 0.1 for every 2 percentage points decrease, and so on. (2) According to the changes of the air environment quality assessment year compared with the previous year in each city and county (city), implement the reward and punishment mechanism for the improvement or decline of air quality, namely: when the X value is 1 percentage point higher than the previous year, 10,000 Yuan will be awarded; on the contrary, for every 1 percentage point decrease of X value over the previous year, a penalty of 10,000 Yuan will be deducted, and so on.

(3) Realization and distribution of funds for transfer of financial resources

After calculating and summarizing the funds for ecological and environmental protection transfer of various cities and counties (cities) based on the above methods, and combining with their financial conditions, different cash subsidy amounts and different cash subsidy coefficients are implemented for each city and county (cities). That is, 24 less developed cities and counties and 27 cities and counties such as Jinhua City, Lanxi City and Anji County were set as 1. Hangzhou, For Wenzhou, Taizhou and other 3 developed cities and 3 economically strong counties (cities) such as Ruian City, Yueqing City and Shaoxing County, the cash subsidy coefficient is 0.3. For the remaining 12 counties (cities), the cashing subsidy coefficient is set at 0.7.

The total amount of ecological and environmental protection financial transfer payment is fixed in one year, which shall be included in the provincial financial budget of that year. After the end of the assessment year, the relevant data of each city and county (city) shall be verified by the relevant provincial competent authorities and delivered to the provincial finance department before February 15 of each year. According to the measures and the data approved by the provincial competent authorities, the provincial finance department shall formulate a specific fund allocation plan and report it to the provincial government for approval of a lump-sum allocation of funds.

[Column 3.2].

Analysis of the basic mode of financial management system below the provincial level-taking Hebei and Zhejiang provinces as examples.

The financial system below the provincial level is an important part of the national financial system and the implementation and extension of the central government to the local financial system. China currently has the world's most hierarchical government system and administrative division system, including the central government, provinces (autonomous regions, municipalities directly under the central government), regions (prefecture-level cities, autonomous prefectures), counties (county-level cities) and townships (towns), totaling five levels. According to the intergovernmental financial relations at all levels, the sub-provincial financial management system can be divided into the following two basic models: First, the province manages the city, the city manages the county. There are six main forms of city and county management: On the basis of the original prefecture-level city, it is divided into several counties; consolidation of prefectures and cities; prefectures changed into cities; The city that does not lead a county originally, is divided into a few counties; County-level cities are upgraded to prefecture-level cities, with several counties under their leadership; County directly upgraded to prefecture-level city, with the implementation of the city management county system. Second, direct provincial control of counties (cities). Due to historical reasons and regional characteristics, Zhejiang and Ningxia have been implementing the system of provincial administration of counties. In addition, since 2003, Hubei, Anhui, Shandong, Fujian, Hunan, Jiangxi, Jilin, Hebei and other provinces have, according to their own conditions, directly assigned economic and social management power to economically strong counties (cities), which are partially subordinate to prefecture-level cities. In terms of financial system, the system of direct provincial control over counties (cities) has been implemented. The main types are:(1) Zhejiang model. Zhejiang has long been implementing the system of direct provincial administration of county finance. City (prefecture) finance and county (city) finance are directly linked to the province in the system. The city (prefecture) level does not have an institutional settlement relationship with the county (city) or the county (city) under its jurisdiction. The main approach is: fiscal and tax integration, hierarchical management. Objectively speaking, Zhejiang's fiscal and taxation system and ranks are still composed of three levels, namely, province, city and county, with distinct Zhejiang characteristics. Give priority to "take", with overall consideration. Since 2003, Zhejiang has adjusted and improved the "two guarantees and two links" fiscal policy. Cities and counties shall, on the premise of ensuring that the fiscal revenue and expenditure of the current year are balanced and the government functions are fulfilled, implement the linkage between provincial subsidies and rewards and the growth and increase of local fiscal revenue. (2) the modes of Hubei, Anhui and Jilin (only take Hubei as an example to illustrate). Its approach: thorough reform, one step in place. Since 2004, the financial management system of counties (cities) under direct provincial administration has been implemented in Hubei province. After the reform, there are altogether 69 units under direct provincial administration. The reform covers six areas, including the budget management system, transfer payments and special fund subsidies, financial settlement, fund reporting and dispatching, debt repayment, and transfer payments. Establish incentive mechanism to support county economic development. In Hubei province, the county (city) system under direct provincial supervision is to concentrate financial resources to support the economic and social development of counties and alleviate the financial difficulties of counties and townships. Hubei province, based on the base of 2003, will return all the incremental contributions made by counties (cities) from 2004 to 2006 to counties (cities) to promote the comprehensive reform of townships and towns and support the development of county economy. For the 11 cities and prefectures with per capita financial resources less than 24,000 Yuan, we will also follow the policies of 69 counties (cities and districts). For 16 cities (prefectures) at the same level (including directly administered cities), when the increment of the four industrial and commercial taxes reach the advanced level of the whole province, the province shall give appropriate rewards according to the absolute amount of the increase of the four industrial and commercial taxes. As a special fund, the city (prefecture) shall use it for the development of new industrialization and agricultural industrialization. Cities (prefectures), counties and provinces that have made outstanding achievements will be rewarded with special funds. (3) Shandong, Hunan and Hebei modes of power expansion. This pattern can also be called the local pilot pattern. Shandong province began to expand its economic and social management authority in stages and batches in 2003. In the first batch, 30 counties (cities) with a good foundation for development and great potential will be selected. In accordance with the general principle of "releasing those can be released", the power of provincial-level economic and financial management will be delegated to counties (cities), and the system of direct provincial management of county finance will be implemented. Subsequently, Hunan province began to implement the system of "direct provincial administration of counties" in 20 economically strong counties (cities) from 2004. Since 2005, Hebei province has carried out a pilot program of "strengthening counties by expanding power" in 22 counties (cities). Pilot power expansion counties (cities) are given the same economic and social management authority as prefecture-level cities divided into districts. The core content of the reform of "expanding power and strengthening counties" in Shandong, Hunan, Hebei and other provinces is also the direct financial settlement under the direct supervision of the province.

Over the years, Hebei province has been in the forefront of financial system reform, which is relatively representative. Zhejiang province is a typical representative of counties directly managed by the province, which has the highest financial efficiency.

(1) Analysis of basic financial support in Hebei province

Starting from 1994, in accordance with the general requirements of the central government for the reform of the tax sharing and fiscal system, and in light of the actual situation of the province's economic development, social progress and fiscal revenues and expenditures, Hebei province has carried out a series of financial reforms, walking in the forefront of financial reform, and realized a historic leap in the financial cause, strongly supporting and promoting the rapid and healthy development of the province's economy and social undertakings.

1. Division of powers below the provincial level

The reasonable division of fiscal expenditure responsibility among governments, as the basic link of vertical fiscal system, is the premise and basis of the division of fiscal revenue among governments. According to the principle of division of administrative power and the actual situation of Hebei province, administrative power at the provincial, municipal and county levels can be divided as follows. Provincial government responsibilities: responsible for the responsibilities related to income redistribution and major economic services, mainly including the adjustment of fiscal revenue within the province and among cities and counties and the social security system, such as the construction and management of basic industries such as energy and agriculture. Since these projects tend to be deployed on a large scale, the overall effect of the macro-view should be considered to strengthen the provincial government's authority in this regard. Municipal government power: mainly responsible for life service power and part of economic service power. These service matters are closely related to people's life, such as environmental health, fire control, public security, culture, medical treatment and basic education of primary and secondary schools. These service matters are assigned to the municipal government, which is conducive to timely listening to the people's requirements and opinions on government services. Thus, continuous improvement and improvement of service level and promotion of efficiency can be achieved; economic service power mainly refers to the cross-county infrastructure construction, including the management of highway construction, agriculture and other basic industrial facilities, as well as the small infrastructure in the city, and the coordination with the construction and management of provincial infrastructure. The powers of the county-level government should mainly focus on maintaining the normal operation of party and government organs, maintaining the social stability of the county and promoting economic development. Education is a special administrative power. In principle, the administrative power of compulsory education lies in cities and counties, and the administrative power of vocational education and higher education lies in provinces.

Since 2005, Hebei province has focused on establishing a set of fiscal system with clear responsibility of inter-governmental expenditure, clear division of income and standard transfer payment, and initiated the specific exploration of the reform plan of inter-governmental responsibility of fiscal expenditure. In terms of specific practice, a series of attempts have been made to define the supporting proportion of financial funds at the provincial, municipal and county levels in a number of fiscal expenditure projects such as compulsory education, public health and family planning. Then, taking the government expenditure item as the clue, it has carried on the comprehensive investigation to the province finance expenditure responsibility. According to the principles of beneficence, compensation and capacity, the allocation of responsibility for fiscal expenditure at the provincial, municipal and county levels has been systematically studied, and a plan for the division of responsibility for expenditure at the provincial, municipal and county levels has been gradually formed, which includes 386 specific expenditure items. In 2008, the provincial government officially decided to take 5 categories and 12 expenditure responsibilities as the first batch of targets for pilot reforms, and adjusted the provincial special fund projects accordingly.

2. Tax revenue division

(1) Tax sharing reform (1994–2001)

In 1994, while carrying out the central government's reform of local tax sharing system, Hebei province implemented the tax sharing system correspondingly. In addition to the central tax revenue, most of the provincial tax revenue is divided into cities and counties. According to the industry and subordination relationship, the provincial share of local value-added tax (including the four major industries of power, petroleum, petrochemical and non-ferrous metals, as well as six major steel enterprises including Tangshan Iron & Steel, JTB, Shijiazhuang Steel, Xingtai Iron & Steel, Chegnde Iron & Steel and Xuanhua Iron & Steel, and North China Pharmaceutical Group), business tax (financial insurance) and provincial enterprise income tax, as well as urban land use tax (50%), resource tax (Tangshan 50%) income. The initial establishment of the framework of the tax-sharing financial system has further mobilized the enthusiasm of organizations at all levels in terms of fiscal revenue, and promoted the development of the market economy and rational adjustment of the industrial structure.

(2) Deepening reform of tax distribution system (2002)

In 2002, Hebei province took the opportunity of the national reform of income tax sharing method to further deepen the reform of tax sharing financial system. Hebei province continued to deepen the reform of the sub-provincial income system based on breaking the subordination relationship of enterprises and standardizing the provincial financial system. The income ranges of provinces and cities shall be divided according to the local income ranges stipulated after the reform of central income tax sharing. Provincial-level governments will share local value-added tax, business tax, enterprise income tax and individual income tax in proportion, and will no longer participate in the income sharing of resource tax and urban land use tax. The division of other fiscal revenues by provinces and cities shall remain unchanged. At the same time, the duties and powers of provincial and municipal governments and the division of expenditure responsibilities will not be changed. After the reform, tax revenue sharing below the provincial level is as follows.

① Scope and proportion of VAT sharing. According to the territorial tax, the central government shares 75%, the province shares 10% and the city shares 15%.
② Business tax sharing scope and proportion. The business tax on local financial business of Industrial and Commercial Bank of China, Agricultural Bank of China, Bank of China, China Construction Bank, China Development Bank, Agricultural Development Bank of China, Export-Import Bank of China and its participating Banks shall be regarded as provincial fixed income. In addition, 10% of the local business tax will be shared by provinces and 90% by cities.
③ Share scope and proportion of enterprise income tax. Income taxes paid by Railway Transportation, State Postal Service, Industrial and Commercial Bank of China, Agricultural Bank of China, Bank of China, China Construction Bank, China Development Bank, Agricultural Development Bank of China, Export–Import Bank of China and offshore oil and gas enterprises continue to be used as central revenue. The income from the central enterprise income tax, which is operated across regions and paid centrally to the Treasury, shall be allocated to Hebei province according to relevant factors as provincial income. The enterprise income tax paid by other enterprises at all levels and of all kinds in Hebei province shall be levied on the basis of dependency and Shared by all levels in proportion. In 2002, 50% was shared by the central government, 25% by provinces and 25% by municipalities. In 2003, 60% was shared by the central government, 20% by provinces and 20% by municipalities. The sharing proportion after 2003 shall be adjusted according to the adjustment of the sharing proportion between the central government and the local government. The following share of enterprise income tax revenue that is included in the scope of income tax sharing in cross-city operation and centralized payment to the treasury in the province shall be

distributed among relevant cities according to the relevant factors of branches (subsidiaries) in various regions.

④ The sharing scope and proportion of individual income tax. Collect according to apanage, individual income tax(including individual income tax on interest earned on savings accounts) shares in proportion at all levels. In 2002, 50% was shared by the central government, 15% by provinces and 35% by municipalities. In 2003, 60%was shared by the central government, 10% by provinces and 30% by municipalities. The sharing proportion after 2003 shall be adjusted according to the adjustment of the sharing proportion between the central government and the local government.

⑤ The division of resource tax and urban land use tax. Tangshan city resource tax is turned over to the provincial finance by quota, and all income is under Tangshan City. Urban land use tax, each city took 2001 provincial income as the base and turned over to the provincial finance by quota, all income was distributed to each city.

⑥ Determination of tax refund amount. In 2002, the return of central value-added tax and consumption tax in each city was calculated according to the central return formula, based on the number of tax returns in 2001, and the growth rate of central "two taxes" in each city was calculated according to the same diameter. Tax refunds for 2003 and subsequent years shall be calculated according to the central formula. The amount of central income tax (including enterprise income tax and individual income tax) refunded from the net income tax of each city shall be approved with 2001 as the base year. According to the income division between the central and local governments after the reform of sharing the actual income and income tax in 2001, the net income of each city in 2001 (the income tax of each city in the central government minus the income tax of each city in the central government) shall be verified, and the amount shall be returned to each city in a fixed amount every year.

The amount of tax refunded by the provincial finance department to the value-added tax, business tax, enterprise income tax and individual income tax of each city (hereinafter referred to as "the four taxes") shall be approved with 2001 as the base year. According to the actual income of 2001 and the income division of provinces and cities after the reform of "four taxes" sharing, the net amount of "four taxes" income of each city assigned to provincial finance in 2001 is verified, and this is used as the base for the return of "four taxes" by provincial finance to each city in future years. In 2002 and later years, the amount of "four taxes" returned by the province to each city shall be increased by an incremental amount (50%) from the previous year's "four taxes". The incremental refund amount of the provincial central city is calculated and determined according to the proportion of the municipal "four taxes" income in 2001. After the province returns to the city, it will concentrate the incremental part of each city, and the provincial finance will use it for the general transfer payment. The subsidized local governments shall make overall arrangements according to their own conditions to meet the basic needs of guaranteeing the payment of salaries and the normal operation of institutions.

On the treatment of tax preferential policies. The central government has introduced preferential policies for levying and refunding value-added tax and business tax at once. After the reform, in principle, each level shall bear its own share. Based on the preferential policies for income tax formulated by the central government, i principle, they shall bear by all levels in proportion to their share. However, the central government will continue to shoulder the responsibility after the reform of the policies of levying taxes on central government enterprises before the implementation of the reform plan and returning them after they are cleaned up. No preferential income tax policies may be issued by all levels.

After the implementation of the new system, if the annual income tax revenue of a city does not reach the amount of 2001, the provincial finance department will deduct the tax rebate base of the city accordingly. If the "four taxes" collected by a city in future years cannot reach the amount in 2001, the provincial finance department shall deduct the "four taxes" tax refund base for the city.

In addition, each city should undertake supporting reform to the financial system below the city level. There are two basic goals to be achieved in the following municipal reforms: first, to initially establish a basic financial expenditure guarantee mechanism for counties (cities, districts) and townships (towns) through institutional reform; Second, standardize the tax distribution system, promote economic restructuring and county economic development. Meet four basic requirements: First, we will establish a standardized tax-sharing and fiscal system. According to the requirements of the standard tax system, we should basically break the practice of dividing income according to the subordination of enterprises, implement proportional sharing according to the principle of territorial tax collection, and divide and determine the sharing proportion according to the nature of different taxes. Second, we need to properly divide revenues and expenditures. Income shall be divided according to the duties and powers of governments at all levels and their expenditure responsibilities. We shall determine the income ranges and sharing ratios at all levels according to the government's responsibilities and powers and the financial resources required for its expenditure responsibilities. We will focus on cultivating the main types of taxes at all levels, mobilize the enthusiasm of the grassroots to raise financial resources and strengthen tax collection and management, and strive to cultivate the ability of counties (cities, districts) and townships (towns) to stand on their own feet and develop themselves. Third, the basic needs of ensuring the operation of grass-roots political power. In determining the income range and sharing ratio of counties (cities or districts), the city shall give full consideration to the salaries, pensions and basic needs of the staff and workers of county (city or district) townships (towns) of government organs and public institutions and the operation of government organs, carefully review and ratify unified standards for wage security and public funds, and reasonably calculate standard expenditures at all levels to determine the reform plan for income distribution. Fourth, formulate the township (town) financial system by classification. According to economic development level and development potential, fiscal revenue scale, per capita financial level, population of townships (towns) and other factors, townships (towns) are divided into different types and different fiscal systems are implemented respectively: For townships (towns) with relatively strong economic strength, relatively large fiscal revenue and relatively high per capita financial strength, a tax sharing system shall be implemented to divide the revenue according to the functions of governments at the first level and their expenditure responsibilities. For townships (towns) with low levels of economic development, small fiscal revenues and low per capita financial resources, the system of unified management of revenues and expenditures at the county level shall be implemented.

(3) Reform of incentive fiscal revenue system (2003–2007)

In 2003, Hebei province implemented the incentive fiscal revenue system on the premise of adhering to the tax sharing system framework. The reforms are as follows: We will maintain the original system for dividing fiscal revenue at the provincial and municipal levels, and appropriately adjust the policies for incremental refunds of VAT, business tax, corporate income tax and individual income tax.

① The province has implemented the policy of "quota sharing and full return of excess income" for the 34 national and provincial poverty alleviation and development key counties under the jurisdiction of Zhangjiakou, Chengde and other cities (hereinafter referred to as anti-poverty counties). That is to say, the province took the actual income sharing of "four taxes" in Zhangjiakou, Chengde and anti-poverty counties in 2002 as the base, and returned the full amount of "four taxes" income exceeding the base after 2003.
② For other districts and cities (anti-poverty counties are excluded), the province has implemented the policy of "return of all incomes exceeding the growth rate". Namely taking 2002 as base year, the province determined "4 taxes" income target growth rate and share growth rate. From 2003 to 2005, the "four taxes" income of each city increased by more than 9%, and share growth rates were 9%, 8% and 7% respectively. For income within the share growth rate, the province will no longer implement the policy of centralized increment of 50%; For the part that exceeds sharing growth rate, the province shares "4 taxes" income returned in full.
③ Revenue below municipal level: First, all districts and cities shall strictly implement the incentive policies set by the provinces, and formulate corresponding incentive policies for counties (cities and

districts) in accordance with the principle of improving the fiscal revenue system and policies of provinces and cities. Zhangjiakou and Chengde cities implement the policy of "quota sharing and full return for excessive income" for their counties and anti-poverty counties for other cities with districts. Other districts and cities have implemented the policy of "return of all incomes exceeding the growth rate" for non-anti-poverty counties.

Second, the proportion of income sharing between cities and counties should be appropriately adjusted. The sharing ratio of value-added tax and business tax between the city and the county shall be adjusted. In principle, the sharing ratio of value-added tax between the city and the county shall not exceed 5%, and the sharing ratio of business tax shall not exceed 15%.

Third, we will implement key incentive policies for economic growth areas such as development zones. High-tech development zones generally have a small income base, large growth space and strong expansion of economic scale, which is the focus of fiscal policy to support the excellent and strong. The city shall implement key incentive mechanism for development zones. Cities with districts should follow the provincial system for general cities and counties, and implement the policy of "four taxes" to share the excess revenue from the growth rate and return all the income. Similar incentive policies should also be formulated for new economic growth points such as science and technology parks, industrial parks and key projects that have a major driving effect on regional economic development.

Fourthly, in anti-poverty counties, there are 6 counties, such as Shexian County, Guangping County, Guantao County, LaiYuan County, Kuancheng County and Pingshan County, with relatively good financial status. Upon the policy support from provincial and municipal governments, the additional incremental financial resources should be mainly used for the construction of poverty alleviation and development projects. Other anti-poverty counties should focus the increased financial resources on improving the guarantee level for the payment of public education personnel and the operation of government.

During this period, Hebei province also carried out three specific fiscal revenue system reform. First, Implement the mode of direct provincial supervision of county finance system for power expansion county (city). Since 2005, the provincial finance has implemented direct financial management mode in 22 counties (cities) with expanded power. With 2004 as the base period, all districts and cities will no longer share the income of counties (cities) with expanded power. Second, further intensify reform of the county and township financial systems. In 2005, in the name of the provincial government, the *Guiding Opinions on Deepening the Reform of the Financial System of Counties and Townships* were issued, requiring the implementation of two specific modes of fiscal revenue system of counties and townships on the basis of reasonable and clear division of expenditure responsibilities: For towns expected to be growing rapidly into those with strong adsorption and radiation driving effect over surrounding areas through self-development and self-accumulation with relatively high economic development level and non-agricultural industry concentration, and relatively large fiscal revenue scale (the total fiscal revenue of the township is more than 5 million Yuan) with strong independent financial resources (the general budget revenue and tax refund at the same level are generally more than 2 million Yuan), implement a relatively standardized tax system to enhance their independent development of the power and financial capacity; For towns and villages with low level of economic development and non-agricultural industry concentration, lacking main tax sources and unable to become regional economic development centers in the short term, implement the system model of unified collection, unified allocation plus incentive. By the end of 2007, pilot reforms had been carried out in 126 counties (cities) in the province, covering 1,439 towns and townships (including 358 towns and townships with relatively standardized tax sharing system and 1,081 towns and townships with unified collection, unified allocation and incentive system). Third, we will implement an incentive fiscal system to promote the formation of economic growth poles. With an aim to promote the formation of the coastal economic boom belt, since 2006, the provincial finance has implemented the preferential policy of "four taxes" income quota sharing and full return in the core areas of Caofeidian new area and Cangzhou Bohai new area, which has accelerated their growth into new economic growth poles.

(4) Further improve the fiscal revenue system below the provincial level (2008–2012)

Based on the principle of promoting advantages and eliminating disadvantages, Hebei province has further adjusted and improved the financial system below the provincial level. With an eye to implementing the scientific outlook on development, we will use the fiscal revenue system to accelerate the development of cities and counties from multiple perspectives. It mainly includes four contents: The first is to implement more accurate classification of incentives to accelerate the development of various regions. It shall change the conceptual classification of regions, according to the main indexes such as per capita GDP, per capita financial resources and per capita net income of farmers, counties are divided into three categories: difficult, average and good, and cities are divided into two categories: average and good. Starting from 2008, we will implement fiscal revenue systems with different incentives based on 2007. We will continue to implement the quota sharing of the four provincial taxes and return all excess revenue to counties with financial difficulties, and return all excess share growth rates to counties with average or good financial conditions and cities. Second, make more extensive use of county and township fiscal systems to promote the scientific development of county economy and society, and extend the pilot reform of county and township fiscal systems to all counties (cities). Third, focus on promoting the formation of the economic growth pole in a larger scope, and expand the scope of application of the provincial fiscal incentive system and preferential policies to the economic growth pole from two perspectives: On one hand, with the establishment of Caofeidian New Area and the expansion of Cangzhou Bohai New Area, the preferential system policy was extended to Tangshan's Tanghai County, Nanbao Development Zone and Cangzhou Huanghua City from 2008. On the other hand, except Tangshan and Cangzhou, the other nine cities with districts can choose a development zone or industrial park with clear zoning and broad development prospects as the new economic growth pole, and enjoy the preferential system for Caofeidian New Area and Cangzhou Bohai New Area. Fourth, promote the optimization and upgrading of the industrial structure and sustainable development, adjust the income division between provinces, cities and counties. It includes: The general business tax sharing at the provincial level will be delegated to counties (cities) to accelerate the development of county tertiary industry; To build and expand the agricultural industrialization of leading enterprises to increase the share of value-added tax at the provincial level to the county, in order to promote the development of agricultural industrialization; The newly built and expanded high-tech enterprises will be left to cities and counties to share VAT at the provincial level to promote the development of high-tech industries; We will change the sharing of resource taxes from cities and counties to 30%, 30%, and 40% at the provincial, municipal, and county levels, so as to reduce the waste of resources and environmental damage caused by excessive mining and digging by the county level out of financial interests.

3. Transfer payment system below the provincial level

(1) Attempt to standardize the reform of financial transfer payment system

After the tax sharing reform in China in 1994, the financial department of Hebei province took the lead in research and exploration since 1995, and successively selected the two important projects of the province's general subsidy to difficult counties and the special subsidy for the "compulsory education project for poor areas" to carry out the reform attempt of standardizing the financial transfer payment system.

① According to the standard idea of transfer payment, improve the general transfer payment funds distribution in difficult counties. In 1995, in order to allocate and use the provincial financial subsidy funds more scientifically and reasonably, the provincial finance department decided to take it as the first "reform experimental field" to standardize the financial transfer payment system. The reform was mainly reflected in the addition of two care factors, one encouragement factor and one restriction factor in the distribution method. Two care factors were: geographical factors. Considering that Zhangjiakou and Chengde belonged to difficult counties with high terrain, low temperature, short frost-free period and long heating period, the calculation standard of their public expenditure was about 10% higher than that of other counties. Population density factor. Some difficult counties were located in mountainous areas or dams with low population density, traffic inconvenience, objectively it needed relatively more public education personnel, and the public expenditure level would be higher. When calculating spending needs, therefore, the proportion of financial providers in the population was added for those counties. Encouraging factor was to increase subsidy amount by grain and cotton output. On one hand, we should compensate the loss of low direct contribution rate of agriculture to fiscal revenue, and at the same time encourage the development of grain and cotton production in agricultural counties to ensure national food security. In addition to the above low population density of counties to give a certain proportion of care, the constraint factor is to all counties in difficulty according to the province's county-level financial support population to calculate the average proportion of counties should be financially supported population. In addition to the give a certain proportion of care above to the counties with low population density, the constraint factor is to calculate the number of financially supported population of each county (except the entitled groups receiving regular and fixed subsidies from the government) according to the average proportion of county-level financial providers to the total population of all counties in difficulty. Through this method, we would encourage counties in difficulty to streamline their administration, reduce their financial burdens, and curb the increase in the number of people provided for by the government. Through this reform, the distribution of general transfer payment funds not only gets rid of the influence of human factors, which is more objective and fair, but also strengthens the function of policy guidance, further enhancing the scientific nature.

② Reform the allocation of special transfer payments in accordance with the formula of relevant factors. In order to achieve the national education development goal, the ministry of finance and the state education commission decided to concentrate financial resources on organizing and implementing the "compulsory education project for poor areas" from 1995, with a view to popularizing nine-year compulsory education nationwide by 2000. In October 1995, the ministry of finance distributed the amount of the subsidy plan for 1995–1997 to Hebei, and asked the provincial finance department to provide 46 poverty-stricken counties with supporting subsidies according to the same amount. After research, Hebei finance department put forward the method to allocate the fund transparently according to the formula of relevant factors. The distribution formula includes one basic factor and six adjustment factors. The basic factor is the number of middle school and primary school students in poor counties. Six adjustment factors giving different weights include: county and township financial affordability; Intensity of county education expenditure; Affordability of farmers; Ethnic minority care factors; World bank loan allocation; The popularization of compulsory education. From 1996 to 1998, similar methods of standardized transfer payments were tried out for the distribution of subsidies for three construction projects: special funds for family planning allocated at the provincial level, the minimum social security fund for urban residents, and basic health care in the old, poor, border areas. After 1998, Hebei province gradually applied this standardized and transparent distribution method to all special social development transfer payments.

(2) Implement the fiscal policy of "grasping both ends, taking the middle, and giving classified guidance"

In 2005, Hebei province reformed the transfer payment system of cities and counties. Starting from the year when the province was in charge of counties, the financial policy of "grasping both ends, taking the middle and giving classified guidance" was implemented for 148 cities (districts) and counties (cities) in the whole province. Specifically it is:

① "Hundred million Yuan county step up" incentive policy. "Hundred million Yuan county step up" policy is to encourage fiscal revenue counties (cities) to grasp the income, step up the incentive policy. The basic idea is: reward developed counties with small money, as a return for big money. Starting from that year, the county (city) with the first hundred million Yuan of local fiscal revenue will be given a one-time reward of 300,000 Yuan. After that, it will take 30 million Yuan as a step every year, and 200,000 Yuan for each step.

② "Two guarantees and two links" subsidy and incentive policy. The "two guarantees and two links" policy is a fiscal policy that combines incentives and constraints and encourages poor counties, economically underdeveloped cities and counties (cities) to increase income, reduce expenditure and guarantee balance, aiming to solve the problem of "food". From that year on, the province implemented a fiscal policy of "two guarantees and two links" for 70 counties (cities). It has stipulated that these counties (cities) under the premise of ensuring the fiscal balance of the year and completing the task of digestion of accumulated deficit over the years (two guarantees), the system subsidies and rewards of provincial finance are linked to the growth of local fiscal revenue (two links). The specific measures are as follows: based on the actual performance of subsidies and local fiscal revenue of these counties (cities) in the current year, for every 1 percentage point increase in local fiscal revenue from the next year, provincial subsidies will increase by 0.5 percentage point. Every time local income increases 1 million Yuan, provincial finance one-time reward is 50,000 Yuan. The first round of implementation will take three years. Three years later, on this basis and in accordance with the principle of "major stability and minor adjustment, neither flogging fast cattle nor encouraging backwardness", the policy of "two guarantees and two suspensions" was appropriately adjusted, and the implementation period was extended to a fixed five years. At the same time of implementing the subsidy and incentive policy of "two guarantees and two links", from that year on, for cities, counties (cities) with "two guarantees and two links", provincial finance implemented technical reform discount subsidy policy for the financial resources construction in order to support these cities, counties (cities) to vigorously develop the economy, open up, conserve financial resources.

③ The subsidy and incentive policy of "two guarantees and two connections". In order to encourage the economic development and the more developed cities and counties (cities) to do a good job in increasing income, saving expenditure and ensuring balance, from that year, the province has implemented the "two guarantees and two connections" policy to the cities and counties (cities) outside the "two guarantees and two links" policy, which is a combination of incentives and constraints. For these cities, counties (cities), on the premise of ensuring the fiscal balance of the current year and completing the task of digesting accumulated deficits over the years, the technical reform subsidies and rewards of provincial finance are related to the increase in the revenue of the local financial system over the previous year (month-on-month). The related ratios of subsidies and rewards for technical reform are: 11% and 4% for the annual local fiscal revenue of prefecture-level cities and some counties (cities) over 200 million Yuan. In other words, the increase of municipal and county (city) local fiscal revenue was paid (month-on-month) 1 million Yuan, and the provincial finance gave a technical reform subsidy of 110,000 Yuan and a reward of 40,000 Yuan; 10% and 5% for other counties (cities). In other words, the increase of municipal and county (city) local fiscal revenue was paid 1 million Yuan, and the provincial finance gave a technical reform subsidy of 100,000 Yuan and a reward of 50,000 Yuan; Three years later, provincial finance appropriately increased the linkage of the policy of "two guarantees and two connections" by 5 percentage points as subsidies for technological upgrading, so as to increase the investment of governments at all levels in technological upgrading.

④ The subsidy policy of "three guarantees and three links". In order to support the development of regional central cities, accelerate the urbanization process, promote the coordinated development of regional economy, and strengthen the distribution function of central cities. From the year when the province was in charge of the county, the province implemented the financial policy of "three guarantees and three links)" for 11 cities above prefecture-level. Six cities, namely Shijiazhuang, Tangshan, Langfang, Baoding, Cangzhou and Handan implemented the policy of "three guarantees and three links". Namely, on the basis of "two guarantees and two links", add "one guarantee and one link": guarantee that the fiscal revenue and expenditure of the counties (cities) under the jurisdiction are balanced in that year and urban construction subsidies (including municipal management and county funds) are linked. The link ratio is 25% (5 percentage points) of 20% (month-on-month) of the city-wide income increase in the province. For Zhangjiakou, Chengde, Qinhuangdao, Hengshui, Xingtai, implemented the policy of "three guarantees and three linksangers", that is, on the basis of "two guarantees and two links", add "one guarantee and one link": guarantee that the fiscal revenue and expenditure of the counties (cities) under the jurisdiction are balanced in that year and urban construction subsidies (including municipal management and county funds) are linked. The link ratio is 25% (5 percentage points) of 20% (month-on-month) of the city-wide income increase in the province.

(2) Analysis of basic financial support of Zhejiang province

Zhejiang region is small, many counties (cities) are developed in economy, county (city) fiscal revenue accounts for 70% of the total fiscal revenue of the province, and the status of prefecture-level city in the province's economy is not as important as other provinces (districts, cities). These characteristics determine that the system of "direct provincial administration of counties" is effective in Zhejiang. Zhejiang province's "direct administration of counties" financial system has achieved the most remarkable results. Its reform has improved the efficiency and level of provincial financial management and promoted the county economy from "fast walking" to "fast running". The experience of this province is worth summarizing and spreading on a large scale. Zhejiang has long been implementing the system of direct provincial control over county finance. The finance of the city (prefecture) and the finance of the county (city) are both directly linked to the provincial system. The municipal (prefecture) level does not have an institutional settlement relationship with the county (city) or the county (city) under its jurisdiction. The main methods are as follows: first, in the financial system, the budgetary funds are settled by the provincial finance and county finance, and the various off-budget "fees" are settled by the provincial and municipal finance; Second, in terms of policy communication and business guidance, the municipal bureau of finance still has an administrative superior and subordinate relationship with the county bureau of finance. In order to encourage the strong counties and help the weak counties, the provincial finance has established the policy of "grasping both ends, taking the middle and guiding by classification", that is to say, different types of policies should be implemented and no one size fits all. Since 1995, after years of exploration, a formulaic, institutionalized, transparent and highly anticipated distribution system has been gradually formed, which is accepted by most cities and counties. That is to say, financial management incentives and constraints combined with the "two guarantees and two links", "two guarantees and one link", "one hundred million Yuan county step up", "two guarantees and two connections" and "three guarantees and three links" policy, put county finance and municipal finance on an equal footing, without discrimination.

Under the premise of determining the fiscal revenue base of cities and counties (cities), Zhejiang province, based on the actual situation, adopts standardized measures such as industry tax categories and proportional sharing to further clarify the sources of government revenue of provinces, cities and counties (cities), and clearly divides them. At the same time, it implements the fiscal policies of "two guarantees and two links" and "two guarantees and one link". The system and policy adjustment does not involve Ningbo city and its counties (cities), and has been implemented since January 1, 2003.

1. Division of powers below the provincial level

Provincial level: provincial administrative management fee, expenditure for public inspection and law enforcement, some funds for armed police, operating expenses for militia, capital construction investment coordinated by the province, technical transformation and trial production of new products of provincial enterprises, and agricultural support expenditure arranged by the provincial finance. Cultural, educational, health, scientific and other operating expenses, price subsidy expenditure and other expenditures borne by the province.

City and county level: city and county administrative management fees, expenditures for public inspection and law enforcement, funds for armed police, funds for technical transformation and trial production of new products of city and county enterprises, expenditures for supporting agriculture, urban maintenance and construction, city and county culture, education, health, science and other operating expenses, price subsidies and other expenditures.

2. Income division

(1) Revenue base and division

The revenue base is based on the 2002 municipal and county (city) fiscal revenue final accounts, which are determined after adjustment the upper and lower levels of income. The upper and lower income shall be based on the actual amount of the income paid into the Treasury in 2002. The amount handed in by the city or county (city) to the provincial finance department or the subsidy provided by the provincial finance department to the city or county (city) shall be accordingly adjusted.

Provincial income: the local share of value-added tax and enterprise income tax paid by electric power enterprises (excluding small hydropower enterprises operated by cities, counties and below), and the local share of the provincial interest income tax on savings deposits, local share of business tax and enterprise income tax paid by provincial Banks, insurance, securities and other non-bank financial enterprises (excluding bank of communications, urban commercial Banks and urban and rural credit cooperatives), provincial income sharing with Hangzhou city, local share of Trans-regional operation and centralized payment of income tax (the income share of cities and counties according to the investment proportion shall be returned by the provincial financial settlement at the end of the year), provincial non-tax income and all kinds of fund income.

Income at city and county level: In addition to the central and provincial income, including city, county (city) enterprise value-added tax, enterprise income tax, individual income tax local share, business tax, urban maintenance and construction tax, agricultural tax and deed tax; each kind of non-tax income and each kind of fund income of city, county (city).

(2) Tax revenue sharing method

Fixed delivery: the delivery under the original municipal and county (city) system and the delivery under the provincial tax distribution system shall be fixed based on the 2002 final accounts. Incremental share: the incremental portion of the fiscal revenue of Hangzhou and other cities, counties (cities) that exceeds the 2002 annual revenue base after 2002. Province and city, county (city) implement "2:8" share, namely 20% for province, 80% for city and county (city). We will continue to give proper care to a small number of poverty-stricken and island counties. Tax refund: The central "two taxes" tax return and income tax return shall be implemented in accordance with the original measures. Share of total amount: the provincial income directly collected by the province and collected by Hangzhou on behalf of Hangzhou city (excluding the local share of value-added tax, business tax, income tax and interest tax on savings deposits paid by the electric power, financial industry and trans-regional operation, and all non-tax income and all kinds of fund income) shall be merged into Hangzhou city, which are collected and managed by Hangzhou tax authorities. The province and Hangzhou city shall share the total income according to their respective share in 2002.

3. Transfer payment system

(1) The subsidy and incentive policy of "two guarantees and two links"

The former "two guarantees and two links" subsidies and incentives, "two guarantees and two links" financial construction technology discount subsidies, "three guarantees and three links" urbanization special subsidies and other policies are integrated and merged into "two guarantees and two links" subsidies and incentives, the scope of application is the

30 cities, counties (cities) that originally implemented "two guarantees and two links".

(2) Incentive policy of "two guarantees and one link"

The former "two insurances and two connections" technical reform subsidies and incentives, "hundred million Yuan county step" incentives, "three insurances and three connections" special subsidies for urbanization policy are integrated and merged into the "two insurances and one link" incentive policy, the scope of application is 33 cities and counties (cities) that originally implemented "two guarantees and two links". For "two guarantees and one link" cities and counties (cities), under the premise of "ensuring that the fiscal revenue and expenditure of the current year are balanced and the responsibilities and tasks of the government are fulfilled", the method of linking the provincial reward with the increase of local fiscal revenue shall be implemented. Specifically: Cities and counties (cities) shall be rewarded according to a certain proportion of the increase in local fiscal revenue over the previous year (quarter-on-quarter). Provincial rewards are divided into two parts: development funds and individual rewards. For Hangzhou, Wenzhou, Jiaxing, Huzhou, Shaoxing and Taizhou, calculate the linked increase of local fiscal revenue, the linked proportion is 5% of the increase, of which 4.5% is used for development funds and 0.5% for personal rewards. For 27 counties (cities), calculate the linked increase of local fiscal revenue of the counties(cities), the linked proportion is 5% of the increase, of which 4% is used for development funds and 1% for personal rewards.

(3) Fixed subsidies

In order to standardize the system settlement and simplify procedures, from 2003 onwards, "third generation" commission and other original single settlement system projects and subsidies calculated by "two guarantees and two links" through Special increase in financial resources in 2001 shall be fixed subsidies based on the 2002 final accounts. We will maintain the policy of increasing urban maintenance and construction taxes, paying taxes and returning subsidies. For the "two guarantees and two links" and "two guarantees and one link" personal incentive funds of the provincial financial subsidies, cities and counties (cities) should strictly control, and the amount of rewards should not be too high. They should make overall arrangements, pay attention to balance, be cautious before and after, and make up for possible shortages with surpluses. At the same time, standardized management and use methods should be established.

4. Transfer payment measures for the reform of rural taxes and fees

In order to ensure the normal operation of rural grass-roots political power antions after the reform of rural taxes and fees, and to ensure the development of rural social undertakings, we shall give overall consideration to the reduction factors of various cities and counties, such as the abolition of township planning fees, the adjustment of taxes on special agricultural products, and the abolition of slaughterhouse taxes. For most of the cities and counties with the net reduction part, the provincial finance shall give appropriate subsidies through transfer payments. After All factors are taken into consideration, after the reform of rural taxes and fees, the provincial transfer payments to cities and counties can be divided into five categories. (the funds needed for the reform of taxes and fees in rural areas of Ningbo city listed separately in the plan shall be raised by Ningbo city, except the transfer funds allocated by the central finance of the province. For the convenience of classification, the classification here includes Ningbo city).

The first category includes 24 economically underdeveloped cities and counties (Qujiang District is incorporated into Quzhou City) and 4 island cities and counties (Zhoushan City, Daishan County, Shengsi County and Dongtou County), with the transfer payment coefficient of 1. The second category is the other two "two guarantees and two links" cities and counties (Jinhua City and Anji County) besides the first category. The transfer payment coefficient is 0.6. In the third category, except for the 30 cities and counties in the first and second categories mentioned above, 8 cities and counties that are given national adjustment wage transfer payment subsidies by the province, namely Tonglu

County, Lin 'an city, Jiande City, Changxing County, Lanxi City, Pujiang County, Pingyang County and Linhai City. The transfer payment coefficient is 0.5. The fourth category is the other 17 general cities and counties, and the transfer payment coefficient is 0.2. The fifth category is economically developed Hangzhou City (including Xiaoshan District and Yuhang District), Ningbo City (including Yinzhou District), Jiaxing City, Huzhou City, Shaoxing City, Wenzhou City, Taizhou City and Shaoxing County, Yueqing City, Ruian City, Yiwu City, Wenling City, Cixi City and Yuyao City. The transfer payment coefficient is 0.

The provincial transfer payment to the cities and counties consists of three parts: the cancellation of the transfer payment to the townships, the adjustment of the transfer payment to the special agricultural taxes and the cancellation of the transfer payment to the slaughterhouses.

According to the 1998 statistics on the number of students in rural primary and secondary schools, the number of women of child-bearing age in rural areas, the number of disabled, demobilized, ex-servicemen and families of martyrs in rural areas, the training tasks of primary and secondary militia, militia emergency contingents and reserve troops in rural areas, as well as geographical areas, after calculating the transfer payment of funds for running primary and secondary schools in rural areas, the transfer payment of funds for family planning, preferential treatment, militia training and rural road construction, the transfer payment amount of rural planning fees is calculated and determined according to the provincial classification transfer payment coefficient.

The adjustment of transfer payment of special agricultural tax mainly considers the transfer payment after the reform of rural taxes and fees due to the adjustment of the impact of special agricultural tax on local finance. The amount of transfer payment for special agricultural taxes shall be adjusted according to the actual number of tax collection on special agricultural taxes of each city and county in 2000, which shall be calculated and determined by multiplying by the coefficient of transfer payment.

The abolition of slaughterhouse tax transfer payment mainly considers the effect of the abolition of slaughterhouse tax on local finance after the reform of rural taxes and fees. The amount of slaughter tax transfer payment shall be calculated according to the number of slaughter tax receipts of each city and county in 2000 and multiplied by the coefficient of transfer payment.

In addition to provincial financial transfer payments, all localities must, in accordance with the relevant provisions of the rural tax and fee reform plan, give comprehensive consideration to the socio-economic development level and financial situation of cities, counties and towns, improve the financial system of townships and towns, adjust the structure of expenditures, allocate a certain amount of funds from the financial resources of their respective levels, increase subsidies to townships and towns, and ensure the normal operation of community-level political power and organizations and the development of family planning and other undertakings. The expenditure necessary for rural compulsory education, in particular, must be budgeted in full and no gaps left. At the same time, necessary measures will be taken to streamline institutions and reduce expenditures.

(3) Basic evaluation

(1) According to the principle of "no offside, no vacancy", redefine the scope of responsibility of finance, and make key breakthroughs and innovations in the financial system below the provincial level. Take "people-oriented, achieve the great with doing little, establish the financial management new mechanism" as the fundamental financial management thought, take "grasp both ends, take the middle, and guide by classification" the basic fiscal policy, take "return finance to the government, empower the system, establish a new order of public finance" as a measure to guarantee and focus on exploring new ideas of reform from practice and theory.

(2) Implement the financial management model of province administrating county according to local conditions. At present, there are four levels of governments below the provincial level, which cannot fully divide revenues by tax categories, but can only follow the situation of increasing revenue sharing tax system and fiscal system. In order to coordinate the administrative and financial powers of grass-roots governments under the framework of rationalization and

legalization, and to further resolve the financial difficulties of counties and townships, we should implement the fiscal system in which the provincial finance directly controls the county finance.
(3) Fiscal reform and innovation should be based on local conditions, and different types of policies should be implemented, rather than one size fits all. For example, Zhejiang province implements a formulaic, institutionalized, open and transparent distribution system with strong expectations. That is to say, financial management incentives and constraints combined with the "two guarantees and two links", "two guarantees and one link", "one hundred million Yuan county step up", "two guarantees and two links" and "three guarantees and three links" policy, put county finance and municipal finance on an equal footing, without discrimination.
(4) Financial reform must put people first. The formulation of financial policies and the design of systems should follow the people-oriented thought of financial management, give full consideration to human factors, and consider the interests of individuals, units and groups in different regions and departments, so as to maximize the enthusiasm of all aspects and effectively deal with multi-angle economic interests.

4.2 Improve the Budget Management System and the Government Budget Management System

Modern government budget system is the foundation of modern financial system. Scientific and complete budget preparation, standardized and effective budget implementation, and open and transparent budget supervision, which are organically linked and balanced, are the core contents of modern budget management system. China has a unified budget system, which aims to provide a single window of guidance for all government departments' budget work in accordance with unified regulations. However, it should be noted that after years of reform, the government budget system is still lack of comprehensiveness, which weakens the role of budget constraint and control to some extent. In addition to the incomplete government budget system, only annual budgets are prepared, making it impossible to link the government's development plans with the budget. At the same time, a cash-based breakdown of the budget method is used to provide relevant data on current revenues and expenditures. However, these figures do not tell the whole story of capital financing and capital expenditure, nor do they tell the whole story of public service provision. For these reasons, it is equally urgent that the system of evaluation and reporting of government budget performance be further improved. The key points of establishing a budget management system suitable for modern financial system are as follows: We will establish a transparent budget system with the focus on promoting budget openness. We will improve the government budget system, and study ways and means to link key expenditures to the growth of government revenue and expenditure or to GDP. Improve the annual budget control method and establish a multi-year budget balance mechanism; Improve the system of Treasury receipts and payments; strengthen budget implementation and comprehensively promote budget performance management.

Continue to Deepen Reform of the Full Bore Budget Management

The ultimate goal of the reform of full-calibèr budget management is to build a full-caliber government budget system with the budget of public finance as the basic basis and the budget of government-managed funds, the budget of state capital operation and the budget of social insurance funds as the auxiliary. As a result, People's congresses at all levels, as legislative bodies, exercising legislative control over all government revenue and expenditure activities at the same level is realized. This means that all government revenues and expenditures should be authorized by the legislature, and only with such authorization can government activities and their corresponding revenues and expenditures have legitimacy.

The main content of the reform of full-caliber budget management is embodied in the following aspects: first, to build the foundation of full-caliber budget management, the financial department is in charge of all government revenues and expenditures. The basis of full-caliber budget management is to form a budget management system in which the financial departments take charge of government revenues and expenditures and the relevant budget units actively cooperate. All government revenue and expenditure activities should be brought into the management and supervision vision of the financial department, and all kinds of government revenue and expenditure should be distributed on the platform of the full-diameter budget system, so as to eliminate partial interests with the overall interests. Budget units can only arrange revenue and expenditure through the platform of the full-caliber budget system, cut off the direct link between the administrative performance of budget units and their funds allocation, so as to truly form a complete government revenue and expenditure management system in which the financial department takes charge of government revenue and expenditure, and the allocation of government funds must go through the budget arrangement. Second, establish the overall planning and approval mechanism among various budgets. We will further explore ways to organically link budgets for public finance, government-managed funds, state capital operations and social insurance funds. For government-managed funds with stable revenue, they can be gradually incorporated into the budget management of public finance. The state capital operation budget should transfer more revenue into the public finance budget, and the financial link with the social insurance fund budget can only be through the public finance budget. Starting from the integrity of the budget, each sub-budget should be unified in the big plate of the government budget to form a specific and total government budget to let people's congresses, the government (finance) and members of the general public truly understand the specific conditions of each sub-budget, ensure that government funds are used in a coordinated way, and work to control the total budget of people's congresses. In addition, we should further explore the operating income budgeting system of state-owned enterprises with Chinese characteristics. Third, we will further improve the classification of government revenue and expenditure. Adjust the specific revenue and expenditure items of each budget under the full-caliber budget management system, so as to form an organic connection between each budget and realize the interconnection of each budget in terms of revenue and expenditure through related items. Fourth, promote fiscal unity within the government. In accordance with the basic rules of the market economy and prevailing international norms, we will gradually put all matters concerning government revenues and expenditures under the unified management of financial departments, and prohibit other government departments from directly carrying out financial distribution activities to enterprises and residents.

The reform of full-caliber budget management involves the most basic power distribution pattern of the country, and the final situation of this power distribution pattern is not only closely related to the political system, but also greatly influenced by history and tradition. China is a unitary country with a tradition of centralization, and a large developing country in the process of transition. The reform of budget management with full scope should be carried out in accordance with the above-mentioned national conditions and in accordance with the principle of starting with the easy ones and then advancing them in stages. The reform path can be divided into three stages.

The first stage: at the level of administrative control, all kinds of revenue and expenditure of government departments shall be brought into the scope of supervision and management of financial departments through the preparation of departmental budget, so as to realize the full scope of budget management of government revenue and expenditure and submit it to the people's congresses at the same level for deliberation.

The second stage: according to the actual situation of different levels of governments, further improve the budget of state capital operation and social insurance fund, and establish a standardized, clear and transparent capital transaction between various sub-budgets dominated by public finance budget. The realization of this goal largely depends on the adjustment of social insurance fund budget. The state capital operation budget depends on its coverage and whether the state capital income distribution system is finally established.

Stage 3: when conditions are ripe, the NPC is responsible for comprehensively reviewing the various government-managed funds and administrative fees charged by central government departments and institutions, and consolidating the number of funds and fees and reducing the number of funds and fees. What is suitable for changing fees to taxes should be converted into taxes. The ultimate goal is to abolish the power of central ministries and commissions to set up funds and charge administrative fees. At the same time, the provincial people's congresses should be responsible for comprehensively examining the administrative institutional fee collection projects approved by the provincial people's governments, and transferring the power of the local governments to the local legislatures.

Improve the Annual Budget Control Method and Establish a Cross-annual Budget Balance Mechanism

The establishment of multi-year budget is a more scientific compilation mode, which is conducive to forethought, comprehensive balance and overall coordination, and is essentially a reflection of the establishment of dynamic budget requirements. China's current budget is a one-year budget (that is, the budget from January 1 to December 31 of the current year), but some expenditures are multi-year and rolling. Therefore, in order to better reflect the management requirements, the preparation of rolling budget, medium and long-term budget or multi-year budget can make the arrangement of expenditure more long-term and systematic, and can also avoid the failure to use up the expenditure arranged at once or the addition of budget to the budget.

The establishment of the multi-year budget balance mechanism is an important improvement in budget preparation, which is not only an important means to prevent and control financial risks, but also a better link between fiscal revenue and expenditure and government planning. At present, the government's five-year plan should be aligned with the budget. We need to optimize government planning through the mechanism of balancing budgets across fiscal years. That is to say, government planning should be based on revenue projections and be planned according to revenue conditions.

The multi-year budget balance mechanism has improved and strengthened the role of fiscal policy in macroeconomic stability. The impact of fiscal policy on the economy cannot be fully shown in the annual budget. Macroeconomic regulation requires fiscal policy to be flexible, sometimes with deficits, but balanced over a period of time.

We will establish a multi-year budget balance mechanism, shift the focus of annual budget review from the balance of revenue and expenditure to expenditure policies, and change the revenue budget from tasks to expectations. The balance of payments determined by the budget may be broken in the course of implementation. In order to ensure fiscal sustainability, it is necessary to establish a multi-year budget balance mechanism. On the other hand, we should establish a mechanism for scientific argumentation of major issues in the medium and long term. We should not make certain policies for major projects in a single year, but take a long-term view. By implementing medium-term fiscal planning and management, we should strengthen their binding on the annual budget, and make fiscal policies more forward-looking and fiscally sustainable. Some regions have already experimented with cross-year budget balancing schemes. It is reported that the current Hebei Province and Henan Jiaozuo city, have adopted a medium-term rolling budget. In view of the actual situation, a simplified version can be adopted at present. For example, the term can be three years. In terms of projects, we can first try budget for investment projects, social security projects and contingent liabilities projects. On this basis, the extension of rolling period and expansion of project scope may be considered in the future. Gradual thinking can also be applied in the scope of promotion. For example, it can start from a certain department, or start from a certain region, gradually expand and carry out gradual progress.

Vigorously Promote Budget Openness and Establish a Transparent Budgeting System

Budget disclosure is the essential requirement of public finance and an important content of government information disclosure. In essence, budget openness is the transparency of government behavior, the need to build a sunshine and responsible government, and the need to administer according to law and guard against financial risks. Promoting budget openness is an important measure to ensure the people's right to know, to participate and to supervise. It is conducive to arousing the people's enthusiasm to participate in social management, strengthening efforts to combat corruption and build a clean government, and enhancing the government's credibility and execution. Drawing on international experience, proceeding from China's actual situation, and following the requirements of "improving openness in party affairs, government affairs and judicial affairs" in the report to the 18th national congress of the CPC, we will pay attention to top-level design, specify implementation steps, and actively yet prudently promote budget openness. We will gradually expand the scope of openness, refine its contents, constantly improve the working mechanism for budget disclosure, strengthen oversight and inspection of budget disclosure, and gradually implement a comprehensive and standardized system for budget disclosure. The newly revised *Budget Law* provides for the first time comprehensive provisions on "budget disclosure". Article 14 sets clear and specific requirements on the scope, subject and time limit of disclosure, explains the requirements for disclosure of transfer payments, government debts, operating expenses of government organs and other matters of great concern to the society, and stipulates the legal liability for violation of budget disclosure standards in article 92. First, we will further refine budget formulation, make it more accurate and scientific, strictly implement budgets, improve the system of budgetary expenditure standards, and vigorously promote performance evaluation, thus laying a solid foundation for budget disclosure. Second, we will further increase the transparency of the government's regular budget, strengthen budgetary management of departmental projects, and fully disclose the use of funds used in project expenditures. In accordance with the main principle of departmental budget disclosure, we will actively promote departmental budget disclosure. All matters that should and can be disclosed according to the *Regulations on the Disclosure of Government Information* should be disclosed in a timely and voluntary manner. We will further refine the release of government budgets and final accounts, and expand the scope and content of the release of departmental budgets and final accounts.

With the exception of confidential information, all central and local departments that use government funds should release their budgets and final accounts. Third, we will urge provincial-level financial departments to further make budgetary information available on their own initiative, fully and completely disclose budgetary information at their level, and strengthen guidance for budget disclosure by lower-level financial departments. Fourth, we will closely follow the progress of the work of making budgets public in various localities and departments, actively study new problems and developments in making budgets public, collect public feedback, guide public opinion, and further improve the work of making budgets public. Fifth, we will push forward the reform of government accounting and gradually establish a government financial reporting system. According to the requirements of the third plenary session of the 18th CPC central committee on "establishing an accrual-based government financial reporting system", the *New Budget Law* in the supplementary provisions puts forward the explicit requirements for governments at all levels to prepare comprehensive government financial reports based on accrual-based accounting on an annual basis. Government financial report, as a comprehensive annual report that comprehensively reflects the government's financial status, operation status and fiscal medium and long-term sustainability, is the stock of government financial situation. It will coordinate with the budget report to jointly reflect the government's performance of various functions and financial performance. The principle provisions of the *New Budget Law* point out the direction for governments at all levels to establish comprehensive government financial reporting system in the future.

Clear Up and Standardize the Linkage Mechanism, and Optimize the Allocation Structure of Fiscal Funds

At present, China's key expenditures linked to the growth of fiscal revenue and expenditure or GDP involve seven categories (education, science and technology, agriculture, culture, medical and health care, social security, family planning, etc.) and 15 regulations. In 2013, such funds accounted for 47.4% of the national fiscal expenditure. As stipulated in *Agricultural Law*, agricultural input takes the proportion of fiscal expenditure in that year cannot be under last year, and reach 15% above step by step; The *Education Law* stipulated that the proportion of education input should be higher than the regular income growth, and later stipulated that the financial educational expenditure should reach 4% of GDP.

The mechanism of linking expenditures has played a positive role in promoting the development of the above-mentioned fields at a specific stage of development, but it also inevitably leads to the solidification and rigidity of the structure of fiscal expenditure, dismembers the budgetary arrangements of governments at all levels, and makes it more difficult for the government to coordinate financial resources. Moreover, it is not in line with the development law of social undertakings, which is easy to cause comparison, and even causes problems such as "two skins", "fund is available but project is not", and "careless spending" of financial input and career development in some fields. This is also the main cause of excessive special transfer payments, budget management cannot be fully disclosed, repeated and inefficient funding.

The *Decision of the Central Committee of the Communist Party of China on Several Major Issues Concerning Comprehensively Deepening Reform* adopted at the third plenary session of the 18th central committee of the communist party of China clearly stipulates that " We will review and standardize the way in which key expenditures are linked to the growth of government revenue and expenditure or to the GDP. Generally, such way of linking is not adopted". The newly revised *Budget Law* has deleted provisions concerning legal expenditures in budget review and implementation, and stressed that in the compilation of general public budget expenditures at all levels, all key expenditures determined by the state should be given priority under the principle of overall consideration and on the premise of ensuring reasonable needs for basic public services.

By reviewing and standardizing the linkage mechanism, we will avoid the formation of a rigid mechanism for fiscal expenditure, improve our ability to coordinate budgets, and make fiscal input more targeted, effective, and sustainable, while continuing to give priority to and ensure the priority of relevant areas.

Further Improve the Treasury Payment System and Treasury Cash Management System

We will continue to improve the centralized Treasury payment system, straighten out the treasury management system, and explore a mechanism for coordinating treasury cash management with treasury bond management. In 2001, we began to reform the treasury management system and introduced it to local governments. The primary goal of the reform of centralized treasury collection and payment is to eliminate the disadvantages of the traditional Treasury, such as the scattered receipt and payment of funds, low operational efficiency and use efficiency, and low transparency so that all the unpaid financial funds are kept in a single account of the national treasury and unified to the national treasury management, so as to realize the effective control of the financial department over the government's cash flow. Up to now, a modern treasury management system has been basically established based on the single account system of the treasury and the centralized collection and payment system of the treasury. In the future, we should continue to deepen the reform of the centralized Treasury collection and payment system, strengthen the control over the expenditure of all fiscal funds, including special transfer payments, and develop the centralized Treasury collection and payment system with a single account into "horizontal to border and vertical to the bottom". By implementing the standard single account system for national Treasury, it can not only reduce the links of government funds receipt and payment, simplify the business process, facilitate accounting and verification, but also effectively avoid capital risks and improve the efficiency of capital operation.

With the great progress of the centralized collection and payment system reform of the single account Treasury, the Treasury funds with high inventory provide a huge operating space for Treasury cash management. But in the actual operation, it must be done step by step, not only to ensure the need for financial payment and the safety of Treasury funds, but also to face up to the possible policy disturbance of Treasury cash management. Further improve the Treasury cash management system, establish the Treasury cash income and expenditure basic database, explore the technical method of accurately predicting the cash income and expenditure flow and cash balance of the state Treasury, determine the minimum Treasury cash balance. We will further improve the cash management system of the central Treasury step by step, and encourage the development of the cash management system of local Treasury on the basis of pilot projects in six provinces and cities. Explore the coordination mechanism between Treasury cash management and Treasury bond management, strengthen the flexible use and management of short-term investment and financing tools of the central Treasury, improve the use of Treasury bond repurchase and reverse repurchase investment tools, and increase the issuance of short-term Treasury bills and other financing methods.

Strengthen Budget Implementation Management and Actively Promote Budget Performance Management

Financial funds are the material basis and institutional guarantee for the government to perform its duties. However, due to the influence of traditional budget management, the problem of "focus more on input, focus less on management, focus more on use and focus less on performance" still exists to a large extent in China's budget management. Performance budget is a new trend in the development of budget system. It can effectively improve the efficiency of the use of government budget funds, improve the openness and transparency of the budget. At present, many countries in the world have been integrated into the reform wave of performance budget. Realizing the "Chinese dream" is a beautiful vision of China's future development, and the "Chinese dream" in the field of budget is to establish an open, transparent, scientific and efficient budget management model. In order to achieve this goal, the implementation of performance budget reform will be an overall direction.

At present, China is constantly promoting the reform of budget performance management. In some fields and departments, our country has carried on the practice exploration and the attempt, has obtained certain result, has initially established the performance management idea, has gradually established the budget reform related system, and has carried on the technical appraisal index improvement and the information system consummation. However, there is still a big gap between the requirements of performance budget. Currently, China's performance budget reform is faced with such practical problems as unreasonable budgeting system, imperfect performance evaluation index system, backward information means of performance reform and imperfect supervision mechanism.

The third plenary session of the 18th CPC central committee put forward the requirement of strengthening government performance management. By 2020, we will comprehensively promote budget performance management and substantially improve fiscal management. To this end, the first is to establish a budget performance management mechanism. Set up the performance concept of "money needs to be asked for effect, and invalidity needs to be held accountable", and establish the whole-process budget performance management mechanism of "budget preparation has target, budget implementation has monitoring, budget completion has evaluation, evaluation results have feedback, and feedback results have application". Second, we will improve the budget performance management system. We will strengthen the construction of laws and regulations on budget performance management, and establish a management system that covers all aspects of performance objectives, performance monitoring, performance evaluation and application of results, improve the systems for budgeting units' final accounts, asset allocation standards, and departmental project expenditure standards, improve the working procedures and operating rules of performance management, clarify the responsibilities and quality requirements of performance management, and standardize the implementation of budget performance management. Third, we will carry out pilot projects to manage budgetary performance. We will strengthen performance target management, increase performance monitoring management, strengthen the collection and analysis of performance information, promote performance evaluation management, improve the application management of evaluation results, establish a mechanism for improving performance reporting, feedback and rectification, as well as an organic combination with budgetary arrangements, promote disclosure of performance information, and gradually establish a performance accountability mechanism. In the near future, people's livelihood projects and major projects with great economic and social impact should be taken as the focus of performance evaluation. Fourth, we will strengthen the basis of budget performance management. We will strengthen research on the performance evaluation index system, further improve the scientificity and rationality of the index setting, accelerate research on the budget performance management information system, improve the construction of expert database, intermediary database, index database, standard database and other databases, increase training efforts, and improve comprehensive quality.

We will actively promote the reform of the accrual basis government accounting system. Government accounting is the basis of budget management. Government accounting not only records and reflects the income and expenditure of budget funds, but also provides the current situation and historical information of the operation of government budget funds. It should also provide information on the government's financial position, including the flow of budgetary funds for the year, as well as information on the government's assets and liabilities. The government accounting reform based on accrual basis can provide more comprehensive and abundant budget accounting and financial accounting information for budget management, which reflects the government assets, liabilities, income, expenses and other relevant information comprehensively, and provides detailed basic information for the scientific calculation of the government's future operating costs, accurate preparation of medium-term financial planning and future medium-term budget, and speeds up the process of performance budget management.

Accelerate the Construction of an Information System for Fiscal Revenues and Expenditures

The establishment of financial information construction is an objective requirement to establish a standardized and orderly modern financial system, and an important technical guarantee to comprehensively deepen the reform of fiscal and taxation systems and strengthen fiscal and taxation management. Since the beginning of 2002, China decided to name the "government financial management information system" planned and established by the ministry of finance as "Golden Finance Project", "Golden Finance Project" has become the main target of the informatization construction of China's financial industry. "Golden Finance Project" is a comprehensive government financial management information system that uses advanced information network technology to support the core business of budget management, centralized collection and payment of the national Treasury and financial and economic prosperity forecast.

However, due to various reasons, a number of independent, closed and independent information application systems have been formed both internally and externally, and the problem of "fragmentation" of information construction exists. The subjects who hold the information still tend to keep the information in the "island state". No one wants to share their "unique value" with other departments. In fact, only by sharing information can scientific and rational decisions be made. For example, the real estate information has not been connected to the Internet and fully reflected, and the information is in a fragmented state. How can we talk about regulating the decision-making and modernization of state governance through the real estate? Now the central government has made it clear that the ministry of land and resources will lead nine ministries and commissions to coordinate the formation of a comprehensive information network for real estate nationwide in 2018, and urban areas should be more advanced. Is the real estate network connected with the acceleration of real estate tax legislation and the subsequent system operation? There is clearly a set of associations in this regard. In order to form an information support platform for scientific policy design and decision-making of public affairs, it is necessary to break down the information barriers of all departments and units and form a more efficient and performance-oriented integrated government regulation and management situation.

We will speed up the establishment of a unified fiscal revenue and expenditure system for finance, state and local taxes, and connect the three information systems. On this basis, a unified and universal system of standardized and unique codes for individuals, enterprises, governments, social institutions and other social and economic entities shall be established. Each department collects basic and original information related to its duties of objects such as land, house, stock, debt and tax corresponding to the above subject, and sets up a professional information system with large concentration and full coverage in the whole country; We will further form a national and comprehensive multilateral sharing platform for legal information, which will share information within limits, constraints and controls.

[Column 3.3]

Local practices:

Information work leading group office of ministry of finance for construction effect and demonstration significance of integrated financial management information system in Fujian Province,:

The second issue of *Golden Engineering Bulletin*, January 27, 2015.

According to the needs of financial management and reform, the finance department of Fujian Province takes golden project construction as the starting point and relies on digital Fujian government affairs network to adhere to the principle of "unified leadership, unified planning, unified technical standards, unified platform and unified organization and implementation". It took three years to build an integrated financial management information system (hereinafter referred to as the integrated system) with unified business standards, safe and reliable system, covering core financial business and radiating financial departments and budget units at all levels. It has achieved initial results, which has a good demonstration significance for improving scientific, standardized and informationized financial management.

(1) Three adherence focus on innovation

In March 2010, Fujian provincial finance department proposed to adopt the "hybrid mode combining access, integration and growth" to coordinate and promote the integration construction.

First, we will adhere to a problem-oriented approach to solving problems in our work. In view of the problems restricting the integration construction, such as overlapping functions of information system, overlapping information repetition and difficulty in data exchange, the department of finance of Fujian province made in-depth research, compiled the *Basic Data Specification of Financial Business of Fujian Province*, and solved the problems of different business system coding and caliber inconsistency. We will upgrade and improve the application support platform, further strengthen its functions in basic data management, information sharing and data exchange, and complete the "multi-year and multi-fiscal" transformation. We shall establish the basic database to uniformly manage the information of financial support units, personnel establishment, salary and other information, avoid multiple collection and data redundancy of the same data, and ensure the integrity and accuracy of basic data.

Second, adhere to the system thinking business system integration and transformation. In accordance with the idea of paying equal attention to closed-loop management and supervision of the core financial business process, based on the application of supporting platform to integrate and reform 6 systems, including budget preparation, indicators and centralized payment of the Treasury, Fujian provincial finance department has developed 11 sub-systems, such as entity fund account monitoring management, budget performance management, project management comparison, etc., and built an integrated system with smooth information and centralized data, covering financial departments, budget units, core financial businesses and financial funds, so as to achieve business operation standardization and data connection and sharing between systems.

Third, we will ensure parallel deployment of systems. In order to facilitate the integration of the system in the city and county to promote the use and management maintenance, Fujian provincial finance department adopts the "centralized" deployment mode of the whole province, which is better to achieve "physic centralization of hardware and logic centralization of software", and establishes the unified operation and maintenance service platform of the whole province, which has effectively alleviated such problems as the weak technical strength of grass-roots personnel and the great pressure of operation and maintenance, saved financial funds and improved work efficiency.

(2) Four enhancements promote improvement.

The integrated system of Fujian province has realized a complete system with budget management as the core and budget indicators as the link, covering budget preparation, budget implementation, feedback of budget implementation results and supervision and evaluation, and the application effect has been gradually manifested.

First, we will strengthen standardized management and make fiscal management more scientific. In the aspect of budget preparation, the system automatically calculates the basic expenditures such as personnel funds and public funds; By controlling the establishment and use of special funds, we will gradually promote the construction of the project database of special funds at the provincial level and the rolling compilation of annual budgets. In terms of budget implementation, the system can grasp the situation of non-tax income in real time, realize the transformation from manual control to automatic control by collecting and spending fixed. Implement electronic management of account opening, alteration and cancellation of budget units.

Second, we will strengthen scientific financial management and improve the use of funds. The subsystem of budget preparation covers all the contents of revenue and expenditure, which enhances the accuracy and completeness of budget preparation; Through each subsystem's mutual restriction, execute budget strictly and strengthen the budget constraint; Carry out implementation analysis of 7 themes, including department budget and bank payment, to further accelerate the implementation of budget; By establishing the budget performance management subsystem covering the whole process of performance management business, we will implement dynamic management of funds in place and expenditures, and improve the efficiency and effectiveness of the use of financial funds.

Third, we will strengthen fiscal oversight and improve the effectiveness of fiscal management. The budget unit can compile and submit the annual budget online through the system, and keep abreast of the review and changes of its annual budget indicators, expenditure plans and fund payment. The financial department can inquire the cause and effect of each expenditure in real time through the system, effectively monitor the operation of financial funds and reduce the factors of human manipulation. The whole process of business handling is managed by "trace", and all the handling information of each business is recorded in detail and can be traced permanently. These measures have put the operation of government funds in the "sunshine" and prevented and curbed corruption at the source.

Fourth, strengthen resource sharing and enhance decision-making ability. Relying on the digital Fujian government affairs network, it integrates the horizontal network of finance, tax and banking, realizes the connection with the provincial population database of the public security department and the data of the people's bank of China, as well as the hierarchical sharing of fiscal and tax policies and macroeconomic indicators of the province. On this basis, it shall carry out project management comparison, which effectively controls repeated declaration; Try to cross-compare the data of departments to prevent the phenomenon of reclaiming, falsely claiming and deceiving financial subsidies, and constantly improve the analysis and utilization level of data resources, so as to provide reference for assisting leaders to make decisions.

(3) Ensuring the implementation of the five measures

The successful operation of the integrated system in Fujian province has accumulated valuable experience and provided useful reference for further financial informatization work.

First is to strengthen leadership. Fujian provincial finance department has established an integrated construction leading group headed by the director of the department, which consists of two working groups: business group and technical group. The leading group of integration construction plans scientifically, puts forward the timetable and road map based on the construction idea, and implements them well to ensure the smooth progress of integration work in an orderly manner.

Second, focus on research. The department of finance of Fujian province went to the grass-roots level to conduct investigation and research, widely soliciting opinions and Suggestions on the integration construction, to get a clear picture of the number, grasp the situation, and find out the crux of the problem, laying a foundation for quickly defining the target and clarifying the key points of work.

Third, take the initiative to consult. Fujian provincial finance department establishes cooperative working mechanism. For the difficult problems encountered in the work, the general integrator puts forward Suggestions and reaches consensus with the developer, and then the integration working group studies and determines the specific solution and establishes weekly meeting system to ensure that the work is efficient and effective implementation.

Fourth, strengthen training. The department of finance of Fujian province organized the training of relevant business and technical personnel at the provincial, municipal and county levels, enabling participants to further understand the construction background, realization concept, functional performance and use method of the integrated system, and improving the operational level and application ability of relevant personnel.

Fifth, steady implementation. According to the idea of "spreading out gradually with points and areas", Fujian provincial finance department promoted the promotion and implementation of integrated system in different levels and steps. At present, the integrated system has been extended and applied to 13 financial units such as provincial level, Sanming City, Ningde City, Longyan City and Youxi County.

[Column 3.4].

Medium-term financial planning: Basic knowledge, local practice and international experience: *Active and Prudent Implementation of Medium-Term Fiscal Planning Management, Research Report of the Institute of Fiscal Science, Ministry of Finance*, no. 5, 2015 (total no. 1836).

Improving budget management and control, implementing the management of medium-term fiscal planning and establishing a multi-year budget balance mechanism are major breakthroughs in the new *Budget Law* and important contents of the *Decision of the State Council on Deepening the Reform of the Budget Management System*. Recently, the state council issued the *Opinions on Implementing the Management of Medium-Term Fiscal Planning*, which plans to accelerate the establishment of a modern fiscal system, improve budget management and control, comprehensively promote the management of medium-term fiscal planning, and study and formulate a three-year rolling fiscal plan. Medium-term financial planning is a profound reform of budget management concept and mode. It is of great significance to the improvement of national governance capacity, the improvement of macro-control to adapt to the new normal of economy, the realization of government governance goals and the budget performance evaluation. To actively yet prudently advance this reform, we need to have a basic understanding of medium-term fiscal planning.

(1) The connotation of the medium-term fiscal plan

The medium-term fiscal plan refers to the multi-year fiscal plan formulated on the basis of determining the medium-term fiscal policy in order to enhance the forward-looking and fiscal sustainability of fiscal policies, according to the needs of national medium and long-term development plan and macro-control. We will implement the management of medium-term fiscal planning, make overall arrangements for policies in some key areas and the government financial resources needed to be used during the planning period, and make annual adjustments and updates in light of changes in the situation, so as to tighten the constraints on the annual budget and improve the ability to coordinate budgets. Medium-term financial planning management includes the following aspects.

1. Scientific forecast of budget revenue and expenditure

According to the economic cycle analysis, forecast the change trend and periodical characteristics of fiscal revenue. According to the choice of expenditure policy, this paper analyzes the change trend of expenditure scale and the periodical characteristics of expenditure structure. Forecast overall revenues and expenditures and overall policies.

2. Mechanism for scientific argumentation of medium-and long-term major issues

Major projects have a long implementation period, and expenditure arrangements must have continuity and consistency. To achieve medium- and long-term budget balance, the key is to have control over major medium-and long-term issues. This requires scientific argumentation of major issues in the medium and long term so as to effectively link up expenditure policies with the selection of major projects.

3. Department rolling expenditure planning

The department rolling expenditure plan is a scientific forecast of the department's career development in the next three years and a rough estimate of the resources needed to achieve the future career development goals. Medium-term fiscal planning and management should be in line with the outline of the national economic and social development plan and the state macro-control policies. The department should consider the career development plan of the future year in advance, and make the medium-term budget plan according to the expenditure limit determined by the ministry of finance, and make dynamic adjustment and rolling management on a regular basis.

4. Medium-term financial planning constraints and guidance of the annual budget

The medium-term financial plan is a rolling financial plan based on the government's medium - and long-term decision-making and activity arrangement, and taking into account the department's career development plan. Medium-term financial planning plays a binding and guiding role in the budget, and the preparation of annual budget must be carried out within the framework of medium-term financial planning.

5. Gradually establish a medium-term budget framework

The medium-term financial planning emphasizes the introduction of the medium-term concept in the financial budget management, so as to link the budget arrangement with the medium and long-term policies of the government, which is in essence the transitional form of the medium-term budget. As medium-term financial planning management matures, it transitions to a true medium-term budget.

(2) Exploring pilot projects for rolling local budgets in the medium term

Since 2009, the ministry of finance has selected Hebei Province, Jiaozuo City of Henan Province and Wuhu County of Anhui Province for pilot exploration of medium-term rolling budget. In recent years, many local governments have actively carried out pilot projects for medium-term budgets. These pilot reforms and explorations have encountered many obstacles and problems in practice. For example, the scope of the pilot is relatively limited, the departments pay insufficient attention to the implementation of the three-year rolling budget, and the promotion of the pilot faces resistance from local governments and departments. However, these pilots have accumulated some experience for the implementation of medium-term financial planning and management. The pilot programs in Jiaozuo in Hebei and Henan Provinces are typical.

In 2008, the Hebei provincial government issued the *Implementation Opinions on Promoting the Preparation of Three-Year Rolling Budgets for Development Expenditures of Provincial Departments*, and began to explore the preparation of three-year rolling budgets for development expenditures. The initial pilot program for 15 provincial-level budgetary departments was gradually promoted. In 2009, it was extended to 42 provincial-level budgetary departments to compile three-year rolling budgets for development expenditures, accounting for more than 70 percent of provincial development expenditures. In 2010, the pilot three-year rolling budget covered all development expenditures at the provincial level, and began to extend to cities and counties. Hebei interim rolling budget pilot main approach can be summarized as three aspects.

(1) Formulate medium and long-term development plans in functional areas of the department. According to the major strategic deployment of the government in a certain period of time and the

medium and long-term plan for the economic and social development of the province, all departments shall study and formulate the medium and long-term plan for their own departments, and define the development goals, investment priorities and expected performance and prepare rolling implementation plans and decomposition targets for three years as the basis and premise for the preparation of three-year rolling budgets for department development expenditures.

(2) Establish a three-year rolling project database of development expenditures. First, carry out careful screening and demonstration of expenditure items. The project selection is required to conform to the major strategic deployment of the provincial party committee and provincial government, the medium and long-term plan for the national economy and social development of the province, and the medium and long-term development plan for the functional areas of the department. Second, standardize the preparation of project budgets. When reporting the project investment and annual budget, each department shall fill in the project budget arrangement of each investment year according to the project implementation years for projects that need to be implemented continuously for many years or annually, and fill in at least three years; For projects that need to be arranged in the next two years, the project budget arrangement in the corresponding year of implementation shall be indicated. In preparing the project budget, the overall and annual performance targets and assessment indicators for three years should be specified, and the final expected effect of the project in the field of economic and social development should also be specified. Third, establish a continuous rolling budget project database. Since the submission of the 2009 budget items, the pilot departments shall submit the contents of the three-year budget items every year, and roll forward year by year. The provincial finance department shall review, appraise or reprove the three-year budget projects of each department every year, and put the projects that meet the requirements into the Treasury of three-year projects respectively.

(3) Formulate a three-year development expenditure proposal plan. Since 2009, all pilot departments, while preparing their annual development expenditure proposals, have compiled and submitted their

development expenditure budget proposals for the next two years in accordance with the required and prescribed formats. The annual cutting limit of all kinds of population development expenditure can be controlled according to 120% of the previous year. Departments should make overall arrangements for development expenditure projects under their respective categories according to the principle of priority and concentration of financial resources in order to accomplish major tasks within the quota, and incorporate major expenditure projects that should be guaranteed within three years into their budget proposal plans, without omission or hard gap. For projects that can be foreseen and should be included in the three-year rolling budget, if it is not included in the department, it will not be arranged in the preparation of the annual budget. The provincial finance department shall examine and summarize the proposed three-year rolling budget of development expenditure reported by the department, and prepare the three-year rolling budget draft of development expenditure of the department, which shall be used as the basis for the department to prepare the budget for the next year upon the approval of the provincial government.

2. Pilot practice of medium-term budget in Jiaozuo City, Henan Province

Jiaozuo city, Henan province began to implement the mid-term budget pilot program in 2009. The pilot program at the initial stage involved 33 departments that were responsible for the heavy central tasks of the municipal party committee and government, responsible for the large expenditure of projects, and had a great impact on the economic and social development of the city in functional areas. Budget items include all projects undertaken by the department of rolling budget to develop the city's economic and social programs and to improve people's livelihood and other key expenditures; Funding sources include general budget revenue, fund budget revenue and debt budget revenue. The pilot of medium - term budget is carried out around 3 link concretely.

(1) Planning. First, we will formulate medium-and long-term fiscal development plans. In accordance with the major strategic arrangements made by the government within a certain period of time and the medium - and long-term plans for the economic and social development of the city, study and formulate medium and long-term plans for the development of economic and social undertakings in the field of financial functions, define development goals and investment priorities, and provide medium and long-term plans for relevant departments, as one of the bases for compiling the medium and long-term plans for the use of municipal financial funds. The draft medium - and long-term financial plan shall be submitted to the ministry of finance for examination and approval to form a formal plan and serve as the basis and premise for preparing a rolling budget. Second, we need to set policy targets for priority development. Feedback to relevant departments by drawing up a list of priority development policy objectives. According to the priority development areas identified in the medium and long term plans, all departments shall determine the annual career development plans and overall arrangement of development expenditures, specify the direction and areas of financial investment, key expenditure projects and performance targets, and submit them to the financial department for approval in the form of project plans.

(2) Evaluation. The financial department shall examine and verify the multi-year rolling budget plan of project expenditure prepared by the department, and summarize and prepare the rolling budget plan of financial project expenditure at the municipal level according to the classification and expenditure subjects, and give the audit opinions to all departments at the same time. Evaluate and demonstrate medium - and long-term budget drafts in accordance with the procedures of expert argumentation and social hearing, discuss the combination and scale of project libraries, and form long-term and long-term fiscal rolling budgets of local governments through adjustment and modification.

(3) Rolling link. According to the project library management requirements, establish the budget project library for rolling implementation. In the compilation and submission of annual budget items, each

department shall, in principle, refine and improve the items reported in the previous year. Except for the policy increase of annual budget which needs to be implemented by the higher authorities, the report is generally not revised. After the financial department reviews the rolling budget projects of each department every year, the projects that meet the requirements will be imported into the financial multi-year project database for standby. At the same time, in accordance with the zero-based budget principle and after the achievement of the phased development targets, all departments should cancel old projects and arrange new ones in a timely manner, so as to ensure the consistency and continuity of expenditures for public welfare and constructive projects in functional areas.

(3) International experience and inspiration on medium-term financial planning and management

The traditional annual budget is not conducive to the implementation of the country's strategic development plan because of the lack of consideration of the medium-term financial arrangement and the institutional arrangement of the multi-annual budget balance mechanism. It will also cause the government to shift the expenditure to the following year in order to achieve the fiscal balance target of the year. The tighter the fiscal constraint is, the more likely it is to delay the difficulty. Since the late 1980s, due to the long-term stagnation of the economy and the rapid increase in the scale of deficit and debt, countries around the world generally pay more attention to the issue of fiscal sustainability. Driven by the new public management (NPM), the United States, Australia, New Zealand, the United Kingdom and other member countries of the organization for economic cooperation and development have carried out large-scale financial budget reform, introduced performance budgeting technology and decentralized management autonomy to expenditure agencies. Medium-term spending frameworks are being introduced in more and more countries as an important mechanism for controlling budgets. At present, all OECD countries have established a medium-term budget framework to conduct fiscal management from the medium-term perspective and achieve sustainable fiscal development. In the past 20 years, many developing countries and some countries in economic transition such as Russia have also introduced the medium-term budget framework. According to the world bank statistics, as of 2008, 132 world bank members have implemented the medium-term spending framework, of which 71 countries have implemented the medium-term fiscal framework, 42 countries have implemented the medium-term budget framework and 19 countries have implemented the medium-term performance framework. From the practice of various countries, the implementation of the medium-term expenditure framework has played an important role in strengthening and improving macro-control, coordinating the use of financial resources, raising the budget level of fiscal year and strengthening the effect of policy implementation.

1. Use the medium-term budget as a link between budget and government planning

In mature market economies, fiscal targets are usually set over a three-year or five-year period, and budgets are usually set in the medium term instead of the traditional one-year budget. The design of medium-term budget greatly improves the certainty of budget funds in the future year, effectively avoiding the deficiency that annual budget only reflects the target of the year, only has a binding effect on the fiscal expenditure of the year, and is difficult to effectively align with the planning in terms of time limit. Ensure the connection between budget and medium - and long-term plan through the standard medium-term budget preparation procedure. First, macroeconomic policy framework should be formulated to forecast macroeconomic income and expenditure in the medium term. Secondly, reach consensus on department objectives, output and behaviors, form department planning and forecast planning costs. Make trade-offs within and between departments to agree on strategic allocation of resources. Then determine the upper limit of medium-term department budget and prepare department budget. Finally, the interim budget report is submitted to the legislature for its review.

2. Budgeting is based on the development strategic plan

In the process of budget management reform oriented by output and result in mature market economy countries, the link between budget and strategic plan is strengthened, and the determination of result and output target in the process of budget preparation should be based on national development strategic plan. Some states in the United States implement strategic planning and performance budgeting system(SPPB), which links strategic planning, performance budgeting and the appropriation process. Strategic planning, performance budgeting and performance monitoring constitute the main contents of SPPB system. Among them, the strategic plan is related to the five-year plan, the goal of government fiduciary responsibility and the means to achieve the goal. The performance budget sets the performance target on the basis of the strategic plan, and all government departments and institutions should report their performance, which is monitored by the budget management department.

3. Establish an economic forecasting model to scientifically forecast budgetary revenue and expenditure

Implementation of medium-term financial planning management is inseparable from accurate revenue and expenditure forecasts. Mature market economy countries generally attach importance to budget forecast. According to the economic growth rate, development speed of various related industries, employment rate, inflation rate, interest rate, real estate value change, transaction activity of various assets, etc. of the next year, financial management departments of the United States, Europe and other countries make forecasts and analyze various factors affecting fiscal revenue and expenditure. Use the economic forecasting model to calculate various relevant economic growth indicators. Based on this, various budgetary income is calculated by selecting factors related to finance, and the calculated result is compared with that calculated by other economic models, and the historical change trend of various income is compared to determine the income budget. The government usually designs economic forecasting models by relying on professional institutions to forecast the revenue and expenditure of its jurisdiction. In recent years, with the general concern about fiscal sustainability, OECD countries have paid more and more attention to the use of long-term fiscal and economic forecasts to assess fiscal risks. For example, the draft annual us budget proposal contains projections for the next 75 years; Norway has published fiscal and economic forecasts until 2060; Britain's annual pre-budget document contains fiscal and economic forecasts for the next 50 years; Germany has issued fiscal forecasts for 2050; Australia has issued a fiscal and economic forecast for 2044/45. The Hong Kong special administrative region of China has implemented a five-year medium-term budget, and recently set up a "long-term financial planning working group" to start forecasting and analyzing the fiscal revenue and expenditure in the next 30 years.

4. Implement the medium-term spending framework in stages according to national conditions

Medium-term expenditure framework is a kind of fiscal policy tool and fiscal management method that the government formulates medium-term fiscal policy, reasonably determines the level and structure of government medium-term expenditure, and takes this as the basis of annual budget compilation, on the basis of medium-term economic and fiscal revenue projections and in accordance with policy objectives and priorities for economic and social development, in order to achieve sustainable economic and financial development,

The medium-term spending framework can be divided into three levels or stages from low to high: First, Medium Term Fiscal Framework (MTFF) refers to the top-down formulation of macroeconomic and Fiscal medium-term targets by the government, including the total revenue and total expenditure forecast of the government in the Medium Term. Second, Medium Term Budget Framework (MTBF) refers to the upper limit of Medium Term expenditure, especially the cost estimation of expenditure projects in the Medium Term, through top-down and bottom-up consultation with the participation of all government departments. Third, Medium Term Performance Framework (MTPF), including the assessment and analysis of expenditure Performance, implementation of output budget, focuses on improving the efficiency of expenditure, fully reflects the output of fiscal revenue and budget, and pays more attention to the consideration of the Performance of fiscal medium-term expenditure. These three frameworks are generally rolled or updated in the light of the annual budget and financial and economic development. In the process of implementing the medium-term spending framework, most countries have gradually promoted from the medium-term fiscal framework to the medium-term budget framework and then to the medium-term performance framework, while a few countries have implemented directly from the medium-term budget framework.

4.3 Deepen Tax Reform and Accelerate the Establishment and Improvement of the Local Tax System

China is in the critical period of completing the building of a moderately prosperous society in all respects and the critical period of comprehensively deepening reform and accelerating the transformation of economic development mode. The new situation of international and domestic economic and social development also puts forward more urgent requirements for tax reform. The third plenary session of the 18th central committee of the communist party of China made a panoramic design on the comprehensive deepening of the reform. As one of the key points of comprehensively deepening reform, the reform of the fiscal and tax systems has been comprehensively deployed in the *Decision of the CPC Central Committee on Several Major Issues Concerning Comprehensively Deepening Reform* adopted at the plenary session. Among them, they also put forward directional opinions on deepening tax reform. From the perspective of the 13th five-year plan period and beyond, the goal orientation of China's tax reform should be to establish a system that is conducive to promoting social equity, can adapt to economic fluctuations and make effective adjustment, and reflects the national innovation-driven incentives, industrial policies and technological and economic policies. It can not only meet the normal demand of government financial resources, but also meet the urgent demand of society, such as optimizing distribution pattern, scientific distribution, coordination and perfect function of various tax tools and tax elements, so as to serve the sustainable development of Chinese economy and the modernization of Chinese society.

The Basic Principles and Roadmap for Deepening Tax Reform

The following principles should be followed to further deepen China's tax reform.

1. Top-level design and step-by-step promotion

For a long time after the reform and opening up, China followed the path of "crossing the river by feeling the stones". Today, however, profound changes have taken place in the structure of society and the pattern of interests. It is difficult to make a successful reform plan without an overall consideration of all aspects, levels and elements involved in the reform from an overall perspective. Therefore, China's tax reform to promote the depth, we need to do a good job of top-level design, careful planning, overall consideration of various factors and supporting system arrangements, to formulate the best system design. However, at the same time, we should also be deeply aware that fiscal and tax reform is a key link and an important breakthrough in economic reform. In the current highly polarized social pattern, it is more difficult to coordinate multiple interests and different goals, and there is growing pressure to coordinate and promote supporting reforms, improve supporting tax collection and management and social conditions. Therefore, according to the priority of reform and the degree of maturity of supporting conditions, it is necessary to reasonably arrange the tax reform process, promote various reforms in an orderly manner, and minimize the impact on the economy and society.

2. Broaden the tax base, simplify the tax system, adjust tax rates, and tighten tax collection and management

"Broadening the tax base", on one hand, requires that on the premise of stabilizing the tax burden, the tax base should be expanded as reasonably as possible, modern taxes on environment, social security and property should be increased, and the range of individual income tax and consumption tax should be expanded. On the other hand, we need to clean up and standardize preferential tax policies and cancel unreasonable preferential tax policies. "Simplifying tax" does not mean that the tax system should be simplified. On the one hand, it requires the simplification of the number of existing taxes and the combination of some taxes with similar or repeated properties. On the other hand, it is required to standardize the tax system in terms of content, and clear up the multifarious policies and regulations currently composed of a large number of regulations, departmental rules and other normative documents. Tax rate adjustment calls for a combination of structural tax cuts and structural tax increases. On the one hand, we need to address the problem of high nominal tax rates and narrow the gap between nominal and actual tax rates. On the other hand, tax rates should also be appropriately raised for certain types of taxes that are significantly lower or less heavily taxed. "Strict tax collection and management" requires strengthening the construction of tax collection and management system, building a scientific, reasonable and efficient tax collection and management system based on information, improving the level and efficiency of tax collection and management, and promoting the coordinated development of tax construction and tax collection and management.

3. Fair tax burden and promotion of income distribution

At present, there are big problems in China's income distribution. Many contradictions caused by different income distribution have become a major obstacle to the healthy development of China's economy and society. How to reduce the inequality of income distribution and realize social equity is the focus and difficulty of comprehensively deepening reform. As an important tool for the government to participate in the distribution and redistribution of national income, taxation is duty-bound in this regard. We will further deepen reform of the tax system, give full play to the role of tax revenue in adjusting income distribution and property distribution, optimize distribution patterns and adjust distribution relations. Reduce the proportion of government departments in the primary distribution of national income by reducing the proportion of indirect tax; Through the reform of income tax and property tax, the income distribution gap and property distribution gap of residents will be reduced. Through tax rate adjustment, the tax burden on basic necessities will be reduced to reduce the living burden on middle and low income people.

4. Improve inter-governmental financial relations

Reasonable income division and tax base allocation are the institutional guarantees for matching financial resources with power, promoting equal access to basic public services, promoting the tax distribution system below the provincial level, improving the national unified big market, and avoiding vicious inter-regional tax source competition. In light of the process of tax reform, we should take into account the nature and characteristics of tax categories, follow the principles of fairness, convenience and efficiency, and reasonably divide tax categories and revenue among governments at different levels. It should not only ensure the leading role of the central government in fiscal revenue and guarantee the central government's regulatory capacity, but also gradually improve the local tax system. Through the reform of property tax, resource tax, consumption tax, environmental tax and other tax systems, local governments will gradually increase their financial self-sufficiency and be fully encouraged to raise fiscal revenue and promote economic and social development.

First, outline a course of tax reform (see Table 4.3) to clarify the implementation steps and long-term goals of tax reform.

Table 4.3 Route and process of tax reform from 2015 to 2020

	Year 2015	The 13th five-year plan period (2016–2020)
VAT	Complete the reform of replacing business tax with VAT	Gradually simplify and consolidate tax rates Appropriately reduce the VAT rate
Consumption tax	Expand the scope of collection	Expand the scope of excise tax collection Adjust the tax rate Appropriately adjust collection link and income sharing method
Resource tax	The price-based charging reform will be extended to other major mineral products	Expand the scope of resource tax collection in due course Levy a water resource tax
Environmental tax	Environmental tax will change fees for air pollution and water pollution, levy an environmental protection tax	Levy an environmental protection tax across the board Impose a carbon tax when appropriate
The individual income tax	Establishe the dynamic adjustment mechanism of expense deduction standard, optimizes and adjusts the tax rate and level	Timely implements the individual income tax system combining comprehensive and classification
The enterprise income tax	The enterprise income tax rate will be moderately lowered	
Property tax	Property tax enters into the legislative process	Takes the opportunity to promote nationwide property tax reform
The social security tax	征收 Collect social insurance premiums uniformly from tax authorities	Implement the social insurance fee to tax and levy social security tax
Inheritance and gift tax	Study the collection plan	Take the opportunity to levy

Make the Tax System More Progressive and Give Play to the Role of Taxation in Adjusting Income Distribution

1. Improve individual income tax

In recent years, the adjustment of individual income tax has always been inseparable from the amount of exemption, but with little effect. From the point of view of scientific and fair tax system design, the goal of individual income tax should be to establish a comprehensive and classified tax system, establish a differentiated expense deduction system, adjust the tax rate appropriately, and strengthen the tax collection and management. First of all, establish the comprehensive and classification combined tax system. In the near future, a comprehensive levy may be implemented on the recurrent income of individuals (including income from wages and salaries, remuneration for labor services, income from production and operation of individual industrial and commercial households, income from contracted operation, property lease and income from author's remuneration of enterprises and institutions). Capital gains and other temporary and contingent income (income from transfer of property, interest, dividends, royalties, contingent income and other income) shall be subject to the current itemized collection method. In the long run, all personal income should be subject to comprehensive taxation except for capital gains. Secondly, implement differential expense deduction system. The personal income tax expense deduction is divided into two categories: one is the basic living and family income deduction (including the basic living, education and medical treatment deduction); The other category is occasional large deductions, such as house purchase costs, mortgage interest and serious medical expenses. The deduction for basic living expenses and family expenses varies according to the number of people who support them. The deduction standard is linked to the consumer price index and adjusted regularly. And the contingent large item deduction, also sets the differential deduction proportion according to the cost attribute characteristic and other factors. Again, moderately adjusts tax rate and classification. Income included in the comprehensive tax range shall be subject to progressive tax rate, and the principle of low bottom tax rate and high high-end tax rate shall be adhered to, reflecting the principle of expanding the coverage of taxpayers and paying more taxes for high-income earners. Lower top marginal tax rate, reduce the tax rate bracket. Consider changing the current tax rate to five brackets: 3, 8, 15, 25 and 35%. Finally, strengthen the monitoring and collection of high income earners. We will continue to promote the system of self-declaration, which is an important measure to strengthen tax monitoring of high-income groups and promote individual income tax to adjust the income gap. In order to make it work better, a series of system reforms are needed, such as the establishment of a permanent single tax number system for taxpayers, promote the real-name system for assets, establish a system for reporting assets, establish an income monitoring system, and share information between Banks and other financial institutions, enterprises, customs and other institutions.

2. Implement property tax reform across the country in due course

Real estate tax is directly related to people's property. The third plenary session of the 18th CPC central committee proposed to speed up the legislation of real estate tax and timely promote the reform. Speeding up the legislation of real estate tax is in line with the implementation of the principle of tax legality, which will better reflect the fairness of real estate tax, build consensus and reduce resistance. In the reform of real estate tax, it is necessary to coordinate the real estate tax and fee system, and gradually integrate many fees and taxes involved in the current real estate development, circulation and ownership, change the current practice of paying more tax in circulation and less tax in ownership, transfer the tax burden in the circulation of housing development to the ownership, and timely levy the real estate tax in the ownership of real estate. First of all, the real estate tax and urban land use tax should be combined to levy a standardized real estate tax. In the unified real estate tax and urban real estate tax, there are two kinds of taxes in China's current real estate ownership, namely urban land use tax and real estate tax. Because the real estate and the land policy are different, it brings many contradictions and the difficulty to the actual collection and management. According to the principle of "broad tax base and simple tax system", it is necessary to combine real estate tax, urban land use tax and other charges related to real estate ownership, and levy a unified and standardized real estate tax. Second, expand the scope and tax base of real estate tax collection. From the perspective of the scope of the real estate tax, it should be designed to include the real estate of all regions and all taxpayers as far as possible. Compared with the original property tax and urban land use tax, this will require an expansion in three aspects: From urban areas to rural areas, from non-residential real estate to residential real estate, and from business units to individuals or families. In the short term, according to the current social and economic development in China, we should expand the scope of property tax reform on individual housing as soon as possible. In the medium and long term, urban land use tax and real estate tax can be combined, and the residential real estate of urban residents and rural residents can be gradually included in the tax range, and the real estate directly used for agricultural production and farmers' housing can be exempted. Again, change estate tax plan tax basis. From the tax basis of foreign real estate tax, most countries tend to collect real estate tax according to the assessed value of real estate, making it have the elastic characteristics of growth with economic growth. China's real estate tax should also be based on the market value of the real estate, the real estate evaluation value as the basis of tax. This not only accurately reflects the tax base and taxpayers' affordability, but also reflects the principle of fair tax burden and reasonable burden. Finally, after implementing the real estate tax reform and increasing the tax burden of the real estate ownership link, it is necessary to reduce the tax burden of the real estate circulation link, and gradually eliminate the land value-added tax, farmland occupation tax, deed tax and other taxes and fees in the real estate circulation link.

3. Replace fees with taxes and levy social security taxes

The reform of social insurance fees to taxes and the introduction of social security taxes will not only help raise social security funds better and reduce the cost of collection, but also help establish a supervision system of social security funds with separation and mutual restriction of collection, expenditure, management and supervision, and improve the efficiency of raising and using social security funds. It is suggested that the social insurance fee can be changed to tax in two steps: The first step, in 1–2 years, the national social insurance premium is uniformly collected by tax authorities. The former social insurance agencies and personnel should be properly redistributed, which can be used for reference in the handling of the road maintenance fee inspection agencies and personnel under the ministry of transport under the reform of refined oil consumption tax. The second step is to implement the social insurance fee tax and levy social security tax. After the social insurance premium is uniformly collected by tax authorities, the social security tax system is established on the basis of summarizing experience through a period of operation.

4. Study the design of estate and gift tax system

Estate and gift tax is an important part of the property tax system, which plays a very important role in regulating the wealth distribution gap. At the same time, it also helps to encourage people to donate, promote the development of charity, realize the "third distribution" of income beyond the regulation of the market and the government, and alleviate the income gap. In view of China's economic development stage, residents' income level and tax collection and management conditions and other factors, China does not yet have the relevant conditions for the introduction of estate (gift) tax. But in the long run, estate and gift taxes are still powerful policy tools to control the gap between the rich and the poor. Therefore, it is necessary to make further research and exploration on its policy design and policy effect and make theoretical reserve. At the same time, we should speed up the construction of property registration system, appraisal system and other relevant supporting systems to prepare for the future reform. As soon as the time is right.

Reduce Tax Distortions and Promote Steady Economic Growth

1. Actively promote the reform of replacing business tax with VAT and improve the VAT system

As an important part of the reform of the socialist market economic system, the tax system reform should be pushed forward in the direction of making the market play a decisive role in the allocation of resources and giving full play to the role of tax revenue in the national macroeconomic regulation. Tax reform should adhere to the principle of relative neutrality. First of all, we will strive to complete the business tax reform in 2015 and gradually achieve full coverage of the industry. Second, improve the VAT deduction system. After replacing the business tax with a value-added tax (VAT) in the real estate industry, enterprises' self-built real estate and newly built real estate are included in the scope of VAT input deduction, making China's VAT become a complete consumption-oriented VAT. Third, a modest simplification and consolidation in tax rates. After the industry reform of replacing business tax with VAT is basically in place, it is necessary to properly clean up and simplify the current cumbersome tax rate range as soon as possible, enhance the "neutral" characteristics of VAT, and standardize the collection and management. In the future, the standard rate of VAT needs to be reduced moderately. The standard rate will be gradually reduced to 13% within 5–10 years, and then the indirect tax rate will be reduced. Simplify the preferential tax bracket. The preferential tax rate is set at 6% only for basic necessities such as food, medicine and books. Finally, improve the export tax rebate system. In principle, zero tax rate shall be applied to the export of all goods and services, with the exception of products with high energy consumption and high pollution and products explicitly discouraged by the state from export. This is not only to maintain a neutral tax system and adapt to the inherent requirements of economic globalization, but also to cope with the current grim international trade situation and the increasing trade friction environment to promote exports and improve the international competitiveness of domestic products.

2. Improve the consumption tax

We will adjust the scope of excise tax. Remove some consumer goods that are already part of everyday life. Some products that seriously pollute the environment, consume a lot of resources and energy, as well as luxury consumption behaviors, such as phosphorous detergents, disposable beverage containers, batteries, excessive packaging materials, products that damage the ozone layer, private jets and so on, will be included in the collection. If the future conditions allow, further coke and thermal power and other products with high pollution and high energy consumption will be included in the consumption tax range. Adjust the consumption tax rate. Implement differential tax rate, there are awards and penalties. Different tax rates shall be applied according to the extent of environmental pollution caused by taxable products and the consumption of resources and energy. High tax rates shall be imposed on products with high energy consumption, high pollution and low utilization rate of resources, as well as consumer goods such as cigarettes and firecrackers that endanger health and the environment; Low taxes or exemptions for clean energy and environmentally friendly products. We will adjust the way consumption taxes are collected and revenue is Shared. Some items suitable for collection in the production link, such as tobacco consumer goods sold exclusively by the state and refined oil products as important strategic materials of the state, are still taxed in the production link, and the revenue is Shared between the central government and the consuming areas, with the central government sharing the majority. For other items, the collection link can be moved from the current production link to the retail link, and the income is assigned to the local government, so as to reflect the consumption tax principle.

3. Accelerate the reform of resource taxes

We will accelerate the reform of AD valorem resource taxes. On the basis of summarizing useful experience in the reform of resource tax on petroleum and natural gas, we will accelerate the reform of price-based resource tax on coal and gradually extend it to non-ferrous metals and other mineral resources. For some mineral resources with stable market price and low value, we can continue to use the current method of levy by volume from the point of view of convenient collection and management. We will moderately raise resource taxes. It is helpful to raise the cost of voluntary use and limit the excessive exploitation and use of resources. According to the needs of economic and social development, the resource tax burden on scarce resources, high-pollution and high-energy mineral products should be further increased. In combination with the reform of the pricing mechanism of resource products, the resource tax burden should be finally reflected in the prices of final consumer products, so that the prices of final consumer products can truly reflect the cost of resources. We will deepen reform of the system of resource taxes and fees, and incorporate mineral resource compensation fees into resource taxes when appropriate. China levies resource tax and compensation fee for mineral resource exploitation at the same time, which have similar properties and functions, resulting in the disorder of resource tax and fee relationship, and the problem of repeated tax and fee collection is very prominent. At present, it has become the consensus of all walks of life to eliminate fees and establish taxes and promote the reform of resource tax. After the reform of price-based resource tax is completed, the compensation fee for mineral resources may be incorporated into the resource tax. Expand the scope of taxation. Currently, the resource tax mainly focuses on non-renewable resources such as mineral resources. If future conditions permit, consideration may be given to including renewable resources such as water resources, forest resources, grassland resources and cultivated land resources in the resource tax.

4. Introduce independent environmental tax (including carbon tax) as soon as possible

In view of the current severe environmental situation and the lack of environmental economic policy means, it is necessary to implement the environmental tax reform as soon as possible and levy an independent environmental protection tax. Determine the tax range. In accordance with international practice and the universality and fairness of taxation, environmental tax should include the behaviors and products that destroy the ecology and pollute the environment, that is, all the behaviors and products that are unfavorable to the environment. On one hand, water pollution control, air pollution prevention and control, solid waste pollution prevention and control will be the focus of China's future environmental protection work. This kind of behavior is the most serious pollution to China's environment. The inclusion of these kinds of pollutants into the collection range of environmental tax conforms to the primary regulation goal of China's environmental tax. At the same time, China's response to global climate change and the development of a low-carbon economy also requires the regulation of carbon dioxide emissions through taxation. On the other hand, taxes on energy products and other products that pollute the environment can be adjusted by existing resource taxes and consumption taxes. On the whole, the collection range of environmental tax in China can be defined as the emission of various pollutants and carbon dioxide. Since the introduction of environmental tax will have an impact on the macro economy and related industries, and the corresponding collection and management capacity is needed as the basis, the scope of environmental tax collection also needs to be implemented step by step and gradually expanded. Reasonable determination of tax rates. The reasonable design of tax rate is the key to environmental protection tax. The design of environmental protection tax rate should follow the following principles: first, the level of tax rate should reflect the marginal cost of pollutant emission reduction to the maximum extent. The tax rate level should be designed in favor of the taxpayers' positive response to the tax, that is, the tax burden is enough to affect their emission behavior. If the environmental tax rate does not meet this standard, it will be difficult to achieve better results. Second, tax rate level should consider the impact on macroeconomic and industrial competitiveness. The excessively high tax rate has a great impact on the macro-economy and industrial competitiveness, so it is necessary to choose comprehensively according to the social and economic development goals of a country. Among them, in order to protect the international competitiveness of key industries and economic sectors, it is necessary to set a lower tax burden. Third, the level of tax rates should be gradually increased. In order to reduce the impact on the economy and social resistance caused by the introduction of environmental tax, the tax rate level should adopt the strategy of gradual progress, that is, implement the low tax rate at the initial stage of the introduction, and gradually increase according to the economic and social conditions in a certain period.

5. Further improve corporate income tax

In 2008, the new enterprise income tax law was implemented, which not only unified the income tax systems of domestic and foreign enterprises, standardized the pre-tax deduction and adjusted the orientation of preferential tax policies, but also significantly reduced the tax rate from 33 to 25%. It can be said that the reform of enterprise income tax is of great significance. From the perspective of policy improvement, the recent focus is to fully implement the new enterprise income tax law and its implementation regulations, and accelerate the formulation and implementation of relevant supporting measures; In the long run, it is necessary to pay attention to the international tax dynamics, improve the international tax source management system, further improve anti-tax avoidance measures, and strengthen international cooperation and coordination.

Improve the Local Tax System and Enhance the Revenue Capacity of Local Governments

Under the socialist market economy system, the purpose of perfecting the local tax system should be to improve the efficiency of resource allocation, promote economic growth and achieve a win–win situation between the central and local governments. The key issue to achieve this result or goal is the normalization and stabilization of the financial relationship between the central and local governments. The key to improve the local tax system is how to reform and improve the tax distribution system, and on this basis to consider the construction of the local tax system, rather than consider the local tax types in isolation. Therefore, the improvement of China's local tax system cannot be limited to these taxes that belong to local taxes. On the basis of the reasonable division of taxes between the central government and the local government, we study the local tax system from a broader perspective. To understand the local tax system from a broad perspective, after the comprehensive implementation of the reform of replacing the business tax with a value-added tax, all kinds of Shared taxes, including value-added tax, enterprise income tax and individual income tax, should be regarded as an important part of the local tax system. To be specific, we can start from the following aspects of reform measures, from near to far, to enrich the local tax revenue, improve the local tax system.

1. Adjust the share ratio of central and local governments in VAT and reform the way of sharing

After replacing the business tax with a value-added tax, VAT revenue will be further increased. Such a large amount of tax revenue is not appropriate for one level of government, but more reasonable for multiple levels of government. It is suggested that value-added tax (VAT) should still be Shared by the central, provincial, city and county governments, and that the share ratio of local governments, especially provincial governments, should be appropriately increased. At the same time, we will reform according to the 75:25 proportional sharing system to eliminate the unfair distribution among regions and distortions in local government behaviors caused by the current practice. The sharing of VAT can be distributed among different regions according to standardized formulas according to the population, consumption capacity, basic public service needs and other factors. At the same time, the VAT revenue sharing budget is made before each fiscal year, so that the local government can formulate the local fiscal revenue and expenditure budget according to this budget, so that the VAT becomes a stable and regular source of fiscal revenue for the local government, especially the provincial government.

2. Reform the tax sharing mode of enterprise income tax and individual income tax, and change the sharing mode from income sharing to sharing rate

To reform the current way of sharing enterprise income tax and individual income tax at the national level, tax rate sharing or local surcharge sharing may be adopted. Corporate and individual income taxes belong to the central government. The central government sets a unified national tax rate, and local governments can impose additional taxes in addition to this rate, but there is a maximum limit on the tax rate. In addition, considering that the flow of income tax sources will cause uneven distribution among tax regions, it is necessary to establish a set of inter-regional tax distribution adjustment mechanism to promote tax fairness.

3. Advance the reform of the consumption tax and make it shared by the central and local governments

We will expand the scope of excise tax collection and adjust the way it is collected and Shared. Some items suitable for collection in the production link, such as tobacco consumer goods sold exclusively by the state and refined oil products, which are important strategic materials of the state, are still taxed in the production link, but the revenue is Shared between the central government and the consuming areas, with the central government sharing the majority. For other items, the expropriation link can be moved from the current production link to the retail link, and the revenue will be allocated to the local government.

4. Promote the reform of property tax and resource tax, and create main tax categories for city and county governments

In the long run, the property tax levied in the link of real estate ownership and the resource tax levied on mineral resources can be used as the main taxes of city and county governments in the developed areas in the east and the less developed but resource-rich areas in the west respectively.

5. Impose environmental tax

The environmental tax is mainly to change the existing pollution fee into the tax. In order to enhance the ability of local governments to control regional pollution and mobilize the enthusiasm of local governments to carry out environmental protection, it is necessary to take the environmental tax as the local tax and make it a stable source of income for local governments.

Implement Tax Collection and Administration Reform and Improve the Efficiency of Tax Collection and Administration

The reform of tax collection and management is an important guarantee for deepening the reform of tax system. As the socialist market economy puts forward new requirements on the macro-control role of taxation, the speed of China's economic integration into the world economy is accelerating, and information technology has been widely and deeply applied in tax collection and management. Tax payers' awareness of law and rights protection has been increasing, and China's tax collection and management reform should adapt to the changing economic situation, keep pace with The Times, and make positive improvements according to the requirements of tax system development. It should be improved from the following aspects.

1. Strengthen the construction of tax collection and management legal system

Based on solving the difficult problems that restrict the practice of tax collection and management, we should be more forward-looking and step up efforts to establish, reform and abolish the tax collection and management legal system. We will complete the revision of the *Tax Collection and Administration Law* as soon as possible, and balance the rights and obligations of tax authorities and taxpayers, so as to not only meet the needs of strengthening tax collection and administration and ensuring income, but also meet the requirements of standardizing power and optimizing services.

2. Establish a complete tax-related information data system

A complete and accurate information system is a prerequisite for tax reform. Under the premise of vigorously promoting information tax fixing, management and taxation, it is urgent for tax departments to share information with relevant functional departments, and such information sharing mechanism should be established among various departments. A unified and universal system of standardized and unique codes for people, houses, land, enterprises, governments and social institutions shall be established nationwide. All departments shall use the unique code to collect the basic and original information of individuals, enterprises, governments and social institutions related to their responsibilities, and establish the professional information system with a large national concentration and full coverage. On this basis, it shall form the bilateral or multilateral information sharing platform between departments. At the same time, establish a national and comprehensive legal information sharing platform independent of all departments, and build an information sharing system and mechanism that can not only communicate information, but also have limits, constraints and control.

3. Improve the construction of tax collection and management system and improve the level of tax collection and management

Take the collection and application of data information as the focus, strengthen tax risk analysis and monitoring. Improve risk analysis methods and strengthen the application of risk analysis. We will standardize tax assessment procedures, improve tax assessment methods, and strengthen supervision and control over tax assessment work. Strengthen data management, make full use of all kinds of information, and constantly improve the level of information management tax.

4. Realize the intensification of tax administration

Through computer network interconnection, information sharing and resource sharing can be realized. On this basis, the tax collection and management organization should be gradually contracted to reduce the management level, promote the flattening of the tax organization system, improve the scope and effectiveness of monitoring, reduce the management cost and improve the management efficiency.

5. Do a good job in tax service

With the focus on safeguarding the legitimate rights and interests of taxpayers, we will effectively optimize tax services and improve taxpayer satisfaction and tax law compliance. We will increase the transparency and certainty of tax laws, regulations and management measures, do a good job in alerting taxpayers to tax risks, reduce their tax burdens, protect their rights, attach importance to tax legal relief, and actively promote the development of tax-related intermediary services.

Supporting Reform Measures to Promote Tax Reform

1. Promote the reform of the intergovernmental fiscal system and improve the transfer payment system

The reform of the tax system needs to be combined with the reform of the financial system, especially the reform of the financial hierarchy, division of powers and transfer payment system. First of all, we need to actively and steadily push forward the reform of direct provincial management of counties, rural financial management of counties and comprehensive township management, and reduce the level of financial entities to three levels: the central government, provinces, cities and counties. Secondly, we should reasonably define the scope of government powers and expenditure responsibilities at all levels. In accordance with the principles of cost efficiency and benefit range, the scope of powers of the central, provincial and municipal governments at all levels should be clarified, and the responsibilities of the governments at all levels for the provision of basic public services should be clarified. From the perspective of international experience, the central government is responsible for national public goods and matters of great importance to national economic and social development, local governments at all levels are responsible for regional and local public goods, and the central and local governments at all levels are responsible for trans-regional public goods. Some of the responsibilities should be borne by the central government or all levels of government, but the efficiency requires the governments at the county level to take specific responsibilities, and the governments at all levels should transfer funds to the governments at the county level that take specific responsibilities. The third plenary session of the 18th CPC central committee has made a relatively clear definition of the division of power and responsibility for expenditure. Next, we need to further refine the lists of powers of governments at all levels, and transfer some powers that should have been assumed by the central government to the central government. We need to properly strengthen the central government's powers and expenditure responsibilities, and rationalize the mechanism for sharing expenditure responsibilities between the central government and local governments. Finally, the transfer payment system should be improved to enhance the basic public service guarantee capacity of local governments. We will strengthen and optimize the top-down system of transfer payments at the central and provincial levels, and cancel tax rebates at an appropriate time. We will improve the mechanism for increasing general transfer payments, gradually increase the size and proportion of general transfer payments, especially balanced transfer payments, improve the current factor-based transfer payments, and increase their objectivity and transparency. We will increase funding for transfer payments to the central and western regions, and increase support for forbidden and restricted development zones with general transfer payments in line with the national plan for functional zones. We will integrate and standardize special transfer payments, gradually reduce the size of special transfer payments, clean up and integrate the various existing special transfer payments, strictly control new projects, and minimize the supporting requirements of special transfer payments on local governments. We will explore the establishment of a system of horizontal transfer payments.

2. Promote the reform of the pricing mechanism and straighten out the tax transmission mechanism

In many cases, tax policies do not directly affect the regulated objects, but connect them through a certain transmission mechanism. Only a sound market and price mechanism can make the change of tax policy pass to the microeconomic subject through the price, and then affect the behavior of the microeconomic subject. If the market system is not perfect and the price mechanism is not perfect, the purpose of tax policy will not be transmitted to the micro subject, and the purpose of tax policy regulation will fail.

After a long period of market-oriented reform, the price of most general commodities in China has been determined by the market supply and demand relationship, but in the field of basic energy, government administrative orders are still the dominant mode of resource allocation. This leads to the distortion of resource and energy price formation mechanism, and the product price cannot truly reflect the scarcity of products, supply and demand relations and production environment costs, thus misleading the upstream, middle and downstream micro enterprises' resource allocation behavior. Therefore, to better play the role of tax policy, it is imperative to take the reform of resource tax as an opportunity to carry out price and tax linkage reform, overcome the major defects in the current pricing system of resources and energy, tax system and financial system, and improve the pricing mechanism of resources and energy so that the price can reflect the scarcity of resources and energy products, internal and external costs and supply and demand relations, the formation of internal incentive mechanism for social subjects.

3. Coordinate the relationship between taxes and fees, eliminate fees and establish taxes to make room for tax reform

It is an important way to standardize tax distribution order and reduce tax burden of taxpayers. In the reform of the tax system, we need to always match fees and taxes, actively cooperate with relevant departments to clear up relevant government fees, change fees of the same or similar nature to taxes into taxes, and fix them in the form of laws and regulations. We will eliminate unreasonable and illegal fees and standardize the way the government participates in the distribution of national income, so as to provide greater space for tax reform.

[Column 3.5]
Investigation and understanding of macro tax burden in China

(1) The connotation and measurement caliber of macro tax burden

The main source of fiscal revenue is tax revenue. The ratio of total government revenue to GDP is usually referred to as "macro tax burden" in a broad sense-a concept that has been accepted by academia and management departments. "Macro tax burden" is an important indicator to measure the scale of government income, reflecting the extent to which a country's government participates in national income distribution in a specific stage of development, economic system and fiscal and tax system. This is directly related to the ability and level of the government to provide public services, which can be used to specifically analyze the characteristics of the "fiscal control by administration and administration through fiscal management" of fiscal distribution and the government's role space of the economy.

China's macro tax burden level can be measured by three different caliber, namely, small caliber, medium caliber and large caliber. Small-caliber macro tax burden refers to the ratio of tax revenue to GDP. Medium macro tax burden refers to the ratio of public financial revenue to GDP. Large-caliber macro tax burden refers to the ratio of government revenue and GDP brought into the budget system.

(2) China's macro tax inspection and international comparison

According to the above three measurement calibers of China's macro tax burden, according to the relevant data published by *China Statistical Yearbook* and the website of the ministry of finance, the macro tax burden level of China's large, medium and small calibers from 2008 to 2012 is shown in Table 4.4.

As can be seen from Table 4.4, China's small-caliber macro tax burden is less than 20%, showing a slight upward trend. The macro tax burden of the medium caliber was about 22%, which also showed a slight increase. Macro tax burden of large caliber is between 27–35%, showing

Table 4.4 China's macro tax burden levels from 2008 to 2012 (unit: 100 million Yuan, %)

Project	2008	2009	2010	2011	2012
National public revenue	61,330	74,933	88,896	103,874	117,254
Among them: tax revenue	54,224	59,521	73,210	89,738	100,614
Revenue from state capital operations	444	989	559	765	1496
Deduction: allocated to public finance			10	40	183
Revenue from social insurance funds	10,805	14,583	17,071	25,758	28,465
Deduction: subsidy from public finance to social insurance fund		1803	1900	5216	6272
Revenue from government-managed funds	14,985	18,335	36,785	41,363	37,535
Scale of government revenue	**87,564**	**107,037**	**141,401**	**166,504**	**178,295**
GDP	**314,045**	**340,902**	**401,512**	**472,881**	**519,886**
Small caliber macro tax burden	**17.3**	**17.5**	**18.2**	**19.0**	**19.4**
Medium caliber macro tax burden	**19.5**	**22.0**	**22.1**	**22.0**	**22.6**
Large caliber macro tax burden	**27.9**	**31.4**	**35.2**	**35.2**	**34.3**

Notes (1) data are collated according to *China Statistical Yearbook* and website data of ministry of finance; (2) the income of social insurance fund in 2008 is the data after deducting financial subsidies; (3) the public financial revenue in 2009 and 2010 includes extra-budgetary revenue, and all extra-budgetary revenue after 2011 is included in budget management. Extra-budgetary revenue data are from the national bureau of statistics website

the trend of rising first and then falling. The macro tax burden was calculated for all 53 countries for which data were available in 2007, based on this index, the *Government Finance Statistics Yearbook 2008* published by the international monetary fund (IMF). The average macro tax burden of these 53 countries is 39.9%, with an average of 45.3% in 24 industrialized countries and 35.5% in 29 developing countries. Compared with other countries, China is an average developing country, much lower than developed economies. Compared with upper-middle income countries with an international population of more than 10 million,

China's adjusted large-caliber macro tax burden is roughly the same as the median of the target countries (see Table 4.5 for details).

(3) Understanding and comprehension of China's macro tax burden

The "high or low" and "light or heavy" of the macro tax burden are not exactly the same. The weight of tax burden of a country must be combined with the boundary of the public function of the government under the influence of various factors such as specific national conditions, stages and strategic design, and cannot be measured only by the level of macro tax burden.

Excluding factors such as the efficiency of fiscal expenditure and the objective differences of public goods supply costs among countries, the so-called high or low macro tax burden mainly depends on

Table 4.5 International comparison of broad macro tax burden in 2011

Upper middle income	Broad macro tax burden	China
Russia	45.59	
Brazil	36.05	
Turkey	34.66	
South Africa	34.34	
Romania	31.30	**32.01**
Tunisia	30.98	
Colombia	29.29	
Kazakhstan	25.95	
Thailand	22.63	
Peru	20.02	
Median	**31.14**	**32.01 (+0.87)**
Reference result		
Arithmetic average	**31.08**	**32.01 (+0.93)**
Weighted by Population	**34.71**	**32.01 (−2.7)**
Weighted by GDP	**36.52**	**32.01 (−4.51)**
Weighted by GNI per capita	**32.72**	**32.01 (−0.62)**

Note (1) macro tax burden includes 3 statistical subjects of tax, social payment and other income of each country, excluding gift income; (2) the selected countries are medium and high income countries with a population of more than 10 million

Data source IMF Government Finance Statistics Yearbook 2012; Per capita gross national income and population data are derived from the WDI database of the world bank.

the positioning of government functions and the scope of government responsibilities. From the practical situation of various countries after the industrial revolution, the long-term performance of the proportion of government expenditure showed an upward trend. This is the conclusion made by the famous "Wagner's law" – the fundamental reason is that with the development of society, economic and social public affairs tend to be complex and services upgrade, the scope of government public functions is gradually expanding.

Under the traditional system, the boundary of the government's scope of authority and function is obviously beyond that of mature market economy countries (there is no discussion on the status of public services in some rural areas under the administrating of city-countryside separately" pattern). Since the reform and opening up, there has been some convergence, but there is still considerable difference. In addition to the offside, vacancy and low fund efficiency caused by incomplete transformation of government functions, the following factors are also included: Specific reform costs in the transition process; To carry out the catch-up strategy and realize the great rejuvenation of the nation to undertake the specific responsibility for economic development; China has been striving to speed up the century-long process of industrialization and urbanization in mature market countries, which has led to the overlapping of public goods (basic system conducive to market development, infrastructure to promote economic development, and livelihood guarantee goods conducive to social stability and harmony) provided by other countries and other factors in the past 30 years of China's reform and opening up.

The above analysis does not negate the problem that the market reform is not in place, the government is offside, and the expenditure efficiency is low, which leads to the improper allocation of public resources, and the waste brings "unnecessary" government expenditure or higher administrative cost. The main purpose of this paper is to explain that the scope of government power is a preliminary cognitive framework to determine the level of macro tax burden. Different countries have different development stages and different national conditions, so the static macro tax burden comparability among countries is not strong. China's specific national conditions and the current special stage lead to a wide range of government powers. In the level of established macro tax burden and government expenditure, apart from some improper factors, there are also some objective inevitability and rationality.

The problem of "tax burden" in China cannot be avoided, but for the optimization of the problem of "tax burden pressure" in China, the key is not to reduce the macro tax burden, nor to point out that the per capita index of macro tax burden does not correspond to the intuitive form of "enterprises handing in 90% tax revenue", but to rationalize the structure distribution of the actual "tax burden pressure" from macro (society as a whole) to micro (individual residents). How to correct the weak function of fiscal and tax redistribution through reform.

On November 13, 2013, the *Decision of the CPC Central Committee on Several Major Issues of Comprehensively Deepening Reform*, adopted in the third plenary session of the 18th CPC central committee, which clearly stated: "reform the tax system and stabilize the tax burden." On June 30, 2014, the *General Plan for Deepening the reform of the Fiscal and Tax Systems*, which was reviewed and adopted by the political bureau of the CPC central committee, again proposed "stabilizing the macro-tax burden". It can be seen that the next step of tax reform needs to be carried out under the premise of stabilizing the current macro tax burden. About "stabilize macro tax burden", it can make the following interpretation.

1. China's macro tax burden is reasonable at present and should be stable at this level in the future

In recent years, there have been continuous discussions on the level of macro tax burden in China, among which doubts and opinions of "excessive tax burden" are frequent. As mentioned above, macro tax burden level of other countries is not the determination standard of China's macro tax burden level, they can only be used as the reference of China's macro tax burden level. The decisive factor of a country's macro tax burden level is the relationship between the government and the market, that is, the scope of the government's power, supplemented by factors such as the stage of economic development and the level of urbanization. For China, a country in transition, the government needs to play a better role in improving the socialist market economy and bear the cost of reform. Therefore, solid financial support is necessary, and the corresponding macro tax burden should not be too low. From the perspective of the actual operation effect of the economy and society since the tax distribution reform in 1994, the current macro tax burden level has not affected the economic and social development, but greatly improved the economic efficiency and promoted the long-term sustained and high-speed growth of China's economy.

2. To stabilize macro tax burden is to carry out structural adjustment on the premise of stable overall tax burden level

With the changes in the economic and social situation, the current tax system plays an obviously insufficient role in promoting the transformation of economic development mode, regulating the distribution of social wealth, saving energy and resources and protecting the environment, which is difficult to respond to the construction of China's "five-in-one" comprehensive well-off society. Therefore, in the future tax reform, on the premise of maintaining the level of total tax burden, we should increase the tax burden on resource use and environmental pollution by means of linkage of tax reform and tax burden reduction. In turn, we will raise the price of resources and the cost of environmental pollution, form an internal incentive mechanism for many market players, strengthen the innovation awareness and ability of market players, and achieve the goal of energy conservation and emission reduction.

4.4 Further Deepen Reform of the Management of Government Expenditures

Improve the Structure of Government Expenditures

Scientific and reasonable structure of public expenditure is an important lever for the country to realize the coordinated development of economy and society. According to Musgrave's "three stages theory" of economic development, different stages of a country's economic development will directly affect the growth and structural changes of public expenditure. In the early stage of economic development, public expenditure focuses on infrastructure and basic industries, while in the mature stage of economic development, fiscal expenditure is mainly inclined to education, medical and health care, social security, environmental protection and other livelihood projects. In addition, the transformation of public expenditure structure is closely related to economic growth. When the economy reaches a certain stage, there will inevitably be corresponding fiscal expenditure structure, and the benign change and scientific adjustment of fiscal expenditure structure can further promote economic development to a new stage. Therefore, the adjustment of public finance expenditure structure must adapt to the stage of economic development and make the expenditure structure fully adapt to the characteristics and requirements of economic and social development in this stage. At present, China's overall economic strength has reached a high level, so fiscal expenditure should focus on the civil projects concerning the overall welfare of the public.

1. Optimize the structure of government investment spending

From the perspective of industrial strategic layout, the primary industry should gradually shift to "intensive operation" in the stability, the secondary industry should pay attention to industrial upgrading and structural optimization, and the tertiary industry, which has more employment potential and is closely related to the improvement of people's welfare, should be vigorously supported. From the cost–benefit perspective, we should reduce industrial investment with high energy consumption, high pollution and low efficiency, and shift the focus of investment expenditure to industrial upgrading and industries with higher science and technology content and benefit prospect. From the perspective of the prospects of endogenous economic growth, except for certain periods (such as economic depression requires the government to expand investment directly), finance should mainly play the role of policy guidance, and investment should drive more "spontaneous growth" effect formed by social capital forces.

2. Strengthen financial support for people's livelihood and public services

Education, health care, medical care, social security, housing, urban and rural community affairs and other public areas are the focus of social conflicts in China. The reform of the financial expenditure structure in terms of distribution should be inclined to people's livelihood, to the less developed areas in the central and western regions, and to the direction conducive to long-term and balanced economic development.

3. Optimize the function of transfer payments and adjust the balanced development of social income distribution and regions

The imbalance of income distribution and economic and social development in China is mainly manifested in the differences between different income groups, the imbalance between regions, the contradiction between urban and rural dual structure, and the differences between monopolistic and non-monopolistic industries. In addition to direct central fiscal expenditure expansion support, the solution to these problems can be more through transfer spending arrangements to support the weak party, fiscal expenditure in the strategic level should be reasonable, unified, orderly, standardized arrangements.

4. Reduce the inflation demand for rigid administrative expenditures, and establish the idea of "lead a thrifty life" and the awareness of economy

No amount of fiscal funds can afford to waste it, let alone the future era of rapid fiscal growth will end. Government departments should pay more attention to results-oriented spending, strictly control administrative expenditures and other general expenditures, strive to reduce administrative costs, and ensure that the limited funds are used to the best advantage. During the rapid growth of fiscal revenue over the past 10 years, many people have become accustomed to spending to buy political achievements, and some people have formed the mindset and behavior mode of carving up "excess income" every year and improving welfare from year to year. At present, with the end of the era of high fiscal revenue growth, we need to have a clear understanding and strengthen governance of these institutional "persistent diseases" that have long existed in China's economic and social operation. The government's "lead a thrifty life" should not stop at slogans, let alone short-term operations, but should be integrated into the fiscal and economic operation process as a long-term strategy.

In a word, considering the reality and trend of the increase of personnel expenditure and the heavy burden of social security expenditure, the scale of fiscal expenditure should strive to maintain the basic stability of administrative cost and seek to reduce it in combination with supporting reforms. The main direction of expenditure should be to strengthen basic livelihood security, general public services and public infrastructure.

Optimize the Pattern of Government Expenditures and Improve the System of Spending Quotas and Standards

We will reduce the use of special subsidies to support the industries and industry development, prudently and rationally adopt tax incentives, and explore ways to incorporate tax reductions and exemptions into budget management in the form of "tax expenditures." The supply of public services should fully integrate the government with the market. The central government is responsible for providing basic public services at the lower limit, local governments provide improved basic public services at the lower limit based on their own conditions, and the market provides higher-level services.

The expenditure standard system is a policy basis and measurement standard established to examine and verify departments' budgetary expenditure in order to ensure the normality, scientificity and rationality of the allocation of financial budget funds. Basic expenditure quota is the arrangement standard of personnel funds and daily public funds in the process of government operation, and it is one of the important bases of budget preparation and implementation. The improvement of China's expenditure standard system should start from the following aspects: First, we need to strengthen the analysis of the macroeconomic situation, grasp the actual needs of economic construction and social development, make scientific forecasts of domestic and foreign economic trends, GDP growth rate, price index and other core economic indicators, define the scope and priorities of expenditure support, and make overall plans and balance the needs of institutional operations and business development when financial resources are possible. Second, we must establish and improve the cost accounting system, fully use information technology means, and objectively and comprehensively analyze government operating costs, on this basis, the further study of business characteristics and development trend of various departments, and improve the pertinence and effectiveness of quota system through the protection scope and standard dynamic adjustment and optimization. Third, we need to implement total allocation and broad category management. On the premise of clarifying the work objectives of all departments in a quantitative or demonstrable manner, we need to consolidate and reduce the itemization of each quota and gradually form a comprehensive quota for basic expenditures. We will increase the proportion of performance-based pay in personnel funds, reflect the characteristics of departments in the use of daily public funds, allow all departments to plan expenditure items according to business needs within the approved budget, and break the boundary between personnel funds and daily public funds when necessary.

Strengthen the Performance Evaluation of Fiscal Expenditure

Our country has carried on some practices and explorations to the financial expenditure performance appraisal, but there are still some problems, such as the lagging of the performance appraisal laws and regulations, the "top-heavy, emphasis on the part rather than the whole", the narrow scope of appraisal, the unscientific appraisal index system and the insufficient application of appraisal results, which need to be further reformed and improved.

1. Improve the standard and method system of financial expenditure performance evaluation, and establish and improve the performance evaluation system

The most important part of financial expenditure performance evaluation is the evaluation standard and method of public financial expenditure performance evaluation. Fiscal expenditure covers a wide range, including direct, tangible and real expenditure, indirect, intangible and expected benefits, as well as social and ecological benefits. It should consider not only the local benefit but also the whole benefit. It should not only be able to evaluate short-term benefits, but more importantly be able to evaluate long-term benefits, to achieve an organic combination of these. To improve the performance evaluation standard and method system of financial expenditure, the following problems should be solved firstly: first, the construction of scientific and standard evaluation standard system; Second, determine the weight of indicators; Third, the selection of reasonable and practical evaluation and scoring methods. The evaluation index system of performance finance includes the combination of commonness and individuality, the combination of qualitative and quantitative evaluation indexes, suitable evaluation standards and correct evaluation methods. In short, scientific, standardized and detailed performance evaluation methods should be used to evaluate the achievement degree and effect of financial expenditure performance targets, directly link the performance evaluation results with the budget funds of the next year, and force all departments to improve the efficiency of financial funds. An assessment mechanism of "implementing annual rolling budget with cost–benefit analysis as the core" should be established to ensure continuous improvement of departmental budget and financial fund efficiency.

2. Expand the objects and contents of performance evaluation, and promote the development of financial expenditure performance evaluation in an all-round and multi-level way

According to the different subjects and objects of financial expenditure performance evaluation, the financial expenditure performance evaluation can be divided into four categories: Financial expenditure project performance evaluation, unit financial expenditure performance evaluation, department financial expenditure performance evaluation and financial expenditure comprehensive performance evaluation. At present, it is necessary to start from the project performance evaluation, reflect the department expenditure performance through the evaluation of large categories of projects, apply the results to constrain the department management behavior, and gradually expand the evaluation scope to the links of budget preparation, budget execution and project arrangement in accordance with the principle of "gradually expanding the scope and advancing in an orderly manner". Taking into full account such comprehensive factors as the characteristics and environment of a specific project or department, combined with the actual economic and social development, promote the development of departmental expenditure performance evaluation to an all-round and multi-level direction, and finally realize the systematic evaluation of departmental expenditure management performance.

3. Standardize the evaluation subject and explore the introduction of third-party evaluation mechanism

Establish effective oversight and accountability mechanisms. Establish an independent budget review team. We will make our review work deeper and more detailed, and move toward substantive review. We will strengthen oversight over the use of budgetary surplus revenue and the management of extra-budgetary funds. The performance evaluation of fiscal expenditure projects is mainly led by the government, which formulates performance evaluation rules and participates in the evaluation of performance evaluation. The government even formulates common indicators, scoring standards and unified evaluation report format for different projects. The government, as the allocating party of project funds, hopes to improve the use efficiency of financial funds through the new method of performance evaluation. However, there are many common interests in both the government departments that allocate funds and the units that implement projects. It is difficult to ensure that the government departments that lead the performance evaluation and its assessment are not in collusion with the project implementation units, so that the performance evaluation becomes a decoration. Excessive government participation in performance evaluation is not conducive to the open, fair and just performance evaluation. In view of this, on the basis of establishing and perfecting the performance evaluation system and the performance evaluation, we should explore the introduction of third-party evaluation subjects, strengthen performance audit and performance accountability, so as to maximize the use of limited financial funds.

4. Strengthen the feedback and application of performance evaluation results

First, summarize the results of various financial expenditure performance evaluation, and take it as an important basis for financial allocation and department budget in the second year, based on which a set of incentive mechanism and constraint mechanism related to financial expenditure performance is established. For those with excellent performance evaluation, priority shall be given to the financial allocation and department budget in the next year; Those with poor performance should be reported and dealt with or even deducted from next year's financial budget. Secondly, in the mid-term implementation of the budget, we can consult and compare the use of funds and their performance according to the evaluation report, further understand the implementation of the department's budget, and find out the problems in the use and arrangement of budget funds in time.

5. Enhancing budget transparency, especially the financial transparency of municipal and county governments, is a key link to improve the efficiency of the use of financial funds

We will accelerate the release of government budgets and make public finance more transparent. The financial departments need to substantially refine the budget and implementation reports submitted to the NPC for deliberation. The current sub-items are too rough and too large for most NPC deputies to understand, let alone the ordinary people. In addition, the acquisition and use of financial funds, all kinds of procedures and information transmission of financial decisions must comply with the rules, and be published step by step. Learn from the experience of capital market, publish not only annual report, but also semi-annual or even quarterly budget performance report. At present, guizhou and other provincial-level departments and units have made public all their budget forms and detailed them into revenue-level subjects. Expenditures on education, medical and health care, social security, employment, agriculture, forestry and water resources, and housing security were made public to sub-level items. Expenditures on official hospitality, official hospitality and official hospitality were made public and explained. The number of employees, the number of vehicles purchased and the number of vehicles possessed were made public. On the basis of summarizing and continuing to improve the publicity of provincial budgets, we will actively promote the publicity of municipal and county budgets.

Improve the Government Procurement System and Actively Promote the Government to Purchase Public Services

The purchase of public services by the government is a new concept, mechanism and method for the government to provide public services in China. It is an important part of giving full play to the role of the market in the allocation of public service resources, transforming government functions and innovating the economic and social governance system. It is also an important way to promote the cooperation and interaction between government and society. The *Decision* of the third plenary session of the 18th central committee of the communist party of China (CPC) explicitly proposed to "intensify the government's purchase of public services… We will promote the purchase of government services.

In principle, we will introduce a competitive mechanism to purchase transactional services through contracts and commissions. The government's purchase of public services is being applied in more and more areas. In 2013, the state council issued the *Guiding Opinions of the General Office of the State Council on Government Purchasing Services from Social Forces* (G.B.F.[2013] No.96), which put forward guiding opinions on government purchasing services. On January 16, 2014, the Ministry of Finance held a national meeting on government purchase of services, which put forward specific requirements for government purchase of services.

The purchase of public services is essentially a contract signed by the government and social organizations to use financial funds to contract services by social organizations to achieve specific public service goals. Its core significance is the contractual provision of public services, and the government and social organizations form equal and independent contractual parties. Its important effects include promoting the transformation of government functions, cultivating the service market, improving the efficiency of financial capital expenditure, and so on. We will accelerate institutional development and improve the systems and mechanisms for the government to purchase public services, mainly including the following: First, improve laws and regulations and formulate regulations for the government to purchase public services. Second, straighten out the relationship between the responsibilities of government departments in the purchase of public services; Third, improve the budget management of purchasing services; Fourth, standardize the administrative procedures for government purchase of public services; Fifth, improve the effective supervision and risk prevention mechanism for government purchase of public services; Sixth, accelerate the cultivation of public service supply market, reshape the relationship between government and social organizations, and promote orderly competition.

[Column 3.6]

The way to alleviate the "trinity paradox" of fiscal distribution.

Through academic demonstration, there is a "trinity paradox" in the process of fiscal income redistribution. That is to say, at any given time, among the three generally "sensible" goals of reducing taxes, increasing entitlement spending and reining in government debt and deficits, people can only achieve two of them at the same time but not all at the same time, and the failure to achieve the goal will limit the achievement of the other two goals at the same time. The "trinity paradox" restriction of financial distribution is a general understanding under certain limited conditions, namely, the established level of fiscal expenditure management, the level of government administrative cost and the multiplier effect of government debt funds, and there is positive and negative correlation: The higher the level of fiscal expenditure management, the lower the level of administrative cost, and the larger the financing multiplier, the more beneficial it is to reduce tax revenue, increase public welfare, and control the debt and deficit.

In view of the existence of financial distribution "trinity paradox", from the perspective of government function transformation, mechanism innovation and deepening reform, it is bound to have the following requirements to ease the restriction of financial distribution "trinity paradox".

(1) Effectively improve the management of fiscal expenditure—"do more and spend less".

Improving the level of fiscal expenditure management requires comprehensive reform of institutional innovation, management innovation and technological innovation interaction. In order to truly achieve the goal of "do more and spend less", we need to start from the following three aspects and strengthen the tripartite reform interaction: First, the system should pay special attention to the deepening reform of the financial system and the construction of the fund performance supervision and evaluation system based on it. Second, expenditure management should continue to carry out scientific and fine management, establish and improve the financial expenditure monitoring system. Related financial expenditure performance evaluation can be considered to introduce balanced scorecard (table) and other methods tend to be detailed and comprehensive. Third, in terms of related technologies, we should continue to comprehensively promote and implement the systematic project applicable to the most advanced information processing technology and upgrade the government financial management system on the basis of "Golden Finance", Golden Tax" and other government "Golden" projects. On the basis of implementing the "twelve golden" project put forward in 2002, we will continue to improve the sophistication, security and comprehensiveness of e-government, and improve the convenience and accuracy of information acquisition, information processing and information transmission. It integrates system information, electronization and performance management systematically to comprehensively improve the level of fiscal expenditure management, do more and spend less, and relax the restriction of the "trinity paradox".

(2) Effectively reduce government administrative costs—"make good use of money and get real work done".

The key to effectively reduce the administrative cost of the government is to promote comprehensive economic, administrative and political reform, which includes: First, we will carry out reform of the administrative system, streamline government agencies and personnel at all levels on the basis of rationalizing the functions and powers of governments at all levels. We will improve the quality of human resources, and at the same time reduce the costs of institutions and personnel in administrative management while raising the efficiency of government work. Second, we will continue to implement the budgetary information disclosure system and strengthen oversight. The disclosure of budget and final accounts information is not only the essential requirement of public finance, but also the important content of government information disclosure. Releasing to the public information on the budgets of the central and local governments for official overseas visits, official hospitality and other public services shows the government's determination to fulfill its commitment and accept public supervision. It has also laid a foundation for governments at all levels to further disclose their administrative funds, practice strict economy and reduce government operating costs under the supervision of the public. Third, further reform the administrative funds related management system. For example, we will push forward the reform of official vehicles, strictly review and approve outbound visits on business, and reduce the number and number of outbound groups. We will strictly control spending standards for official business trips and receptions, and prohibit gifts. Fourth, we will work hard to improve the supervision, evaluation and accountability system for government funds, so that every penny of taxpayers' money will be spent where it is needed and maximized, so that the saved financial funds can be invested in the areas most needed by people's livelihood.

(3) Expanding the multiplier for government borrowing—"borrow less and do more"

Multiplier of government debt financing refers to the degree of chain reaction caused by the change of government debt. The larger the financing multiplier, the better for reducing taxes, increasing public welfare, and controlling debt and deficit levels. Raising the financing multiplier of government bonds or local government bonds inevitably requires a series of management and mechanism innovation, especially the comprehensive supporting reform related to policy-based financing system mechanism. One of the key points of implementation is to build a risk-sharing mechanism among financial institutions, policy-based financial institutions, enterprises, commercial Banks and credit guarantee institutions (rather than a bottomless financial mechanism). Under the market economy environment, the government USES policy-based funds, market-oriented operation and specialized management mechanism to pursue the "credit amplification" of funds, that is, "achieve the great with doing little" to drive social funds and private capital to follow up, and improve the efficiency of capital use. It is feasible and necessary to explore the potential of this aspect in the market economy environment, which is conducive to easing the restriction of the fiscal "trinity paradox", "borrowing less" and "doing more", that is, to increase the multiplier effect and strive to bring about and transfer social funds to form a more substantial force.

(4) Substantive transformation of government function type—"expanding financial resources and optimizing administrative power".

In the process of the sound development of market economy in China, the rationalization adjustment of government functions is imperative. The implementation mode of national political power governance will mainly reflect the management of social and public affairs. Finance, as a distribution system of fiscal control by administration and administration through fiscal management", must serve this historic transformation and carry out its own corresponding transformation, that is, to improve public finance. The substantial transformation of government functions calls for the reform of government system, institutions and social management. For example, in terms of government system, it is necessary to gradually clarify and reasonably define the functions of governments at all levels from the central government to local governments, form detailed lists of powers from rough to fine, and establish and apply a complete, transparent, scientific and reasonable modern government revenue and expenditure classification system in the budget, so as to provide basic management conditions for the performance of government functions. In terms of government social management, we should continue to build and improve the basic education system, basic medical and health care system and basic housing security system that cover all the people, and stress the transformation of government into a service-oriented one. We will encourage and guide the development of various types of non-governmental bodies and intermediary organizations oriented to the market and public welfare, and improve institutions and systems for public–private cooperation. PPP (public–private partnership) model of public works and public goods supply should be a model worthy of special attention and development in the process of government transformation. These include at least a variety of public–private contracts, including design and building (DB), operation and maintenance (O&M), design, building, financing and operation (DBFO), building, ownership and operation (BOO), building, operation and transfer (BOT), purchase, building and operation (BBO), building, lease, operation and transfer (BLOT), etc.. With the improvement of China's market economic system and economic and social development to form a more extensive application and optimization. It will encourage non-governmental entities and non-governmental financial resources to inject new vitality into the transformation and optimization of government functions, open new financial resources and potential space for the improvement of public welfare level, and effectively alleviate the pressure of government debt and deficit.

4.5 Improve the Government Debt Management System

There are many reasons for the expansion of local government debt in China. To solve the problem of local government debt, we should establish a reasonable local debt financing channels, perfect the financial management system below provincial level, ensure the basic-level government basic funding needs, promote equal basic public services, and narrow transverse longitudinal financial gap between regions, increase local fiscal sustainability, promote financial reform deepening, and implement the comprehensive control of local debt.

We will regulate local government financing platforms and gradually reduce outstanding debt, especially by controlling the excessive growth of new debt. We will improve the evaluation model of GDP, including the growth of the debt ratio of local governments and GDP in the evaluation of top party and government officials at the municipal, county and township levels, prevent the moral hazard of excessive debt, and change the unreasonable incentive mechanism that is not conducive to the performance and promotion of officials without too much debt.

Establish and Improve the Local Debt Management System

We will give local governments limited rights to issue debt and give full play to the leading role of financial departments in local government debt management. We will establish a comprehensive mechanism for local government debt risk management, carry out fine management of government cash and debt, establish a unified national system and information system for local government debt statistics, a system for real-time risk monitoring indicators, and an information disclosure mechanism, and identify responsible institutions for controlling the size of local government debt and supervising its operation.

Improve the Operation of National Debt and the National Debt Balance Management System

We will further clarify specific measures for managing the size and maturity of debt, give full play to the role of Treasury bonds in coordinating fiscal and monetary policies and stabilizing market expectations, build a debt governance framework that meets the country's borrowing needs and is conducive to risk control, and optimize the management and use of the central budget stabilization fund.

[Column 3.7].

The international practice and enlightenment of local government debt management.

In developed countries such as the United States, Japan, France and Germany, the local government financing system is very developed, and local government debt has become an important part of government bonds. With the accelerated development of market economy, the scale of local debt in some emerging industrialized countries and other rapidly developing countries keeps expanding, and its impact on social economy cannot be underestimated. This part sorts out and analyzes the local debt management situation of developed countries like the United States, Japan, newly industrialized countries like South Korea and representative developing countries like Brazil and Colombia, and then puts forward the beneficial reference and inspiration for improving the local debt management of China.

(1) Local government debt management in the United States

The United States is a federal country with perfect market economy system and strong financial and economic strength. State and local governments have their own fiscal systems, with substantial financial support from the federal government. State governments get most of their revenue from sales and income taxes, while local governments rely on property taxes.

1. Scale and composition of local government debt

Local governments in the United States mainly finance their debts by issuing municipal bonds, bank loans and financial leasing. Among them, municipal bonds are the most important form of local government debt in the United States. The United States was an early issuer of local government bonds and a country with large local debt. Since the 1960s, local government debt in the United States has been on the rise. The scale of debt and the size of local government economy and fiscal revenue has been maintained a relatively stable proportion. For local governments, the proportion of direct debt borne by local municipal agencies is relatively low, and the proportion of contingent debt formed by government guarantee is relatively high.

According to their purposes, the short-term bonds issued by states and local governments in the United States can be divided into prepaid tax bonds, prepaid income bonds and urban reconstruction bonds. Both prepaid tax bonds and prepaid income bonds are issued to make up the difference between state and local government revenues. Urban reconstruction project bonds are short-term bonds issued by urban reconstruction institutions to raise short-term funds for urban reconstruction projects, which are generally guaranteed by state and local governments. The vast majority of state and local government bonds are long-term bonds with maturities of more than one year, typically 10, 20 or even 30 years. Historically, long-term debt has accounted for more than 90 per cent of us local-government debt. Long-term bonds include general obligation bonds and revenue bonds. General obligation bonds pay debts and interest on the basis of the issuer's creditworthiness, that is, taxes. Revenue bonds pay debts and interest based on a specific income earned by a government enterprise. The size of state and local government debt and the proportion of the two kinds of bonds are shown in Tables 4.6 and 4.7. Local bonds are bought almost entirely by households, funds, commercial Banks and insurance companies.

Statistical Abstract of the United States.

Table 4.6 The size of state and local government debt in the United States (unit: $1 billion)

Year and grade		Accumulated debt		Debt activities	
	Total	Short-term	Long-term	Debt issuance	Debt repayment
1980: Total amount	336	13	263	42	17
	122	2	80	16	6
Among them: state places	214	11	183	26	12
1990:	858	19	474	108	65
Total amount	318	3	126	44	23
Among them: state places	540	17	349	65	42
1995:	1115	27	697	129	95
Total amount	427	6	205	53	37
Among them: state places	688	21	492	77	58
2000:	1452	24	960	185	122
Total amount	548	6	267	75	44
Among them: state places	904	18	693	110	78
2003:	1813	40	1243	346	215
Total amount	698	16	366	149	86
Among them: state places	1115	24	876	197	129

Note in the United States, local government refers to governments below the state level (excluding states)

Table 4.7 Annual new municipal long-term bonds issued by U.S. state and local governments (unit: $1 billion)

Year	Total	General bond	Revenue bond
1980	46	14	32
1985	202	40	163
1990	126	40	86
1995	156	60	96
1997	214	72	142
1998	280	93	187
1999	219	70	149
2000	194	65	129
2001	284	101	182
2002	356	126	230

Note in the United States, local government refers to governments below the state level (excluding states)

2. Budgetary system for local government debt management

Strengthening budget management and budgetary restraint is the most important means to effectively control the expansion of local government debt. After a long period of exploration, the United States has formed a relatively effective budget system to strengthen local government debt management.

In the United States, almost every state constitution or law requires the implementation of the balanced budget rule, that is, the governor submits the balanced budget implementation bill, which is passed by the state legislature, and signed and issued by the governor. Five states-Indiana, Texas, Vermont, Virginia and West Virginia – require their governors to submit balanced budgets to their legislatures each year. Of these, 15 states have specific requirements in their constitutions and statutes, while the remaining 30 states only have provisions in their constitutions or statutes. The second level of fiscal restraint is reflected in the balanced budget act enacted by the state legislature. Currently, 41 U.S. states have this requirement, 11 of which have specific constitutional and statutory requirements. If the budget is in deficit, the state can borrow and carry the current deficit over to the next fiscal year. Since there are no restrictive fiscal constraints at the end of the fiscal year, these states are legally allowed to run deficits, another type of "prior rule" that is in effect in eight states. The third limit is to allow states to run deficits at the end of the year, but to reflect them in their budgets for the next fiscal year and ensure that they can be repaid. This is known as the "ex post facto rule", which applies in all 10 states. The most restrictive of the balanced-budget rules is the legislature's balanced-budget law, which requires deficits to be absorbed at the end of a fiscal year and prohibits carry-over to the next. Government borrowing is allowed only during the budget cycle. The "ex post facto rule", which requires balanced budgets in 35 American states, is strict. The long-term practice of the balanced budget rule in the United States shows that the rigorous budget rule and its strong enforcement mechanism can help regulate the fiscal expenditure of local governments, reduce or avoid the excessive expenditure of local governments, and prevent the excessive debt of local governments.

3. Local financial risk warning and prevention mechanism

The United States has accumulated rich experience in dealing with the local government financial crisis and formed a relatively sound mechanism for early warning and control of local government debt risk. In Pennsylvania, for example, chapter 30 of the *General Local Law* (local recovery act) provides a clear idea of how to prevent local fiscal crises. The *Local Recovery Act* sets out clearly the powers and responsibilities of all relevant parties, the recognition of local financial crises, the initiation of emergency financial assistance, and the necessary integration of local financial rights and resources. When evaluating local financial stability, the following criteria should be taken into account: Local governments have been in deficit for more than three years, and the deficit ratio has been more than 1% (including 1%) in each fiscal year. Local expenditure exceeds income by three years or more; Payment of principal or interest on bonds or notes in arrears; the local has 30 days in arrears; For 30 days the locality fails to pay the creditors' expenses on a specified date; Local governments negotiated with creditors for an adjustment of more than 30% of the debt, but the negotiations were unsuccessful. The local government deficit to GDP ratio has been 5% or higher for two consecutive years; Where a local government fails to pay the minimum pension expenditure within a specified period of time as required by the *Local Pension Plan Funding Standards and Recovery Act*, it may adjust its liabilities under chapter 9 of the bankruptcy code; Local taxes on general purpose real estate have reached the highest level, while the number of local services has been significantly reduced. Ohio and other states have also established a relatively sound risk warning mechanism model. The *Local Financial Emergency Law* specifies in detail the operation procedures of risk warning monitoring system and crisis resolution mechanism.

4. Local government debt information is transparent and the role of market supervision and guidance is emphasized

By formulating and improving relevant laws and regulations, the United States strengthens legal constraints and improves the transparency of municipal bond issuance by local governments. State and local governments in the United States must follow the basic standards for government debt reporting established by the government accounting standards board in *Government Accounting, Auditing and Financial Reporting* (1983), and record and report government debts. Municipal authorities are required to disclose any significant changes to the city's financial and legal situation during the term of the municipal bonds. In 1989, the securities and exchange commission amended relevant rules of the *Securities Law* to further improve the quality and timeliness of municipal bond information disclosure. To further prevent abuses in the municipal bond market, the SEC adopted new market transaction disclosure principles in 1990 and 1995, requiring issuers and users of municipal bonds to update their disclosure information in a timely and regular manner. The public disclosure of these information has greatly improved the information situation on which municipal bond credit risk judgment is based. In addition, in local debt management, emphasis should be placed on the role of market supervision and guidance. For example, when raising funds in the capital market, American state and local governments must be supervised by credit rating agencies, and the rating results affect the cost of government debt.

5. Case analysis and enlightenment of the bankruptcy of orange county government in the United States

Under the market condition, the local government is not infinite government, once the fiscal expenditure is seriously improper, the debt is excessive, it will go bankrupt. There have been many cases of local governments filing for bankruptcy due to excessive debt and inability to pay off debts in the United States. These events are instructive for China to strengthen local government debt management.

Orange county in southern California declared bankruptcy in December 1994. Orange county is a southern California county with a GDP of $118 billion and a per capita income of $70,000. However, on 6 December 1994, this wealthy county had to declare financial bankruptcy. The reason orange county went bankrupt was because, Robert Citron, treasurer of the orange county Treasury for tax revenue and public deposits borrowed \$14 billion from all parties for derivatives speculation, which was extremely sensitive to interest rate fluctuations. Due to poor judgment, the investment failed, resulting in a loss of \$1.7 billion in the financial resources of orange county, which was beyond the financial capacity of the government. Due to payment crisis, orange county government had to declare bankruptcy.

After orange county declared bankruptcy, the federal government and the state government decided that the root cause of the bankruptcy was poor financial management and asked the county government to solve the problem itself. After bankruptcy, orange county government took the following measures:(1) after bankruptcy, the government reorganized and set up a crisis management team. (2) cut government employees and retrench. Orange county cut 12% of its workforce, and more than 2,000 of the county's 17,000 civil servants were laid off to save money. (3) cut investment in fixed assets and public services. Many important construction projects have had to be postponed, and public services have been cut or delayed, with the exception of schools and police. (4) extend the repayment period through negotiation. The new county government negotiated a new repayment agreement with creditors, asking for an extension and promising to repay the debt with the county government's local taxes for several years to come. The above emergency measures have worked successfully in the short term. Eight months later, orange county was out of bankruptcy and back to normal.

2008 Jefferson county, Alabama, declared bankruptcy. The county government's public infrastructure spending is huge, and many officials are suspected of corruption, resulting in serious financial problems. The total fiscal liabilities are \$3.2 billion. With Jefferson county unable to resolve the crisis any time soon, it filed for bankruptcy with the state of Alabama. Moreover, the state of New York has repeatedly been on the verge of bankruptcy. In the current financial crisis, several state and local governments, including New York, are on the verge of bankruptcy. The financial bankruptcy cases of orange county government and other places in the United States give us the following enlightenment: First, we need to strengthen local government debt management, strictly control debt risks, and establish an early warning mechanism for local government financial risks. We need to integrate this mechanism with auditing and oversight by local people's congresses. Second, in the face of local government financial crisis and bankruptcy, the higher level government and the central government should be careful to use the means of aid, first of all, the local government should be self-reliant, self-rescue mainly.

(2) Management of local government debt in Japan

Japan is a unitary country implementing the system of local autonomy. In 1879, Japan established the principle that "the borrowing of local government debt must be decided by the parliament". From 1888 to 1890, it successively promulgated the *Municipal System and Township System, Prefectural System* and *Prefectural System*, and the local government debt management system was constantly improved. In 1940, the total annual amount of local government debt was controlled for the first time, and the main issuers of bonds were mainly big cities, with large Banks and trust and investment companies with strong strength. As early as in the 32nd Meiji (1899) law, it recognizes the claims of governments at the county level, but the specific items of borrowing, such as the amount of borrowing, repayment method, etc., is subject to the approval of the Home Secretary and Minister of Treasury. At present, the issuing bodies of local government debt in Japan are mainly in prefectures, cities, towns and villages. In addition, in article 283 and article 314, paragraph 2 of the *Local Autonomy Law* of Japan, special local public organizations, such as joint organizations of local public organizations and local development enterprises, are granted creditor's rights.

1. Scale and composition of local government debt

Japan's overall local-government debt is small and concentrated in the central government, with local government borrowing accounting for about 9% of total government revenue. Local bonds are divided into two basic types: local bonds and local corporate bonds. While local public enterprise debt has the nature of both partial government bonds and partial enterprise bonds, so it does not constitute the direct debt of the government, but it is undoubtedly the contingent debt of the government. The proportion of Japanese local government bonds and local corporate roughly 5:1. There are two main ways of borrowing local government debt, namely issuing bonds and borrowing money. There are two ways to issue bonds: public offering and private offering. Before 1979, most of them were issued by private offering. After 1979, the use of public offering began to increase. The issuing objects are mainly financial institutions; Bond denominations of 10,000 yen, 100,000 yen, 1 million yen mainly, mostly for interest-bearing bonds, bond interest rates are usually set with reference to the same term of the national bond interest rate, at the same time private bond interest rate shall be slightly higher than the public bond, in principle cannot be listed in circulation. Since July 1972, all local government bonds have been repaid with a 10-year repayment period by lottery. They are repaid every six months, each time paying 3% of the amount issued, paying interest twice a year and enjoying certain tax advantages.

2. Source and use of local government debt

Japan's local government debt sources mainly include the central government, public enterprises financial Treasury, Banks and other funds. Central government funds mainly include ministry of capital utilization and simple life insurance funds. Among them, the fund utilization department's fund sources are postal savings fund, accumulated fund and surplus fund of central business special accounting such as welfare annuity and national annuity. The fund source of simple life insurance is the idle fund of the postal department to develop simple life insurance system by the post office branches. The public finance fund of public enterprises is the financing fund specially provided for local public enterprises. Bank funds are mainly the loan funds of the Japanese city bank (Metrobank), local Banks and long-term credit Banks. Other funds mainly include fraternal associations, insurance companies and other companies. According to the data since the 1990s, central government funds have always accounted for about half of the outstanding debts of local governments. If we add the financial funds of public enterprises that actually belong to financial investment and financing funds, local government debts provided by the central government account for about

65%.Since 1999, the Japanese government began to reform the financial investment and financing plan. Affected by this, the share of the new debts of local governments from the central government has been decreasing year by year, which has decreased from 45.37% in 1999 to 32.03% in 2004. If we add in the funds from the public financial pools of public enterprises, the share of local government debt provided by the central government decreased from 55.52% in 1999 to 41.26% in 2004.

Japan's local government debt funds are mainly used for constructive spending, not recurrent spending. Specific uses include: funds needed for transportation, gas, sewage and by other enterprises operated by local public utilities; rollover of local government debt; Expenses for disaster fighting, emergency response, post-disaster recovery and disaster relief; Expenses for the construction of public facilities or for the use of land for such facilities. In addition, local government debt of other enterprises can be decided by making special laws when necessary. In recent years, more local borrowing has been used to help implement fiscal policies.

3. Local government debt management is dominated by administrative control

The Japanese government has implemented fine management of local government debt through strict local government debt plan and agreement approval system. (1) the issuance of local government debt shall be subject to planned management. After the second world war, the central government of Japan (mainly composed of the Ministry of Finance and Ministry of Home Affairs) has prepared the local government debt plan every year, which mainly includes the total amount of local government debt issued, its purpose and the amount of debt issued in various ways. The local government debt plan is only submitted to the parliament as a reference, and does not belong to the object of congressional review and resolution, so it has no legal basis and no enforcement effect. However, since it was formulated through consultation between the minister of the Ministry of Finance and the minister of the Ministry of Home Affairs, and stipulated the scale of the central government's subscription of local government debt and the specific use of local government debt, the minister of the Ministry of Home Affairs took this plan as the basis when examining and approving the application of local governments to issue bonds. (2) implement a strict agreement approval system for local governments to borrow money, so as to control the scale of debt, prevent the expansion of local government debt and ensure the healthy operation of local finance; prevent excessive spending in rich regions and ensure reasonable allocation of funds; Coordinate the supply and demand of central government, local government and private funds. According to the *Local Autonomy Law*, when a local government requests to issue bonds, it shall report to the autonomous province in advance, and propose the construction projects to be developed, the sources of funds and the amount of bonds to be issued. After the review by the autonomous provinces, the issuance plans of various regions will be summarized, and after consultation with the Ministry of Finance, the issuance quotas of different regions will be issued uniformly. If public debt bonds are issued, after the approval of the local council and the Ministry of Home Affairs, the meeting of the Ministry of Finance, the Ministry of Home Affairs, the entrusted bank and the securities company shall jointly decide the total amount of issuance each month and the amount of issuance by different regions. The key point of examining and approving local government borrowing by the ministers of the Ministry of Finance, the Ministry of Home Affairs is to determine the list of local governments that do not approve or restrict the issuance of bonds. The basis for such determination generally includes: local governments that do not repay the principal of local government debts on time or find that they have been approved to issue bonds through applications that are obviously inconsistent with the facts are not approved to issue bonds; Local governments with a debt dependency (debt balance/general fiscal expenditure) of 20–30% may not issue bonds for infrastructure construction, and local governments with more than 30% may not issue bonds for general undertakings. It is stipulated that local governments with the tax rate of the local tax being less than 90% or that have more income from horse racing may issues bonds; Local governments with fiscal deficits and loss-making public enterprises are strictly restricted from issuing bonds.

(3) Local government debts of the Republican of Korea

South Korea is a newly industrialized country. According to article 7 of South Korea's *Local Finance Law*, local governments cannot borrow in principle, but it also stipulates: Where necessary, special treatment may be given to the unavoidable local government debts. The specific scope of borrowing includes: First, public works projects with long-term benefits; Second, projects that have sufficient investment returns and can repay capital and interest; Third, projects to resist natural disasters and post-disaster reconstruction; Fourth, raise funds for the previous round of debt repayment; Fifth, other projects to improve the welfare of residents. These specific provisions, in fact, made the local government get a lot of debt financing space. Specifically, the situation with regard to local government borrowing is as follows:

1. Management of local government debt

Local government borrowing must be approved by the central government. Every year, the central government determines and issues the basic guidelines for local government borrowing, and formulates the *Medium-Term Plan for Local Government Borrowing*. Most of the local debt is borrowed from the central government. The specific form is to consult with the government departments that manage the state housing fund, the special account for rural development and the special account for environmental protection before submitting it to the central government for approval. In the examination and approval, some indicators must be controlled within a certain range, such as the debt repayment rate (the average debt repayment amount in the first four years/the average fiscal revenue in the first four years) must be less than 20%, and the income and expenditure balance rate must not be less than −10%. After the central government approves the local government debt plan, the specific amount of the plan must be approved by local municipal authorities (only less than the amount approved by the central government).

2. The overall composition and scale of local government debt

According to different purposes of borrowing, Korean local debt can be divided into general account debt, special account debt and public enterprise debt. The funds raised from the general account debt are mainly used for road and bridge construction, public facilities repair and disaster relief projects. The funds raised from the special account debt are mainly used for housing, water supply and drainage, rural enterprises and other projects. The funds raised by public enterprise bonds are mainly used for projects such as subway and water works. At the end of 2001, the total balance of local government debt in South Korea reached 17.7 trillion won, among which general account debt, special account debt and public enterprise debt amounted to 7.5 trillion won, 5.4 trillion won and 4.9 trillion won respectively, accounting for 42%, 30.4% and 27.4% respectively. The ratio of local debt to local tax revenue and non-tax revenue averaged 70.4%. The situation of local government borrowing varies greatly. The ratio between the balance of borrowing and the total revenue of local finance taxes and fees is 160.6% in Taegu and 32.0% in Gyeongju.

3. Sources of financing for local government bonds

Local government debt is mainly financed by borrowing and issuing bonds. Loans can be borrowed from the central government, local public funds, financial institutions and foreign countries; Bonds can be divided into conventional bonds, obligation bonds, contract bonds and foreign bonds. According to the situation of local government debts in South Korea in 2001, most of them are loans, accounting for 86.1%, which are mainly loans from the central government and local public funds, accounting for 58.6% and 22.6% respectively. More than half of the local bonds in South Korea are in the form of compulsory bonds, such as local development bonds, public road bonds and Seoul city railway bonds, which are purchased by motor vehicle buyers, land developers, etc. at the time of transaction. The so-called contractor bonds are a small amount of bonds that local governments use to cover payments to contract suppliers. The total scale is not big. Conventional bonds account for just 4.6% of total local government debt, while smaller local bonds issued abroad account for 2.1%.

Table 4.8 shows the debt scale of local governments in South Korea in 2001 and their ratio to local tax revenue scale. Table 4.9 reflects the specific amount and structure of local debt in South Korea.

Ministry of Government Administration and Home Affairs.

(4) Control of local government debt in Brazil

1. Local government debt crisis

Brazil is a large developing country located in South America. Since the 1980s, as federal budget constraints softened, Brazil has suffered three big fiscal crises triggered by local government debt. The first debt crisis occurred in the 1980s. In order to implement the strategy of import substitution industrialization, Brazil, whose economy was in the take-off stage, borrowed heavily in the international financial market. In the late 1980s, the second oil crisis triggered an international debt crisis. Soaring interest rates greatly increased the pressure on Brazil's debt service, and states were forced to stop paying their foreign creditors. As a guarantor, Brazil's central government has had to strike a deal with foreign creditors to take over \$19 billion (2% of GDP) of the states' foreign debt for 20 years. In 1993, state governments defaulted on their obligations to federal financial institutions, triggering a second debt crisis. In the wake of the crisis, the central government and state governments agreed again to have the federal Treasury repay some of the \$28 billion owed to federal financial institutions for 20 years. After the initial resolution of the crisis, the federal government began to take measures to regulate state debt, but did not fundamentally establish a comprehensive and effective debt risk control mechanism. The third debt crisis began when state governments refused to meet their debt obligations, causing financial market turmoil. Once again, the central government promised aid and authorized the states to exchange their bonds for those of the federal or central Banks. The central government issues central bonds to reconfirm local government debt and become a creditor to state and municipal governments. 25 of the 27 states and 183 municipalities (with 95% of their outstanding debt) have entered into debt restructuring agreements.

2. Major measures to control local government debt

Table 4.8 Balance of local debt and local revenue (December 2001) (Unit: 1 billion won)

Regions	General account	Special account	Public enterprise account	Sub-total	Subway debt	(A) Total debt balance	(B) Local tax revenue and non-tax revenue	A/B (%)
Seoul	200	1580	117	1897	4320	6218	9203	67.6
Busan	774	1168	532	2474	—	2474	2099	117.8
Taegu	595	942	376	1914	367	2281	1420	160.6
Inchon	273	20	421	714	592	1306	1544	84.6
Kwangju	482	266	199	948	—	948	702	135.0
Daedeok	286	285	243	814	—	814	799	101.9
Ulsan	259	96	159	514	—	514	616	83.4
Gyeongju	1156	193	910	2259	—	2259	7056	32.0
Kangwon	425	63	223	712	—	712	918	77.5
Chungcheongbuk-do	233	39	118	390	—	390	785	49.7
Chungcheongnam-do	417	99	325	840	—	840	976	86.1
Jeollabuk-do	483	101	269	853	—	853	905	94.2
Jeollanam-do	279	202	144	625	—	625	892	70.1
Gyeongsangbuk-do	813	118	282	1213	—	1213	1438	84.4
Gyeongsangnam-do	436	99	452	987	—	987	1840	53.7
Cheju	393	127	95	616	—	616	466	132.1
Total	7506	5399	4865	17,770	—	23,050	31,748	70.4

Sources Ministry of Government Administration and Home Affairs

Table 4.9 Sources of local debt revenue (December 2001) (Unit: 1 billion won)

Borrowing					
177696 (100%)	Sub-total	Government	Public funds	Abroad	Financial institutions
Total	152918 (86.1%)	104089 (58.6%)	40218 (22.6%)	3916 (2.2%)	4696 (2.6%)
		Bond			
	Sub-total	General bond	Mandatory bond	Contractor bond	Abroad
	24778 (13.9%)	8251 (4.6%)	12578 (7.1%)	221 (0.1%)	3728 (2.1%)

After three local government debt crises, the central government of Brazil has resolutely implemented the fiscal stability plan since 1998, and comprehensively strengthened the management of local government debt. The main measures taken are:

1. Establish public finance rules and strengthen fiscal and debt management responsibilities. Since 1998, the central government of Brazil has decisively implemented the fiscal stabilization plan and implemented the fiscal adjustment policy to increase the surplus of the public sector. We will accelerate institutional reform in the areas of social security and administration. In May 2000, the Brazilian government promulgated the *Law on Fiscal Responsibility*, which establishes public finance rules and strengthens fiscal and debt management responsibilities. The *Law on Fiscal Responsibility* and its supporting ACTS have established a general framework for three-level government budgeting, execution and reporting systems on finance and debt, and formulated highly operable quantitative indicators to regulate local government debt.
2. Improve the legal system and strengthen the direct control of local government debt. The government studied and formulated a system of laws and regulations on debt management, and comprehensively strengthened local government debt management. After the crisis, the senate signed the bill No. 78. In 1999, the financial regulatory commission of Brazil promulgated the regulation No. 2653, which authorized the central bank to control the total amount of credit from

domestic Banks to local governments and to review the loan application of local governments. Then came the *Law on Fiscal Responsibility*, which included a strict set of measures to control local government borrowing. Its main provisions include: local government suppliers and contractors shall not provide credit to local governments or their affiliated entities; The amount of borrowing by the local government (except for the enterprises and suppliers mentioned above) must be less than or equal to the size of the capital budget; The new debt must not exceed 18% of the current net income, the debt service cost must not exceed 13% of the current net income, the total debts of the state government must be less than 200% of the current net income, and the total debts of the city government must be less than 120% of the current net income; Borrowing government revenue exceeds non-interest expenditure (maintain primary surplus); Defaulters are not allowed to borrow money; The balance of the guarantee issued by the government must be less than 25% of the recurrent net income; Short-term income advance shall not exceed 8% of recurrent net income; The issuance of new bonds is prohibited except for the extension of maturities; When the bond matures, it shall repay at least 5% of the balance. If the debt repayment expenditure of the borrowing government is less than 13% of the current account net income, it shall repay more than 10% of the balance when the debt matures, or increase the debt repayment expenditure to 13% of the current account net income. Even if the amount of debt is within the above limit, local governments need to meet certain conditions and pass the senate resolution before they can borrow new debt. State and municipal governments are not allowed to raise new debts for eight months before the government transition. The law also stipulates that the ratio of outstanding local government debt to the bank's net assets must be less than 45%. Banks are prohibited from lending to states that borrow money illegally, exceed the deficit limit, or fail to repay the federal government or any other bank; Brazil's state-owned Banks and local government-owned Banks cannot lend to the government.

3. Establish a regular debt reporting system to improve transparency. Brazil's local governments are required to report to the federal government each year on the balance of their fiscal accounts, and every four

months to issue a report on government debts signed by the local administrator. If a local government fails to adjust its debt to the legal limit within the eight-month grace period, it will be blacklisted by the ministry of finance. Disclosure relies heavily on national information systems linked to all Banks. All lending transactions must be registered in the information system or they will be considered illegal. The information system is open and transparent, and any government or bank can see the information. The system runs automatically and cannot be manually adjusted.

4. Formulate strict punishment measures to restrain local government debt management. According to the *Law on Fiscal Responsibility*, those who fail to fulfill their obligations will be punished with personnel punishment, and those who fail to fulfill their obligations will be dismissed from their posts, banned from working in the public sector, fined or even sentenced.

3. Scale and composition of local government debt in recent years

Brazil's *Law on Fiscal Responsibility* and its supporting measures have achieved certain results in controlling the scale of local government debt and curbing the continuous expansion of local government debt. While debt levels have also increased, their share of GDP has declined, from 3.1% in 1999 to 2.6% in 2001. Both the size of the fiscal surplus and its share of gross domestic product have increased. After the debt restructuring and economic stabilization plan, Brazil's economy continues to grow. In recent years, the debt scale has been controlled, but the overall scale is still high. In 2004, Brazilian government revenue was $140.6 billion, government expenditure including capital expenditure was $172.4 billion, and fiscal deficit was $31.8 billion (see Table 4.10). The government owed $219.8 billion in foreign debt. Issuing public bonds was the main means by which the Brazilian government paid interest on its debts. In 2005, Brazil's debt ratio was 60% of gross domestic product (GDP), interest on debt was 12% of GDP, tax revenues were 39 to 40% of GDP, and 25% of that was used to pay interest on foreign debt. In 2005, the total external debt of the government was 187.3 billion us dollars, and the balance of short-term debt was 23.993

Table 4.10 Government revenue and expenditure of Brazil and Colombia in 2004 (Unit: $100 million)

	Brazil	Columbia
Government revenue	1406	153.3
Government expenditure (including capital expenditure)	1724	210.3
Fiscal deficit (a positive number is the surplus)	−318	−57

Source: http://www.worldbank.org

billion us dollars. In the same year, the total local financial debt was 444.0 billion us dollars, of which the domestic debt accounted for 84.2% of the total debt (see Table 4.11 for details). In 2006, the total external debt of the government was $194.1 billion, and the balance of short-term debt was $20.325 billion (see Table 4.12).

(5) Local government debt management in Colombia

Colombia is one of the countries with the highest degree of decentralization in the Americas. Its government structure is divided into three levels: central government, provincial government and municipal government. All levels of governments have their own expenditure responsibilities and financial resources. Its local governments account for about 40%

Table 4.11 The proportion of domestic debt in Brazil's local financial liabilities and the scale of local liabilities

	2003	2004	2005	Total liabilities of local finance(Unit: $100 million)
Brazil	78.7%	81.1%	84.2%	4440

Source http://www.standishmellon.com/public/documentsnewsEMLM_W2006.pdf

Table 4.12 External debt situation of Brazil and Colombia from 1999 to 2006 (Unit: $100 million)

Year	1999	2000	2001	2002	2003	2004	2005	2006
Brazil	2000	2320	2510	2224	2149	2198	1873	1941
Columbia	350	340	390	384	382.6	387	377	397

Note year-end statistics
Source http://www.worldbank.org

of national spending. The main features of local debt management in Colombia are:

1. Place equal emphasis on administrative and legal means of local debt management

Colombia's debt management is dominated by administrative control, allowing local governments to borrow domestic and foreign debts. According to different ways of borrowing, the central government has different degrees of control over local government borrowing.

While local governments need approval from the ministry of finance to issue bonds, other ways of borrowing, such as by commercial Banks, are not strictly restricted. In addition, Colombia rules that local governments cannot borrow to finance current spending. The ministry of finance, banking regulators and commercial Banks are responsible for overseeing the implementation of the rules.

Colombia has banned the central bank from lending to local governments. If the local entity violates the provisions of *Law No. 617* and *Law No. 358*, or owes debts to the government, then the government is prohibited from lending to the local entity or guaranteeing its debts. In addition, loans to local entities by financial institutions and regional development agencies must meet the restrictions of different legal norms such as *Law No.358*, *Law No. 617* and *Law No. 817*. Otherwise, the credit agreement is invalid and the borrowed funds must be repaid immediately without interest or any other expenses.

2. Establish an early warning system for local government debt risks

In order to control and manage local government debt, Colombia has established a quantitative debt risk warning index, which improves the scientificity of local government debt management. Between 1993 and 1997, the Colombian government established the "traffic light" system, which links the debts of local governments with their solvency, and uses the two indicators of "traffic light" to warn the potential local debts to be borne by the central government. *Law No. 358* of 1997 clearly stipulates specific restrictive provisions on local government debt, which is bound by two indicators: first is the ratio of local government debt interest expenditure to current surplus, which represents the liquidity of local governments. The second is the ratio of debt balances to recurring revenue, which is used to assess the sustainability of medium-and long-term debt. *Law No. 795* of 2003 eliminated the yellow light classification in the original system (Sect. 120), and the revised law imposed stricter borrowing restrictions on local governments. As Table 4.13 shows, local governments in (heavily indebted) red-light districts are prohibited from borrowing. Local governments in the green zone are allowed to sign their own borrowing contracts. *Law No. 819* of 2003 (the fiscal transparency and accountability act) added another layer. In addition to the initial liquidity and solvency indicators, a third indicator has been added, namely, that the current surplus should be greater than or equal to the interest on the debt.

3. Strengthen the management of local contingent liabilities

Since local governments in Colombia do not have their own Banks, fees are recognized on an accrual basis. Thus, management of contingent liabilities has traditionally been limited to the central government. *Law No.448* (1998), *Law No.617* and *Law No.819* (2003) extend the scope framework of contingent liabilities. *Law No.448* requires the central government, provincial governments and all categories of local entities to include budgetary allocations to cover contingent liabilities. The Ministry of Finance plays a central role in the quantitative management

Table 4.13 Colombia's "traffic light" system for local debt (warning system)

Indicator	Green light (%)	Red light (%)
Liquidity (debt interest expense/current surplus)	<40	>40
Solvency (debt balance/recurring revenue)	<80	>80

Note current surplus = current revenue-current expenditure (excluding interest expenditure) - transfer payments to lower levels of government. Recurring revenue mainly includes tax revenue, non-tax revenue, transfer payments from the central government, revenue sharing between the central and local governments and interest income. Current expenditure includes salary, social welfare and social security expenditure of these liabilities. The law also establishes a special fund (the venture fund of a regional entity) to cover the costs incurred by the regional debt, which is an agreement secured by the central government. Under *Law No. 617*, non-earmarked revenue must be used to fund the running costs of local entities, which include not only recurrent expenses, but also contingent and pension liabilities and funds for some capital investments. *Law No. 819* requires that any contingent obligations relating to concessions, sovereign debt guarantees and legal legality be reported to congress annually as part of the medium-term fiscal framework.

(6) Reference and inspiration for local debt management in China

With the continuous expansion of national and local debt, various countries have adopted different management modes and practices according to their national conditions, with successful experience and failure lessons. From the practice of local debt management in various countries, the following points are worth our reference.

1. The tax-divided and graded fiscal system required by market economy contains the necessity and rationality of local government borrowing appropriately

Raising creditor's rights is the property right of governments at all levels under the standardized tax sharing system. This is the experience obtained from the long-term practice of countries implementing the tax-sharing financial system. In most market economies, a tiered (tax-sharing) fiscal system exists between the central (federal) and local governments. Local finance is independent of the central finance. The central budget and local budget are prepared and run independently. It is very common for local governments to issue bonds. For example, in the United States, Japan, France, Germany and the United Kingdom, local governments are allowed by law to issue bonds, and the local government bond market has become relatively mature and perfect, becoming an important way of local financing and an organic part of the capital market, playing a very important role in the national economic development, especially the development of local economy. Therefore, it is reasonable and necessary for China to implement the tax classification and fiscal system and entrusts local governments with creditor's rights. It is an important step to deepen the reform of the financial system to entrusting local governments with the due financial power, including raising the debt right, on the basis of dividing the inter-governmental powers. Giving local governments the right to raise debts moderately, and allowing local governments to borrow on an appropriate scale and raising necessary construction funds through standard legal procedures and under conditions of transparency and supervision is helpful for local governments to cope with the high expenditure of municipal construction and other aspects in the short-term in the operation of graded budgets, spread the expenditure peak into a longer period of time, and exert the function of providing quasi-public goods with the help of social funds and market mechanism, so as to effectively make up for the shortage of local government revenue.

2. Improve relevant laws and standardize local debt management

The investigation of foreign local government debt management practice shows that most countries have made clear provisions on the division of administrative and financial rights of governments at all levels by the constitution and laws, and clarified the responsibilities of governments at all levels, avoiding unnecessary buck-passing and unfair means of fighting for funds. In addition, there are clear legal provisions on the sources of financing, fund management, the scope of investment and debt repayment. In strengthening the management of local government debt, China should learn from this experience, improve the budget law and transfer payment regulations, clarify the administrative and financial rights of governments at all levels in the form of legislation, tighten budgetary constraints, regulate government debt and guarantee behavior, and strengthen the legal management of local debt.

3. Strengthen the central government's supervision over local government debt, and establish an early warning and control system for local financial risks

Local debt crises in countries such as Brazil and Argentina illustrate the risks that local government borrowing can pose. Without proper fiscal rules to rein in excessive spending by local governments, they may go bankrupt from excessive borrowing. Therefore, the central government must strengthen local government debt management. China and Brazil are both large developing countries. At present, the scale of local government debts is huge and the management is poor. Therefore, it is urgent for the central government to strengthen management and formulate effective management measures to prevent debt risks. The experience of the United States, Colombia and other countries shows that the establishment of feasible local financial risk warning and control mechanism is of great significance for early warning and identification of local financial risks and effective prevention of local debt crisis and even financial crisis. On the basis of perfecting the local debt statistical accounting system, China should establish the local financial risk warning and control system as soon as possible, so as to effectively identify, warn and prevent the local financial risk.

4. Promote relevant fiscal reform and comprehensively address local government debt problems

The practice of debt management in Brazil and other countries shows that debt management measures are comprehensive. It has not only mobilized almost all powerful control means including law, administration and judiciary, but also reconstructed the financial framework, adopted corresponding financial supporting reform measures, further improved the inter-governmental financial relations and restricted the proportion of personnel funds in the expenditure structure. At present, there are many reasons for the expansion of local government debt in China. In order to solve the problem of local government debt, we should establish a reasonable place to debt financing channels, perfect the financial management system under provincial level, ensure the basic-level government basic funding needs, promote equal basic public services, and narrow transverse longitudinal financial gap between regions, increase local fiscal sustainability aspects, promote financial reform deepening and implement the comprehensive control of local debt.

5. Improve the transparency of local finance and debt information, and give play to the supervision and guidance role of the public and market mechanisms

Improving the bond market mechanism and enhancing the transparency of debt information are effective means to control local government debt. Developed countries have generally formed a relatively sound bond market mechanism. For example, in the United States, the credit rating system, information disclosure system and private bond insurance system constitute three important mechanisms in the municipal bond market, reducing the default risk of the market and effectively preventing the potential debt crisis. Most developed countries pay attention to the transparency of financial information, especially local debt information, and have established regular and standardized local debt information disclosure systems. New Zealand and other countries have also established contingent liability reporting systems. After Brazil resolved its third local-government debt crisis, fiscal transparency played an important role in the federal government's efforts to control the size of local government debt. At present, China's local government debt management is still lack of unified accounting methods and information management system, local government debt situation is difficult to grasp in real time, information asymmetry, which is not conducive to national macro management. We should learn from the successful experience of other countries and gradually establish a national unified information system for local government debt management on the basis of necessary accounting and statistics, establish and improve a system for reporting debt information, and improve the transparency of debt management. Gradually improve the bond market mechanism and cultivate a long-term mechanism to prevent risks.

5

Risk Prevention and Control and Supporting Linkage

Based on the analysis and evaluation of the basic situation of financial risk, this paper puts forward the idea of treating the root causes of local government debt, and puts forward the framework and essentials of defusing local debt risk and establishing financial risk prevention system from three aspects. The problem of local government debt is rooted in China's unique administrative structure and operating system. Only by fundamentally changing the guidance and incentive mechanism of performance assessment and eliminating the non-cooperative game between the central and local governments can local governments' impulse to borrow be effectively restrained. We need to combine short-term measures with long-term institutional building, step up efforts to guard against problems at the source, clearly fulfill our responsibilities, and do a good job in addressing risks of local government debt. Meanwhile, a standardized local government debt mechanism of "central regulation + market constraint" should be established to provide a regular and transparent financing channel with institutional guarantee

J. Kang and L. Wei, *Transformation of the Fiscal and Taxation Systems*, The Great Transformation of China,
https://doi.org/10.1007/978-981-16-2590-9_5

for local infrastructure construction. At the end of this paper, suggestions are given on the coordinated promotion of fiscal and tax reform, price, land, finance and other reforms.

5.1 Evaluation of the Basic Situation of Financial Risks

Local Government Debt has Increased Substantially, and the Overall Risks are Under Control

Since 2009, in line with the proactive fiscal policy and the implementation of the 4 trillion Yuan investment plan, local governments at all levels have set up a large number of local financing platforms and borrowed heavily in various forms. As a result, in recent years, the rapid expansion of local government debt has become an important concern of financial risks. Financing platform debt of local governments has also become the convergence point of the accumulation of fiscal and financial risks in a recent period.

According to the audit results of the national audit office, the outstanding debt of local governments nationwide reached 10.72 trillion Yuan by the end of 2010. Among them, 62.6% of the debt was owed by the government. The contingent liabilities of the government under guarantee accounted for 21.8%; other debts for which the government bore some responsibility for which it was liable amounted to 15.6%. Later, on June 10, 2013, the national audit office released the results of spot checks on the government debt situation of 36 local governments since 2011. By the end of 2012, the outstanding debts of 36 local governments had reached 3.847581 trillion Yuan, an increase of 440.981 billion Yuan or 12.94% over 2010. According to the audit, local governments raised a total of 218.087 billion Yuan in disguised debt financing, accounting for 15.82% of the total new debt raised by these regions in two years. The disguised means of debt financing include not only trust loans, financial leasing and after-sales leaseback, but also the issuance of financial products, BT (construction-transfer), construction with advanced funds and even illegal fund-raising. These financing methods are highly hidden and difficult to regulate, containing new risks and hidden dangers. The results of the survey also showed that problems such as excessive reliance on land sales revenue for local government debt, false investment by financing platforms and illegal acquisition of debt funds still exist.

Generally speaking, China is still in a period of strategic opportunities for development, and the economy will maintain a medium–high growth rate in the future. The sustained economic development will bring an increase in fiscal revenue, which lays an important foundation for the prevention of government debt risks in China. In addition to fiscal revenue, local governments in China have fixed assets, land, natural resources and other realizable assets, which can enhance debt paying ability. In addition, many local government debts are incurred in support of operational projects, which can also generate revenue to repay debts. Therefore, the risks of local government debt in China are generally controllable from the perspective of fiscal capacity and local government assets.

Outstanding Problems Existing in Local Government Debt

At present, the large debt scale and unreasonable debt distribution structure of local governments in China, as well as the loose debt management may lead to excessive debt of local governments, trigger the financial crisis of local governments and thereby endanger the safety of central finance. The current local government debt mainly has the following problems:

First, the local government debt financing lacks the standard and the financing cost is high. Since the existing law does not directly endow local governments with borrowing powers, there is no standard for the existing debt financing behavior of local governments, local debt financing channels and different ways, with long debt and the debt procedures are not transparent. According to the audit, most local governments borrowed through financing platform companies and other disguised means. Some government agencies provided guarantees without obtaining debt funds in violation of regulations, and some government departments and units even borrowed directly in violation of regulations. Compared with issuing local government bonds, the cost of financing by other means is too high, which further increases the burden on local governments. According to relevant investigations, the financing cost of local government bonds is generally high, most of which are above 10% (in EU countries, 7% interest rate is considered as high-risk financing). For example, the comprehensive financing cost of BT project in Sichuan Province is over 20%, and some even reach 30%.

Second, revenue and expenditure of local government debt have not been included in the regular budget management, and debt supervision is not in place. In addition to local government bonds and debt transferred by the government, most local government debt revenues and expenditures are not under budgetary management, and the relevant management system is not sound. The problem of imperfect debt management systems for municipal- and county-level governments is more prominent, and some local governments have long had problems such as unclear debt size and unfulfilled debt repayment responsibilities.

Third, some regions and industries are under great pressure to repay their debts, and debt risks continue to accumulate with hidden risks. First, individual local governments have a heavy debt burden. Second, part of the local debt repayment funds has great dependence on land transfer income. By the end of 2012, the outstanding debts of the four provinces and 17 provincial capitals, which had pledged to use land transfer revenue as the source of debt repayment, amounted to 774.697 billion Yuan, accounting for 54.64% of the outstanding debts of these regions, an increase of 118.397 billion Yuan or 3.61% points over 2010. In 2012, the income from land sales in these areas decreased by 13.508 billion Yuan, or 2.83%, compared with 2010. After deducting the expenditure and various incomes extracted in accordance with state regulations, the disposable income from land sales decreased by 17.956 billion Yuan, or 8.82%. Third, the debt scale and debt repayment pressure of expressways, universities and hospitals in some regions are relatively large. The 12th five-year plan period is the peak period for local government debt repayment. As the growth of local government revenue declines, the pressure on key expenditures such as people's livelihood increases, making it difficult to arrange funds through public budgets to repay debts. The decrease of land transfer fee income will also reduce the amount of land transfer fee income that can be used for debt repayment. Risks continued to accumulate in some areas with high debt burdens, and the number of local government debts overdue continued to rise. By the end of September 2012, the amount of overdue local government debt was 125.85 billion Yuan, up 33.9% over the year before, and some of the overdue debt may turn into bad debts. For example, Yunnan reported that in addition to the 43.36 billion Yuan of overdue debts, there would be 47.01 billion Yuan of additional maturing debts for secondary roads and other projects in 2013. In addition to resolving the debt of colleges and universities, government and legal organs, other public welfare debts in rural areas, and the upcoming debt settlement of senior high schools, the debt repayment pressure was greater.

Fourth, in recent years, the local government non-standard financing is more serious. Some local governments have raised funds in violation of laws and regulations. For example, borrowing funds and BT to build public welfare projects in violation of regulations, providing capital injection or guarantee to financing platform companies in violation of regulations, and borrowing government debts through financial companies, trust companies and financial leasing companies in violation of regulations.

A Fundamental Approach to Local Government Debt

The strict notional prohibition of local governments from directly financing in the capital market and the institutional arrangement that takes the development of local economy as the priority assessment target make local governments create a lot of new financing methods, leading to considerable implicit and explicit debts. The problems arising from the application of these financing methods are: (1) lack of transparency in capital financing; (2) fragmentation of local budgets; (3) increasing uncertainty of local financial resources; (4) increased risks in the financial sector and macro-finance; (5) missed opportunities to learn and develop capacity to manage sustainable debt financing.

First, local government debt and its risks should be viewed dialectically. First, we need to objectively recognize that the scale of debt is very high, easy to go wrong. If you ignore the risk of debt, it could be a real problem. The Chinese government has plenty of resources and tools to deal with the problem if it recognizes the risks of debt and prepares for a rainy day. Second, we need to see the particularity of China's system. Local government debt is prone to go wrong, but it does not necessarily go wrong. The real risk lies in the process identification, the key is to correctly identify all kinds of debt and its risk points, and timely take measures to control.

Second, the current Chinese government debt problem is highly correlated with the local economic development model and closely linked to land and real estate. It manifests itself in two aspects: First, land transfer fees and real estate taxes are the main source of income for local governments. About 70% of local government financing platform belongs to the platform at the county level. Due to the limited financial strength of county-level governments, especially in central and western regions, it is difficult to repay the principal and interest of loans by relying on platform cash flow and local general budget revenue. Therefore, land transfer income has become an important source of debt capital. The total revenue of the five major taxes on the real estate industry increased by more than 10 times from more than 90 billion Yuan in 2003 to 1.01 trillion Yuan in 2012. Second, many local government financing platforms borrow at land prices or as collateral. As house prices rise, debt can be eased, covered by land finance. When housing prices fell and land finance became unsustainable, local rescue policies will be introduced immediately. As can be seen from the dependence of the Chinese government on real estate, huge investment should be earned from the appreciation of real estate to maintain fiscal and debt sustainability. Local government debt, property regulation and stable investment growth are already bound to each other. Of the 10.72 trillion Yuan of local government debts disclosed in the audit report of the national audit office in 2011, the government is responsible for 6.71 trillion Yuan of debt repayment, while local governments have pledged 2.55 trillion Yuan, or 37.9%, to use land transfer revenue as a source of debt repayment, involving 12 provincial, 307 municipal and 1,131 county-level governments. The solvency of local governments will be largely affected by the property market. In the past two years, land transfer income has decreased due to the sharp rise in demolition costs. In 2012, the proportion of land transfer fee in local fiscal revenue decreased to 27%, of which the net income only accounted for 5.9%. With land-related tax revenue, the net income of government land only accounted for 20% of the total fiscal revenue in 2012, which was significantly lower than the peak of 31.7% in 2010. From 2010 to 2012, interest rates on local government debt were 0.86 trillion Yuan, 0.9 trillion Yuan and 0.96 trillion Yuan, respectively. In 2010, the net revenue from local government land peaked at 1.57 trillion Yuan, then fell to 0.95 trillion Yuan in 2011 and 0.58 trillion Yuan in 2012. In 2012 net land income covered only 60% of interest payments. So a very real proposition is that if China's property bubble bursts, the impact on local government debt will not be negligible.

Third, it should be noted that the biggest risk of local government debt lies not in its static scale, but in its formation mechanism and management mechanism. The background of local government debt this time is the investment-led economic model led by local government. No matter from the aspect of total factor productivity or fund use efficiency, it shows that the current investment development model is a debt trap piled up by a lot of funds. First is to analyze where government debt "goes". According to previous audit results, government debt is generally used for public infrastructure construction, such as railways and roads, rural and urban infrastructure construction, as well as education, medical care and other livelihood expenditures. Second, we should also consider whether the high-quality assets or non-performing assets formed after the expenditure of government debt. Third, we should look at the ability to repay debt, whether cash flow can realize repayment of principal and interest. China's local governments have huge assets, in addition to land, but also a variety of factories, mines, hotels, tourism resources, instruments and equipment. By the end of 2012, a total of 953 state-owned holding companies had been listed on the A-share market, accounting for 38.5% of the listed companies on the A-share market, with a total market value of 13.71 trillion Yuan. Adding up the assets of local governments, several hundred thousand billion Yuan is out of question. Therefore, from the perspective of assets, local government debt is not a big problem. The key point of risk lies in its irregular and unsustainable formation mechanism.

Based on this, the root cause of the governance of local debt risks is to build open channels and plug tunnels, accelerate the establishment of local government debt financing mechanism with open and transparent government bonds as the main body, implement classified management and limit control, early warning for areas with high debt risks, and effectively prevent and defuse financial risks.

5.2 The Framework and Key Points of the Financial Risk Prevention System

Addressing local government debt risks is a systemic project. Local government debt problem is rooted in China's unique administrative structure and operating system. Only by fundamentally changing the guidance and incentive mechanism of performance assessment and eliminating the non-cooperative game between the central and local governments can the local governments' impulse to borrow be effectively restrained. We need to combine short-term measures with long-term institutional building, step up efforts to guard against problems at the source, clearly fulfill our responsibilities and do a good job in addressing risks of local government debt. Meanwhile, a standardized local government debt mechanism of "central regulation + market constraint" should be established to provide institutional guarantee, regular and transparent financing channels for local infrastructure construction.

Speed up the Improvement of the System and Eliminate the Mechanism of Local Governments' Improper Borrowing

The causes of local government debt problems are various. Existing local governments need to raise funds to promote local economic and social development. There are also institutional factors such as the unclear boundary between the government and the market, local governments' financial power and administrative power, which lead to local governments' capital shortage, as well as the irrational investment impulse of local officials caused by the deviation of government officials' performance appraisal orientation, as well as management factors such as the lack of overall supervision and effective supervision.

First, we should promote the transformation of local government functions, change the incentive mechanism that relies on investment and development, and restrain unreasonable investment projects and project construction. Fundamentally solving the local government debt investment impulse needs the transformation of government functions. First, we should reasonably define and divide the functional scope of local governments, accurately grasp the boundary between the government and the market, and turn the government functions to provide public goods and services. According to the basic requirements of constructing the socialist market economy system and public finance system, we should change the phenomenon of "offside" and "absence" in the scope of government activities. Second, we will standardize the investment and guarantee activities of local governments, implement a strict decision-making mechanism for debt investment, stop local governments from violating their guarantee commitments, and strengthen accountability for making investment and guarantee decisions in violation of regulations.

Second, we need to accelerate the improvement of the fiscal system. Institutional reforms that properly and clearly define spending responsibilities and match the resources available to local governments with spending responsibilities are essential. We will properly divide fiscal and administrative powers at all levels, promote tiered fiscal and tax reforms that aim to equalize spending responsibilities and establish a strict system for local budgetary oversight on the basis of establishing a unified fiscal distribution system that combines fiscal and administrative powers.

Third, fundamentally correct the one-sided performance evaluation and inappropriate economic incentive mechanism, eliminate the bad debt impulse of local governments. For a long time, the performance evaluation standards of the higher level government to the lower level government still mainly focus on the regional GDP, tax revenue, employment, investment, social stability and family planning indicators, etc., which provides a powerful stimulus for excessive investment and irresponsible borrowing. Although these performance standards have been revised to increase the proportion of people's livelihood and public services, economic growth is still the most important consideration when promoting cadres. Local government officials are rewarded for the number of projects they invest in and the metrics that go along with them, but the size and structure of the debt they generate is ignored, and almost no penalties are associated with irresponsible borrowing. In terms of the direction of reform, it is necessary to learn from the local *Government Performance and Results Act* of the United States (1993), the *Local Government Act* of the UK (1997) and the *Government Policy Evaluation Act* of the Japanese government (2002). Improving the evaluation mechanism of government performance appraisal is a systematic project involving multiple departments and mechanisms. Legislation at the national level is very important and should be vigorously promoted so as to make the government performance appraisal scientific, institutionalized and routine.

Fourth, we will accelerate the development of a legal system for local fiscal responsibility. Draw lessons from relevant international experience and establish corresponding error correction and accountability mechanism. For example, Brazil's *Law on Fiscal Responsibility* of 2000 provides for personnel punishment for local government responsible persons who fail to fulfill their obligations. Failure to comply with the relevant fiscal rules on debt and deficits is a serious dereliction of duty, bans from working in the public sector, fines and even jail (up to four years). Article 92- 03 of part III of the *Local Government Debt Act 1956* provides that: In the event that the local authority is unable to pay the principal or interest of the special bond in full and continuously, an additional 5% of the default amount will be paid to the holder of the bond or stock as compensation. In the event that the local authority is unable to pay the full and continuous installments of the sinking fund for 28 consecutive days, the local debt committee will recover the debt with the local authority or request the high court to appoint a financial trustee to recover the debt.

Govern the Stock and Control the Increase, and Establish a Sunshine Local Debt Classification Management System

To control the stock of local government debt, we need to carry out classified management of the huge stock of local government debt that has accumulated in recent years. The key is to solve the problem of debt repayment sources: Distinguish which projects may directly become financial burdens and which projects can be repaid directly through the platform to accurately grasp the real debt burden information of local governments. The general principle is that public welfare debts should be included into the scope of local government debts and be repaid gradually with public financial revenue. For platform debt, income debt supported by cash flow should be paid back with income. Meanwhile, the construction of new financing platforms should raise the threshold and strictly control the new debts of local governments.

First, we need to distinguish borrowers and ensure their repayment responsibilities. Debts incurred by government departments, institutions and institutions with full allocation, as well as debts incurred by institutions with differential allocation and financing platform companies due to the provision of public services and without sources of debt repayment, local governments should bear direct debt repayment responsibilities. For debts incurred by various financing platform companies due to the construction of infrastructure and public welfare projects, which have sources of debt repayment funds, local governments should urge them to strictly fulfill repayment obligations according to the plan and the requirements of the contract, and try their best to avoid transforming into direct government debts. As for the debt generated by the market behavior unrelated to public services, the principle of "who borrows, who pays" should be followed, and borrowers repay themselves, the government does not assume the responsibility to bail out.

Second, ensure repayment sources and fully defuse risks. On the basis of distinguishing debt-raising entities and fulfilling repayment responsibilities, it is necessary to formulate repayment plans in a timely manner, raise debt repayment funds scientifically and fulfill debt repayment obligations on time. Among them, local governments should arrange debt repayment funds in a timely manner according to their financial situation, debt scale and maturity for debts that bear direct repayment responsibilities. For debts for which it is obliged to bail out, for example, project debts with income borrowed by institutions of higher learning, hospitals, transportation and other public welfare projects should be gradually resolved through project income. When the debt service demand cannot be met, local finance should give appropriate subsidies to control the risks within a certain range. For debts for which it is not obliged to bail out the debt, local governments should urge local government financing platform companies to improve the legal person governance structure, standardize the operation and management, improve their own sustainable operation ability and gradually repay through their own earnings. In addition, private capital can be introduced to optimize the equity structure and improve the solvency.

Build a Standardized Sunshine Financing System for Local Governments as the Basic Point to Promote the System Construction

To standardize local government debt, the key is to grasp the "root cause" system construction in the treatment of both symptoms and root causes, make all local government debt under the sunshine operation and change the implicit borrowing behavior of local government.

The tax sharing financial system required by the market economy contains the necessity and rationality of local appropriate borrowing. In the world, governments are generally endowed with creditor's rights by countries implementing the tax sharing financial system. Based on the gradual improvement of the current tax sharing fiscal system and the actual financing needs of local governments, it is an important step to further deepen the reform of fiscal system and the fundamental way to regulate the management of government debt to endue local governments with the right to finance including raising debt rights on the basis of the division of inter-governmental powers. The central government should leave some financing space for local governments and allow them to issue local bonds publicly so that local governments have more ways to borrow money besides loans. In this way, on the one hand, local governments can avoid excessive reliance on bank financing, diversify risks and promote the explicit rationalization of implicit debt; on the other hand, due to the strict approval conditions for issuing bonds, local governments can improve governance, improve the standardization of government affairs and financial transparency, and standardize debt management. At the same time, because bond issuance is a market behavior, through the choice of public purchase, it can improve the social welfare and economic efficiency of government-invested construction projects.

Considering that the peak period of infrastructure construction in China will continue in the urbanization process, and the negative effect of the existing financing mechanism of "land finance + local financing platform" is prominent and cannot be sustained, we need to accelerate the innovation of investment and financing mechanisms in the field of infrastructure, actively develop the local sunshine financing system and reconstruct the public investment financing system of "municipal debt + policy-based finance". On the basis of regulating existing local government debt, especially local financing platforms, we will adopt a market regulating local government debt system based on the central government's total allocation. We will officially launch the binding issuance of local government bonds by provincial and county governments in the open market, with the municipal governments issuing municipal bonds independently. We will build a public investment and financing system with municipal bonds as the main body. We will launch the issuance of municipal revenue bonds, expand financing channels for local governments through asset securitization, introduce institutional investors such as insurance and pension funds, and continue to develop policy-based finance to fund infrastructure construction in a standardized manner.

Establish and Improve the Local Debt Risk Control Mechanism of "Central Regulation + Market Constraint"

Internationally, local government debt management can be roughly divided into two categories. The first category is market constraint, that is, local governments issue bonds independently at their own risk. This model requires tough market and budget constraints. The actual conditions are full local autonomy, a clear division of responsibilities between the central and local governments, no intervention by the central government in local affairs, no debt exposure, no bailout by the central government, and even with the local government bankruptcy as a hard constraint. The second type is central control. Under this model, the central government measures the debt issuance capacity of local governments and controls the debt ceiling, which is approved by the central government. The background is that local governments are not fully autonomous. As far as China is concerned, due to the unclear division of powers and expenditure responsibilities between the central government and local governments, the central government has to rescue local governments after they incur debt risks, and budgetary constraints are not strong enough. In addition, due to the interest rate control and the lack of development of market rating in China's capital market, market constraints do not have the conditions to prevent debt risks. So now we're basically in a centralized mode. With the continuous improvement of China's inter-governmental financial relations, the strengthening of local government control and binding force, and the development of the capital market, the central government's control over local government bond issuance can be gradually reduced. At present, the central government approves the issuance of local government bonds in a standard way, but it cannot be issued by the ministry of finance for a long time, otherwise, it will easily aggravate the "moral hazard" of local governments to the central government.

According to the actual situation of our country, the local debt management system of our country should choose the mode of institutional constraint, supplemented by a certain degree of market constraint. In short, the central government manages local government debt through a series of systems, while giving local governments the power to issue, use and manage debt in accordance with regulations, normally without interference. Specifically, it includes the following aspects:

1. Incorporate Local Government Debt into Budget Management, Reform the Government Accounting System, and Prepare and Disclose Local Government Balance Sheets

(1) We will implement a budget for government debt, and put debt receipts and expenditures under budgetary management. We may consider adding a debt budget to China's overall budget, and at the same time set up a separate "firewall" between the debt budget, the general public budget, the social security budget, and the budget for state capital operations, so as to effectively control debt risks.
(2) We will bring revenue and expenditure of local government debt into budgetary management by category. We will gradually establish a financing mechanism for local government debt that is controllable in risk, low in cost, efficient in operation and open and transparent.
(3) Strictly apply the "golden rule" of debt management. It should be clearly stipulated that in addition to short-term debts strictly authorized, local government debt can only be used for capital expenditures related to the development of public utilities or to replace existing debts, not for recurrent expenditures. In addition to administrative responsibility, violators will be put on a debt management "blacklist", reducing or canceling the qualification and amount of the next debt issue.
(4) Reform the government accounting system, prepare and disclose local government balance sheets. The modern accrual accounting standard has gradually replaced the cash accounting standard to prepare the government balance sheet. Identify, measure and report government debt. Prepare and disclose local government balance sheets. By compiling and disclosing the government balance sheet, we can find out the "background" of the government, analyze the structure, proportion and term of government assets and liabilities, and reveal the risk of government debt. In addition, check how much of each local government's assets are truly realizable. Some assets may be part of basic public services, and treating them as assets that can be turned into cash gives a false sense of security. In addition, which assets can be realized through which specific financial means (such as asset securitization). This gives a real idea of the solvency of local governments.

2. We Will Implement Strict Procedures for Examining and Approving Local Government Bonds and Formulate Access Conditions for Issuing Local Debt

In principle, only local governments that are solvent and financially sound can issue bonds. Local governments need to follow a strict examination and approval system, follow the principle of prudence and necessity, fully demonstrate the necessity of borrowing, and must not borrow at will. The purpose and direction of funds raised by debt must be clear and meet the requirements of the government to perform public service functions. We will clarify the authority of local governments to borrow, and establish a financing mechanism for local governments to borrow mainly from government debt. With the approval of the state council, provincial governments (including cities specifically listed in the plan) may issue bonds, and provincial governments may borrow debts if they really need to. The examination and approval procedures for local government debt issuance are as follows: The state council shall determine the limit of local debt, report to the National People's Congress for approval and then release it to the lower levels; the provincial governments shall borrow according to the limit issued by the state council, and as deficits shall be included in the budget adjustment plan at the corresponding level, and report to the standing committee of the people's congress for approval. Within the debt warning line and the debt ceiling approved by the central government, the governments at all levels shall, in accordance with the budget year, determine the scale and mode of the annual debt borrowing, the use direction of the debt funds, the debt repayment arrangement (including the debt repayment reserve) and the repayment of the principal and interest of the stale debt, report to the higher level government for examination and verification and prepare the annual debt budget, and then submit it to the people's congress at the same level for examination and approval.

3. Implement Debt Classification Management and Limit Control

We will divide local government debt into general debt and special debt, and adopt corresponding management measures. General debt is debt for the development of public welfare undertakings, and it is debt financing for public budget deficit. Try out the "offline" operation method before the budget law is not authorized. Special debt is debt for the development of profitable quasi-public welfare undertakings, with special funds or income as a limited guarantee, so as to strictly control the rules and approval level of debt issuance. Generally, exploration should be allowed for financing not for deficits by the countries. While allowing local governments to regulate borrowing, local governments are forbidden to continue borrowing through financing platform companies. We need to get rid of the government financing functions undertaken by financing platform companies. Pure public welfare projects are mainly financed through general debt, while quasi-public welfare projects are financed through special government debt and PPP mode, and we will actively expand the PPP mode. At the same time, the contingent debts of local governments' outstanding debts will be included in the monitoring scope, and the risks will be calculated according to a certain proportion of the total debt size.

4. Establish and Improve Risk Warning and Prevention Mechanism

We will establish a local government bond rating and information disclosure system. Introduce the market rating system of local government debt, and professional rating companies will evaluate the grade of local government debt to introduce market forces and form external constraints.

(1) Establish a local debt monitoring index system. Gradually build a reasonable space for local government debt financing evaluation system. The first is to reflect the debt capacity of local governments related indicators, such as deficit ratio, debt ratio, debt bearing ratio. Second, the relevant indicators to reflect the solvency of local governments, such as debt dependence and debt repayment rate. Third, relevant indicators reflecting the structure of local government debt, such as term structure and repayment period structure, can be further specified.
(2) Establish a systematic regulatory framework and responsibility mechanism for government debt risks. Establishing an early warning system for local debt risks, pre-regulation and early warning system

can help mitigate fiscal risks. In this regard, it is necessary to study and set risk monitoring indicators, such as debt ratio, debt guarantee and fiscal revenue ratio, new debt ratio, debt repayment ratio, interest expense ratio, debt dependence ratio, asset-liability ratio, debt ratio, short-term debt ratio and guaranteed debt ratio.

(3) In addition, the establishment of a sinking fund system should be accelerated. Local governments are required to set up a special sinking fund, in which the proceeds of projects supported by debt funds, the surplus of local fiscal revenues and expenditures and the surplus of reserve funds are all entered into the sinking fund in accordance with regulations. Sinking fund shall be under closed off management, and improper withdrawal and use shall be strictly prohibited.

5. Establish Strict Debt Reporting and Auditing Systems

First is to require local governments to conduct comprehensive debt statistics, all debts directly liable for repayment by local governments shall be included in the scope of necessary statistics, and the debts with guarantee liabilities and joint and several liabilities shall be specified separately in the form of annexes. Second, establish a mechanism for early warning and resolution of debt risks, strengthen constraints on creditors such as financial institutions, and establish an assessment and accountability mechanism. Third, regular auditing of local government debts. Fourth, we will implement a system for reporting local government debts. Statistics and auditing of local government debts must be regularly reported to the National People's Congress, and at the same time be included in the scope of releasing financial information to the public.

In addition, we should strengthen the post-event accountability system for government debt risks. In order to prevent "moral hazard" and slack debt management, it is necessary to strictly limit the conditions and procedures of debt relief, such as temporarily taking over local finance, stipulating that the local government in debt crisis must correspondingly reduce expenditure and sell off assets. At the same time, relevant responsible persons should be held accountable and given different punishments according to the circumstances to maximize the prevention and control of local debt risks.

[Column 5.1].
An empirical analysis of local government debt management from the perspective of market: *Research Report of* institute of fiscal science, Ministry of Finance, 2013, 179 issue, *Credit Risk Research of Urban Investment Bonds of Local Governments* in China, author: Jin Hainian, doctor of economics, Chief Research Officer of Noah (China) Holdings Co., LTD.

With the deepening development of market economy and urbanization process, local government debt in China has been rising rapidly. In recent years, it has become a hot topic in China and even in the world, which is one of the core issues concerning whether China's economy can maintain rapid growth. The proportion of urban investment bank bonds in the whole bond market has increased from about 1% in 2008 to about 8% in 2013. In the next five to six years, the repayment pressure of China urban investment bank bonds will increase by 4–7 times, and the total repayment principal and interest of current outstanding debts will exceed 500 billion Yuan in 2019. If future new debt is taken into account, the total pressure on debt servicing in 2019 could reach 1 trillion Yuan, about seven times that of 2012. From the perspective of existing debt repayment and new debt management, a report from the market puts forward the idea of gradually replacing land finance with the income from state-owned assets and profits of state-owned enterprises. It puts forward the idea of debt package marketization of urban investment bond project, and puts forward systematic solutions and policy suggestions in the aspects of government debt management system, financial system and even the division of government and market functions. This paper will analyze and study the development and credit risk of urban investment bonds of local governments in China in recent years. This report is of great policy reference value for the future countermeasures and solutions of local government debt risks in China.

(I) analysis of the development status of urban investment and debt of local governments in China.

1. The Background of Local Government Financing

The financing needs of local governments come from the gap (deficit) between fiscal expenditure and fiscal revenue, while fiscal revenue is determined by the national and local fiscal and tax systems and regional economic aggregate, and fiscal expenditure is determined by the functional positioning of local governments and the government planning of the region.

On the whole, the fiscal system of tax distribution and the orientation of government function in our country determine that local governments have more power than financial power. In recent years, China is in the stage of rapid urbanization development, and the construction of infrastructure, public services and local economy has generated huge capital needs that are quite different from those of developed countries. In this stage of rapid economic development, large-scale government financing needs are inevitable. In the first few years of local government financing, it is basically based on bank loans. When the total amount of bank credit is in conflict with the market demand for credit, some local governments gradually turn to bonds, equity, BT/BOT and other financial channels for financing, resulting in the current coexistence of credit, bonds, equity, trust, finance lease, asset securitization and other financing methods.

Due to the current legal constraints in China, local governments must issue government bonds through the agency of the ministry of finance instead of issuing bonds directly. Therefore, the financing subjects are also transformed from the government to the platform companies such as urban investment companies, industrial investment companies or project companies with government responsibilities. These platform companies can more flexibly and quickly conduct debt or equity financing activities to solve the problem of fund gap in urban construction, which also brings more complex risks and hidden dangers.

On March 7, 2013, Shang Fulin, chairman of China banking regulatory commission, disclosed that the loan scale of China's local financing platforms was 9.3 trillion Yuan. The *Approval Power of the Double Lines "of Loans and Bonds to Reduce the Old and Control the New Platform Financing Must be Transferred to the Head Office, 21st Century Business Herald*, April 16, 2013. According to CBRC statistics, by the first half of 2013, there were 10,853 platform companies at provincial, municipal and county levels.

2. Analysis of Urban Investment and Debt Development and Change

Urban development investment bonds (UCBS) are currently the most important form of debt financing for local governments in China besides loans. Since the opening of the bond market, the development of urban investment bonds of local governments in China has gone through three stages (see Fig. 5.1). The first phase was in its infancy before 2004, issuing negligible amounts of debt each year. The second stage was the initial stage of development from 2005 to 2008. The annual issuance amount increased rapidly by 10 billion Yuan, accounting for about 1% of the total bond market. The third stage is the rapid development stage since 2009. Unless otherwise specified, the data of 2013 in this report are all up to September. Due to the response to the financial crisis and the acceleration of urbanization process, urban investment and debt rapidly increased from more than 300 billion Yuan in 2009 to nearly 900 billion Yuan in 2012, accounting for nearly 8% of the whole bond market. Issuance more than doubled in 2012 from 2011.

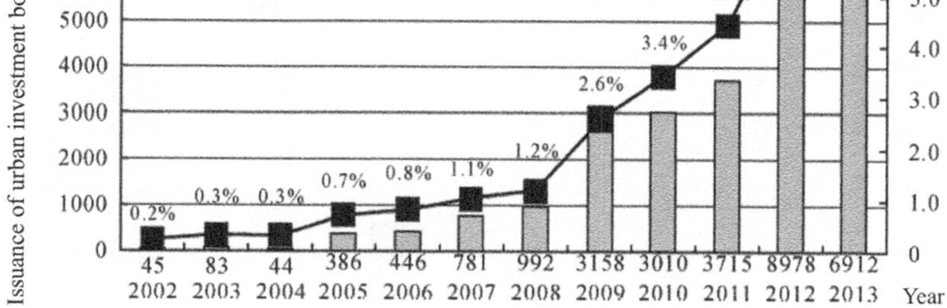

Fig. 5.1 Ratio of Urban investment bonds and bond market from 2002 to 2013

城投债发行量/亿元	Issuance of urban investment bonds/ 100 million Yuan
年份	Year
城投债发行量	Issuance of urban investment bonds
比重	/% Ratio/ %
图5-1 2002-2013	年城投债及债券市场比重

It can be seen that the development of urban development bond in recent years has two important features: First, in response to the impact of the international financial crisis on China's economy, the growth of urban investment and debt since 2009 has been in an ultra-high speed and unconventional development state; second, the proportion of the city's debt to the whole bond market is rising. Under these two characteristics, the growth of urban investment and debt is unstable. As an important means of government financing, its risk management and overall planning are seriously lagging behind.

From the perspective of the issuance types of urban investment bank bonds (see Fig. 5.2), due to the long period of government capital demand and the short establishment time of urban investment bank, the issuance of urban investment bank bonds is mainly enterprise bonds and medium-term bills, and the proportion of short-term financing bonds within one year is relatively small, while the proportion of corporate

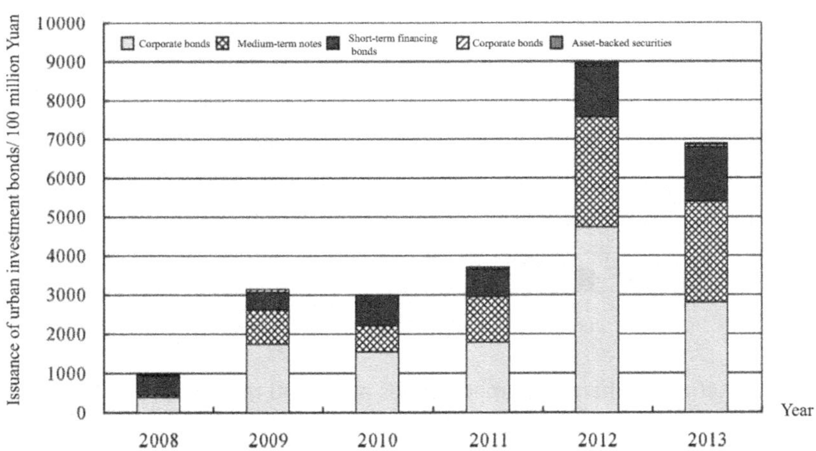

Fig. 5.2 Change of issuance types of urban investment bonds

城投债发行量/亿元	Issuance of urban investment bonds/ 100 million Yuan
年份	Year
企业债	Corporate bonds
中期票据	Medium-term notes
短期融资券	Short-term financing bonds
公司债	Corporate bonds
资产支持证券	Asset-backed securities
图5-2	城投债发行种类变化情况

bonds issued by listed companies is even lower. But since 2012, local governments have been experimenting with more financial instruments, such as asset-backed securities and trusts.

In terms of the industry direction of the use of urban investment bond funds (see Fig. 5.3), from the initial emphasis on public utilities, industry (capital goods), transportation and diversified finance (government funds or investment companies), the proportion of industrial, transportation and diversified finance has increased significantly in recent years. By September 2013, industry accounted for 42% of the total urban investment and debt, diversified finance 23%, transportation 22%, real estate 4.5% and public utilities only 6%.

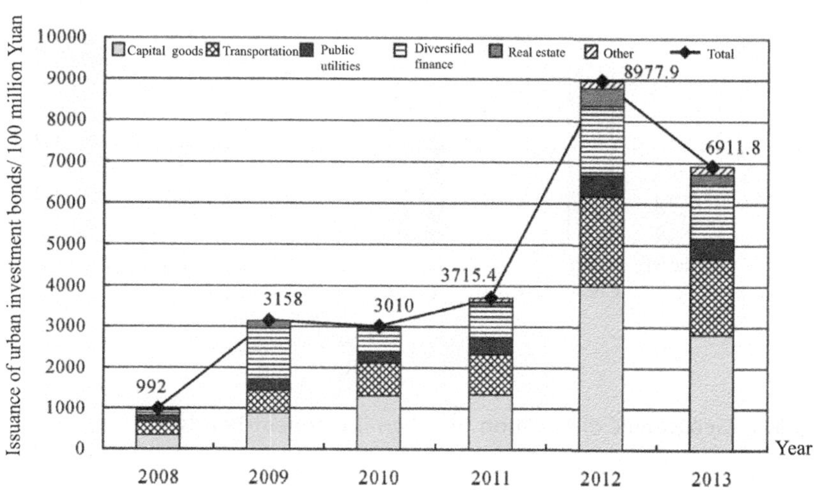

Fig. 5.3 Structural changes of urban investment bond industry

城投债发行量/亿元	Issuance of urban investment bonds/ 100 million Yuan
资本货物	Capital goods
运输	Transportation
公用事业	Public utilities
多元金融	Diversified finance
房地产	Real estate
其他	Other
总计	Total
年份	Year
图5-3	城投债行业结构变化

From the regional distribution of UCB (see Fig. 5.4), it is mainly concentrated in the eastern coastal region, the middle reaches of the Yangtze river, the northern coastal region and the southwest region, while the southern coastal region, the middle reaches of the Yellow River, the northwest region and the northeast region are relatively small.

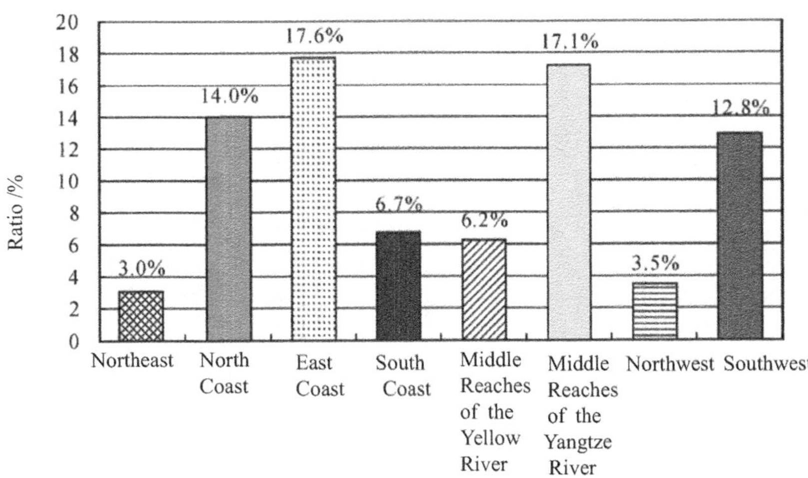

Fig. 5.4 Geographic distribution of urban investment bonds

比重	/% Ratio /%
东北	Northeast
北部沿海	North Coast
东部沿海	East Coast
南部沿海	South Coast
黄河中游	Middle Reaches of the Yellow River
长江中游	Middle Reaches of the Yangtze River
西北	Northwest
西南	Southwest
图5-4	4 城投债地域分布

(2) Credit risk status of urban investment bonds of local governments in China.

Below, we make a preliminary analysis of the credit risk status of urban investment bonds from the credit rating and risk changes of urban investment bonds.

1. Credit Rating of Urban Investment Bank Bond

From the credit rating of urban investment bank bond issuers (see Fig. 5.5), most of them are above AA-, with AA accounting for 56.11%, which indicates that the main credit of urban investment bank and the local government they rely on have good overall credit, strong solvency and low default risk.

From the credit rating of urban development investment bank bonds (see Fig. 5.6), the main body of urban development investment bank has a higher level, among which AAA accounts for more than one-fifth and AA + is twice as much as the same level of main body. This shows that the debt itself has good income or asset credit enhancement measures, making the debt with stronger solvency and lower risk.

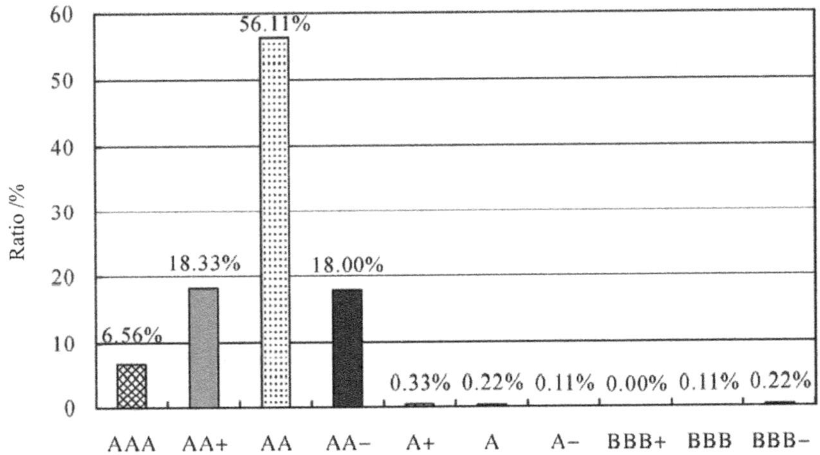

Fig. 5.5 Main credit rating distribution of urban investment company

比重 /% Ratio /%
图5-5 城投公司主体信用级别分布

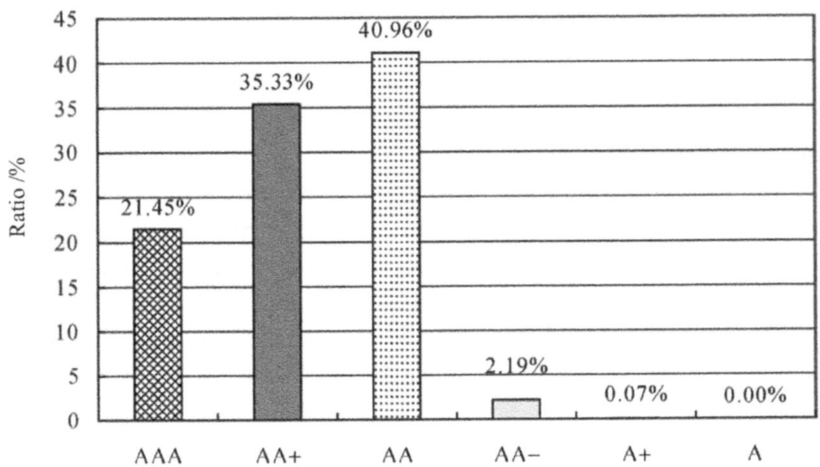

Fig. 5.6 Credit rating distribution of urban investment bonds

比重 /% Ratio /%
图5-6 城投债债项信用级别分布

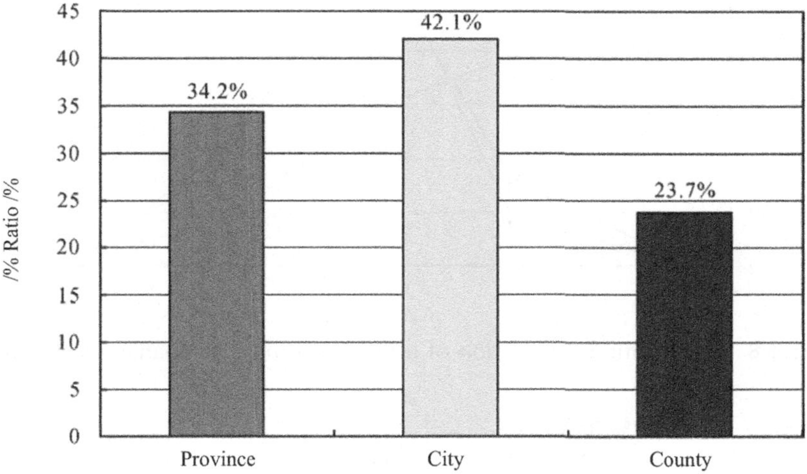

Fig. 5.7 Distribution of stock urban investment bonds of governments at all levels

比重 /% Ratio /%
省 市 县 Province, City and County
图5-7 各级政府存量城投债分布

From the perspective of the main background of urban investment companies (see Fig. 5.7), urban investment companies at the municipal level account for 42.1%, indicating that urban investment companies at the municipal level are the most active in China's urbanization construction and economic development. Provincial urban investment companies followed, accounting for 34.2%. County level is the least, at 23.7%, because of its low financial resources and decision-making status. This proportion roughly describes the distribution of government functions in economic development at all levels in China.

Among the three levels of urban investment companies (see Fig. 5.8), the credit rating of municipal and county level is roughly the same, and the credit rating of provincial level is relatively higher, which is closely

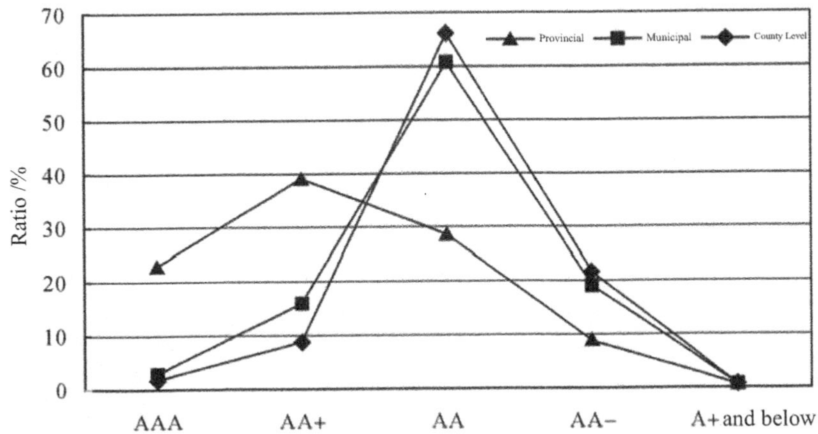

Fig. 5.8 Credit rating distribution of urban investment companies at all levels

比重	/% Ratio /%
省级 市级 县级	Provincial, Municipal and County Level
图5-8	各级城投公司信用级别分布

related to the stronger financial resources and resource allocation power of provincial governments.

From the level distribution of the industry in which urban construction investment company is located (see Fig. 5.9), transportation, real estate and public utilities have high credit ratings, while diversified finance and industrial (capital goods) industries have similar credit ratings, similar to other industries in China's private sector, but with the largest proportion of AA, about 40% ~ 60%. This difference also shows the difference in the credit rating of public services supported by government finance and industries supported by market.

2. Credit Grade Change of Urban Investment Bank Bond

Now we analyze the main risk points of urban investment bonds from some typical cases of credit rating adjustment in recent years, especially the reduction.

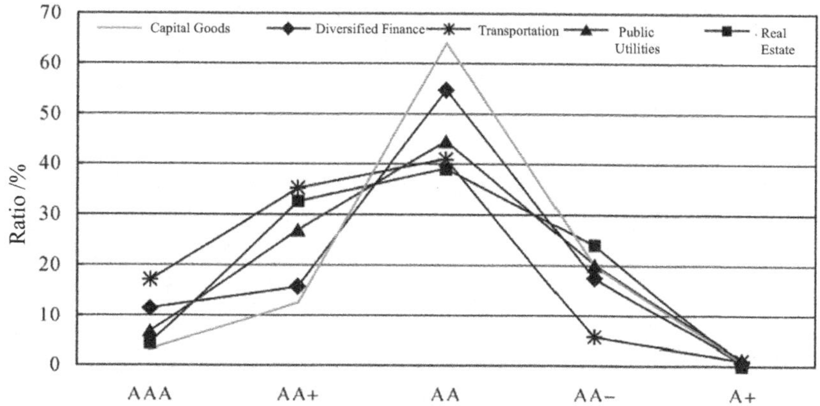

Fig. 5.9 Credit rating distribution of urban investment bonds in various industries

比重	/% Ratio /%
资本货物	Capital Goods
多元金融	Diversified Finance
运输	Transportation
公用事业	Public Utilities
房地产	Real Estate
图5-9	4 城投债地域分布

It can be seen from Table 5.1 that core business stripping, franchise change and land value change are the main types of risks of urban investment companies at present, and the largest source of credit for urban investment companies is the government's franchise, good asset injection and fiscal revenue endorsement. These are the biggest risks for local government financing vehicles such as urban construction investment company and their debt.

3. Credit Risk Status Quo of Urban Investment Bonds

Through the analysis of the overall credit rating of the above subjects and debts, the credit rating of subjects at all levels, the credit rating of various industries and other aspects, it can be concluded that the risks of urban investment bonds of Chinese local governments are generally

Table 5.1 Typical cases of downgrading of urban investment companies in recent years

Issuer	Rating agencies	Downgrade date	Level adjustment	Reason for downgrade
Guangzhou Construction Investment Development Co., Ltd	United credit	2013/7/8	AA + → AA	The assets of major subsidiaries were stripped in 2011, and the injection of compensatory assets and franchise rights did not improve the company's profitability
Chongqing Transportation Tourism Investment Group Co., Ltd	new century	2012/12/31 2013/6/30	AA + → AA AA → AA-	The overall divestiture of the tourism business has led to a decline in the company's profitability and an increase in the asset-liability ratio; the quality of land reserves is poor
Inner Mongolia High-tech Holdings Co., Ltd	new century	2013/6/28	AA + → AA	The subsidiary "Binhe Construction", which is mainly engaged in the construction of urban infrastructure, has been controlled by the Finance Bureau of the Rare Earth High-tech Zone, which has received less support from the government and reduced profitability
Xinjiang Investment and Development (Group) Co., Ltd	大公 DAGONG	2012/12/28	AA + → AA	The atomic company "Zhongtai Chemical" was transferred to another investment and financing entity "Xinjiang Zhongtai (Group) Co., Ltd." of the SASAC of the autonomous region, and the bond holders' meeting was not approved before the transfer

controllable, the main risks are lower than the average market situation, and they have better credit status than bonds in other markets.

From the perspective of the current potential risk points, the following six aspects need to be paid attention to:

(1) Core business transfer: for example, subsidiaries or core business spin-off leads to reduced profitability and solvency of the company.
(2) Government support for changes in franchise management.
(3) Overall changes in the industry caused by industrial policies and cycles.
(4) Changes in the financing chain caused by high debt ratio.
(5) No new projects of the project company lead to business sustainability problems such as slowing down of revenue.
(6) Changes in the value of core assets such as land asset price or quality.

From the perspective of various industries, it is necessary to pay attention to the influence of industrial policy adjustment, regulatory policy changes of relevant departments on government financing platform, financial system reform, and Internet financial innovation and other recent hot spots and new situations.

In 2012, the state council issued the *12th Five-Year Plan for Energy Conservation and Emission Reduction*, which eliminated the production capacity of small thermal power plants, iron making, steel making, cement, coke and paper making, and imposed total emission controls on major pollutants in the power, steel, paper making and printing and dyeing industries. The overall impact on these industries needed attention.

At the same time, according to the *National Development Plan for Strategic Emerging Industries During the 12th Five-Year Plan Period*, the support for seven major industries, including energy conservation and environmental protection industry, information technology, biological industry, high-end equipment manufacturing, new energy, new materials and new energy vehicles, would also improve the profit prospects and credit rating of relevant industries.

For public utilities, due to various levels of government and various forms of external support, public utilities and local government investment and financing platform enterprises have lower credit risk than industrial and commercial enterprises and local government investment and financing platform.

Expressway, port, aviation and other industries are greatly affected by the economic downturn cycle, and their financial strength has declined. Cash flow and solvency of railways, power grids, airports, rail transit and water utilities remain stable. In 2012, the profitability and solvency of the thermal power industry were significantly enhanced, and the growth trend continued in 2013.

In the short term, the debt repayment environment of urban investment corporation and industrial investment and financing platform is more stable than other bonds, and the optimization of industrial structure, growth of domestic demand and tax reform will all constitute strong support for the growth of local government fiscal revenue. With the continuous implementation of the reform of local government financing system, urban construction investment company will still maintain a strong solvency. In the long run, due to the pro-cyclical performance of fiscal revenue exceeding expectations, the overall trend of fiscal revenue growth slowing down due to the slowdown of macroeconomic growth rate, there will be more worries about local financing platforms. Some county-level platform companies, second-and third-tier city platforms, and some industrial investment and financing platforms may have significantly higher credit risks.

(3) Outlook on the risks of urban investment bonds of local governments in China.

The above is a preliminary analysis of the risk status quo of urban investment bond. Next, we further study its future risk from the pressure of future urban investment bond repayment principal and interest.

1. Forecast of Future Repayment Burden of Urban Investment Bank Debt

Bond repayments tend to have a larger share of principal. In Fig. 5.10 according to the information of bonds issued each year, the amount of urban investment bank bonds that need to pay the principal at maturity

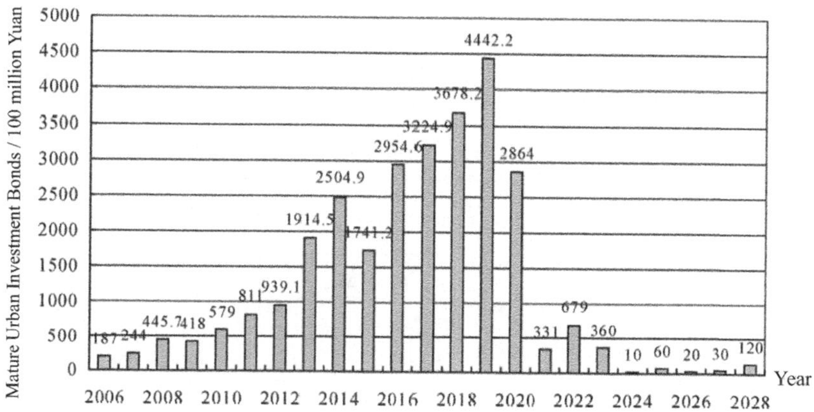

Fig. 5.10 Maturity of urban investment bonds issued before 2013

城投债到期量/亿元	Mature Urban Investment Bonds / 100 million Yuan
年份	Year
图5-10 2013	年前发行城投债到期情况

in each year is sorted out. It can be seen that although the new debt data after October 2013 has not been taken into account, since 2013, urban construction investment bonds has entered the peak of principal repayment. Among them, the recent extreme value reached more than 250 billion Yuan in 2014, which gradually increased after 2016. The principal amount to be repaid in 2019 will be 2.32 times that of 2013. This has caused great concern about the fiscal capacity and solvency of local governments.

Moreover, the annual repayment of urban investment bonds is not only the principal itself, but also the interest of the outstanding debt. Figure 5.11 shows the growth of the stock debt since 2006. By the end of September 2013, China urban investment bank debt has exceeded 2.3 trillion Yuan, and such huge debts are still increasing at an average annual rate of about 60%. This led to the interest payments of urban investment bank bonds over 140 billion Yuan in 2014, which will continue to increase as the debt stock grows.

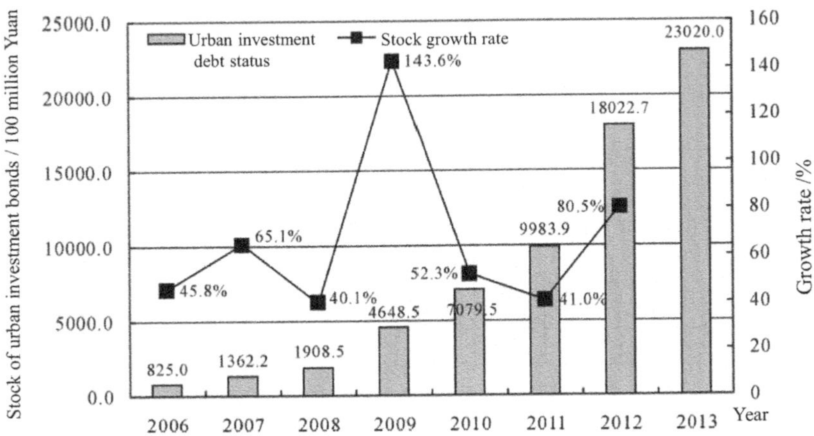

Fig. 5.11 Growth of stock of urban investment bonds

城投债存量/亿元	Stock of urban investment bonds / 100 million Yuan
年份	Year
城投债现状	Urban investment debt status
存量增长率	Stock growth rate
增长率	/% Growth rate /%
图5-11	城投债存量增长情况

In 2012, the total repayment principal and interest of urban investment bank was 150 billion Yuan. According to the current issued urban investment bank bonds, the total repayment principal and interest of urban investment bank would reach 400 billion Yuan in 2014, 2.67 times of the total repayment in 2012. In 2019, the principal payment of the existing urban investment bond will reach a peak of 444.2 billion Yuan. If the new urban investment bond is added every year from 2014 to 2018, according to the forecast in this paper, the total amount of principal and interest payment of urban investment bond in 2019 May reach 1 trillion Yuan.

The huge and rapidly growing pressure on repayment of principal and interest, along with the slowing economic growth and fiscal growth rate, will be the largest direct risk to China's local government urban investment bonds in the future.

2. Analysis of Future Risk Factors of Urban Construction Investment Bonds

There are eight risks in the future urban investment and local government debt: Economic environment risk, financial environment risk, government function reform risk, regional economy and fiscal revenue risk, cash flow management and other liquidity risk, debt repayment mechanism and other willingness risk, land and other government debt core asset value and stock change, external support policy change.

First, in terms of economic environment, the regional and industrial division of local economy is affected by the international economic situation and domestic macroeconomic trends, as well as the upstream and downstream industries at home and abroad. Local economy is the source of local government fiscal revenue, which is influenced by macroeconomic cycle and regional industrial division of labor. Supply factors such as capital, resources and manpower flow according to the influence of local relative competitiveness, which is the background factor that determines the local economy up to the local fiscal revenue and expenditure and financing demand. The local division of labor status determined by the economic environment and the local industrial structure changes are the important risk factors affecting the local financing demand and supply. Second, in terms of financial environment risks, monetary and fiscal policies mainly including macroeconomic environment, financial and fiscal system that affects local financing mode and scale, are the direct influencing factors of local government financing activities. Macro-monetary policy not only affects the cost of government financing, but also affects the scale of government financing in general, which is a factor of capital supply. Fiscal policy, especially tax policy, affects the gap of government fiscal revenue and expenditure, which is the factor of capital demand. Policy differences on financial industry and regional aspects are the influencing factors on the structure of total financing scale. In December 2012, the Ministry of Finance, the National Development and Reform Commission, the People's Bank of China and the China Banking Regulatory Commission jointly issued the *Notice on Stopping Local Governments from Financing in Violation of*

Laws and Regulations, which had a great impact on government financing channels and total amount.

Third, the reform of government functions is an important factor determining the structure and scale of government expenditure. Streamlining administration and delegating power to the market will reduce government spending. Generally, the government will focus on non-profit livelihood expenditure and other aspects, which will also make the government investment reduce the debt repayment sources of projects and rely more on fiscal revenue. In practice, streamlining administration and delegating power will generally significantly reduce government expenditure and have obvious governance effects on fiscal deficit and debt burden.

Fourth, regional economy and fiscal revenue and expenditure are the direct and medium- and long-term factors that determine the sources of government debt service. The local regional economy is the source of the local government finance. Non-tax income, whether tax or land, is directly determined by the local economy. The development planning of local economy and society is also an important demand direction of local government expenditure. The scale, structure and development trend of regional economy, as well as the local fiscal revenue system jointly determine the local fiscal revenue and its growth potential. Together with the future expenditure planning of the local government, it has become the main factor to analyze the source of local government debt service and debt growth.

Fifth, liquidity management, such as cash flow, is the short-term direct factor to analyze the term structure and repayment arrangement of government debt, which directly affects the default probability and default loss rate of urban investment bank debt and other local government debt.

Sixth, in terms of debt repayment intention, such as debt repayment mechanism, it is necessary to consider the continuity of local policies and legal responsibilities relying on debt repayment subjects and debt items. Since the debtor of urban construction investment bonds is not directly the subject of the government, the impact of the change of government or the change of principal decision-making officials on its debt obligations and legal responsibilities should also be paid special attention to.

Whether it is direct debt, implicit debt or contingent debt, solvency willingness and solvency are both core risk factors. The decision-making and management mechanism and its changes in core business, core assets and core business qualification of debtors are an important risk factor closely related to local government debt. Seventh, the value change and stock change of the core assets of government debt are not only the core factors of credit enhancement calculation of local government debt, but also the important guarantee of debt repayment source. The value of income protection and credit enhancement contents such as land, mineral resources, franchise rights and core business assets are not only influenced by macro-environment, economic cycle and industrial trend, but also determined by its own quality and quantity.

Eighth, external support policies, including transfer revenue, mainly make up for the fiscal deficit caused by debt service and fiscal expenditure. From the provincial, prefectural and county levels, the dependence on transfer revenue is increasing. In some prefectural and municipal governments, the dependence of fiscal expenditure on transfer support even exceeds 60%. This is determined by China's characteristic system of vertical management between central and local governments and below the provincial level and it forms the elements of systemic risk with the country's overall financial situation.

To sum up, in the process of comprehensively investigating the future risk of local government debt in China, it is necessary to focus on the analysis of the balance relationship between the expenditure pressure of paying principal and interest and the change of fiscal revenue growth every year, and systematically pay attention to the eight risk factors related to it.

(4) Problems and policy suggestions on local government debt management from the perspective of urban construction investment bonds.

After analyzing and studying the development and changes of urban construction investment bonds, risk factors and other aspects, the problems existing in local government debt are sorted out and analyzed, and then the systematic solutions and policy suggestions are put forward from the two aspects of debt repayment and new debt management.

1. Main Problems of Local Government Debt in China

Currently, China's local government debt mainly has six problems: unclear base, unreasonable industrial structure, uncontrolled scale growth, disordered financing channels, increased credit risk and lack of systematic payment management.

The first is the problem of not knowing the base. The central government, competent departments and even local governments themselves lack timely, accurate and consistent statistics of direct, hidden and contingent liabilities undertaken by their own governments and their subordinate governments. The information is not comprehensive, the statistical caliber is not consistent, the records are not timely, and there is a lack of coordination and management among different regions and levels. Relying only on irregular auditing can only be used as a means of supervision, and it is impossible to conduct timely and effective management of its own debts. It is urgent to establish a standardized and real-time government debt information and statistics system at all levels. Without a clear understanding of the debt base, it is impossible to establish an effective government debt management system, and the risk of debt is bound to be out of control. Like an unknown time bomb, it may cause immeasurable impact on the region, macro-economy and even social stability at any time.

The second is the structure of the industry. In terms of the existing urban construction investment bonds industry composition, industrial capital goods account for 42%, diversified finance for 23%, transportation for 22%, real estate for 4.5%, and public utilities as the core work of the government is only 6%, which reflects the offside and absence of government functions. In terms of industries that can operate in the market, government financing not only crowds out social financing resources, but also crowds out market allocation, affecting the effective allocation of market innovation resources. For public utilities and social security and other public services that should be undertaken by the government, there is an obvious shortage of supply. In the diversified financial industry, the functions of the government should gradually play a greater role in maintaining and increasing the value of social security fund and should reduce the involvement of investment in the profit-making field.

Third, the rapid growth of government financing and debt is out of control. After the global financial crisis in 2008, the financing of local governments grew at an ultra-high speed, and its proportion in social financing increased even faster. The ratio of urban development investment and debt increased from about 1% in the previous crisis to nearly 8% at present (see Fig. 5.1), and the ratio of government debt to national economy gradually became unbalanced. This is also an important reason for the sharp increase in the annual payment of principal and interest and the excessive financial burden even far beyond their own financial solvency.

The fourth is the lack of effective management of financing channels. Local government financing in China has gradually expanded from bank credit to corporate bonds, short-term financing, and then various financial instruments such as trust, asset securitization and financial leasing. The relevant departments have to urgently inform and stop local governments' illegal financing activities. The current disorder of local government financing channels will further complicate risk management.

The fifth is credit risk. The overall credit risk of China's local government debt remains a mystery due to database issues. For risk management, calculable risk is not the problem; uncertainty and uncertainty are the biggest risks. In addition, most of the current debts of governments at all levels have not been assessed with the government as the main subject of credit risk, and it is impossible to reveal the risks of local government debt systematically and comprehensively by only carrying out detailed credit rating on the financing platform of urban development investment corporation.

The sixth is the issue of solvency management. At present, local governments at all levels in China lack systematic, professional and effective management of their own and their subordinate responsible debt projects and repayment of principal and interest. The resulting loss of value, cost of capital and liquidity risk is also increasing.

Because of these six aspects of the existence of problems, we must take systematic and effective measures to solve.

2. Solutions and Policy Suggestions

Aiming at the problems existing in the six aspects of local government debt in China, the solutions are aimed at solving the existing debt repayment problem and managing the new debt in the future.

(1) For the existing stock of debt, the main challenge lies in the contradiction between the huge pressure to repay principal and interest in the next six years and the unsynchronized growth of fiscal revenue. As can be seen from the industry composition of urban construction investment bonds (Fig. 5.3), more than half of the debt comes from profitable industries (capital goods), transportation and other fields. These projects can generate their own income through good operation to repay the debt. Such debts can be packaged with project or operating companies for marketization, such as bidding for sale or outsourcing to non-government responsible departments. As long as government departments set standards and requirements for project progress, quality and operating services, the market will make the optimal allocation of resources. In this way, 60% of the debt burden can be easily solved, and the remaining 40% is within the range of financial sustainability and management.
(2) For the new responsibilities and debts in the future, it is suggested to carry out systematic reform and optimization from the perspective of the positioning of the government and the market and the whole financial system. The specific suggestions are as follows:

First, establish a modern standard local government financial information disclosure mechanism. For different levels of government, including direct debt, implicit debt and contingent debt, it shall make statistics of the information in the prescribed format, uniform caliber, prescribed period and prescribed scope, and make classified and classified disclosure to the relevant departments of the state, the government at a higher level, creditors, authorized risk assessment institutions and the society. Relevant departments of the state shall be uniformly responsible for establishing a modern and standardized mechanism for local government financial information disclosure.

Second, establish a modern standard local government financing management system. On the basis of establishing certain information disclosure standards, it shall carry out risk assessment and early warning of government financing information to achieve a balance between development and stability in terms of financing and risk control, build a credit risk evaluation system for local governments and realize the whole process monitoring of local government debt (overall planning, quota issuance, project management and repayment management), so as to establish a modern and standardized local government financing management system and systematically and sustainably solve the problem of local government funding supply in the process of urbanization.

Third, establish a modern standardized local government financial management system. In view of the demand of local government funds, we should accelerate the reform of national financial system, establish a system of fiscal expenditure management, such as budget, final accounts and deficit management of governments at all levels, and carry out the central and local tax sharing reform according to the balance of administrative power and financial power in tax revenue management and so on. At present, many local governments are excessively dependent on land revenue, and the limited nature of land itself, differential rent and fluctuation of value need to be replaced. Of course, real estate tax is a method, and the profit distribution mechanism of state-owned assets and state-owned enterprises at all levels can also be considered here. State-owned assets and profits of state-owned enterprises themselves are the legal income sources of governments at all levels. In this respect, the system design can completely replace the land income and become an important part of the local government revenue.

Fourth, gradually adjust and optimize the role of local governments. Of course, the positioning of government functions is the fundamental to determine government expenditure and is the basis of positioning government funding needs in a reasonable structure and scale. Government functions should be positioned in terms of system supply and public services, such as security order, social justice, maintaining fair market competition, external supplement, and the functions that can be realized by the market should be released, and the special functions endowed by the special period should be withdrawn at the due time. At the same time, attention should be paid to the changes of government responsibilities and expenditure structure at different stages of economic development. For example, in the accelerated stage of urbanization, a relatively high proportion of funds will be spent on infrastructure construction, while in the middle and later stage of urbanization, the use of funds should gradually turn to the social security and welfare system. Of course, innovation environment and market competition order will be the eternal topic of system supply, and the government's diversified financial platform should gradually shift its focus to government innovation fund, social security fund and environmental protection fund. In short, China's urban construction investment bonds and overall debt of local governments are growing rapidly and will reach a new peak from 2014 to 2019. The risks and consequences are far beyond current social expectations, which should attract wide attention from all sectors. But this problem can be solved, and effective solutions need to address both symptoms and root causes, long-term and short-term combination. We believe that the management and control of local government debt risk will be closely combined with China's financial system reform and financial system reform, accompanied by China's urbanization construction, and lead to China's modernization and the realization of the Chinese dream.

5.3 Coordinate and Promote Fiscal and Tax Reform and Other Reforms

On the basis of comprehensively serving the reform in economic, political, social, cultural and ecological fields, we will deepen fiscal and tax reform in adjusting the distribution structure, especially in properly defining government functions, straightening out inter-governmental financial relations, reforming the tax system, optimizing the structure of expenditures, strengthening budget management, standardizing government debt and improving the information system. At the same time, we will strengthen fiscal and tax reform and reform of prices, land, finance and opening up.

Price, Tax and Fiscal Reform Linkage

To accelerate the reform of the tax system, it is necessary to carry out the reform of the overall design in line with the key points of the pricing mechanism of basic resources and products and the financial system, and to coordinate with the reform of interest rate liberalization, the sound development of the capital market and the construction of the state-owned assets management system, so as to rationalize the allocation of production factors.

First, take the reform of resource tax as an opportunity to improve the pricing and regeneration mechanism of resource products in China, and straighten out the price comparison relationship and price formation mechanism of coal and electricity, reflect the scarcity and non-renewable nature of resources as well as the intergenerational equity of resource income, so as to encourage enterprises to innovate the process, technology and products of energy conservation and consumption reduction under economic pressure, and promote the reform of monopoly sectors (such as the supporting reform measures of "coal to electricity").

Second, we will further improve the reform of the tax sharing system. We will flatten the five levels of government to three through direct provincial management of counties, rural financial management of counties and comprehensive supporting reform of townships. According to the "first-class power, first-class governance, the first-class finance, first-class tax base, first-class budget, first-class property rights, first-class creditor's rights" principle, a tax-based and graded fiscal system is constructed in the manner of reconciling financial power and governance and matching of financial power and governance.

Third, we will improve the income sharing system and the local tax system, and foster local tax sources. With the gradual reform of resource tax and property tax, their income capacity is also gradually enhanced, and they will eventually become the main types of local taxes in county and municipal governments. At the same time, with the expansion of the scope of consumption tax and the backward reform of the collection link, some consumption tax revenue will be assigned to local governments. In the transition period when the reform of resource tax and real estate tax is not completely in place, we should improve the national one rate tax revenue sharing system and gradually increase the proportion of enterprise income tax sharing of local governments, so as to guide local governments to change the direction of economic development from quantity to quality. We will take VAT as a central tax, cut off the link between local government revenue sharing and economic scale, and take it as the income source for the central government to implement general transfer payments in accordance with the factor law, making it an important income source for local governments, especially provincial governments.

Fourth, we will advance market-oriented reform in the financial sector and the management of state-owned assets, such as actively promote financial deregulation in the financial sector, accelerate the pace of interest rate liberalization, gradually break up administrative monopolies in fields such as oil, railways and finance, lower the threshold for access to social capital and diversifying property rights, lay a micro-foundation for improving the further marketization of commodity pricing and interest rate marketization, and gradually form a new round of supporting arrangements for the "minimum package" of reforms that will promote the flow of factors, fair competition, and structural upgrading and optimization that are matched by prices, taxes and finance.

Establish a Reasonable Sharing Mechanism for the Proceeds from the Transfer of Public Resources

First, in combination with the reform of the state-owned economy, we will strengthen the budgetary management system for revenue from public resources. To solve the problem of loss of public resource revenue, firstly, we should bring all public resource revenue into budget management and strengthen budget constraints; second, we need to strengthen the livelihood orientation of public resource revenue expenditure, promote the sharing of all people and explore the establishment of a relatively independent "public property rights revenue budget". For example, we should consider using the proceeds from the transfer of public resources to establish a system of "basic social security package for the whole people" with equal standards. In addition, we will establish a management system for funds derived from the transfer of public resources to promote intergenerational equity.

Second, we should bring the income from public resources into the scope of normal financial system distribution, that is, we should reasonably "share production" on the basis of the tax sharing system and promote the sharing by all the people.

Establish a Complete Financial and Tax Information Data System with Big Data

We will speed up the establishment of a unified fiscal revenue and expenditure system for finance, state and local taxes, and connect the three information systems. On this basis, a unified and universal system of standardized and unique codes for individuals, enterprises, governments, social institutions and other social and economic entities shall be established. All departments collect basic and original information related to their duties related to the objects such as land, house, stock, debt and tax, corresponding to the above subjects, and establish a professional information system with a large concentration and full coverage in the whole country. To form a multilateral information sharing platform among various departments, namely a national and comprehensive legal information sharing platform that is based on and independent of all departments, and to build an information sharing system and mechanism that can not only share information but also have limits, constraints and controls. Use big data and cloud computing technology to establish a complete tax-related information data system.

Actively Deepen Reform of the Administrative System

We will advance reform of the administrative and fiscal and tax systems at the same time. We will move faster to formulate rules and regulations for dividing responsibilities and powers at three levels of government, and improve performance evaluation indicators. The pace of the advance should be based on provincial situation. We will deepen reform of the administrative system, including the fiscal reform to put counties under direct provincial control. The first problem to be solved is the "baton" problem, the core is the official promotion indicator assessment system; second, there is the issue of oversight and accountability, including fiscal transparency or public governance. "Direct provincial administration of counties" and other reform measures should first improve the performance judgment standards of officials, especially the promotion mechanism of party and government leaders, and introduce the divisor of GDP growth rate and debt growth rate. It involves environmental indicators such as soil, water quality and air (such as PM2.5, COD, nitrogen and ammonia values, and heavy metal content), people's satisfaction degree, income distribution and other indicators, and evaluates leading cadres more comprehensively and objectively. We will promote the implementation of the scientific development concept of "green mountains and clean waters are also political achievements" from the mechanism, and weaken the impulse of provincial, municipal, county, especially municipal and county governments to pursue the growth of low-level GDP at all costs. At the same time, we will accelerate the development of community-level democracy and accelerate the formation of competitive elections for leading officials at the county and township levels, so that community-level people have more channels and power to influence the promotion of community-level officials. From the mechanism, we should encourage leading cadres to look down, pay more attention to the provision of basic public services by the masses and strengthen the functions of county-level governments in providing basic public services and safeguarding political power.

Improve the incentive system for administrative promotion of officials. With the increasing financial resources and transfer payments of local governments, the proportion of local government expenditure has remained stable at 82%, 10% higher than 20 years ago. In 2010, the total amount of local fiscal expenditure reached 7.36 trillion Yuan, and in 2012, the total amount of local fiscal expenditure exceeded 10 trillion Yuan, reaching 10.5 trillion Yuan, a 30-fold increase compared with 333 billion Yuan in 1993. If you add in the extra revenue that local governments still have, the total amount of money they control is enormous. In this case, the shortage of basic public services and goods is largely due to the lack of incentives for local governments under the current system. At present, since the promotion and appointment of local officials are decided by superiors, the main indicators related to GDP are assessed, including GDP growth rate, industrial added value, fixed asset investment and fiscal revenue. As a result, grassroots governments compete with each other for GDP, land and environment to attract investment, thus forming the basic public services that attach importance to short-term economic benefits and ignore human capital. Practice shows that the improvement of local financial conditions alone cannot fundamentally change this situation.

Deepen the Reform of the Land System and Establish a Virtuous Circle of Land Finance

We will comprehensively improve the system of urban and rural land ownership, right of possession, right of use, right of assignment and relevant rights and interests, and straighten out the whole process of real estate formation, transaction, holding and tax adjustment starting from land development in the process of urbanization, as well as the relevant interest distribution relations. In the future, real estate tax will be an important part of local tax. At present, the widely criticized local government land finance is a focal point. However, from a practical point of view, the goal of deepening the reform of local financial system is to transform the current land finance mode, rather than land finance itself. Even in developed regions such as Hong Kong, local fiscal revenue is largely related to land finance. The land fiscal revenue of local governments in China includes taxes and fees related to real estate, and the revenue from state-owned land use right transfer. The current mode is not sustainable, which is the consensus. We should accelerate the implementation of government monopoly level land reserve, and then balance the finance of "people's livelihood, development and efficiency" through assets and liabilities, so as to curb the unreasonable income and expenditure contradictions that commonly exist in local areas. On the basis that the central government has defined the direction of property tax reform, governments at all levels should accelerate the reform of the property tax with the housing stock as the subject of tax, reduce the excessive dependence on the one-time land sale income, turn the incentives of local governments to improve the basic public services in cities and improve the investment environment, so as to enable local governments to obtain long-term, stable and predictable property tax revenue is the key. The difficulty of collecting real estate tax is higher than that of value-added tax and other turnover taxes. In addition to the good design and careful preparation of financial and tax departments, the coordination and cooperation of housing construction, land, law, finance and supervision departments are also needed to solve the problems of information collection, real estate assessment and legislative guarantee.

Accelerate financial Reform and Coordinate with Fiscal and Taxation Reform

Accelerate the liberalization of deposit interest rate, establish and improve the deposit insurance system, reduce the threshold of financial monopoly and build a firewall to transform financial risk into financial risk; develop and improve the capital market, use tax means to guide its healthy development, lower the overall level of taxes and fees in the capital market and form a stable mechanism to curb short-term speculation and encourage long-term investment. Strengthen the construction of anti-money laundering system, strengthen the control of large cash transactions; set up local financial regulatory agencies, implement tiered management of financial supervision, and vigorously develop local financial institutions.

Establish a Mechanism for Coordinating International Fiscal Policies

We will promote the orderly and free flow of factors at home and abroad, efficient allocation of resources and deep integration of markets. We will accelerate efforts to foster new advantages in participating in and leading international economic cooperation and competition, and promote reform through opening up. We will unify laws and regulations on domestic and foreign investment, and maintain stable, transparent and predictable policies on foreign investment. Actively promote the "One Belt and One Road" strategy. Finance should build a favorable external development environment in line with China's diplomatic situation, further enhance China's voice in the formulation of international economic rules, establish a mechanism to coordinate international financial policies and safeguard national interests.

Postscript

The book is published under the organization and coordination of China (Hainan) Institute of Reform and Development and Zhejiang University Press. The book is closely combined with the theme of comprehensively deepening fiscal and tax reform. It analyzes and discusses how to deepen fiscal and tax reform and promote the systematic construction of modern fiscal system during the 13th five-year plan period. Based on the previous internal research results, especially the research on fiscal and tax supporting reform conducted by Liu Kegu, former Vice President of China development bank, the cognitive framework has been formed. Heartfelt thanks is offered to Xu Lin, Director of the Planning Department of the National Development and Reform Commission, who has also given guidance and support to the research of this book. Liu Junmin, Director of Research Office, National Audit Office, and Wang Guijuan, Deputy Director of Political Research Office, Ministry of Finance, participated in the discussion and research of this book. Ms. Yang Rui and Ms.

J. Kang and L. Wei, *Transformation of the Fiscal and Taxation Systems*, The Great Transformation of China,
https://doi.org/10.1007/978-981-16-2590-9

Yang Ruoxi, China (Hainan) Research Institute of Reform and Development, Zhu ling, editor of Zhejiang University Press, did a lot of work on the book. I would also like to express my heartfelt thanks to them.

Due to the limited time, the writing of this book still has a lot of shortcomings, readers are kindly requested to correct and criticize.

Jia Kang Liuwei
July 2015 Xinzhi Building

References

1. Feng Yuding, et al. Money Sharing or decentralization: Re-discussion of Tax Distribution System. *Southern Weekend*, 20130815.
2. Research Group of Development Research Center of the State Council. Basic Ideas and Action Plan of the New Round of Reform. *China Reform*, 2013(10).
3. Hou Yilin. Government Functions, Power and Responsibility and Financial Power and Financial Resources: Theoretical Analysis of the Division of Financial Power and Administrative Power in China's Financial System Reform Since 1978. *Public Administration Review*, 2009(2).
4. Jia Kang, Bai Jingming. County and Township Financial Relief and Financial System Reform. *Economic Research*, 2002(2).
5. Jia Kang. Fiscal Flattening Reform and Inter-Governmental Power Division. *Journal of CPC Central Party School*, 2007(12).
6. Jia Kang. Re-understanding of Financial Function and Balance Principle. *Financial Research*, 1998(7).
7. Jia Kang, et al. Basic Ideas and Policy Suggestions for Deepening Fiscal and Tax System Reform. Fiscal and Tax Reform Subject Report of China International Economic Exchange Center, 2013.

J. Kang and L. Wei, *Transformation of the Fiscal and Taxation Systems*, The Great Transformation of China,
https://doi.org/10.1007/978-981-16-2590-9

8. Jia Kang. Basic Understanding of Public Finance. *Tax Research*, 2008(2).
9. Jia Kang. Tax Sharing Reform Needs to Be Further Deepened. *China Reform*, 2006(2).
10. Jia Kang. The Relationship between Tax Sharing Reform and Central and Local Governments. *Reform*, 1990(4).
11. Jia Kang. Public Finance and Social Harmony. *Economic Research Reference*, 2006(45).
12. Jia Kang. Reflections on Public Finance. *Journal of Graduate School, Chinese Academy of Social Sciences*, 2005(6).
13. Jia Kang. Discussion on Establishing Public Finance Framework. *Journal of National School of Administration*, 2005(3).
14. Jia Kang. Jia kang's Anthology. Beijing: People's Publishing House,2013.
15. Jia Kang, Liang Ji. Comprehensive Review under the Supporting Reform Orientation: Re-discussing the Tax Distribution System. Research Report of the Institute of Fiscal Science, Ministry of Finance, 2013.
16. Jia Kang, Liang Ji. Analysis of the Institutional Logic and Representation of the Distribution Relationship between Central and Local Governments. *Financial Research*, 2011(1).
17. Jia Kang, Liu Wei. Paying Attention to People's Livelihood, Optimizing Structure, Innovating System and Promoting Development: the Road of China's Public Finance Transformation. *Economic and Management Research*, 2007(10).
18. Jia Kang. Taking Flat Reform as the Starting Point to Reform China's Current Financial System: Reflection and Discussion on the Path of China's Financial Reform. *China Finance*, 2008(8).
19. Jia Kang. Correctly Grasp the Big Idea and Promote the Tax Sharing System: and Proposition of "Divide it into Two Sections Lengthwise and Two Sections Horizontally". *Journal of Central University of Finance and Economics*, 2005(12).
20. Jia Kang. 30 Years of Fiscal and Tax Reform in China: A Brief Review and Comment. *Fiscal Research*, 2008(10).
21. Jia Kang. China's Fiscal Reform: Thoughts on Government Level, Authority, Expenditure and Tax Arrangement. *Research on Local Finance*, 2004(1).
22. Jia Kang. Decentralization after China's Fiscal System Reform. *Reform*, 2013(2).
23. Jia Kang. New Supply: China's Innovation of Economic Theory. Beijing: China Economic Press,2013.

24. Li Ping. Illustration of China's Intergovernmental Fiscal Relations. Beijing: China Fiscal and Economic Press, 2006.
25. Liu Shangxi, Xing Li. Solving Financial Difficulties of Counties and Townships Depends on Different Places. *China Reform*, 2005(12).
26. Lou Jiwei. An Overview of Fiscal and Tax Reform. Beijing: Economic Science Press, 2014.
27. Lou Jiwei. Establishment of Modern Financial System. Guidance Reader of the *Decision of the Central Committee of the Communist Party of China on Several Major Issues of Comprehensively Deepening Reform*. Beijing: People's Publishing House, 2013.
28. Lou Jiwei. The Key to Solve the Contradiction between Central and Local Governments is to Implement Economic Decentralization. *Economic and Social System*, 1991(1).
29. Lou Jiwei. Review and Prospect of China's Fiscal and Tax Reform in the Past 30 Years. China's Economic 50 People Look at the Past 30 Years: Review and Analysis. Beijing: China Economic Publishing House,2008.
30. Lou Jiwei. China Needs to Continue to Deepen the Reform of the Six Systems. *Comparison*, 2011(6).
31. Lou Jiwei. Rethinking the Fiscal Relations between the Governments of China. Beijing: China Financial and Economic Publishing House, 2013.
32. Ma Jun, Bai Chongen. Thoughts on the Reform of Fiscal and Taxation System. Major Issues within the 40-person Forum on China Finance, 2013.
33. World Bank: International Experience beyond the Annual Budget: Medium-Term Spending Framework. Department of Finance, translated by. Beijing: China Fiscal and Economic Press, 2013.
34. Wang Baoan. Deepening Tax Reform // Guidance Reader of the *Decision of the Central Committee of the Communist Party of China on Several Major Issues of Comprehensively Deepening Reform*. Beijing: People's Publishing House, 2013.
35. Zhang Xuedan, Liang Ji, Shi Wenpo. Perfecting the Core of the Tax-Sharing Financial System: the Reform of the Intergovernmental Tax Division System. Research Report of the Institute of Fiscal Science of the Ministry of Finance, 2013.
36. China Center for International Economic Exchange Fiscal and Taxation Reform Research Group. Basic Ideas and Policy Suggestions for Deepening the Reform of Fiscal and Taxation System. *Financial Research*, 2014 (7).

The manufacturer's authorised representative in the EU is Springer Nature Customer Service Centre GmbH, Europaplatz 3, 69115 Heidelberg, Germany. If you have any concerns regarding our products, please contact ProductSafety@springernature.com

Printed and bound by CPI Group (UK) Ltd, Croydon, CR0 4YY

30/09/2026

02225234-0002